D1209935

The Autobiography of
CECIL B. DEMILLE

CECIL B.

THE AUTOBIOGRAPHY

OF

DeMILLE

Edited by

DONALD HAYNE

PRENTICE-HALL, INC. ENGLEWOOD CLIFFS, NEW JERSEY

ACKNOWLEDGEMENT

is gratefully made to the following for permission to quote from the copyrighted books listed:

Bobbs-Merrill Co., Inc.: Francis X. Busch, *Enemies of the State.*

Miss Agnes deMille and Miss Margaret deMille: William C. deMille, *Hollywood Saga.*

Doubleday & Co., Inc.: Daniel Frohman, *Memories of a Manager;* Jesse L. Lasky, *I Blow My Own Horn;* and Mary Pickford, *Sunshine and Shadow.*

E. P. Dutton & Co., Inc.: Bosley Crowther, *The Lion's Share.*

Mr. Samuel Goldwyn: Samuel Goldwyn, *Behind the Screen.*

Little, Brown & Co. and Atlantic Monthly Press: Agnes deMille, *Dance to the Piper.*

Liveright Publishing Corp.: Percy MacKaye, *Epoch.*

W. W. Norton & Co., Inc.: Maurice Bardèche and Robert Brasillach, *The History of Motion Pictures.*

Prentice-Hall, Inc.: Julian Dana, *A. P. Giannini: Giant in the West.*

Princeton University Press: Robert Hamilton Ball, ed., *The Plays of Henry C. DeMille, written in collaboration with David Belasco.*

Random House Inc.: Alva Johnston, *The Great Goldwyn;* and Lloyd Morris, *Curtain Time.*

Unless otherwise noted, all illustrations courtesy Paramount Pictures Corporation.

Library of Congress Catalog Card Number 59-15367

Printed in the United States of America

05455

Contents

Editor's Preface

This is Cecil B. deMille's book.

He had started work on it long before I began working with him in 1945. His method was much like that which he used in preparing a motion picture: first the accumulation of a vast quantity of data on every aspect of the subject, then the construction and preliminary drafting of the story, finally the finished script. This book was well into that final stage at the time of Mr. deMille's death. My main duty, as editor, has been the selection and arrangement of material from the voluminous collection of Mr. deMille's handwritten and dictated notes and his preliminary drafts of those portions which he had not yet put in final form.

For the painstaking labor of assembling, expanding, classifying, and cataloguing most of that material, editor and reader alike are indebted to Mr. Art Arthur, who worked closely with Mr. deMille on all phases of preparation for this book from January to December, 1957. Over the years, the late Gladys Rosson, Miss Berenice Mosk, Mrs. Lynn Hayne, and Mrs. Doris Turner made an indispensable contribution by transcribing and preserving Mr. deMille's dictated autobiographical notes. To Mr. Jack H. Dawley asknowledgement is due for his research in published sources, undertaken at Mr. deMille's request in 1956 for the purpose of verifying and coordinating Mr. deMille's personal recollections; and I know that Mr. Dawley seconds the expression of thanks to Miss Elizabeth Franklin, librarian of the Academy of Motion Picture Arts and Sciences, for her assistance in that research. For the history of his family, Mr. deMille depended principally upon the diaries, scrapbooks and other papers of his father, Henry Churchill DeMille, and the genealogical researches of Mr. Louis P. deBoer. An unpublished "Index to the Films of Cecil B. DeMille" by Mr. George Geltzer, edited by the late Theodore Huff, has been of constant and timesaving use.

To facilitating the editor's work in every way Miss Florence Cole has given the same daily, tireless devotion which marked her years as Mr. deMille's secretary. My own secretaries, Mrs. Lynn Hayne, Miss Mary Bennett, and Mrs. Jane Mounts, have been of the help which only a writer blessed with such assistance can adequately estimate. A special word of appreciation is due Prentice-Hall, Inc., for an understanding and patient helpfulness far beyond a publisher's normal call of duty.

Members of the "deMille staff," relatives, friends, and former associates of Mr. deMille and his family were most gracious in volunteering data or in responding to inquiries or interviews conducted while work on this book was in its early stages: their names are too numerous to mention individually, but they will see in the finished work that Mr. deMille was gratefully cognizant of their contribution to its completeness. Work on this book was so far advanced at the time of Mr. deMille's death that only one formal interview (with Mr. Farciot Edouart on some technical aspects of film production) has been necessary since then; but for their help in clarifying some few points on which Mr. deMille's notes were somewhat obscure, I must also express my thanks to Mrs. Edith Anderson, Miss Anne Bauchens, Mr. A. G. Cook, Dr. James H. Cryst, the Duke of Devonshire, Mr. Y. Frank Freeman, Mr. Samuel Goldwyn, Judge Edgar J. Goodrich, Mr. Jesse L. Lasky, Jr., Mr. Neil S. McCarthy, Mr. Jeremiah Milbank, Mr. Henry S. Noerdlinger, Mr. LeRoy Prinz, Mr. Russel A. Treacy, Mr. Charles F. West, Miss Sydney Whitmore, and Mr. Henry Wilcoxon, none of whom, however, is to be held responsible for the final interpretation of the points in question.

Above all, I am most grateful to Cecilia deMille Harper (Mrs. Joseph W. Harper) for giving me, in connection with this work, the same confidence which made my association with her father one of the most deeply gratifying relationships of my life.

DONALD HAYNE

The Autobiography of
CECIL B. DEMILLE

1

P‌RESIDENT G‌ARFIELD ate some toast, soaked in the juice of a care‌fully broiled steak.

Even though Garfield was a Republican, my father would have been glad to know that the wounded President was able to take some nourishment. Father was a Democrat, but he was a good Christian and a gentle man. He would have felt better after read‌ing that encouraging report from the White House. He would certainly have read it, if only he had had time.

He was always reading. He had one of those rare minds that not only devoured but retained. He was interested in everything. If only he had had time, after reading about the President's con‌dition, he would have found much else to interest him in that day's paper in the summer of 1881.

He would have agreed with George S. Coe's statement to the Bankers' Association that public sentiment favored the early and entire extinction of the national debt. Public sentiment was due for some disappointments. President Garfield was going to die of his bullet wound, in spite of the juice of that steak so carefully broiled. As for those hopes about the national debt, it was the hopes, not the debt, that were going to be extinguished.

Father was much too poor to own a horse, but he would have strongly disapproved the fact that horse thieves were active again around Port Jervis. He would never have bet on a race either, but it would have been almost un-American not to be glad that Maud S. had lowered the record of 2:10½ at the Rochester Driving Park the day before.

Father was a schoolmaster by profession. He would surely have glanced at the educational advertisements if he had had time to read the paper, but he would naturally be most interested in the New York schools and tutors. He would not have stopped to read Colonel Theo. Hyatt's announcement that the Pennsylvania Military Academy at Chester was scheduled to open September 14th. It would not have had any personal meaning to him if he had read it; for by the time I was a young pupil in Colonel Hyatt's school, father was dead. That was a part of the future that no one, happily, could see on August 12, 1881, the day when father had too much on his mind and heart to read the newspaper with his usual thoroughness.

It was summer and school was out, but schoolmastering in 1881 did not pay enough to allow for much vacation. It was pleasanter to be in the Berkshires, in Mrs. Bronson's house in Ashfield, Massachusetts, than in steaming New York; but work went with him. Four of his private pupils from New York were there in Ashfield with him, to be tutored in Latin, Greek, and mathematics. I imagine father gave them their lessons on August 12th the same as any other day. Father was like that. His heart was in the large front room upstairs in Mrs. Bronson's house, but if his sense of duty told him his mind belonged with the four boys bent over their books in some other room downstairs, that is where father was at lesson time.

It had been very different when William was born three years before. Then mother had gone down to Washington, North Carolina, to the warm southern welcome of the old family home. Father had a lonesome time of it in New York, but they wrote to each other every day until he could take the Norfolk steamer and join his young wife, in good time for the arrival of his first-born in the same old house on Bridge Street where he himself had been born.

The day William was born, July 25, 1878, father had time to write "joyful letters" to mother's parents and a handful of close

2

relatives and friends in New York, as well as record all the details of the event in his diary.

My arrival is recorded with starker simplicity:

"August 12th my little boy Cecil was born."

But I cannot feel slighted, when I remember those four pupils and the Latin, Greek, and mathematics, and Bill running around Mrs. Bronson's unfamiliar house, and the anxiety that must have hovered in that large front room upstairs. For I knew my father, so I know all that he compressed into those eight hurried words.

Eight words, after all, are a longer history than most of the world's population has had or will have. It is good for the soul to try to imagine how many human beings have lived on this world, and then to subtract one from that number, and see how much difference it makes. Very little; and yet very much, for each one is a link in a chain. If any one who has ever lived had not lived, the whole history of the world might be different, for who knows where the chain may go, what others it may cross, or where a broken link might have led?

2

A hundred and fifty years ago, one of my great-great-grandfathers was a small merchant in Liverpool, England. Another was busily losing his modest fortune in New York. They could not possibly have known each other. They had neither nationality nor business ability nor anything else in common. Yet Ralph Samuel's success in Liverpool and Peter DeMill's failure in New York were linked by their effects. I should know. I am one of the effects.

When I cannot sleep at night, instead of counting sheep, I try to count those links, to travel back and live with them. After all, they are living with me. If they had not been what they were, I would not be what I am. I am not suggesting that the critics of my next picture place the blame on Gillis deMil, born in Flanders around the year 1280. Gillis probably had enough to answer for without that.

Gillis is as far back as I can go. There is little known about him, beyond the fact that he married Anna van de Walle. That is comforting, though. I am glad the lady accepted him. You would not be reading this book if she hadn't.

When we begin to get more facts about these Flemish deMils,

3

certain characteristics begin to appear. They were ambitious, sometimes pugnacious, and usually religious. In the fifteenth century, Anthony deMil was Abbot of Eeckhout. When he died in 1438, his monks buried him in the fine choir that he had built for them. He built well. His choir outlasted the unified religious world he lived in.

One of the sixteenth century deMils, François, left some precious advice to his later namesakes. He had a pretty taste for puns. When he died in 1544, his tombstone was inscribed with this double play on the family name and the name of his manor of Vaerden:

"Wees MILDE van Herte,
VAERD naer Uwen Staet,"
which has been translated, "Be mild of heart; behave according to your standing."

Mildness of heart, however, does not exclude vigor of action, as we find nine years after François's death, in the account of Adam deMil's trial for killing his stepfather, Gillis Zoetins. Adam was a quiet, well-behaved young man, a glovemaker. We might not have known anything about him if his stepfather had not stopped on his way home, one June evening in 1553, and imbibed too freely of some potent Flemish brew. To put it plainly, Gillis was fighting drunk by the time he got home. Mild-hearted Adam said to him peaceably, "Father, nobody wants an argument," but Gillis responded by taking after his stepson with a knife. I have always believed that Adam was only raising his hand to defend himself, as the mildest of men might do, and that somehow the axe by the fireplace happened to fall into his hand and so find its way to Gillis's head. Anyway, two lusty chops with the axe restored Gillis to sobriety long enough to forgive Adam and take on himself all the blame for the altercation; but only long enough for that. Adam was finally acquitted by edict of the Emperor Charles V, but he was sentenced to pay a small fine and costs. I have often wondered about that odd verdict. Perhaps the emperor thought it was all right to dispose of an obnoxious stepfather, but took a more serious view of leaving axes lying carelessly around the house.

Such little domestic interludes did not distract the deMils from that religious quest which runs all through their history. We come across a rash of Old Testament names, tokens of the family's Mennonite period. At the same time there were deMils who clung to the old Church of Abbot Anthony, deMils who were priests and friars, deMils who carefully noted in their wills bequests for Masses for their souls. It was a time of religious ferment, which left no one untouched. As I think back to it on those sleepless nights, my sympathies go in both directions, with those who were loyal to the majestic, age-old Mother Church and with those who ventured all the way to following Menno Simons in his lonely, persecuted flight from all things worldly.

By the turn of the seventeenth century the ferment was beginning to settle. The modern shape of Christendom was becoming fixed. Reflecting his time, Isaac deMil withdrew from the Mennonite flock and joined the Dutch Reformed Church. No doubt he thought he was making a purely individual decision; but I wonder how different my own life would have been if Isaac's son, Anthony, had been raised a Mennonite. The Mennonites were adventurers of the spirit, but of the spirit only. They carried their unworldliness to the point of refusing to take oaths or hold civil offices or bear arms or have anything to do with earthly courts of law. Constant persecution made them a close-knit, clannish group. I doubt that Anthony deMil would have come to the New World if his life had been bound up with theirs. If he had not come to the New World, I would not be here to tell this tale.

Anthony deMil was a baker in Haarlem when he married Elisabeth van der Liphorst in 1653. Five years later, he and Elisabeth and their two small daughters set sail from Amsterdam to New Amsterdam in the *Gilded Beaver*. In 1945, when we were writing the script of *Unconquered*, I needed a good name for an inn in Colonial Virginia. We called it the Gilded Beaver. The timbers of the little sailing vessel that brought Anthony deMil to America have rotted away somewhere centuries ago, but millions, without knowing it, have heard its name, through a medium unthought-of in Anthony's most adventurous dreams.

It took some six weeks to cross the Atlantic then. It was the middle of May, 1658, when Anthony and Elisabeth deMil caught their first sight of the New World. New York is always lovely in the spring.

Anthony prospered there. He worked at his trade as a baker.

5

He and Elisabeth had four more children born in New Amsterdam. They were faithful members of the Dutch Reformed Church. The first deMil house in America stood near the tip of Manhattan, in what is now Bowling Green.

Anthony plunged early into the political life of the colony. He was among the leading citizens who urged Peter Stuyvesant to surrender to the English and who mingled socially with the conquerors after the English moved in. Somehow he was able to do this without losing his sturdy Dutchness. His neighbors must have thought so anyway, for when Dutch rule was restored in 1673, they chose Anthony for the office of *schout*, or sheriff, who seems to have been the chief law enforcement officer of the colony.

He was obviously no mere time-server, anxious to be on the good side of whoever was on top. When the English returned to power, they not only got themselves a new *schout*, Governor Edmund Andros also clapped Anthony into jail. His crime has a curiously modern ring. He was imprisoned for refusing to take a loyalty oath. He would pledge allegiance to the English Crown, he said, only if he could make a reservation for freedom of religion and exemption from military service. Was this stubborn Dutchness or the old Mennonite love of liberty and peace coming through? Probably a little of both. In any case, it was an assertion that there is an authority higher than that of any state: the voice of a man's conscience. That is the root and heart of freedom. I am proud of old Anthony for taking his stand there in 1675. I had to face something like it 269 years later. The first American deMil left a good example for one of his descendants.

Before following Anthony's son, Peter, up to Connecticut, it is time to talk, once and for all, about spelling. Every so often someone asks me if my name should be spelled with a capital D or a small "d." He usually asks in a shy, tentative sort of way, as if he did not really expect me to be sure myself. There are about a dozen different spellings in the family records. The oldest seems to be deMil. I have used that so far in these pages to avoid confusion, although DeMille, with an "e" on the end, appears for the first time in 1747, but DeMill, Demill, and other variations keep cropping up until my father's time. He spelled it and made it well known in the theater as DeMille. Sometime after his death, the family went back to the original small "d" for personal use, but kept the capital D for professional use. My brother and I have followed that rule. By the time I finish this explanation, my polite questioner is usually ready to retire, slightly dizzy and probably wishing he had not brought up the subect. I never blame anyone who misspells my last name. He could probably find precedent for the weirdest variations somewhere in the past seven hundred years. I do squirm a little, though, when I receive letters addressed to me as "Cecile." My spelling may be dubious; but I have never had any doubts about my sex.

With that spelling lesson out of the way, I return to Peter, now DeMill, taking his share of his father's estate, a little more than £30, and establishing himself in Stamford, Connecticut, early in the eighteenth century. The Stamford DeMills became millers and grain and flour merchants. Perhaps they reasoned that there was more profit in selling flour to a number of bakers than in following old Anthony's trade themselves. They also became Episcopalians, the last of the family's changes of religion. Like the previous changes, this one must have been a matter of conviction, not conformity, for the Congregational Church was the established church of Connecticut apparently. Peter's name is on a petition asking to be excused from paying tax to the Congregational Church, another assertion of a DeMill's belief in freedom.

Some who know me well have accused me of being positively Chinese in what they call my ancestor worship. It is not worship. It is, I think, a decent respect for those who begat me; and I think there is something to be learned from them, even from the few relics and mementos that come down from them.

At the foot of a fine old tree on my ranch, I have the tombstone of one of the Stamford DeMills, Joseph, who died in 1800. On the tree, above the stone, I have a bronze crucifix. I often sit there in the late afternoon, when the sun is slanting through the leaves, falling upon the cross and stone, and think about what they represent, mortality and immortality. They are both wholesome thoughts for a man who will soon be joining Joseph DeMill and, he hopes, the Other also. How important now are the problems that worried Joseph DeMill when his political loyalties drove him away from his Connecticut home during the American Revolu-

7

tion? About as unimportant, in the light of the crucifix, as the problems that worry his twentieth century descendant. Ancestors have their uses.

3

My grandfather, William Edward DeMille, died eight years before I was born, but he is as real to me, from my father's stories, as if I had known him. After all, the Civil War, in which he served, was only 16 years in the past when I was born.

Before the War, my grandfather had been a flourishing merchant in Washington, North Carolina, mayor of the town, and one of the pillars of St. Peter's Episcopal Church. My father has left in manuscript a pleasant account of the way a boy grew up in such a family in the ante-bellum South, where the most memorable events in a boy's life were visits to his father's steamer, *Pamlico*, when it was in port; family dinners at Aunt Betsey Blount's a mile from town; gathering hickory nuts on a hill opposite their house; and Sunday school, always preceded by Sunday morning breakfast, with plenty of fresh butter, down at his Grandmother Hoyt's. The great event of each year was the visit to New York, where his Grandfather Thomas Arnold DeMill lived. Once home from that long trip, the placid round of safe, happy home life began again—until 1861.

For four years members of the family were displaced persons. My grandfather joined the Confederate Army early, as post commissary under General D. H. Hill at Greenville, North Carolina, where he had taken his young wife and children for safety in March, 1861. Shortly after, he was appointed by Jefferson Davis commissary of Martin's brigade, Hoke's division. This meant separation, and all the burden of keeping the family together in the midst of war fell on my grandmother, still in her twenties. The contrast with their old life comes through in father's account of learning to knit his own socks and plait the straw for his hats. Fat pork was almost the only available meat. To make it slightly more palatable as daily fare, the children were offered one cent for every slice of it they would eat. Father earned about $11 this way. Facing and downing those 1100 slices of fat pork was surely one of the unsung minor heroisms of the lost cause.

In the spring of 1864, the Confederates recaptured Washington, North Carolina. Father, ten years old, drove down from Greenville with his aunt and the minister, Mr. Harding, as soon as they heard that the Yankees had gone. It was sunset on a Sunday afternoon when they reached home. Washington was free of the invader; but, standing on the river bank opposite the town, father could see, across the burned bridge, his childhood home still smoldering from the fire left in the wake of the fighting. Fortunately, most of the house was saved. It survived a second fire the same year and still stood there on the corner of Bridge and Second streets, a comfortable three-story brick with a wooden porch, until a few years ago when it gave way to progress in the form of a gas station.

The second fire did destroy St. Peter's Church, of which Thomas Arnold DeMill had been one of the first vestrymen. As the wooden steeple burned, the church bell tolled by itself until its supports were burned away and it fell, a shapeless, molten mass of bronze. An old Negro carried the wrecked bell away in a wheelbarrow and kept it until the War was over, when he brought it back to be sold as old metal and the proceeds put in the building fund for the new church. The sturdy brick structure was largely designed by my grandfather and is still standing, now thickly hung with the vines he planted when the church was built.

After the second fire, father went back to Greenville. There, on my grandmother's 30th birthday in February, 1865, my grandfather was captured by a detachment of Federal cavalry raiding the town. He was kept a prisoner of war until August.

While my grandfather was a prisoner, my grandmother supported the family by investing all her Confederate money in a small tobacco farm. Confederate money has been a subject for thousands of tired jokes. It comes as a surprise to realize that there really was a time when you could buy a farm with it. All through this period, while supporting her family, and all through the terrible Reconstruction after the War, my grandmother indomitably kept her children at their lessons, hearing their recitations every day, except when interruptions like the Federal raid or her husband's capture broke in on them. Father began to learn Greek from his Uncle Richard's Greek Testament; and he writes, "Then it was too, that I first became interested in elocution."

9

When peace came, the family returned to our home. There was nothing left. Grandfather's business was gone. He was deep in debt. The half-burned home had to be restored. The children went barefoot to save socks and shoe leather. The whole land was prostrate in defeat.

My grandfather refused to take advantage of the bankruptcy law, as he could have. He buckled down to pay his debts, repair his home, build a new church, and give his children whatever advantages he could scrape from the hard work that was shortening his own life. It is a remarkable tribute to his parents that my father remembered 1866 as "a very happy year of my life." He was 13. He started school, for the first time in his life, at the Academy taught by the rector of St. Peter's.

But I think what made 1866 happiest for father was his first appearance on the stage, in an amateur production of *Nan the Good For Nothing*. What gives a better picture of the defeated South than the fact that, beaten and broken, they had time and spirit for amateur theatricals? I have never read *Nan the Good For Nothing*. But I always think kindly of that old and probably very bad farce. It was the virus that inoculated father with love of the theater.

He had a severe case of that disease, from his first exposure to it. The same year of his debut in *Nan*, he gave up a trip to New York rather than miss playing a sailor in *Pocahontas*. The sailor's part consisted of two words. Love of the theater is an incurable disease. It is also hereditary, I fear.

But father had his trip north the next year. It took nine days, by schooner to Baltimore and rail from there to New York. It was intended to be only a short visit to his grandfather, Thomas Arnold DeMill, but father, like everyone else in Washington, had contracted fever and ague from the marshes across the river, stripped of their trees during the War. Being a grandfather myself, I can imagine the arguments Thomas Arnold DeMill used to persuade father's parents to let the boy stay in New York and go to school and put some flesh on his bones. They yielded finally. In September, 1867, father entered the Adelphi Academy in Brooklyn, conducted by a classmate of his Uncle Richard's, John Lockwood. He was just 14 years old.

Father writes about John Lockwood's "thorough welding of religion and learning," about his teaching on "the brotherhood of humanity," about the sane and balanced program of a school which neglected neither body, mind, nor soul. "That humble beginning of light in my soul has since developed into the belief of an *all* merciful God in Heaven." When father was writing, years later, this account of his schooldays, he underlined "*all* merciful." This belief was perhaps the strongest single motive of his whole life.

In 1871 he entered Columbia College, aided by a grant of $175 from the Society of New York for the Promotion of Religion and Learning. I have tried to find the Society of New York for the Promotion of Religion and Learning, but it seems to have gone out of existence. I wanted to make some return on its investment in my father. I have never been able to give it that return in money, but perhaps it has been given in other ways, not out of keeping with the Society's object. When I sign the contracts involving millions of dollars for motion pictures like *The King of Kings* or *The Ten Commandments,* and still more when I receive letters from all over the world, witnessing to the religious values of those pictures, I remember the Society for the Promotion of Religion and Learning and the $175 it gave my father. I should like to think the good men who voted that grant might not be displeased with what has grown from their investment.

Father did not have money for much expensive fun, but somehow he managed to hoard pennies enough for the Saturday matinees at Barnum's Museum. He dreamed of being an actor; but it was apparently a hopeless dream. Boys from nice southern families, with strong religious leanings, did not go on the stage in the 1870's. Once he said to his mother, lightly but with his heart in his mouth, "What would you say to my becoming an actor?" "It would break my heart" was her reply. That answer never left father's mind in those young years; but neither did the hope that that answer seemed to crush.

Meanwhile, though, there were college programs at the Academy of Music and there were amateur theatricals, which even the strictest Episcopalian could enjoy. And there was a girl.

11

All his life father preserved the cheaply printed program of the 14th Weekly Entertainment of the Philokalia Musical & Literary Association of Brooklyn, presented on November 4, 1872. His name does not appear on the program, but, if he was not backstage, I feel sure he was not far away; for another name does appear. Miss Tillie Samuel is listed for a recitation, "The Vital Spark," for the part of Laura in the Irish comedy that concluded the evening, and as a member of the Association's entertainment committee. Being a good Greek scholar, father probably found more than one meaning in the Association's name that evening, while he waited impatiently between the two appearances of Miss Tillie Samuel. Philokalia means love of beauty.

He never called her by her first name or by the teen-age nickname she used among the Philokalians. He always called her Beatrice. I am not sure that Columbia students read Italian literature as well as Greek, but father's instinct was right, whether he knew Dante's Beatrice then or not. That slim, bewitching English girl, Matilda Beatrice Samuel, dark-eyed, vivacious, different somehow from all the American girls who had momentarily caught his "too susceptible heart," was to be his Beatrice, like Dante's, his guide as well as his enduring love.

When he spoke on the topic, "What's In a Name," at the Columbia Semi-Annual in 1875, she threw him a bouquet, with a card reading, "What's in a name? Would a rose from another smell as sweet?" There are roses that do not lose their fragrance. Father noted in his diary, about that evening, "Beatrice was with me." Those four words could have described all of the 18 short years he had left to live.

When he took his B.A. degree at Columbia in 1875, there he was, on the threshold of life, a good scholar, a devout churchman, an unusually serious-minded young man, whose two most ardent ambitions were about as far removed from everything in his background as could be imagined. He wanted to be an actor and could not; and he was in love with a girl whose family opposed their marriage.

He had resigned himself to his mother's opposition to his going on the stage. He would become a teacher. Books and learning were congenial to him anyway. But all the fire in his intense young soul and his wire-thin body rose up against the opposition to his marrying his Beatrice. Mother was strong and determined, too. I can see them meeting every morning in that fall of 1875, walking the two miles to Lockwood's Academy, where they both taught— father (let it be confessed) a little prim-looking, soberly dressed, very earnest; mother, I imagine, wearing a touch of color somewhere and breaking into the serious conversation to point out amusing sights along the way or tell something funny that had happened in school; but both looking ahead, planning, determined to win what they both wanted. They did.

They were married July 1, 1876, at St. Luke's Church, Brooklyn, and had their honeymoon at the old home in North Carolina. Then, in the fall of 1876, back to their teaching at John Lockwood's school and to begin housekeeping in rented rooms on Madison Street, near Tompkins Avenue, in Brooklyn.

The year 1878 was one of changes and decisions for father. He was twenty-five. His first son, my brother William Churchill de-Mille, was born. He left Lockwood's Academy and moved to Manhattan to teach in the Columbia Grammar School, with a welcome increase of salary to $900 a year. He also taught calisthenics to the orphan children at the Church Charity Foundation, apparently as a labor of love, but it was rewarded by bringing into his life a powerful influence: the Rev. Dr. Charles H. Hall presented him with a copy of the life of Charles Kingsley. For the next decade Kingsley helped form father's thinking on the deepest things in life. He gradually acquired Kingsley's works, read them, annotated them, made them his constant companions. When he read the Sunday service at St. Stephen's, Brooklyn, he could not preach a sermon of his own, since he was a layman; he invariably read one of Kingsley's sermons, a practice he kept up whenever he conducted services, as long as he lived. His devotion to Kingsley is nowhere better shown than in an incident duly recorded in his diary for 1878, which certainly did not strike that earnest young diarist the way it does us: when he went for a day's outing to Coney Island, he took along a volume of Kingsley's sermons to read! Of the millions who have made Coney Island a byword for frivolous amusement, I am reasonably sure that very few have thought to take reading matter along with them. I am positive that there was only one whose idea of appropriate reading for such a day's outing was the sermons of Charles Kingsley. That was my father. That was, indeed, and most characteristically, my father.

Father first became acquainted with Kingsley early in 1878. On May 27th of that year, he was accepted by the Standing Committee of the Episcopal Diocese of Long Island as a candidate for Holy Orders.

I do not think that Kingsley was responsible for his decision to become a priest of the Episcopal Church. That must have been growing in him for some time. It was a natural decision, given his background and convictions. It was a decision which must have pleased his family infinitely more than his notion of becoming an actor. What we can learn from Kingsley's influence on father is the kind of priest he would have been. It shows in the kind of playwright he was, and the kind of man.

Father was never ordained. He studied theology and Church history diligently, but he never presented himself to the Board of Examining Chaplains to qualify for ordination. The *Long Island Diocesan Journals* list him as a candidate for the priesthood for eight years, from 1878 to 1885. Then in 1886 he is not listed. By that time, the lines of his life were definitely cast in another direction. He was beginning to reach, as a playwright, a far wider congregation than he would ever have reached from the pulpit.

I never heard father say exactly why he finally chose the theater instead of the ministry as his vocation. I have always believed that mother influenced his decision; but he was not a man to yield to influence unless it agreed with something in his own heart.

One day, after a religious argument with his uncle, father exclaimed in his diary, "Prejudice! Prejudice! Unwillingness to think for self." Freedom to think for himself and to make war on prejudice was something he could not lose. It was too much a part of him. I think he came to see that the stage gave him more scope for it than the ministry would have done in those days. I think we can see it in his plays.

6

Father's transition from teacher to playwright was gradual. His $900 a year from the Columbia Grammar School and the small fees from his private pupils were hardly enough to meet the doctors' bills that poured in, on top of living expenses, in the months after William was born. An 18-part serial story published in *Leslie's Weekly* brought a welcome $400, but even this and an increase of another $100 a year from the school were not enough when I came along in August of 1881. Father was putting in all his spare time on his first play, *Robert Aclen*. Finally, in March, 1882, he secured an introduction and an appointment to read his play to that formidable gentleman of the church and stage, the Rev. Dr. George S. Mallory.

Never before nor since has either the church or stage presented a phenomenon quite like Dr. Mallory. An Episcopal clergyman, editor of *The Churchman*, a shrewd, hard-headed businessman, he and his brother, Marshall H. Mallory, had taken over the Madison Square Theatre in July, 1879, after that ill-starred genius, Steele MacKaye, had had to close it in May for lack of funds.

The Mallorys knew a good thing when they saw it. Steele MacKaye had remodeled the Madison Square and made it an example of the most advanced theater construction ever seen up to that time. But his visions always outran his pocketbook, and he was desperate when the Mallorys came to the rescue with a contract that gave them an unbreakable grip on the Madison Square and a mortgage on the genius who had created it.

We still have the manuscript of the play that father read to Dr. Mallory. The title page is revealing. It shows that father was not burning any bridges. It reads: "*Robert Aclen* an original comedy-drama in four acts by Churchill deMille." If the doctor happened to frown and shake his head sadly at the end of the fourth act, well, at least the name of Professor Henry C. DeMille, M.A., would not have been involved in the hope-blasting venture. But the doctor did not frown. It may strain the imagination a little to think of him smiling, but he did tell the young author to come back again and read his play to Marshall Mallory and the stage manager, William Seymour. *Robert Aclen* was never produced, but something else was written: a contract, giving father a job on the Madison Square staff as play reader at $1,500 a year, plus an additional $1,000 for any original play he wrote, provided it ran 200 nights. He began his duties in April, 1882. He had found his place.

One of the aims of the Mallorys was to encourage American

playwriting. They let it be known that they would consider original manuscripts from any source, thereby setting amateur pens moving across paper all over the United States. In one period of three months father read 200 manuscript plays (if I may chivalrously call them plays). We may forgive some of the caustic comments in his carefully kept notebook. Father never shirked hard work. Again the Mallorys shrewdly had known a good man when they saw him.

But father had no intention of spending his life reading other people's plays. I do not know where he found the time, but he began another play of his own, his first venture in modern comedy, *John Delmer's Daughters*.

My brother William, who was the scholar of the family, liked to point out that the great change to what we know as modern drama did not come until after father's death, so that there was less difference between father's work and the drama of the eighteenth century than there was between father's plays and the plays that appeared on Broadway within ten or twenty years after he died. I do not entirely agree. I think that father was a part of the change, even if I cannot go as far as *The New York World's* drama critic, Nym Crinkle, who in 1891 compared father with Ibsen, to Ibsen's disadvantage. There is occasional dialogue in *The Charity Ball* (1889) and *The Lost Paradise* (1891) which, to me at least, is suggestive of the style of Oscar Wilde, but which cannot have been imitative since Wilde's first real success, *Lady Windermere's Fan*, did not appear until 1892. But all this was to come. When father was snatching time to write *John Delmer's Daughters*, he was still learning; and he had much to learn.

7

There were to be other distractions, though, before father could finish his own play. Along with the Madison Square Theatre itself, the Mallorys had inherited from Steele MacKaye three very noteworthy assets, named Charles, Daniel, and Gustave Frohman. Dan was business manager of the theater. Charles and Gustave between them managed the road companies—another Madison Square innovation which for the first time put "playing the road" on a sound and reliable business basis. In San Francisco, Gustave Frohman had spotted a young man whose flair for the theater

16

immediately kindled the unerring Frohman instinct. Gustave said to him in effect, "Go east, young man"; and in August, 1882, after passing the inevitable interview with Dr. Mallory, the young westerner was hired by Dan Frohman as a stage manager of the Madison Square.

Dan Frohman's judgment was as sharp as his little pointed beard or the keen small eyes behind his pince-nez. He knew that he had in father a scholar, a literary man, a man whose background and taste fitted perfectly into the Madison Square scene, but a man completely without professional theater experience. The new stage manager from California had showmanship written all over him, but it was the kind of spectacular showmanship that needed tempering to fit the Madison Square. Dan Frohman was the chemist who mixed those two elements in an amazingly successful compound, when he introduced father to David Belasco and put them to work together.

Their first collaboration was in remodeling Fred Marsden's play, *Elsie Deane*, while father went ahead with writing his own *John Delmer's Daughters*. After all the interruptions and delays, the management finally decided in a hurry to produce father's play in December, 1883. Father's mother came up from North Carolina for the opening night, full of pride in her son and the expectation they all had that *John Delmer's Daughters* would be a hit. It lasted exactly six nights. Father worked feverishly all through the week, cutting the script and trying to compensate somehow for the inadequate rehearsals and the illness of two of the cast, but the management insisted on ringing the final curtain down on Saturday night. It was father's first professional venture as a playwright; and the Madison Square's first failure. It could not have been a very happy Christmas that year. Mother felt it most. Father wrote in his diary, "The failure was worth having to know the number of friends the author had." To him there were always things in life more important than failure or success.

His family was always one of them. Amid all the harassment of getting ready to produce his first play, father took time to paste in his scrapbook a program of *The Rajah*, played at the Madison Square on November 24, 1883, and to write beside it in the margin, "Baby Cecil's first entertainment at the M. S. Theatre," noting also that about three months before I "had sat through part of a

17

performance of Callender's Genuine Colored Minstrels." I do not remember these historic events. But I was stage-struck early, and have been ever since.

Around the same time there were worries and changes I was too young to know about. The Frohmans left the Madison Square to join Steele MacKaye, who was still dreaming great dreams and, for a moment, realizing them at the new Lyceum Theatre, the first New York playhouse to be completely equipped with electricity, personally installed by a friend of MacKaye's, Thomas A. Edison. Belasco soon followed the Frohmans. To counteract these defections from their none too happy little family, the Brothers Mallory brought A. M. Palmer to the Madison Square as director with a half-interest in the house. The Mallorys did not know it, but their theatrical days were numbered when Mr. Palmer, with his precisely triangular side-whiskers in full sail, moved into the Madison Square.

Father saw some storm warnings. Fortunately he had acquired a port, a summer home at Echo Lake, New Jersey, an old pre-Revolutionary house still held together by its original wooden pegs, the first home I remember. He went on reading and doctoring plays and doing a little acting at the Madison Square and on the road, until his contract ran out in the summer of 1885. Mr. Palmer, then in complete control, did not renew it. We spent that summer at Echo Lake, "at liberty." Father wrote of it, "I had to get along by borrowing and other such doglike means of living."

The end of summer brought a summons from A. M. Palmer for father to play a role in *Sealed Instructions* for a few weeks, but his contract was not renewed, so he and mother both engaged with George W. Sammis to play in *Young Mrs. Winthrop* on a long road tour. Mother appeared on the programs as Miss Agnes Graham. The mother of the company's ingenue, Etta Hawkins, came on from Minnesota to Echo Lake with her two younger children, to take care of Bill and me.

None of the rigors of the road dampened father's interest in everything around him. He managed to see all the historical sites in the towns they played. He apparently never missed church on Sunday. He took note of all such remarkable phenomena as the fact that in Bradford, Pennsylvania, "natural gas burned everywhere, even for heating the rooms." And all the while he was working on another play, *The Main Line,* in collaboration with Charles Barnard, a well-known writer at the time, one of the editors of *The Century* magazine.

The Main Line is far from being a deathless drama, even if I cannot agree with the pronouncement of the St. Joseph, Missouri, *Daily News* that "the play from beginning to end is simply rotten." Critics, then as now, were seldom diffident about their judgments. The play is crude and dated, by our standards. Its principal situation turns on the hero's shocked revulsion when he makes the unspeakable discovery that the girl he loves plays cards. But in 1886, when *The Main Line* was produced at the Lyceum under Belasco's direction, it represented in many ways a revolutionary advance in realism. The subject alone was cause for comment: some critics scorned the idea that any romance could be found in so prosaic a subject as railroading. There would not have been controversy over the realistic railroad effects in *The Main Line* if they had not been regarded as comparatively new.

Today, motion pictures have made all audiences take realistic effects for granted. They demand them on the stage no less than on the screen, but it would not be accurate to say that motion pictures have created the demand for authenticity and realism. Motion pictures responded to that demand, which had been born in the theater of David Garrick and grew into the theater of David Belasco. Beyond Belasco's realism the stage could hardly go. There the camera was needed. But the public taste which only the camera could satisfy had been fostered and taught by men of the theater like Boucicault, Daly, MacKaye, Belasco, and my father. That, I think, is the historical importance of a play like *The Main Line,* dramatically mediocre, but theatrically a definite step forward.

Financially for father, however, it was a large step backward. It was not until a year or two later that the play caught on, to such an extent that four companies played it in Chicago in four different theaters in two years. Father ended the first season nearly $7,000 in debt.

Dan Frohman came to the rescue. He was organizing a stock company at the Lyceum and looking around for a new play to open its first season. He remembered how he had first brought together the spectacular young man from the West and the staid young man from the South, at the Madison Square. He already had Belasco as stage manager of the Lyceum. Now he turned again to father. Would he and Belasco write a play together for the new company? Father was glad to accept $25 a week in advance of royalties. He and Belasco immediately repaired to Echo Lake and buckled down to work. As Frohman put it in his memoirs, "Thus began one of the most famous of dramatic collaborations."

2

David Belasco was practically a member of our family for the next five years. I can just remember my first impressions of the slender young man, with his shock of coal-black hair, his deep, dark eyes, and the high-standing clerical-looking collar he always wore. To me, at six years of age, this newcomer was an exciting addition to our household. He had the spirit of fun that children love, and with it the rarer gift of taking children seriously, treating them as persons.

When Belasco and father were working together at our Echo Lake home, they wrote and talked, at desks facing each other, for about four hours every day. Then they handed their rough and heavily marked-up day's work to mother, to be copied out in her neat longhand. They could not afford a typist or a typewriter. Late in the afternoon, Bill and I would be called in to hear the day's writing read aloud. I can never remember a time, no matter how young Bill and I were, when we were not encouraged to voice our opinions of what had been written; and more than once our boyish suggestions went into the final script. It was a good apprenticeship, one I have never forgotten. When I am making a motion picture, I will take a suggestion from one of my youngest grandchildren or from a studio mail boy as readily as from the highest paid writer. One of the best things I learned from father and Belasco was a willingness to learn—from any source.

I cannot say that my contributions to father's work with Belasco were all constructive, however. It was impressed upon me that, while father and Belasco were writing together in their room overlooking the barnyard, my most constructive contribution would be to keep out of the way. One day in particular, I was told that I must in no circumstance enter the yard. No reason was given, which was rather unusual. I am afraid that I was never as docile and obedient as Bill, who once carried a piece of candy from North Carolina to New York to get mother's permission before he would eat it. Anyway, I crawled under the bottom bar of the barnyard fence and walked in. The reason why the yard was off limits for me that day was soon evident. A large bull had been brought down to visit our solitary cow. I looked at him. He looked at me. I had no ill will toward him at all. I had been taught to love animals. But the bull's education had been neglected, as far as kindly dispositions toward little boys were concerned. He reared, then charged. Ty Cobb never slid for home faster than I went over that fence. Fortunately, the fence was strong. The bull hit it with a crash that brought father, mother, and Belasco running out of the house, to find a stunned bull leaning groggily over the top rail and a studiously nonchalant little boy strolling away from the barnyard, with an occasional backward glance at his victory. I probably interrupted father and Belasco at their work more than once thereafter; I do not remember ever venturing again to interrupt a bull.

Only twice in my nearly fifty years of friendship with David Belasco did he ever disappoint me; and I am glad that that experience came early. When I was perhaps seven or eight years old, he promised me, many months before my birthday, that he would give me a pony. What boy would not nurse that promise to his bosom for any number of months? When the 12th of August dawned, I was downstairs early, I think before anyone else was up. I looked out in the barnyard. No pony. I waited all day. I said nothing. No pony. There were other presents, of course, and all the other excitement of a small boy's birthday: but underneath it I was having my very first experience of a forgotten promise. I wonder how many times I have unintentionally forgotten, as Belasco surely forgot, some promise I have lightly and confidently made to my children or grandchildren. I could not understand that then as I do now. It was a bitter experience, as only a childhood sorrow can be bitter; but I learned from it not to expect the world to be as sure or as dependable a place as the family circle with father and mother at the center and all the grandparents, aunts, and uncles making a comforting circumference. Every child learns that sooner or later. It must be learned. I am glad, in a way, that I learned it from a man whom I have so many other and greater reasons to respect.

The first of the DeMille-Belasco collaborations was *The Wife*, produced at the Lyceum on November 1, 1887. The reviews on the whole were good, but the first week's receipts were disappointing. Dan Frohman called father and Belasco into his office to tell them that he would have to close the play. Both young authors were ready to fight for their child. They argued. Frohman was adamant. They saw that only direct action could save the thing they loved. Belasco took Dan Frohman by the throat. Father's customary mildness gave way to the fury of a mother bear defending her cub. He picked up a heavy, sharp-edged octagonal ruler from Frohman's desk and held it poised over the startled manager's head. This tableau did not dissolve until Frohman regained his power of speech and consented to keep the play on, provided the authors agreed to cut and tighten it. They did. *The Wife* ran for 239 performances. It paid all the debts of the Lyceum Theatre and all the debts father had carried from the failure of *The Main Line*. Belasco and DeMille were commissioned to write a new play for the next Lyceum season. And Dan Frohman presented the ruler to father, as a souvenir of the happy result of father's persuasiveness.

There was in the Lyceum company a young actor whose fame was still due mainly to his father's name, which was Sothern. Since the elder Sothern had created the immensely popular role of Lord Dundreary, father and Belasco decided to write a play around the character of another comic English lord for the son, but with a significant difference. *Lord Chumley*, the play that Belasco and father wrote for E. H. Sothern, is the story of a rather blundering fop, but underneath the conventional silliness of the comedy nobleman they wrought a character of self-sacrifice, fidelity, and strength. There again father and Belasco pushed American drama a step forward. I think that the idea of finding strength of character behind a façade of apparent weakness is one that would have appealed particularly to father.

Father and Belasco were soon at work on another play, *The Charity Ball*, and on other projects which must have appealed to father as much as his growing success. One of Steele MacKaye's dreams had been a professional school for actors. Together with Franklin H. Sargent and others, MacKaye had founded the Lyceum Theatre School in 1884. Sargent continued it under the name of the New York School of Acting after MacKaye had left the Lyceum. Father became its associate director in 1888, and gave it its present well-known name: the American Academy of Dramatic Arts.

One of the Academy projects into which father put his whole soul was the first American production of Sophocles' *Electra*, in March, 1889. Belasco staged it, from a text arranged by father from the original Greek and various translations. After its Lyceum run, *Electra* was taken to Boston and played by invitation at Harvard University. I like to think of father helping to produce a play of Sophocles at Harvard, just as I like to think of him conducting the divine service of the Episcopal church. His life was becoming rounded out. He was by now a successful, even a famous, playwright. He remained always the scholar and the earnest Christian.

His sense of humor seasoned the hard work of writing and teaching. In one of his notebooks there is a penciled caricature which must date from this period, for it shows Belasco tearing his hair, father sitting dejectedly with his head in his hands and books strewn on the floor in front of him, Franklin Sargent lying on his back exhausted, and Bronson Howard making an exit, with a gesture of despair. Some of the newspaper accounts of their early efforts to train budding thespians are amusing too; but the fine work of the present-day American Academy of Dramatic Arts is their lasting monument.

In the third Belasco-DeMille play, *The Charity Ball*, father was feeling his way toward the dramatic presentation of social problems which was to be the theme of his last and best work. The manuscript revisions of *The Charity Ball*, in father's and Belasco's

24

handwriting, give a clear picture of what they owed to each other. Father had the ideas he wanted to express, but he tended to preach and to paint in too heavy colors. Belasco was pure theater. He did not check the flow of father's ideas: he quickened their pace and heightened their audience appeal. Father was still learning. But I can see Charles Kingsley smiling in the wings when the curtain rose on *The Charity Ball*.

It was not Charles Kingsley, though, that the players on the stage saw when they looked into the wings one matinee, during one of the most affecting scenes. It was the playwright's younger son, sucking a very large piece of candy, but so engrossed and moved by the play that his face was contorted with sorrow, tears, and taffy. It almost broke up the performance, until father noticed that something was wrong onstage and snatched me out of sight of the distracted players.

2

I wish I could tell that I vividly remember the day when a striking-looking, red-haired lady descended on our quiet home at Echo Lake, demanded to see Mr. Belasco, threw herself at his feet, and exclaimed, "If being hurt by people can make me act, I can act!" However, this is a truthful book; and I have no recollection whatever of my first meeting with Mrs. Leslie Carter. I am sure she took no notice of an eight-year-old boy. She was after bigger game.

Is Mrs. Leslie Carter remembered at all today? In 1889 she was perhaps the most talked-of woman in America. After what *The New York Times* called "a particularly repulsive divorce case in Chicago," Mrs. Carter came to New York to seek a career on the stage, for which she had no experience whatever. She set siege to Belasco. She was not the first or last society woman who sought his guidance for a stage career. As usual he fought shy of taking on a private pupil who was more used to giving directions than receiving them, but the emotional interview at Echo Lake broke down his resistance. The next 16 years of his life were mainly devoted to the career of Mrs. Carter.

The story of their long association and final break has never been fully told. This is not the place to tell it, except as far as it touches my father's life or mine. If Mrs. Carter was the most talked-of woman in America, most of the talk was violently unfavorable. That, if anything, is what is remembered about her. It seems only fair to recall a witness for the defense. Steele MacKaye wrote of her that she was "a woman of sensibility and refinement who has been outrageously stretched upon the rack." MacKaye was a man of independent and fearless judgment, not given to flattery.

In February, 1890, the stockholders of the Lyceum Theatre, instigated, it has been said, by Georgia Cayvan, the leading lady, objected to Mrs. Carter's using the Lyceum stage to rehearse the acting lessons Belasco was giving her. A curt exchange of notes between Dan Frohman and Belasco ended that arrangement. A month later Belasco resigned from the Lyceum.

Meanwhile Charles Frohman had leased F. F. Proctor's new 23rd Street Theatre with the intention of forming his own stock company, and had asked Belasco for a play to open the 1890 season. In Belasco's words, "I was strongly tempted to write the opening play alone, but when I saw how much depended upon it, I had a touch of stage fright. Naturally, my thoughts turned to Henry DeMille." It was 5 o'clock in the morning when he turned up at our house at 119 Waverly Place to ask father to work with him on another play. His loud knocking on the front door awakened us all. Father went to the door armed with a heavy cane, but instead of having to beat off an invader, he opened the door to the last of the DeMille-Belasco collaborations, the play called *Men and Women.*

Charles Frohman particularly asked Belasco and father to write a good part into their play for a young actress who had briefly played a small role in *Lord Chumley.* He brought the girl down to meet father again, to impress him with the possibilities that Frohman saw in her as an actress. She was just a slip of a thing, not above playing with little boys while their elders talked about her prospects for a career on the stage. She let me pull her around on my sled, I remember, but even then she had that gently shimmering magic that later on made the name of Maude Adams the greatest name in the theater in her time. A whole generation gave Maude Adams a kind of worship that no actress has enjoyed since. I seldom use the word "proud," but I confess I am rather proud that she rode on my sled when I was eight years old.

26

Belasco and father did write the part of Dora in *Men and Women* for Maude Adams. The play opened on October 21, 1890, and ran till the end of March, 1891. The critics were divided, but even those who disliked it acknowledged painfully that it would probably be a success. Like all the Belasco-DeMille collaborations, it was.

But it was their last together. Father wrote in his diary for 1890: "It was during the last few days of this year that I found that David's interest and mine no longer lay together, and in perfect amity and with mutual regard for each other we determined not to work together for the present."

The New York papers hinted that Mrs. Carter was the cause of this split in a successful partnership. In an interview with a *Daily Continent* reporter, father said that he preferred writing for a stock company rather than for an individual star, but that his personal relations with Belasco continued friendly. It was characteristic of father that his public statements and his private diary should be perfectly consistent.

When I think of the DeMille-Belasco plays or glance at them again after all the years, I like to remember what Professor Robert Hamilton Ball wrote about them as recently as 1941:

> It is easy from our vantage point of the present day to smile knowingly at what is old-fashioned in them, to criticize the formula upon which they were written, or in fact any playwriting to formula, but to judge them properly we must see them in relation to the times and conditions for which they were written. The factor which determined the nature of these plays was the stock company. For that purpose they were admirably suited. They gave great and enduring pleasure to a large number of people.

To give pleasure to people is any playwright's goal. "Great and enduring" are words that a scholar like Professor Ball does not use lightly. I think father and Belasco would have been well satisfied with that summing-up of their work together.

3

Now it was time for father to strike out on his own. He had learned much since the day he took his courage and his first script in hand and read *Robert Aclen* to the formidable Dr. Mallory. He was something of a celebrity by now. Newspaper artists sketched him; people pointed to him in public places. We were far from rich, but comfortable, with the flat on Waverly Place for the winters, when father was busy in the theater and Bill and I were at Horace Mann School, and with plans being made to buy land in New Jersey for our first real home.

Father had been able to bring his mother, his brother John, and his sisters Bet and Stannie to live in New York. How close his family ties were, how much it meant to him to have his family near, we can judge from the fact that he and John, who was then 19 years old, kissed every time they met or parted. In our own family, mother and father were expecting a baby, hoping it would be a girl, I suppose. The future was very bright for father at the end of 1890, when he was thirty-seven years old, approaching the height of the powers that had already made him a success.

One evening in December, 1890, father took mother and Mildred Dowling, a young protégée of his since she had been a student at the American Academy of Dramatic Arts, down to Amberg's, a German theater in New York, to see Ludwig Fulda's *Das verlorene Paradies,* which Charles Frohman had asked him to see with a view to making an English adaptation of it. The theme of the German play, the rights of labor, appealed at once to father, who was becoming more and more interested in social and economic problems. Kingsley's influence on him was being reinforced at this time by the writings of Henry George, which I can remember father reading aloud to us. I cannot say that at 9 years of age I understood Henry George's economics, but this early introduction to his works eventually had a decided influence on my brother Bill: he married Henry George's daughter, Anna.

Bill and I used to play with the George children at their house. In fact, my theatrical career began there, as an extra in a family play in which Bill took the lead. Henry George was an extremely controversial figure, passionately admired by some and as passionately condemned by others; but I remember him as a kindly, bearded man who never complained that the children romping downstairs disturbed his profound and philosophic thoughts.

By agreement with Ludwig Fulda, father began an English adaptation of *Das verlorene Paradies.* Mildred Dowling worked with him on it in the early stages, but the last two months of work, putting the play in final form, were father's alone. He wrote in his diary: "We soon found that an adaptation was not sufficient. We drew out a scenario of a new play, using whatever we found good in the German."

While father was working on *The Lost Paradise*, my little sister, Agnes Beatrice, was born at the Waverly Place flat, April 23, 1891. Again mother was near death. Twice father had to stop work and clear his desk so the doctors could use it as a table for their surgical instruments.

After delivering *The Lost Paradise* to Charles Frohman, father in one week's time rewrote *The Main Line*, changing its title to *The Danger Signal*. Then he left for Denver to meet the Charles Frohman Stock Company and begin rehearsals of *The Lost Paradise*, which opened at the Columbia Theatre, Chicago, on August 17, 1891. The enthusiastic audience called father out for speeches after the second act and at the end of the play. At the first curtain call he came out in his shirtsleeves, as the Chicago *Inter-Ocean* remarked, a workman among the workmen whose lives and struggles his play depicted.

Here at last was success all on his own. How deeply he felt about it can be seen in a letter he wrote to Edward Freiberger three days after the Chicago opening:

"Your note on the card was most welcome. The dear old mother shall see it. How can I ever express my gratitude to Chicago for what she had done for me? My heart is so full that I confess it now and then runs over at my eyes."

The comment of *The Inter-Ocean* on *The Lost Paradise* was typical of the critics' reaction: "*The Wife, The Charity Ball* do not compare to it in real worth for either natural sentiment, dramatic construction, absolute breadth of idea, or deep undercurrent of human interest." The *Tribune* called father "one of the most talented of contemporary playwrights."

The success of *The Lost Paradise* confirmed his belief in himself and in what he had to say. He started work on another play, *The Promised Land*, whose very title shows that he meant it to be an answer to the problems he had proposed in *The Lost Paradise*.

In *The Promised Land*, father's talent as a dramatist reached

29

its height. There can be no question of his originality in this work. The characterizations he created for this play have a dimension of depth and inner reality surpassing anything he had previously written, with or without collaborators. His writing of *The Promised Land,* however, was delayed a whole year too long because he was busy, for the first time in his life, putting down roots in land of his own.

4

Early in 1891, while traveling down to Oakland, New Jersey, to work with Mildred Dowling on *The Lost Paradise,* he had come for the first time upon Pompton Lake. The beauty of the lake, framed by the Ramapo Mountains, stayed with him. In April, he bought a site of 76 acres on a hill above the lake. In August, Bill and I turned the first sod. We lived nearby, in the old home of the Ryerson mining family, until our own house was finished in April, 1892. With his thoughts going back to his own boyhood on the river that ran through little Washington, North Carolina, father called our new home Pamlico. It was a large white frame three-story house, handsome by Victorian standards, with turrets and wide porch, surrounded by lawn, overlooking the lake and the Pompton Plain. Father traveled the countryside, selecting the fittings and furnishings for it. Soon after we moved in, he planted an orchard behind the house. Young as I was, I could see the love and pride he built into Pamlico, especially at times like our first Christmas there, when he and Bill and I went through the snow to cut our Christmas tree from our own woods by the lake.

It was like father, too, that the roots he was putting down for himself and all of us should not be material only. He identified himself at once with the struggling Episcopal parish of Christ Church at Pompton. At the first annual meeting of the parish after we moved there, on Easter Monday, 1892, father was elected senior warden and delegate to the diocesan convention. He did not miss a meeting of the vestry until a few weeks before his death, and he conducted a men's Bible class in our home every Sunday afternoon.

The congregation of Christ Church was small and poor, consisting largely of steelworkers' families. The sexton was paid $3 a month, raised to $4 during father's term as senior warden. Obviously so poor a parish could not support a resident clergyman, so father was called upon to conduct service as a lay reader during the summer and fall of 1892. I know how much he loved that too. When he stood in that small chancel, reading the *Prayer Book* and a sermon of Kingsley's Sunday after Sunday, his life had, so to speak, come full circle to completion. There, anyone would have said, was a man who had achieved success in his profession, who had his family about him in a beloved and lovely home, who had in his church a trysting-place with that "all merciful God" who was never far from his thoughts: there was a happy man. And so he was.

I remember him best there at Pompton, for I was then 11 years old. I remember best the evenings, I think, when he read to us a chapter from the *Old Testament,* a chapter from the *New,* and often a chapter from American or English or European history or from Thackeray or Victor Hugo or some other classic. He liked to have his head rubbed while he read, and Bill and I used to take advantage of that to prolong the evening's reading. Father had a beautifully modulated voice and a fine sense of the dramatic values in what he read. He made everything real.

He once said, "The dramatist is a camera, and his photography of life must be true if he would reach men's hearts." His reading of the Bible and the classics of literature reached a boy's heart; and he was unconsciously prophetic when, back in 1889, he spoke of his work in the terms of photography and a camera. I have had a good deal to do with photography and cameras since then. *The King of Kings* and *The Ten Commandments* were born in those evenings at Pompton, when father sat under the big lamp and read and a small boy sat near his chair and listened.

For father it was a time of contentment. The time of struggle was over. He was on the crest of life. My mind keeps going back to that Christmas, 1892, our first at Pamlico. Millie Dowling had given father a complete set of the works of Ruskin. Father wrote in his diary about this: "Not since Kingsley have I met an author who has so taken hold of me. Strange to say, he comes just at the time I need him, as Kingsley came when I needed him. God is over all." It was a very happy Christmas. It was father's last Christmas on earth.

He was in his usual health. I cannot think that he had any premonitions; but on December 29th he paid off the last of the mortgage on Pamlico and shortly afterward took out a new life insurance policy. New Year's Eve he spent, as usual, at The Players in New York, with Edwin Booth, Joseph Jefferson, Wilton Lackaye, and the rest of that good company; Grover Cleveland, about to begin his second term as President, made the traditional speech, just at midnight. The early part of January, 1893, was taken up with the varied tasks of supervising the building of an icehouse at Pamlico and working with Mildred Dowling on a play she was writing for John Drew.

On January 8, father held service for the last time at Christ Church, Pompton. He read Kingsley's sermon, "The Light"; and he wrote this note on his copy of it, "Excellent—Whatever makes clear is light. Christ gives light, but we must open our eyes to use it."

Later in the month he went in to New York again, to dine with friends and attend the theater. On the 25th, he went to the opening of the Empire Theatre at 40th and Broadway, to see *The Girl I Left Behind Me*, by Belasco and Franklin Fyles. The following day he lectured at the American Academy of Dramatic Arts, saw two plays at the Theatre of Arts, and spent the night in good talk with Wilton Lackaye and other friends at the Lambs Club.

When he came home a few days later, he complained of feeling ill. He remarked that the street had been dug open in front of the Ashland House, where he stayed in New York, for repairs of the sewer. He thought the fumes had upset his digestion, always delicate and nervous. But this was more serious. He had to go to bed. The doctor was called, and gravely pronounced the dread word, "typhoid." In 1893, that was a sentence of death.

I cannot forget those hushed days. In what moments she had away from father's sickroom, mother tried to keep life as normal as she could for Bill and me, but none of us had heart for the normal routine. Everywhere in and around the big new house were reminders of father's presence—his love and pride in the home he had just built for us. And upstairs in the big bedroom father was dying.

Once he sent for me. I stood there by the bed while he talked. I have no recollection of what he said. I was too torn by overwhelming emotion to take in what he was saying; and I could

32

not speak. After a few minutes he sensed that. He smiled, and told me to go and play.

Henry Churchill DeMille died at 4 o'clock in the morning of February 10, 1893.

The day before the funeral at Christ Church, while his body was lying in state in the same room where we had celebrated Christmas with him, mother brought Bill and me in to stand beside his casket, just the three of us. She put her arms around us and spoke, not to us but to him: "May your sons be as fine and noble and good and honest as you were. May they follow in your steps, helping God and their fellow-man, never turning from the right as you saw it."

For mother and her three children, life had to go on.

3

MOTHER'S ENERGY and resourcefulness stood her in good stead. It took her no time to realize that, with three children to raise, her vocation was not to be a genteel widowhood, but work. She had father's insurance money and his plays, a large house free and clear, and her own talent. With them she went to work at once.

She had already been instrumental in starting a school in Pompton, renting space first in a store near the Susquehanna Railroad, then over Durling's grocery, hiring a Miss Acker as teacher, and rounding up the neighborhood children to attend. This had been her characteristic way of providing schooling for Bill and me when we moved to Pompton. She could have taught us herself, but I think she realized the importance to two rather gentle boys of being thrust into the mill of regular schooling. Certainly one of my most vivid recollections of Miss Acker's school is of being beaten up by a little boy named Lester Smith. He did it quite competently with his left hand, while holding a baseball bat in his right. While defending myself as well, or badly, as I could, I begged Lester, "Don't use the bat!" He answered calmly, "I don't need to." He didn't. Mother was right. I needed school.

It was, then, natural for many reasons for mother to think of moving the school from Durling's grocery store out to Pamlico and taking charge of it herself. Mother never thought in small terms.

Within weeks after father's death, she was having an addition built to house boarding pupils and making plans for a tennis court and a baseball diamond. Meanwhile she was busy securing the patronage of such persons as the Bishops of Newark and North Carolina, former Mayor Hewitt of New York, the rising young Dr. Nicholas Murray Butler of Columbia, and others, who let her use their names as references. By April of 1893, the Henry C. DeMille School was ready to receive its first pupils.

Early in the school's history, an observant prophet might have predicted its eventual fate. Mother was a fine teacher, but a spectacularly bad businesswoman. Among her investments for the school was a horse-drawn carryall to pick up day students in the neighborhood, a forerunner of the modern school bus. It was priced at $300, which mother promptly paid. Bill, though only in his teens, saw that she had been outrageously overcharged for the carriage and remonstrated with her for paying so much. Mother's bland defense was, "These people must learn that I will not haggle." Purveyors and creditors learned quickly.

I still hear from some of the girls who attended the DeMille School. Mother comes vividly to life again in their letters, for they continually speak of her mental alertness, her motherly wisdom, her taste for bright colors, and the excellent table she set. The latter was probably due in part to her own good taste in food and in part to reluctance to "haggle" with the butcher; but whatever its effect on the school's budget, it is good to remember that mother's schoolgirls were not fed like those in Dickens' stories of nineteenth century schools.

But I think mother's qualities as schoolmistress and woman show best in her dealings with the most famous pupil the De-Mille School had, a breathtakingly beautiful girl of sixteen who was sent to the school in the autumn of 1902 by a distinguished New York architect who had taken an interest in her.

I do not know how Stanford White happened to select the De-Mille School as the place to send Evelyn Nesbit in an attempt to put her out of reach of the attentions of John Barrymore. That, at all events, did not succeed. Barrymore soon found his way to Pompton and, when Evelyn declined to see him, left ardent notes addressed to her on the tennis court and at various places around

35

the property, which must have made exciting reading for the girls who found them.

I was not at Pamlico when Evelyn Nesbit arrived, but my brother was. He was standing on the porch. Evelyn dutifully acknowledged mother's introduction of "my son William" and then went up to her new room to write in her girlish diary her first impressions of the school, including the description of Bill as a "pie-faced mutt," which District Attorney Jerome read out with such relish in a passion-darkened courtroom four years later.

John Barrymore was not Evelyn's only visitor at Pamlico. There was a rich young man from Pittsburgh who succeeded not only in seeing her but in ingratiating himself with mother. Mother had told Evelyn that she should study the drama, that, while her beauty would give her a start in the theater, as it had done in *Floradora*, only study and hard work would bring her real success. She may have divined from that talk that Evelyn, in spite of an eager mind and artistic ability, did not really want theatrical success. Whatever the reason, mother took another tack. She asked the girl how she felt about marrying the rich young Pittsburgher, who was evidently madly in love with her, and who could give her wealth, security, and everything she might want all her life long.

"But I don't like Harry Thaw," Evelyn said. "There's something wrong with him." She could not then have known what. But what she said was enough for my mother, who firmly told her, "Then you must not marry Thaw. A girl's instincts in a thing like this are more important than all the money in the world."

Evelyn Nesbit was telling this story to someone a few years ago. Her hearer remarked, "Mrs. DeMille must have been a very wise woman." Evelyn, an old lady then, sitting in her little studio overlooking a parking lot in downtown Los Angeles, thought for a minute, and all her tragedy of fifty years was in her answer, "I only wish I could say today that my mother had been so wise."

I have been speaking exclusively of girls at the DeMille School. Where did Bill and I fit in? After a year or so, Bill was sent to a *gymnasium* in Germany, to prepare for college. Mother had to empty my small savings account to bring him home, on a cattle boat. The family fortunes were usually at that ebb, but mother never let that stand in the way of providing the best she could for

36

us. Her mind was always fertile in stratagems. When I grew too old to continue attending classes with the girls at Pamlico, she arranged a deal to "exchange" me for the daughter of Colonel Charles E. Hyatt, the president of Pennsylvania Military College.

Meanwhile she saw to it that I had a boy's upbringing, in spite of the feminine atmosphere of the school. I learned to ride, to shoot, to fence, and to box. We were very fortunate in our nearest neighbors, the family of the Dutch Reformed minister of Pompton Lakes, the Reverend Edward P. Terhune. Mr. Terhune had a son, some years older than I, who worked on one of the New York papers, but who always had time to impart to the boys of the neighborhood the deep and virile knowledge and love of nature which was to make his name, Albert Payson Terhune, famous among American writers. We boys all idolized Bert Terhune; and it was an idolatry well placed and well deserved. Whether he was teaching us how to defend ourselves with our fists or how to read the wonder of all living things in woods and fields and lakes, Bert Terhune was more than a teacher or leader. He was the kind of friend every boy, especially every fatherless boy, ought to have.

My brother, too, helped to fill father's place as best he could. Bill was always the intellectual of the family. It tells something about both him and mother to remember that they set right to work to finish father's last play, *The Promised Land*. That they never did finish it is no reflection on a young widow with her hands full of building and running a school or on her 15-year-old son. What I admire is the fact that they tackled it at all. With the same young seriousness of purpose, Bill taught me much. I remember especially his initiating me into the world of music, the pains he took to familiarize me with all the great themes of the Wagnerian operas. If I sometimes surprise or annoy the Paramount music department nowadays by saying that I want something like this or that obscure Wagnerian theme worked into the score of one of my pictures, Bill is to be thanked.

Not that he was ever solemn or pretentious or overprotective with his little brother. His wits were always so sharp that I had to keep mine about me. When, one July 3rd at Echo Lake, he shot off all his fireworks and then inveigled me into swapping all mine for what was left of his burnt rocket sticks, exploded crackers, and exhausted Roman candles, I was left to celebrate an in-glorious Fourth, sitting glumly on the porch and watching my clever brother thoroughly enjoy the ill-gotten fruits of his trade.

Another kind of fireworks provided more frequent fun, how-ever, when I used to make mud balls and toss them into the air to be shot at by another of our neighbors, Miss Annie Oakley, who was then living at Pompton and still keeping her shooting hand in practice.

As I have watched my own children and grandchildren grow up, I have sometimes wondered how much adults know of what is going on in a child's mind. One good rule is never to be sur-prised. My mother and aunt followed that rule one August 12th. I happened to be the first one up that morning. I came downstairs confidently expecting that somehow the world and nature, not to say my devoted family, would have produced some wonderful phenomena to set the day apart from all other days, since it was my sixth birthday. But nothing was different. The weather was normal. The house looked the same. The furniture stood in its accustomed places. The rest of the family were sleeping as calmly as if it were an ordinary day. Well, I thought sadly, if others for-get, I will not. I went out and tore from the fence across the road long strands of wild clematis, long enough to drape and festoon my chair at the breakfast table, in what I thought was only fitting honor to him who sat thereon. When my family came down there was the chair, all suitably bedecked in its floral beauty, a lovely tribute to myself, a silent, sad rebuke to those who had been able to sleep soundly till breakfast time on such a day. No one so much as flicked an eyelid. It would have been cruel to scold. It would have been worse to laugh. It was Cecil's day after all. If he wanted to eat his breakfast on a clematis throne, all right.

2

Sixty years ago boys had movies and radio and television, be-fore movies or radio or television were invented. We had them in our heads. We were our own producers, stars, propmen—and audi-ence. I doubt that mother or Bill or Bert Terhune or anyone knew about the Champion Driver; but he was active all through the years at Echo Lake. In my imagination, fed with the heroic tales my father read us, I was the Champion Driver.

Mother was extremely fond of Jerusalem artichokes. She had a bed of them in our yard at Echo Lake. She cared for them tenderly. Whenever she looked out of the window at their tall, sunflowerlike stalks, I suppose she thought comfortably about the full rows of succulent roots beneath, waiting there for her to enjoy, one after the other.

One afternoon mother and father and Bill were away from the house somewhere, I was alone. When they came home, the artichoke bed was leveled to the ground. It looked as if a fury had struck it. Chopped, hacked, and twisted, every last proud stalk lay over the earth in confusion, obviously the victims of a ferocious assault.

Mother called me.

"Cecil, look at the artichokes."

I looked.

"Cecil, you were here alone this afternoon. Nobody else could have done it. Did you?"

"Yes."

"Why?"

"I was playing and . . . and . . . cut them down."

I was not punished. I do not think mother was remembering George Washington and the cherry tree. I think she saw, without the help of an expensive child psychologist, that something was boiling, too deep for further questions. Something was. The tortures of the Gestapo could not have dragged it out of me. I never told it to anyone till I was 71 years old. And yet, come to think of it, I have told it to the whole world.

Those were not Jerusalem artichokes. They were the enemy. They were the Saracens at Acre or the Union Army at Bull Run. No little boy had cut them down. The Champion Driver had reached the scene, alone, just in the nick of time.

The Champion Driver was a Robin Hood whose Sherwood Forest was the world. Wherever evil was massed against good, wherever beauty was in peril, wherever justice languished under a tyrant heel—listen, can you hear the distant hoof-beats, louder now, and louder? Thank heaven! The Champion Driver has heard the cry for help.

There were no jeeps or tanks or planes then, much less ICBMS or satellites. The Champion Driver rode a tireless, magnificent

Arabian. Foam flecked the steed's mouth and sweat glistened on his shanks when the Champion Driver finally arrived, pulled hard on the reins, took in the situation in one quick glance, and, careless of the odds, plunged in, to conquer for the right.

Jerusalem artichokes? Desperadoes, every one. Why, the whole village of Echo Lake might have been put to the sword that very night, if the Champion Driver had not cut them down.

But of course I could not tell my mother that.

Later on, at Pompton, on the bitter winter day when the ice jammed so high and hard against the Ramapo Dam above the Ludlum Steel Mill and the men told me to ride to Haskell for dynamite, I could not have told them that they could stop worrying as soon as I was in my saddle. I cannot imagine why they sent a twelve-year-old boy on that errand. The more sensible characters among them must have been sure that I would break my horse's leg on the icy roads or perhaps stop to get in a snowball fight, while the dam broke. Little they knew who was astride that horse, hugging the dynamite in a big, old-fashioned camera case. Little I knew myself, I suppose, for I thought I had outgrown the daydreams of the Champion Driver by this time. But it was not the twelve-year-old DeMille boy who saved the Ramapo Dam. It was, still, the Champion Driver.

It was a camera case in which I carried the dynamite that day. I have been closely associated with cameras on other occasions since. So has the Champion Driver. Richard facing Saladin in *The Crusades,* Jean Lafitte at Barataria in *The Buccaneer,* Jeff Butler driving the rails westward in *Union Pacific,* Chris Holden appearing in a cloud of smoke at Guyasuta's camp in *Unconquered*— different names, different stories, different times; but yes, come to think of it, I have told the world the Champion Driver's secret story before this.

There are numerous professional critics who would say that my mother's Jerusalem artichokes died in vain. They may be right, though the Champion Driver in me denies it fiercely. I somehow think my mother was right, when she looked sadly at her devastated garden, and then at me, and decided to wait and see. Hindsight is the professional critic's stock in trade. Foresight is a mother's.

Our little sister, Agnes Beatrice, was a ray of brightness in

40

mother's life during those years. Too young to realize what father's loss meant, Agnes was, in a way, the only unchanged link between our life as the family of a successful playwright and the struggle mother had to support us after he died. To Agnes, the schoolgirls who suddenly flooded our house were only so many more delightful playmates. And then, Agnes too was taken away. She died on February 12, 1895. As mother had done when father died, so she did again: she brought Bill and me into the parlor where our little sister's body was lying in its pathetic small white coffin. Mother made each of us boys put our hand over the dead child's heart and pledge that we would never treat any woman other than we would have wanted Agnes treated, if she had lived. Mother had a high sense of the dramatic. A more sophisticated age might call it too highly colored. I do not. Rather I think that this more sophisticated age has lost something genuinely valuable, in its anxiety to decry and suppress the gestures that express deep feeling.

Agnes was not with us long, but neither Bill nor I ever forgot her, thanks largely to the memorable way that mother impressed upon us her purity and sweetness. I carry a miniature of her on my watch chain always. Bill made her name live. He named his first daughter after her; and Bill's daughter has lived to make the name of Agnes deMille world famous as that of the foremost American choreographer of our time.

And there was one other link between our old life and our new: Christ Church, to which father had given so much of himself. It is a sign of the depth of father's influence upon us all that our family's intimate connection with Christ Church continued for as long as we were at Pamlico. Mother was president of the Women's Guild. The minutes of the vestry duly record that, amid all the struggle she was having to make ends meet, she was able to manage an entertainment put on by the Guild and turn over as its proceeds $64, a large sum for a parish which paid its minister less than $60 a month, when it could afford a resident minister at all.

It was in Christ Church, during our first year at Pompton as I remember it, that I had one of the most memorable experiences of my whole life. The parish could not afford a permanent minister at that time; in fact, the vestry wrestled for months with the problem of paying a $5 livery stable bill contracted when the bishop had visited the parish the year before. But somehow a clergyman was found who was willing to come and officiate for Holy Week. He was a big man with a full red beard; I never knew his name. The parishioners must not have greatly appreciated his willingness to serve them, for one morning that Holy Week I found myself the only person in church for the early service. The church seemed very big to a very small boy, but I went in and took my place in one of the pews, and waited. When the hour struck for the service to begin, the red-bearded minister came out, in his surplice, went to the altar, and conducted the entire service exactly as if he had had a congregation of a thousand people. I felt some awkwardness when the time for the collection came. I had a nickel for the purpose, but my problem was how to get it on the plate. The minister rose to the occasion. Before time for the offertory, he gravely came down out of the chancel and put the collection plate on the first pew, then as gravely returned to the altar. I went up and deposited my nickel. The minister returned at the proper time, carried the plate to the altar, and offered my gift as solemnly as if it had been gold. Then he concluded the service and went his way; and I went home.

Why has that incident stayed with me all these years? Not only because of that red-bearded minister's tactful consideration for a little boy. He could have said, "Run along, little boy. No service today"; or he could have thought that a little boy's nickel was not worth bothering about. But there was more to it than that. What I saw that morning was a man's faith—alive. He was not reading that service to me or for me, or to or for himself. It was for Someone Else, whose Presence was more real to him than mine or his own. I think he would have read the service just the same if there had been no one in the church but himself—and God. Young as I was, that minister's conduct gave me a deep sense of the reality of God; and it has never left me since that day.

3

Thus the years passed at Pamlico, until I was 15 and mother decided that it was time for me to go away to school. After arranging to pay for my tuition by taking Colonel Hyatt's daughter into the DeMille School, she took me down to Chester, Pennsylvania, to enter me in Pennsylvania Military College, in the fall of 1896. We went on bicycles. Mother saved train fare that way, but I think that cycling from Pompton to Chester appealed to her spirit of adventure too, as it did to mine. It was a fine September day when we wheeled up to the red brick buildings of the college and presented ourselves to Colonel Hyatt.

In spite of his short stature Charles E. Hyatt, in his blue uniform, was a fine looking man. In character, he was as fine as he looked. He was undemonstrative, a real Christian soldier of the old school—but no boy was at P.M.C. long before the president knew him intimately and knew how to guide him individually through the shoals of adolescence, that "space of life between" when the guidance of a good man can do so much for any boy.

My room, as I remember it, was on the second floor of the five-story Main Building, above the offices and library. My roommate was a boy named McMurtrie. He became a cartoonist in later life, but at P.M.C. he was already showing another note of resemblance to Rube Goldberg. He was always inventing things. Some of them were a comfort to his roommate—for example, his devices for turning the lights on or off or shutting the window on cold mornings without leaving his bed. Others, like the cascade of water over the door, ready to be tipped and drench the luckless watchman who checked the building at night, were more hazardous. McMurtrie once blew off part of a finger while experimenting with a model of an automobile engine. I told him he was wasting his time: the horseless carriage would never amount to anything. I did not know that the year I went to P.M.C. also saw the first carriage, drawn by no visible horse, being driven on the streets of Detroit.

That was not the last time that I have been a bad prophet. I might have dismissed as airily another invention that had its first public exhibition in 1896, the Edison Vitascope. Yes, of course, it was an interesting novelty to see photographs move on a screen in Koster and Bial's Music Hall in Herald Square; but it could never replace vaudeville.

My old schoolmate, Clarence Starr, who later gave P.M.C. many years of fine service as athletic director, visited me in Hollywood many years later and brought with him a list of some of my final grades, from the school records. To my surprise, and the greater surprise of my studio staff, they were all in the 90's. But I have said that Colonel Starr brought only some of my grades. Mathe-

43

matics was mercifully omitted from his list. The passing grade was 60; and the mathematics teacher, Colonel Comfort, said to me sadly, "I'll give you 59 and 10/10ths. My conscience won't let me give you 60." What surprised my staff most, though, I think, was that my grade in deportment was 100.

Friday night was the busiest of the week. That was the time that cadets who had been demerited were required to explain their delinquencies to Colonel Hyatt in person and receive his admonishments, at once all-soldierly and all-paternal. It was also the time for writing home. We could write at other times as well, but, knowing boys, Colonel Hyatt insisted that we must all write to our parents every Friday, and he made sure of it by collecting and inspecting the letters himself before they were sent. Friday was also bath night. The tubs were ingeniously arranged under the floor of the washroom. Throughout the week, we stood on the floor and washed from spigots flowing into troughs around the walls. On Fridays the floor was lifted, and our tubs awaited us. That was my first, but not my last association with sunken bathtubs.

The social amenities at P.M.C. were equally spartan. I was allowed to call on the daughters of the Episcopal rector, I remember. There must have been others too; the rector's daughters could not have furnished the entire collection of feminine handkerchiefs that decorated the walls of my room at P.M.C. There were vacations at Pompton too, of course, and mother's pupils were charming. My brother Bill, an older man of 19 and a Columbia College man as well, was naturally the more fascinating figure; but I found that a cadet uniform and a willingness to teach fencing and riding were not exactly despicable either.

There was one girl in particular. How I remember her delicate grace, her wealth of lovely hair, her fair young face, her slender hands, her poetry of movement as she walked. I planned very carefully the proper setting for laying at her feet my smitten heart. It was to be at sunset. I hitched up mother's horse and buggy and slowly drove the precious object of my affection through the green-bordered Jersey lanes to a spot where we could sit and watch the slow darkening of the gold-red western sky. We stopped. I sighed, waiting for the gentle word that would give me

44

the courage to declare myself. It came at last. She said, "My, ain't the road dusty!"

If love's young dream expired there in the dust of a New Jersey road, another dream, this one of glory, died young at P.M.C. The Spanish-American War broke out during my second year there, my first year of college proper. We knew, if anything, less than the general public did about the realities behind that utterly unnecessary war. We remembered the *Maine*.

We execrated the well-advertised cruelties of Cuba's oppressors. We also remembered President McKinley's visit to Philadelphia, when I had the honor of marching in the guard of that fine frock-coated figure of a statesman. When he called for volunteers to liberate the Cubans and avenge the *Maine*, the Champion Driver was down at the recruiting station in Chester bright and early. I do not know who found out that I had rallied to the colors. Perhaps the recruiting officer raised a questioning eyebrow to Colonel Hyatt. However it was done, the news traveled quickly north; and Bill was despatched to Chester to explain to the United States Army that Cuba would have to be freed without the help of the Champion Driver since he was still four months on the tender side of 17. And that is how it was someone else, not the Champion Driver, who carried the message to García.

But I had reached an age when it was time for me to be thinking about some career. Bill, at Columbia, was already veering away from his engineering studies toward the theater, as a budding playwright. Mother encouraged him, setting aside a room at the top of the house at Pamlico as Bill's inviolable sanctuary for writing. The schoolgirls romantically called it the Dreamery. On my part, I was infected with the same virus. With mother's encouragement, it was decided that I should leave Pennsylvania Military College in the summer of 1898 and enroll that fall in the American Academy of Dramatic Arts.

4

For the next two years I lived at Pamlico, going back and forth to New York every day except when I stayed occasionally overnight with my brother at his rooms near Columbia. I learned to know every tree along the Greenwood Lake railroad line and every squeak in Ezra Evans' open surrey, in which I drove in all weathers from our house to the depot to catch the 7:15 train each morning.

At the Academy, I kept myself to myself, as the English say, following all the regular courses but making few friends. That was a mistake, I think. I have never been hail-fellow-well-met. Polonius' advice to Laertes on friendship has always seemed congenial to me. I have had, and I have, a few very close friends, grappled to my soul with hoops of steel; but I have never had that gregarious instinct or that fund of small talk which enables people to enjoy a limitless crowd of casual acquaintances. To this day, a cocktail party is an ordeal for which I have to nerve myself; and the usual evening at a night club comes close to being my idea of purgatory—or it would if I ever went to night clubs.

My father's friend, Franklin Sargent, was still head of the American Academy of Dramatic Arts when I went there. Acting was taught by Charles Jehlinger. I respected the tough fiber of Jehlinger's character and teaching, and we came to like each other in later years when we were no longer teacher and pupil; but at the Academy we were usually at odds. Jehlinger had a technique of direction with which I never agreed. He believed in imposing upon actors his own conception of a role, making them do, in every detail of voice, movement, and business, exactly what he thought they should. That is one way to get a well-articulated performance out of a cast. It is not the way to teach the art of acting. Nor, I believe, is it the way to bring out the best performance of which an actor is capable, assuming that he is gifted with a reasonable amount of understanding, authority, and competence to start with.

Of course, the director must direct. He must guide and fit each actor's performance into the over-all conception of the play as a whole. But I do not believe that the director should ever do violence to a competent actor's inner understanding of a role. Good, not to say great, acting is a creative art; else why do we go to see half a dozen different Hamlets and find them all true? I enjoy a clever puppet show; but that is not acting, and the puppet master is manipulating, not directing.

As a director, I have tried consistently to follow the principle that my job, once I have cast an actor in a role, is to help him bring out the finest expression, of which he is capable, of his own understanding of his role. Before I ever let an actor see a script I tell him the whole story from the point of view of the character he is to play. Thus he does get his original conception of the role from me; but his interpretation may differ from mine in some respects. I may think mine objectively better. But the performance must be his or it will not be real.

One of the few lifelong friendships I did form at the Academy was with Wilfred Buckland, who had been a pupil of my father's and who was on the Academy faculty, teaching make-up, when I went there. He later became Belasco's set designer. Later still, at my mother's suggestion, I brought him to Hollywood to design sets for motion pictures. As the *Encyclopaedia Britannica* says of him in its article on motion picture sets, "Wilfred Buckland was the first man of recognized ability to forsake the theatre for the motion picture. He brought to the screen a knowledge of mood and a dramatic quality which until then was totally lacking." Set design today is one of the most important elements in motion picture production. If anyone is ever inclined to catalogue contributions I have made to motion pictures, I hope that my bringing Wilfred Buckland to Hollywood will be put near the head of the list.

The Academy teacher to whom I owe the most was Wellington Putnam. He taught me something that can make all the difference in the world between a middling good actor or public speaker and a great one. He taught me the vowel sounds of the English language. For the benefit of my grandchildren's generation, which seems to me to speak some other language consisting of a number of feeble consonants, let me record that English, as Mr. Putnam taught it, had many more vowel sounds than they have imagined. Mr. Putnam's method was simple. It was drill. He taught us to run over the vowel sounds aloud and distinctly over and over and over again, then to put each of the consonants before the vowels, then to put combinations of consonants before and after, through nearly every combination and permutation of real words and nonsense words that the 26 letters of the alphabet could make up.

I have practiced Mr. Putnam's drill steadily for 60 years; I fear that fellow passengers on trains or passers-by in the street may have been startled sometimes to see my lips moving vigorously and, if they were close enough, to hear me emitting a rapid stream of Putnam vowels. But I always think of Mr. Putnam when I hear well educated and otherwise good speakers saying "Oi" for "I" or "Tho" for "Thou."

Belasco was another stickler for enunciation. It was after his time that the modern stage practice of muttering into the orchestra pit developed. You can tell the difference if you are fortunate enough to catch on television one of Mrs. Leslie Carter's old motion pictures or a performance by one of the still living actors or actresses trained by Belasco. The acting may be stagy to modern taste, but you know what they are saying.

5

I was graduated from the Academy in 1900. The climax of each student's two-year course was the graduation play. Staged in a Broadway theater, attended by some of the leading producers looking for talent, it was, though unpaid, our first professional performance.

When we stepped from the wings of the Empire Theatre into *The Arcady Trail*, our thoughts were on a plump little gentleman in the audience, whose shrewd appraisal would have much to do with whether the next Academy catalogue listed us as working or, as the catalogue delicately put it, "resting."

Charles Frohman was his name; and to our minds his power in the theater was godlike. Four years before, he had brought together the regional giants of the American theater business: Al Hayman from the Pacific Coast, Marc Klaw and Abraham L. Erlanger from the South, S. F. Nixon and J. Fred Zimmerman from Pennsylvania, and, with himself representing New York, had forged a nationwide theater chain which for years dominated the business side of the American drama. Not even the opposition of great individualists like Belasco, Bernhardt, Mrs. Fiske, Joe Jefferson, and Richard Mansfield had shaken Frohman's dominance.

The life or death of the average play depended upon its being booked by Klaw and Erlanger into the theaters controlled by the Frohman syndicate; and whether or not we aspiring young actors ate or "rested" depended largely upon whether we were cast in a play that played or one which expired for lack of bookings.

And there he was, looking us over. I was one of the fortunate ones. Together with three of my classmates, I was engaged for a small part in Frohman's production of Cecil Raleigh's *Hearts Are Trumps,* which opened at the Garden Theatre on February 21, 1900, and ran for ninety-three performances.

I shall spare the reader a synopsis of *Hearts Are Trumps* and the other plays to which I made my quite forgettable contribution as an actor. Kind-hearted publicists who have written about me have sometimes said that I became an actor in order to learn play production. The facts are more elemental. I became an actor in order to eat. I wanted to be in the theater, somehow. My whole family lived and breathed it. While I was at the American Academy of Dramatic Arts, mother was collaborating with Harriet Ford in writing *The Greatest Thing in the World,* which had a short run at Wallack's Theatre in the autumn of 1900. Bill was starting to write plays. Father's habit of sharing all the phases of his work with us paid dividends. We were all interested in every aspect of the theater. Acting happened to be the door that opened to me.

I am by no means sorry that was the case, even if I never intended to make acting my exclusive career. There is no better training in self-confidence than appearing on a stage; and I needed self-confidence. Inside the Champion Driver, there was still the solitary student of the Academy, who kept to himself and had few intimates. On stage, you are protected by your role. It is not you there on the boards; and yet through your role you are in contact daily with the changing audience, you are projecting something to them, it is you who are making them laugh and cry, fear and hope. You learn to play on them as on a great organ; and their response, that indescribable feeling of contact and communication that a responsive audience gives an actor, is one of the most satisfying of human experiences.

After its New York run, *Hearts Are Trumps* took to the road. There were some changes in the cast of the road company. One of the new faces was that of a girl whose father, a New Jersey judge, had finally succumbed to her campaign to go on the stage against all objections. Her name was Constance Adams, and the New England ring of her name fully expressed what her family thought of one of its members being an actress.

Constance Adams joined the *Hearts Are Trumps* company in Washington. As an old professional by this time, I did not pay much attention to the newcomer, except to notice that she was

49

beautiful. Then one day, a few towns later, I happened to sit next to her at a lunch counter, eating a piece of pie. We talked. I suppose I thought I was being gracious to a novice. I discovered that she had wit as well as beauty. Then I found myself, after every performance, waiting to walk with her from the theater to the modest supper which was all either of us could afford.

By the time the company reached Boston, we were wondering what Judge Adams would say if we told him that his daughter was in danger of entering into a contract longer and more binding than the one he let her sign with Mr. Frohman. On the 31st of December, 1900, at midnight, sitting together on the steps of a theatrical boarding house at No. 9 Beacon Street, Boston, completely oblivious of the cold, we celebrated the beginning of a new year and a new century by becoming engaged.

Many years later, when I was visiting Boston, I made a sentimental journey to Beacon Street, to see the spot where Mrs. deMille and I had become engaged. I thought I might sit for a few minutes of nostalgic meditation on the old stone steps if they were still there. They were; but I did not sit on them. No. 9 had been turned into a plumbers' supply house, and the new show windows were displaying the latest thing in gleaming porcelain fixtures. I felt it might be too much of a good thing if a reporter or photographer chanced along and found C. B. DeMille meditating before a shrine of bathtubs.

The spring of 1901 brought me parts in two other Charles Frohman productions, *To Have and To Hold* and Leo Ditrichstein's farce, *Are You a Mason?* The summer, to put it delicately, gave me more time for calling at the home of my prospective father-in-law, Judge Adams, in East Orange, New Jersey. When Charles Frohman called me to rehearse for *Alice of Old Vincennes,* to open at the Garden Theatre in early December, I was ready to echo my father's pun that Charles was "the noblest Frohman of them all." December 31st, that year, was the eve of the most fortunate year of my life, for, with *Alice of Old Vincennes* going strong and Judge Adams, however reluctantly, giving his blessing to having an actor for a son-in-law, Constance and I were able to begin thinking about setting a date. Engagements to marry lasted longer in those days. So did most marriages. Ours has lasted for 56 years.

50

4

WE WERE MARRIED August 16, 1902, with an Episcopal ceremony at the Adams home at 77 Washington Street, East Orange. A man can write what is in his heart about his parents or his brother or his dearest friends. He cannot write about his wife. If he is foolish enough to try, he must fail, no matter how honest he tries to be or how gifted the language he tries to use. I will not be that foolish. I will only repeat that Mrs. deMille's name is Constance. In the whole history of the world, no one has ever been more fittingly named.

It is a standing joke among my family and staff that in almost any large city in the United States, if I am called upon to make a speech, I can begin by saying that Mrs. deMille and I were there on our honeymoon. By revealing why, perhaps I am depriving myself of a pleasant opening for speeches, but truth must be served! We have E. H. Sothern to thank for it; and for much more.

After his initial success in *Lord Chumley* by my father and Belasco, Sothern had gone on to become one of the most distinguished figures on the American stage. By 1900 he was ready for that summit of an actor's ambition—*Hamlet*. By a happy coincidence he decided to revive his *Hamlet* the year I was married and to follow it with an extensive road tour of Justin Huntly McCarthy's *If I Were King*. When assembling the company, Sothern and Dan Frohman, the producer, remembered Henry DeMille's younger son, who had been cutting his thespian teeth in Charles Frohman productions. I played Osric in *Hamlet* and Colin de Cayeulx in *If I Were King*.

Traveling with E. H. Sothern was like going back to school, the best school a future director could attend. What I learned from him, and later from David Belasco, can still be seen in any of my pictures, I think. It is commonplace, and not particularly revealing, to say that they were both perfectionists. Merely being a perfectionist can result in being merely fussy. Their infinite attention to detail was always directed toward the single, total objective: the play was the thing.

Once, on the very last night of a tour, something went wrong with the performance. Sothern called a full rehearsal immediately after the final curtain. In the darkened, empty theater, with only the stage lights on, starting near 11 o'clock at night, we did the whole second act that no audience would ever see us do again; and we did it right. That was Sothern.

Kindly critics (there are some) have said that I know how to direct a crowd. I learned that from Sothern. Other directors, in laying out a crowd scene, might tell the extra players to babble *ad lib* when crowd reactions were called for. Sothern gave every single extra an appropriate distinct, individual line to say. The audience could not hear the lines, but they saw and heard a crowd of real people acting and talking like real people. The way to direct crowds of extras is never to think of them as "extras." They are individuals, they are players, they are parts of the whole, with a function as important in its way as the function of the stars. They respond—and you can see the difference on the stage or screen.

Not all the drama of those tours with Sothern was enacted on the boards of the theaters we played in between New York and California; at least not all the comedy. I never cross the continent on the Super Chief and the Twentieth Century Limited now without remembering the wooden railroad coaches of 55 years ago with the windows that were called poker windows because it took jacks or better to open them. Perhaps it was the tight windows that kept our day coach from splintering when our train crashed in the middle of the West Virginia countryside. Mrs. deMille had

52

been admiring the wild flowers along the right-of-way. When the train crashed to a halt and the fire extinguisher fell on my head and broke and covered me with vile-smelling chemicals and all the other passengers screamed and a traveling salesman in the coach began to chase the conductor down the aisle yelling that he didn't care about the wreck but he wanted his mileage ticket back, Mrs. deMille was heard to murmur through the din, "Oh, now we can get out and pick wild flowers." Mrs. deMille has always been a stabilizing influence. From that moment I have never lacked confidence in her ability to handle any situation calmly.

However, maybe I should not have sent her the message I did one night when we were stopping at a little town in Idaho. I was downstairs in the hotel playing poker; Mrs. deMille was up in our room, with a bulldog that we had picked up somewhere along the way and managed to smuggle into the hotel. Suddenly a bell boy appeared at my shoulder with the urgent news that Mrs. de-Mille was terrified because someone had tried to get into her room. She had the door locked, but she wanted me to come up right away in case the intruder came back. I said to the boy, "Well, ask Mrs. deMille if she can't depend on the bulldog for a while. Tell her I'm winning and if it keeps up, we can pay our bill."

Paying the bills was always a tight squeeze, as it has been with strolling players since the first player strolled. E. H. Sothern would hardly have tolerated the dodge which a too bright company manager successfully used crossing Canada with a *Lord Chumley* company a few years later. There were, if I remember correctly, 21 people in the company. The manager regularly bought 20 railroad tickets. When the conductor came into our coach, the company manager was always on his feet to meet him and escort him to my seat with "I want you to meet our star, Mr. De Mille. Mr. De Mille is playing the lead, you know, in *Lord Chumley,* written by his father. Shake hands with Mr. De Mille." I was expected to respond graciously. Then, after the conductor was presumably charmed and dazzled by these attentions, our manager would begin handing him the tickets for 20 passengers, pointing out and naming the 20 other members of the company as he did so. On rare occasions, when a conductor ploddingly counted the tickets and the people and then looked at me and said, "But what about—did you say his name was Mr. De Mille?" the manager was lavish with apologies for his oversight; and somehow enough cash was forthcoming to pay the 21st fare.

My strongest impression of those winter travels in Canada is that we were never warm. That was not the fault of hospitable Canada. We could not afford to stay in hotels with heated rooms. We would walk, of course, from the railroad station to the hotel, which always seemed miles away. There may have been hacks for hire, but not for us or our luggage. We would thaw a little in the lobby and corridors of the hotel, which were heated, but our rooms were as icy as the street in Montreal where I froze an ear because I stood looking too long and too longingly at a fur collar in a shop window. A fur-collared coat was just what "our star, Mr. De Mille" needed, but of course there was no chance of being able to afford it. It cost $7, I seem to recall.

It is easy to say that one would not exchange the hardships of youth for anything in the world. I wonder if anyone really means it. I think what anyone means when he says that is not the hardships themselves, but the knowledge, including the self-knowledge, that came with them. I have the reputation of having little patience with alibis. Maybe that stems in part from the explanations the theater managers on the road had for sparse attendance at some of our efforts. There was always a reason, which never had anything to do with bad acting on our part or bad showmanship on the manager's, why the public stayed away in such large numbers that particular night. If it had only been some other night, if we had only come to town on a Saturday instead of a Wednesday, why, Madison Square Garden could not have held the multitudes that would have turned out to see us. In five towns out of six, we were told that Saturday night was the night we should have come. That was the big night. I reminded one theater manager of that on a Saturday night when we had played to a half-empty house. "Well, you know, Mr. De Mille," he said, "on Saturday night everybody in this town goes to the barbershop to get shaved. That's why they weren't here." Whenever I am offered an alibi— or am tempted to find one to excuse myself—I remember that Saturday night.

Playing on the road was not easy, but it gave one a feeling of

My mother, in riding habit,
around 1892.

My father in 1887.

With our little sister, Agnes Beatrice, and William
turning the first sod for our home at Pompton, New
Jersey, 1892.

My Aunt Bet's wedding to John R. Pitman at our home in Pompton around 1897. Standing: William, Mother, C. B. deM. in uniform, my Uncle John deMille; my Grandmothers deMille and Samuel behind the bride.

My fencing pupils doing their homework, DeMille School, around 1897.

Constance and I about the
time of our marriage.

Mrs. deMille in costume for *Madame Sans-Gêne*.

One of my touring roles; this is as the sheriff in *Tess of the d'Urbervilles.*

With Bruce MacRae, right, rehearsing for *Hearts Courageous* around 1905.

Partners hoping to avoid pitfalls in 1915. Jesse Lasky, Adolph Zukor, Sam Goldwyn and Albert Kaufman at my left.

My brother Bill and I at Echo Lake, N.J., around 1886, with our pup, Major Homer Q. Putnam, named after a character in one of Father's plays.

With my brother Bill, newly arrived in Hollywood. This pose in the autumn of 1914 is a "remake" of the one at Echo Lake.

Hal asks for Naturich.

34:   Foot Hills - Naturich silhouette in moonlight -
(250)
251   kneeling - arms out looking up.

35:   Hal's bedroom - Hal asleep - Jim looks - then
(254)
252   kneels by bed - collapses -

REEL 6

Scene 1:   Ranch House - "Dawn" - Budd and Clark sneak on -
(252)
253   Toby bus. - Clark into barn - Toby on - Bud to
door. Toby follows - enters house.

2:   Bed room - Ray of sunlight through window -
(253)
254   Bud sneaks on - searches - finds gun in drawer -
out -

3:   Ranch House - Toby against wall - Budd on. Toby
(254)
255   grabs the gun - struggle - Bill on - grabs small
gun - Clark drops down from barn - Bill demands
explanation - Budd demands the gun - Bill asks how
he came by it - "This gun belongs to Naturich".
Budd elated. Toby pantomimes how Budd stole the
gun. Bill sends Toby off - Bus.bullet and pouch.
Jim on - Scene - Jim sends Bill into house with
gun.

4:   Bed room - Bill puts gun back in draw.
(255)

5:   Ranch House - End of sheriff scene - Jim tells
(256)
257   Budd to get out - Clark off - goes to house -
meets Bill - tells Bill to escort sheriff out -
Jim out - Budd puts foot on grindstone - starts

A page from our script of the first *Squaw Man*. Scripts are more
complex today, but the director's pencil still comes in handy.

How many Westerns have followed *The Squaw Man* of 1913 would be almost impossible to calculate, but of their continuing popularity there is no question. Dustin Farnum and Dick LaReno are the principals in this scene where I can be seen seated at right playing a faro dealer.

Considering script questions with Adolph Zukor and Jeanie Macpherson.

Wonderful Victor Moore as *Chimmie Fadden* with
Mrs. Lewis McCord in 1915.

Sessue Hayakawa and Fannie Ward helped make *The Cheat* a popular and critical
success. Film historians include this among the most important silent films.

Earlier day flexibility allowed us to write Irvin S. Cobb into *The Arab* with Edgar Selwyn in the title role.

Wallace Reid took my point much more seriously than Geraldine Farrar as we prepared a scene for *Carmen*.

Of the many conceptions of Joan of Arc, few have equalled Geraldine Farrar's. *Joan the Woman* (1916).

Lovely Mary Pickford made two pictures for me in 1917. Here she is supported in *The Romance of the Redwoods* by Elliot Dexter and Charles Ogle.

"The faces" in *The Whispering Chorus* (1918).

Gloria Swanson, one of the most popular stars the screen has known. Julia Faye at left in our 1919 production *Male and Female* based on Barrie's *The Admirable Crichton*.

The altimeter on my wrist recorded our altitude; the only other instrument, a gas gauge, told Jesse Lasky and me how long we might stay there.

DeMille Field No. 2, now in the heart of Wilshire Boulevard's "Miracle Mile."

Al Wilson watching as I prepare a doubtful Sam Goldwyn for his first flight.

Gloria Swanson joined Mrs. deMille and me at one of the Mercury Aviation Company's fields.

Our original Pathé camera mounted on a makeshift camera truck.

Anne Bauchens, Karl Struss, Alvin Wyckoff and Peverell Marley shown with camera equipment grown increasingly complex—and flexible.

Since 1916 we have lived in this home in Hollywood.

and for America—the America between the coasts—which actors, directors, and producers have sometimes seemed to lack since "the road" died. That experience was invaluable to me, for that America is still there; and now it goes to the movies.

Mrs. deMille and I attended a murder trial in one small county seat in the Northwest. The sheriff of the county was on trial. There was no doubt that he had killed his man; the question was whether or not the killing was in self-defense. The accused sheriff took the stand while we were in the courtroom. He was quite self-possessed. His answers were as brief and positive and unemotional as you would expect a sheriff to be in a western film. But all the while he was testifying he had one leg crossed over the other and he was slowly honing a large and serviceable knife on the sole of his huge boot. Every once in a while he would just glance over at the jury, then give the knife another whet or two as he answered the pending question with a monosyllable.

Another night, in a Montana mining town, Mrs. deMille and I were walking from the railroad depot to the hotel. I was carrying our two suitcases. Up out of the darkness came the great bulk of a burly miner. He stopped us, looked at the suitcases, jerked his head toward Mrs. deMille, and said, "Which one is hers?" With a suitcase in each hand, I was not in a desirable defensive posture. All I could do was indicate which case was Mrs. deMille's. The miner took it, turned on his heel, and fell in step with us all the way to the hotel, without a word. When we reached the steps of the hotel, he put the suitcase down and went about his business. I could no more have offered him a tip, even if I had had one to offer, than I could have offered one to a prince.

Rough justice, rough chivalry. Frontier qualities, they were still not far below the surface of that America between the coasts. In a motion picture, sophisticates would call them "corn," the same accolade sophisticates of the shallower sort give to honor, decency, patriotism, and all the ancient pieties. But in the real America, they are still real.

I do not mean to disparage the coasts. I am the child of one, and by choice I am going into my old age on the other. I love them both. I am still always exhilarated by a trip to New York; and always happy when a trip anywhere finally brings me home to California. But I am very glad that I know the America between the coasts, too, thanks to the months and years of trouping on the road. The next time I make a speech in Butte, Montana, or Burlington, Iowa, or Biloxi, Mississippi, I probably will, after all, say that Mrs. deMille and I were there on our honeymoon. It was a delayed and prolonged honeymoon, if you like, but that is how I remember it; and how better can I thank the Buttes, Burlingtons, and Biloxis for all they taught me about America than to remember them in that happy aura?

It was on the tour of *If I Were King* that Mrs. deMille and I made our first visit to California, when the Sothern company opened the new Mason Opera House in Los Angeles in June, 1903. On that visit we did not venture far out of downtown Los Angeles. There was not, in fact, far to venture. There was certainly no reason for us to make what would have almost amounted to a safari, out through the open country to Hollywood. Los Angeles was a compact little inland city, thriving in its modest way. The people were gracious to us. I am touched when old residents tell me now that they remember the opening of the Mason Opera House. They are uniformly too polite to say whether or not they remember me.

2

One of the secrets of my life in the early 1900's came out when I appeared on the *What's My Line?* television program a few years ago. The panelists, blindfolded as usual, were almost thrown off the scent when I truthfully answered yes to the question, "Have you ever had anything to do with musical entertainment?" That is, all of the panelists, except Bennett Cerf, who knows so much about so many things and who may have heard echoes of the rumor which it is now my sad duty to confirm. I was, for a mercifully brief space of time, an opera singer.

It had never been my intention to make acting a lifetime career. I always wanted to write, direct, and produce as well as act. I did write, steadily, plays in which the New York producers showed a remarkably consistent lack of interest, until my brother and I collaborated on *The Genius, The Royal Mounted,* and *After Five,* which were produced, in 1906, 1908, and 1913, respectively. Together with Cyril Scott, who starred in the play, I also staged *The Royal Mounted,* but I had no opportunity to produce a legitimate play all on my own until 1911, when the program of Lee Wilson Dodd's *Speed* carried my name as producer for all 33 of its performances at the Comedy Theatre. Archie Selwyn tried me out as a director once, but sadly had to let me go. Because I let the actors give their own best interpretation of their roles, Mr. Selwyn told me flatly, I lacked the intestinal fortitude—only he used a shorter word—ever to be a successful director.

But meanwhile there was the Standard Opera Company. In that I was a little of everything. We toured in *The Bohemian Girl, The Chimes of Normandy, Martha,* and *The Mikado.* I acted, sang, booked theaters, managed, and carved my niche in musical history. One night the conductor, Rudolph Berliner, was suddenly taken ill shortly before a performance of *Martha.* Panic descended. How to present an opera without a conductor? The wildest flights of the Champion Driver's dreams of glory had never carried him that far—but he was there. I called the orchestra together and asked them one question: did they know the score of the opera? Of course they did. When overture time came. I stepped to the conductor's small podium in the pit, suavely acknowledged the audience's applause, tapped the baton in a most professional manner, and for the rest of the evening managed to keep my hands and the baton going more or less gracefully in time with what the orchestra was playing. Bennett Cerf may have heard that story, but the Metropolitan Opera Company or the New York Philharmonic never did. At least I had no offers from them.

Between plays, there were still rent and grocery bills to pay. At one desperate time I answered an advertisement for a house-to-house book salesman. But I got so enthralled with the sales manager's talk about his wares that my mind ran off sketching out plays based on the books, instead of listening to the techniques for getting housewives to sign on the dotted line. I did not get the job. I still have among my papers notes to my brother William and to B. F. Claggett for sums of money that tided Mrs. deMille and me over some of the lean months. The notes have long since been marked paid; but there is no way of repaying adequately the generosity of a brother like Bill or a friend like Ben Claggett.

A call from David Belasco to play Arthur Warren in *The Warrens of Virginia,* written by my brother, was more than an easement of our financial problems. It was the beginning of one of the richest and most beneficial associations of my career, or rather it was the renewal of the association between Belasco and my father which had begun some 20 years before.

The Warrens of Virginia opened at the Belasco Theatre in December, 1907. Frank Keenan played the lead, but the member of the cast who was destined for the greatest fame was a very young girl named Smith who played my younger sister Betty. For her New York debut in *The Warrens of Virginia,* little Miss Smith wisely decided to use a more distinctive professional name than her own, though, even if she had remained plain Gladys Smith, I think that Mary Pickford would still have become America's sweetheart. Her winsome, girlish loveliness captured the hearts of that first-night audience at the Belasco Theatre 52 years ago, as it would win the hearts of the world some years later. Mary has never lost that loveliness.

Probably millions of words have been written about David Belasco as writer, producer, director, and man. Some thought of him as the greatest figure in the American theater, towering over two generations. To others, he seemed almost a charlatan, an admittedly magical showman, but one who contributed next to nothing to dramatic art. As a boy, I knew Belasco when he was taking the first solid steps on his climb to success. At the time of my closest association with him, between 1907 and 1911, he was near the long-sustained height of his power in the theater. What was the secret of that power? Which estimate of him was true? The best answer I can give is to tell the story, which I have never told in full before, of *The Return of Peter Grimm.*

In 1910 Belasco engaged me to write a play. The weekly stipend he paid enabled me to go to the Maine woods to think out my plot in solitude. One day while I was there, sitting in a rowboat on a lake, I saw enacted on the gunwale of the boat a drama which gave me the idea for my play. What I saw was a little grub turning into a brilliant dragonfly. It was the drama of eternal resurrection: when it was completed, the dragonfly darted off, shimmering in the sunlight, to a new life, leaving behind only the drab little husk from which it had emerged. I suppose that half-elusive fragments from the Gospels drifted into my mind: Our Lord's sayings about the lilies of the field and the single sparrow that falls. Here I had seen life come from death. If Our Father does this for a

58

dragonfly, what must He not do for us? I would write my play, I decided, on the theme of survival after death.

I set to work. If a man survives the death of his body, I asked myself, why in the world would he want to return to the world? The strongest motive I could think of for wanting to return would be to undo, if possible, the wrong a man had done in this lifetime. So I made my principal character a manufacturer, a hard businessman of the old school, used to having his way in everything, so driven by the love of power that even his love of his ward, a young girl, was subordinated to his desire to dominate her life. Then he died, and saw how wrong he had been. The play was the story of his efforts to return and acknowledge his wrong and set the girl free to follow her own heart rather than the dictates of his ruthless will. I had a séance in the play, which I still think was something more than a good comedy scene. I had the returned spirit of the old manufacturer on the stage, invisible to the other players, vainly trying to get someone to pay attention to the urgent message and plea he had for them, while the medium babbled inconsequential nothings about how lovely everything was on the other side. Eventually the message and the plea came through—not through the medium—and everything was straightened out.

I gave my manuscript to Belasco. The result was *The Return of Peter Grimm,* produced at the Belasco Theatre in October, 1911, with David Warfield in the title role. My hard-driving businessman had become a gentle, lovable nurseryman, famed and cherished in his little community for his loving skill with flowers and his generosity in sharing the beauty he produced. The séance and a subordinate theme of a stolen invention were eliminated. The supporting characters, though evidently based upon those in my script, were muted down, so to speak, to focus attention upon Peter Grimm. The way Belasco chose to get Peter's message through was a brilliant improvement on my play; he did it through a dying little boy who had loved Peter in life and now, dying, was close enough to the border of the next world to see and hear beyond. The play ends with Peter carrying the little boy off stage, across the border of this world to the next, singing the funny old song, "Uncle Rat has gone to town to buy his niece a wedding gown, ha, h'm." The play was staged with all the wonderful lighting effects for which Belasco was famous. It was an enormous success.

The program described it as a play by David Belasco. There was a note in very fine print giving credit to Mr. C. B. DeMille for the idea. I was hurt when I read that. I was young. I was poor. I had a wife to support and a baby daughter, Cecilia, whom I had had to help the doctor deliver at home because we could not afford a hospital or a nurse. Belasco had paid me well enough while I was writing for him, but when that stopped I had had to borrow on my life insurance to make ends meet; and I often walked from Times Square to 110th Street to save the nickel carfare to buy milk. It was evident from the first night that *The Return of Peter Grimm* would be a greater success than any play I had been associated with up to then. It would have meant much to have joint author's credit. Neither the audience nor other producers paid much attention to fine print on a program; and, if they did, the credit to Mr. C. B. DeMille for an idea could have meant anything or nothing.

And yet I understand why Belasco did what he did to my play; and what he did was a perfect example of his methods, his talent, his deficiencies, and his success.

First, the theme of the play was, for those days, one which the public would probably have accepted only from someone with a well-established name. Belasco had told me that. So had Lee Shubert when I showed him my manuscript. Throughout his whole life, Lee Shubert was always both friendly and honest with me. He always showed confidence in me—something I remember with warm gratitude. He had said to me, "Only Belasco can make the public take a play on this subject."

Then, David Belasco had David Warfield. He had found that great actor playing German low comedy. He wanted to bring him out in another dramatic role of great sympathy, to build upon his great success in *The Music Master*. Peter Grimm was a less consistent character dramatically than my original iron-willed manufacturer. If an audience subjected Belasco's magic to analysis, they might have found it hard to believe that the lovable old German nurseryman could have done in life any wrongs that he would have to undo after death. But David Warfield could not have played my manufacturer believably. He played Peter Grimm splendidly; and his artistry and the magic of Belasco's production took care that the audience were not too critical of the character. Belasco's minor characters—though based on mine, but weaker than my originals in some instances—made the central character more vivid and memorable; and Belasco had Warfield's future in mind. Dropping the invention theme and the séance, good as it was, gave the whole play a straighter line. Belasco's ending, with its heart-breaking accompaniment of the little boy's death with the childhood song about the wedding breakfast of "hard-boiled eggs and a cup of tea," was, for the purpose Belasco intended, simple genius.

I had written a good play. Belasco made it, as only Belasco could, an outstandingly successful play. I still have my manuscript. It still reads well. But I know that it would never have had the success that greeted *The Return of Peter Grimm*.

Nor can I accuse Belasco of breaking his word. He had not promised me joint author's credit. He had promised me acknowledgment on the program. Literally, he kept his promise. There was my name, even if it was buried in fine print among learned references to Professor William James and other authorities on the subject of psychical research.

I do not for a moment believe that Belasco deliberately chose to cheat. He was not small. When it came time to print the programs, after revision and rehearsal and all the thousand absorbing details of production, very probably he believed in all sincerity that *The Return of Peter Grimm* owed more to his work and less to mine than was actually the case. Perhaps it was like the pony he promised me when I was seven or eight years old. Perhaps he just forgot.

Certainly that incident is very small in comparison with the immense debt that the American theater and I personally owe David Belasco. It amuses me that some critics find in DeMille pictures the same faults that similar critics two generations ago found in Belasco plays. If the same faults are there, so are the same virtues. In both cases, I am willing, as Belasco was, to let the public judge which is which.

3

Belasco's methods of work left a lasting impression with me.

Strong individualist as he was, it was not congenial to him to work alone. He liked to talk his work, to construct the way he had constructed with my father when, in an empty theater with Belasco on the stage and father at a table, they plotted, wrote, and acted their plays all at once. When I worked with him, Belasco had surrounded himself with a permanent staff, as loyal as they were efficient. He depended upon them more, probably, than he knew. Personal loyalty stood high among his values. He was a benevolent despot. He fought the advance of organized labor in the theater; but he kept his own people on the payroll even when there was nothing for them to do. He confidently expected actors to work for him for less money than other producers would pay them; and the wisest among them did, and profited by it more than the difference in money. Sothern was the only man I ever knew who approached Belasco's insistence upon nothing less than perfection; and Belasco's range was the wider of the two.

From the strict viewpoint of dramatic art, I suppose that Belasco may have been to some extent a victim of his own success. There was never a rigid Belasco formula, but there were Belasco ingredients that the public came to expect from him always; and he did not disappoint them. That, to my mind, is not a small achievement, in the competitive and risky business of the theater.

Our difference over *The Return of Peter Grimm* did not break our friendship. I never worked with Belasco again, but, when he was ready to sell the motion picture rights to his plays, it was to our company that he entrusted them. When he died, I suppose that I had known him longer than most of his living contemporaries in the theater. Echo Lake was a long way from both of us then, but the "Old Man" still had the respect a young boy had formed for him in the days when he shared our home. He still has it.

A month before *The Return of Peter Grimm* was presented in New York, I produced Lee Wilson Dodd's *Speed* at the Comedy Theatre, but my effort gave no competition to Belasco's production. If the 33 performances of *Speed* were remembered at all today, it would probably be only for the fact that a stout young man named Sidney Greenstreet appeared in it, helping to lay the foundations for his future career as one of the most menacing and at the same time most lovable villains in motion pictures.

My brother Bill was considerably more successful at this time. His play, *The Woman,* also produced by Belasco, even outran *The Return of Peter Grimm.* Bill had already had successes with *Strongheart, Classmates,* and *The Warrens of Virginia.* He never reminded me of the fact that his most outstanding non-successes, *The Genius* and *The Royal Mounted* (and, later, *After Five*) were the plays on which I collaborated with him!

Mother, meanwhile, had also been inevitably gravitating toward the theater. The school at Pompton did not give full scope to her gifts; and, though she was a fine teacher, managing a school demanded other abilities which she conspicuously lacked. The De-Mille School always tottered on the economic brink. When mother saw it languishing into certain death, she turned her ever active mind in another direction. She bravely opened an office in New York and became one of the first women to go into business as a play broker and agent.

When the name of Mrs. H. C. deMille, Authors' Representative, went up outside mother's first little office in the Knickerbocker Theatre Building on Broadway, she had father's plays to handle and Bill and me as clients. But she also had courage and ideas and a flair for bringing ideas to life. Never a successful writer herself, though she never stopped trying to write, she knew writing talent when she saw it and she knew how to nurture and develop it in others. She discovered a young writer named Avery Hopwood and took him into her home and helped him to find the distinguished place he later occupied in the American drama. Rachel Crothers was one of the charter members of the Women Dramatists' Society which mother founded. Before long, mother's list of clients included Mary Roberts Rinehart, James Montgomery Flagg, Wilson Mizner, George Sylvester Viereck (not yet involved with the Kaiser, I believe), Zoë Akins, Beulah Marie Dix, Frank H. Spearman, and Charles Klein.

When Charles Klein wrote *The Lion and the Mouse,* mother took his manuscript to Henry B. Harris and read him the first two acts. She knew the third act was bad; but she turned that to advantage. After whetting Henry Harris' appetite with the first two acts, she abruptly stopped reading and offered a deal for the play, insinuating, I presume, that the third act was so stupendously good that Harris would be well advised to snatch the play then

63

and there instead of hearing it through and then "haggling." Henry Harris took the bait. Mother took the manuscript back to Charles Klein and made him completely rewrite the last act. It was, of course, an immense hit.

By 1910 Mrs. H. C. deMille, Authors' Representative, had become the DeMille Play Company, with offices in the Astor Theatre Building. I enjoyed the title of general manager of the company at that period, but mother remained the real general. She also remained as allergic to keeping accounts as she had been at the DeMille School, with the result that thousands of dollars undoubtedly got lost here or there, but eventually the DeMille Company was profitably sold to the American Play Company. While it lasted it gave mother something she enjoyed more than the money it brought in or the money it might have brought in: it gave her the chance she had not had, since father's death, of encouraging and helping to mold creative talent—of being, in her own small but special way, a real contributor to the theater she loved.

The DeMille Play Company broadened my experience in the theater. I had written plays and acted in them. Now I had the opportunity to become acquainted intimately, if at times painfully, with the business side of the theater, with financing and all the phases and the headaches of a production from writing a first act to ringing down a final curtain, for there was nothing in the theater that the DeMille Play Company would not attempt to undertake, given the chance. There were experiences upon which I look back with unalloyed pleasure and a touch of pride, like giving the youthful, courtly, but unknown Walter Hampden his first leading role, in Mary Roberts Rinehart's *Cheer Up*. There were other experiences that left a bittersweet remembrance, as when Lee Shubert had enough confidence in my production of *Speed* to put $3000 in it, hoping that would keep it running long enough to catch on with the public, only to be disappointed.

I have boxes full of contracts and correspondence from those days, dusty dreams now, but then each of the theatrical projects they represent seemed as if it might have been just the one that would really strike that elusive fire that blazes into a hit. And then I have to remember, rather wryly, the contracts that were not signed, as when I failed to take much notice of Theodosia

Goodman although she used to come to our office hopefully when she heard we might be casting. She had to come to Hollywood and change her name to Theda Bara before she had her chance to add a new symbol, "the vamp," to American mythology.

<h2 style="text-align:center">4</h2>

It is to my mother, in her capacity as literary agent, that I owe one of the longest and warmest friendships of my life. I think that to the end of his life Jesse L. Lasky agreed that our friendship had been good, but certainly no one ever entered into an association more reluctantly than he did with me. I had heard of Jesse Lasky long before I met him. Everyone in the theater had. Vaudeville was at its height; and the height of vaudeville was in the Lasky productions of musical plays, short but always well constructed, well cast, well mounted, well directed. There was a Lasky touch, a Lasky finish and polish about his productions that made them unique. The song-and-dance teams might be dreary and the acrobats unexciting, but if the bill included a Lasky musical, you left the vaudeville theater well satisfied and with a lilt. Lasky was a showman's showman.

One of the ingredients of the Lasky touch was Jesse Lasky's appreciation of good writing and good construction. His musicals were not slap-dash concoctions of pretty songs and pretty costumes. They were plays. In his quest for good dramatic writing as the foundation for good musical plays, Lasky decided to reach into the legitimate theater for an author whose already established reputation was a guarantee of the quality he was looking for. He came to my mother and asked for William deMille.

I have often imagined the scene. Mr. Lasky, the producer, natty with his high stiff collar and pince-nez, at once charming and businesslike, expansive yet intent. I feel sure that he must have opened the conversation with a graceful reference to father's plays, and then to Bill's. Mrs. H. C. deMille, authors' representative, seated behind her desk, in one of her flowing yet for the occasion not over-feminine velvet gowns, smiling, accepting the family tribute; but I am sure that her quick brain was already putting the finishing touches on the plot she was about to spring. Yes, to be sure, William was a good writer, wasn't he? Successful too, as Mr. Lasky himself had pointed out. So successful, in fact, that he was already heavily committed; Mr. Belasco, you know, Mr. Henry B. Harris too, why, you might almost say that William's future work was already optioned for years ahead. But Mrs. deMille had a younger son, Cecil, who wrote too. Mr. Lasky could never be anything but urbane, but he made it quite clear that he did not want Cecil; he wanted William. But, Mr. Lasky . . . mother had a way with her; and mother had her way. When the conversation ended, Mr. Lasky, without quite knowing how it happened, was saddled with Cecil.

Thus, inauspiciously, began the association and the friendship which wore so well for nearly 50 years. There have been times when that friendship was strained. Jesse and I never spoke of those times, but I think we both remembered them; and I think we both realized that they perhaps were the greatest proof of our friendship's strength. What Jesse Lasky and I had was more than friendship. It was an affection warmer and closer than that of many brothers.

Surprisingly, we hit it off fairly well from the very first meeting, though I went to that meeting with some misgivings and I imagine Jesse came to it, understandably, with a somewhat trapped feeling. Our first collaboration was on a musical play with the prophetic name of *California*. Its plot was about running a railroad through one of the old missions. I wrote the book and shared the direction with Jesse. William Le Baron wrote the lyrics; Robert Hood Bowers composed the score. Blanche Lasky, Jesse's sister, did the costuming. The Belasco influence could be noted in the fact that we had on the stage a real orange tree, from which the characters picked oranges and peeled and ate them—an expensive piece of business for the two-a-day! *California* was a success, followed by others, including *In the Barracks* and *The Antique Girl,* all put together by the same team. The casts always included contemporary headliners like Mae Busch and the marvelous Bavarian tenor, Fritz Sturmfels.

Between the Lasky operettas I tended the numerous other irons I had in the theatrical fire, some of which I have described, none of which approached anything resembling white heat; but Jesse and I fell into the habit of lunching together almost daily at the Claridge Grill, even when we were not working together, and of taking our vacations together in the Maine woods nearly every

66

summer. Jesse was at my side during the time of *The Return of Peter Grimm* and when *Cheer Up* notably failed to cheer up either the audience or its producer. I followed sympathetically the rise and crashing fall of Jesse's venture with the Folies Bergères, an attempt, too many years ahead of its time, to introduce the European cabaret, a restaurant with entertainment, to America.

I think that part of Jesse's genius for friendship lay in his spirit of adventure. I always found that one of his most appealing traits. The world was new to him every morning. For Jesse life was a sparkling road full of unknown curves, round any one of which might lie untold adventure. We had a sort of watchword that we applied to everything from the plot of our next operetta to a swim in the cold waters of some lake in Maine: Jesse or I would propose something by saying, "Let's do thus and so," and the other would instantly respond, "Let's," and it would be done.

And so we came to the fateful year of 1913.

We could not know that 1913 was the end of one era and the beginning of another, for the world no less than for ourselves. For the world it was the last of the years of peace, the years of optimism. King George V was on the British throne, but the morals and manners of the civilized world were still largely Victorian; and there was, in Sir Winston Churchill's phrase, a tranquil glory about that last Indian summer twilight of the Victorian age, which still looked to us like high noon. Here, Woodrow Wilson was inaugurated in March. To my brother's disgust, I took little interest in politics, but I voted for Wilson and his orderly vision of a New Freedom; perhaps I unconsciously saw something of my father in that scholarly, intense southerner who had also left his quiet academic life to preach to a larger student body from the political rostrum, as my father had gone from the schoolroom and pulpit to the stage. Of course there were a few barbarous anachronisms left in the world, like Turkey, "the sick man of Europe"; there were flare-ups in the Balkans now and then; there were many who thought that the obstreperous Mexicans needed a good scolding from the schoolmaster in the White House. But these were minor irritations. The sinking of the *Titanic* might have warned us that nature was not yet wholly tamed; but surely that, like civilization and universal peace, was only a matter of time and inevitable progress. If we thought of atoms at all, we imagined them as in-

67

destructible little billiard balls, out of which our quite stable and manageable universe was firmly built.

It was, in fact, just the kind of time when one might safely feel adventurous. I was 32, Jesse a year older. I was, quite seriously, thinking of going to Mexico to join a revolution. I forget what revolution was brewing or boiling at the time there. Any revolution would have done the Champion Driver in his mid-1913 mood. Jesse did not go quite so far as that; but he was ready for something new.

There was one in our circle of friends who did not greet Woodrow Wilson's inauguration with any hosannahs. That was Jesse's brother-in-law, Samuel Goldfish. Sam, at 29, was a successful glove salesman; but the new Democratic Congress was lowering the tariff on imported gloves, to the consternation of the domestic manufacturers and Sam, who saw the bottom dropping out of the business. Sam in turn had a lawyer friend, appropriately named Arthur Friend, whose legal practice and acumen gave him an insight into developments in the world of business.

Among the four of us a ferment was at work. Jesse and I had our own reasons for being ready for something new. Sam Goldfish felt that the time had come for him to get out of a business which was going to be economically hard pressed by foreign competition. As he looked around for new fields, he came across one which was still young, still so undeveloped that opportunity was unlimited to a man of his energy and enterprise, a new business which Arthur Friend opined could have a great future and great rewards.

5

The thing that was going to bind the four of us together was a flimsy strip of celluloid. The new business, in which Sam and Arthur had such daring faith, was the infant industry of motion pictures.

I was not a party to the earliest conversations among the other three. I was in fact, again, a second choice. Just as Jesse had wanted my more distinguished brother to write his operettas, so Sam wanted an experienced motion picture director to go into this new venture with them. With that keen perception of motion picture values which has made him one of the best producers Hollywood has ever known, Sam went to see a young director

68

who was already on his way to becoming one of the greatest directors America has given to the world; but David Wark Griffith was not impressed with the eager young glove salesman's plans. Griffith asked to see a substantial bank balance to the account of the proposed new company; and a bank balance was just what the proposed new company lacked. It was then that Jesse Lasky, finally persuaded to lend his name to the company, suggested that I might possibly do as a director.

I had seen a few motion pictures. The earliest I recall was a picture of a bull fight, lasting only a few minutes, which I had seen at the Eden Musee long before. The bull was about the size of a flea and hopped around the screen very much like one; but it was a picture and it did move. Another picture, of a durbar in India, showed me that spectacle could be put on the screen more strikingly than it could ever be put on a stage. When I saw *The Great Train Robbery* in a little house on 6th Avenue near 23rd Street, I discovered that you could tell a story in this medium and, in the telling, achieve both greater speed and greater detail than the stage allowed.

I did not need much persuading, as far as I alone was concerned. I had a family, though. Mrs. deMille and I had been married for 11 years, 11 years of almost unremitting struggle to keep our heads above water financially, but we had roots in New York and New Jersey and in the theater, which this new venture would mean tearing up, for it was part of the plan that if I joined the new company, I should go west to make the first picture. I talked it all over with Mrs. deMille, in one of the two most fateful conversations we have ever had. She said, as she has always said, "Do what you think right and I will be with you."

Somewhere in the Adams family's staid New England background there must have been a buccaneer or a bohemian or an adventurer of some kind, whose blood has stirred in Mrs. deMille's veins when I have proposed outlandish or quixotic courses. She has always said "Yes." Perhaps that is what she had in mind when she remarked to a friend a few years ago, after living with me and putting up with me for nearly 50 years, "Life with Cecil is not always placid—but it's always interesting!"

A day or so later I met Jesse Lasky for lunch at the Claridge Grill. He looked at me and said, "Let's do it." And I said, "Let's."

We turned over the menu and on the back of it wrote out in pencil the terms of my joining the Jesse L. Lasky Feature Play Company as director-general.

Jesse would head the company. We were all glad to have his name on it, for his was the only one of our names which meant anything as a theatrical producer. I would make the picture, or pictures, if the company survived the first one. Sam Goldfish would sell them. Arthur Friend would handle the corporate and legal side.

There were, of course, a few little details to take care of first, such as the fact that I had never been inside a motion picture studio. Sam arranged for me to spend a day at the old Edison Studio in the Bronx. I watched the director and cameraman set up the camera and point it toward a stone wall alongside a road. The director called for action. The cameraman cranked. A girl emerged from a hedge, climbed the wall, and ran down the road, looking back in terror from time to time at some unseen pursuer. A man met her, stopped her, and they talked, in pantomime of course, with much emotive gesticulation. I went back to Jesse and Sam and reported, "If that's pictures, we can make the best pictures ever made!" That was my apprenticeship as a director.

I had no money to put into the company. Fortunately Jesse and Sam and Arthur Friend were willing to take youthful confidence as my investment, in return for which I was voted a block of stock and the title of director-general. We capitalized the company at $20,000, but could raise only $15,000. We tried to interest my brother Bill in putting up the other $5,000, but he said he thought he had better keep his money to pay my fare home from the West when, as he confidently expected, the company folded up.

So we had a company, with a director-general who had spent nearly a whole day as a guest in a studio. Then all we needed was a subject for our first picture, a cast, a camera, and a location.

Most of our friends, like my brother, thought we were crazy. We had not yet heard the now ancient line that one does not have to be crazy to be in motion pictures, but it helps. A cousin of Sam's said to him, "I don't think you ought to go into this picture business because there are too many pitfalls." We found that warning so hilarious that afterwards, whenever anything untoward happened, we would all say to each other "Pitfalls!"—and proceed to climb out of whatever the latest pitfall happened to be. That, after all, is the best way to deal with pitfalls, especially when one is young.

On one thing we were all agreed—and that practically all the older and wiser heads in the business thought was the craziest idea of all. We expressed it in the name of the company, when we called it a feature play company. We determined to make it a policy of our company that all our pictures would be, as we called it, feature-length, long enough to tell a real story, with the same elaboration of plot that an audience could expect from a stage play.

It was natural, I suppose, that Jesse and I should look to the stage for our first subject. A play of Edwin Milton Royle's had had success on the stage a few seasons before, *The Squaw Man*. It was a western, with many of its scenes laid in Wyoming: that appealed to us because it meant that most of it could be filmed outdoors at less expense than in a studio, a consideration not to be overlooked by a group of young men who did not have a studio. It was a good story too, virile and exciting. Its dramatic value had been tested on the stage. Its title was known to that part of the public which followed the theater, and that was a part of the public we wanted to attract, along with the already existing and growing motion picture audience. Mr. Royle was willing to sell us the motion picture rights for a price we could pay. Best of all, Dustin Farnum, an established star of the stage, was at liberty and, un-like most stage stars of the time, he was willing to spend a few weeks in the underworld of motion pictures. In our enthusiasm at getting Dustin Farnum as our first star, we offered him the same quarter-interest in the company that we had tried to sell my brother for $5,000, but Dusty also was too good a businessman to take stock. He preferred to be paid $250 a week for his four or five weeks' work. A quarter-interest in the company which later became Paramount would have been worth millions in a very few years.

When we rounded up Oscar Apfel, a young director with ex-perience in the eastern studios, and Alfred Gandolfi, a cameraman, both of whom could be counted upon to keep the director-general from toppling into too many pitfalls, we were ready to go. Where? Well, we thought, Arizona might be good. It was western. Some motion picture companies had been going to California, we knew; but California was still farther west than Arizona and railroad companies had the unpleasant habit of charging by the mile. Arizona it was.

Mrs. deMille, we decided, should stay in New York with our five-year-old daughter. If Bill did have to pay my fare back, there was no reason why he should have to pay two fares and a half. But Mrs. deMille played a very large part in my trip out: she bundled up the family silver and gave it to me to take to Simpson's pawn shop.

That was not my first visit to Simpson's or to that other estimable institution, the Provident Loan. The family silver had been ensconced in one or other of those places more than once, to pay rent and buy food. Now it was buying me a career—or would it be another failure, like Bill's and my play, *After Five*, which opened at the Fulton Theatre that same autumn of 1913 and closed after 13 rather sad performances?

Of the five of us who took that train to Flagstaff, Oscar Apfel and Al Gandolfi could have got jobs in any of a half-dozen existing motion picture companies; Dustin Farnum was an established star of the stage; Fred Kley was Farnum's dresser and factotum. Only the director-general was staking everything on those knives, forks, and spoons in Simpson's vault; only the director-general and his brave wife and trusting little daughter, that is.

I was at an age when most men have found their groove in life, even if the groove is only a rut. I do not know if the Junior Chambers of Commerce had begun the practice of making awards to the most successful and promising young men in their communities in 1913, but, if they had, they would not have sent a committee looking for the director-general in the crowded station that day we went all aboard for Flagstaff. But hope—and a certain amount of blissful ignorance of pitfalls—rode with us.

5

D<small>A</small> V<small>INCI</small> . . . Kircher . . . Newton . . . Davy . . . Daguerre . . . Roget . . . Plateau . . . Uchatius . . . Sellers . . . Hyatt . . . Muybridge . . . Edison . . . Lumière . . . Eastman . . . Friese-Greene . . . Latham . . . Méliès . . . they, and many others, were also riding with us to Flagstaff, though we did not know all their names then.

I am not a scientific historian, but as a layman I cannot think of any other invention into which so many diverse streams of thought and experiment poured and united, as into the creation of motion pictures. Physicists, artists, photographers, businessmen, scholars, dabblers, all kinds of men, for 400 years, brought their small or large pieces of new knowledge, their curiosity, their hunches, their chance discoveries, and their patient experiments to the cauldron of ideas out of which finally emerged "the movies."

The motion picture industry is sensitive about that word, "movies." We almost never use it without quotation marks. But I wonder if we are wrong there. I wonder if there is not a deep significance in the fact that the people so quickly gave a popular nickname to what has become the most popular and influential of the arts. People give nicknames only to what they love; and it is what we love that has the greatest influence upon us. "Movies" is an affectionate term; and already in 1913 "the movies" were

73

firmly winning their place in the affections of the great mass of people, to a degree never anticipated by the inventors of motion pictures.

I say inventors advisedly. There is credit enough for all. When Edison ordered his first film from George Eastman in May, 1889, for example, did he know that William Friese-Greene in England had already taken pictures on perforated celluloid four months earlier? Did Friese-Greene know that, three months earlier still, Edison had perfected a method of "photographing continuously a series of pictures . . . on a cylinder or plate," producing images 1/32nd of an inch wide, which had to be viewed through a microscope, but which were the obvious forerunner of the Edison kinetoscope? Did either Edison or Friese-Greene know in any detail what Marey and others were doing at the same time in France and elsewhere?

These are fascinating questions for the historian, but what really matters is that all this widely scattered research was coming to a head at the same time—and at the same time that a public taste for a new kind of entertainment was forming. Simultaneously, not in one place nor in the mind of one man, but in many places and many minds, in the early 1890's, a new art form was being born. By the time we took the train to Flagstaff, an infant industry had come into being to bring the two together.

It is remarkable that few, if any, of the inventors of motion pictures fully realized the potential of their brain-child. Edison opined that the United States might provide a market for about 12, or at most 20, motion picture projectors. My brother's characterization of motion pictures as "galloping tintypes" accurately represented how most people in the theater felt about them. One dramatic critic showed himself a prophet, when Hillary Bell wrote of the chariot race in *Ben Hur*, staged on a treadmill in front of a moving painted panorama at the Broadway Theatre in 1899, "The only way to secure the exact sense of action for this incident in a theater is to represent it by Mr. Edison's invention." But for the most part the only men in America who saw the commercial possibilities of "Mr. Edison's invention" were men with no theatrical, scientific, or artistic background.

It is fashionable in some quarters to sneer at those men. I do not sneer at them. Some of them were shortsighted. Some of them were ruthless. Some of them saw in motion pictures only another way to extract nickels from the poor. Most of them were entrepreneurs, not creators. But if they had the defects of businessmen, they had also the virtues of businessmen. They took risks. They had drive. They had organizing ability. And the best of them had vision.

As usual, the men of vision among the pioneer organizers of the motion picture industry had to suffer at the heavy hands of those who had no vision. Adolph Zukor tells of sitting, hat in hand, waiting to be given audience by the tycoons of the Motion Picture Patents Company, which dominated the industry in 1912. They finally heard what he had to say, but they brushed away his idea of giving the public good plays on film, in pictures running perhaps as long as four reels. Nonsense, they said; no one would look at a picture longer than one reel. When a daring director did make a picture in two reels or more, the distributors broke it up and released one reel at a time. When Mr. Zukor imported from France the four-reel *Queen Elizabeth*, starring Sarah Bernhardt, he was forced to engage legitimate theaters in which to show it. The Trust, as the Motion Picture Patents Company was known, would not let it run in the motion picture houses. The Trust controlled production through monopoly of the Edison patents and controlled the exhibitors by the threat of cutting off their supply of pictures if they dared run any not distributed by the Trust.

Again, however, the old Biblical adage was proved correct: it was those without vision who finally perished. Adolph Zukor's success with *Queen Elizabeth* in 1912 was one of the turning points. It proved that an audience would sit through a four-reel picture, if it was good. It proved that people would go to a regular theater and pay more than a nickel or dime to see a good picture. It encouraged mavericks like Lasky, Goldfish, deMille, and others to produce pictures independently of the Trust; and it helped make exhibitors restive under the Trust's iron control, when they saw not nickels but dollars being taken away from their nickelodeons. The monopolists put up a hard fight, both in the courts of law and by such lawless methods as sending strong-arm men to smash the cameras of independent producers; but they were doomed by their own lack of vision, their inability to grow and develop as the public taste in motion pictures was growing and developing.

I was convinced that the future lay with what, in the name of our company, we called "feature plays"; pictures several reels long, telling a well-constructed story, well acted, and intended not as conglomerate items on the daily changing programs of the nickelodeons or as "chasers" in the vaudeville houses, but precisely as "feature" attractions which could stand on their own merits as a real and new form of the drama. In this aim we were charting a new course in American motion picture production. We were not alone in this belief. I do not claim for myself or for the Jesse L. Lasky Feature Play Company a monopoly on the idea of feature-length films. Perhaps the first man in America to have that idea and do something about it was George Kleine, who made, interestingly enough, *The Life of Moses* in several reels in 1908; but *The Life of Moses* was released under the Trust's policy of one reel at a time and was not a success. The same George Kleine in 1913 imported the Italian *Quo Vadis*, which ran for eight or nine reels, and exhibited it at the Astor Theatre, New York, for several months. The same year, Hobart Bosworth's production of Jack London's *The Sea Wolf*, in seven reels, and a six-reel film, *Traffic in Souls*, based on the Rockefeller report on prostitution, were shown in New York. David Wark Griffith had the same faith in the feature-length film at this time, though, still employed by the Trust, he did not venture beyond four reels in his production of *Judith of Bethulia*. Adolph Zukor's company, Famous Players, was making *A Lady of Quality* in five reels. As happened with the invention of motion pictures, when many minds were working along the same lines at the same time, the feature-length picture was also the brain-child of several fathers. We were among them.

2

We were staking everything not on a single long picture or an occasional one, but on the settled policy expressed in the name of our company. We had nailed our faith to the masthead. We had to make a success with our first picture or it would very probably be our last. If we failed, we had nothing to fall back upon. The wiseacres of the Trust would have laughed off another trio of broken upstarts. The budding movement toward feature-length films would have suffered a somewhat clamorous defeat.

76

Oscar Apfel and I were very conscious of all this, as we settled down on the train to write a shooting script from the play *The Squaw Man*. We were conscious too that the possible pitfalls were not only literary and photographic. We hoped that Flagstaff might escape the notice of the Trust's strong-arm squads and that we might finish the picture with our Pathé camera intact. But I had a revolver in my luggage, just in case. In my innocence I had yet to learn that there were more refined methods of dealing with an upstart competitor; and also that there was in the Trust at least one honorable and chivalrous man.

A shooting script today is likely to run to several hundred typed pages. By the time our train was chugging over the last miles of Arizona desert, Oscar Apfel and I had perhaps as many as 20 pages of penciled script and the hope that we could find a typist in Flagstaff, cheap. Apfel knew a great deal about motion pictures, 1913 vintage; I was supposed to know something about dramatic construction. The script, we hoped, embodied the best of both. No two parents ever clutched a precious only child tighter than we did that penciled script, when we stepped off the train at the Flagstaff station.

It was a beautiful day. Somehow the story has got about that it was raining. It was not. I suspect that, years later, some press agent may have felt that it made a better story to picture the four of us standing on the station platform drenched and discouraged. Like St. Peter's mother-in-law with the physicians, I have suffered much from many press agents; not that I condemn them all, indeed, any more than that lady, I presume, gave up all medical aid. But the press agent, or whoever it was, who made up the story about the rainstorm at Flagstaff, was particularly unkind to us, I feel. We should have been a sorry lot if a little rain discouraged us. What actually happened was that we made a far more disastrous discovery than any sprinkle, any downpour, of rain.

Today, if we were going on location, an advance party from the location department would have preceded us and reported back, with photographs and full descriptions, long before we left or packed a camera. In 1913, the only location department we had was our imagination. We had blithely assumed that the West was, after all, the West. Our story was laid in Wyoming. We knew that, in the fall of the year, Arizona was warmer and sunnier than Wyoming, so we had come to Arizona. It was warm enough. It was sunny. But some of us had been in Wyoming; and knowledge is always the enemy—or is it rather the friend?—of innocence. With one accord, we saw and knew that for our purposes Arizona, beautiful, healthful, sunny Arizona, was all wrong. It did not occur to us to rewrite the script and send the young man in the play to, let us say, North Africa instead of Wyoming; perhaps there were no squaw men among the North African tribes anyway. It would, of course, never occur to a motion picture producer to place a story in Arizona just because he happened to be in Arizona and have his script, star, and camera with him.

There was little time for second thoughts in any case. The train was beginning to practice puffing its lungs and pulling itself together, the way trains used to do, before continuing its westward journey. There was time only for a very quick decision.

I remembered that at the end of the railroad line was Los Angeles and that other picture makers had been working there on and off for some years. The California climate was good, there was a great variety of scenery there, and it was that much farther away, so we thought, from the minions of the Trust, in case any of that inquisitive fraternity decided to take too personal an interest in what we were doing.

3

The quick decision was made. When the train puffed out of the Flagstaff station, we were back on it. Some more of the Jesse L. Lasky Feature Play Company's capital assets were in the conductor's pocket, for our fares to the end of the line. All unknown to its corporate officers in New York, the Company was on the move; and all unknown to a quiet village of orange groves and pepper trees, out there to the northwest of Los Angeles, "Hollywood" was about to be born.

But would the end of the railroad line be for us the end of a rainbow, or a convenient jumping-off place if we failed and decided that swimming the Pacific would be a more feasible adventure than the production of galloping tintypes?

No such doubts, however, appeared on the brave faces we

wore when we stepped off the train and went, of course, to the elegant splendors of Los Angeles' leading hotel, the Alexandria.

We knew not a soul in the city, but the Hollywood grapevine must have been in existence before Hollywood existed as a cinema center. It was just about as accurate then as now. The word soon spread that a group of rich easterners had landed at the Alexandria, dripping dollars and panting to make pictures. We soon had many, many friends.

Among our visitors were two enterprising gentlemen named L. L. Burns and Harry Revier. They owned, they told me, a little laboratory about ten miles out. They would like to develop our film. In the course of conversation something else must have developed, namely, the fact that while we did have film and a camera too, we were still looking for some place, other than the Alexandria Hotel's baggage room, to use them. Messrs. Burns and Revier had an answer for that, too. In and around the building that housed their laboratory there was space that could be rented for a studio. There was a stage, equipped with diffusers, and room to build another one if we wanted it. I forget whether I nodded wisely at the mention of diffusers or whether I really knew then that diffusers were the strips of cloth hung above an outdoor stage to control in some measure the brilliance of the California sun.

If I have sometimes been mistakenly called the father of the Hollywood film industry, Burns and Revier deserve to be called its obstetricians. After a long drive through the straggling outskirts of Los Angeles and then through a stretch of open country, they delivered me at last to the somnolent village of Hollywood, to have a look at their laboratory and studio. Turning off the sparsely-settled main thoroughfare, grandly called Hollywood Boulevard, we drove down a broad, shady avenue more appropriately named Vine Street; and there it was.

It was a barn. Unmistakably, it was a barn. That did not bother me, though. I was not unfamiliar with stables. In Pompton, as a boy, I had lived over the stable for awhile. Besides, I expected to be working like a horse: what did it matter being housed like one?

On the credit side, it was a surprisingly large barn. L-shaped, one of its yellowish heat-beaten wings ran along Vine Street and the other stretched back, parallel with Selma Avenue, into an orange grove. The owner was a man named Jacob Stern, who lived in a white house near-by. Gently, the news was broken to me that while Mr. Stern was entirely willing to let us devote most of his barn to the art of the cinema, for a reasonable consideration, he did reserve the right to keep his carriage and horses there. After all, they were there first; and, when we went in to look over the interior of our prospective studio, the horses looked me over, with mild curiosity, as a prospective fellow tenant.

While I was coming to terms for the use of the barn and the laboratory services of Burns and Revier, back in New York Jesse and Sam had begun to worry. Worrying in the New York office about what the studios are doing in Hollywood has since become a firm tradition in the motion picture industry; but I must admit that Jesse and Sam had cause. Sam had already begun to sell exhibition rights to our first picture. Buyers had bought, laying cash deposits on the line. And all Sam and Jesse knew was that the director-general had gone beyond Flagstaff, beyond the end of the line, to a barn in a place they had probably never heard of, called Hollywood. With a prudent warning to make no long-term commitments, however, they approved the renting of part of the barn. Soon a large sign announced to the occasional traveler along Selma Avenue that the Jesse L. Lasky Feature Play Company had acquired a local habitation as well as a resounding name.

A partition was set up within the barn to form a small room, a desk was brought in for the director-general and a kitchen table for his as yet nonexistent secretary, and we were ready for business. The most important article of furniture, however, I found to be the wastebasket. It provided a very convenient refuge for my feet whenever Mr. Stern washed his carriage and the water ran under my desk.

Our first employee engaged in Hollywood was a secretary-bookkeeper, a little young lady named Stella Stray. She sat behind the kitchen table, perched on a straight wooden chair, with a couple of city directories added so that she could reach the typewriter keys. Stella was thoroughly capable; but she was to be an early victim of one of the first of the economy waves which periodically take their rise in the New York offices and sweep

80

over the Hollywood studios. Someone decided that the salary I was paying Stella, $15 a week, was much too high. A good male secretary, I was told, could be had for less. Stella was given her choice of taking a cut or taking leave of the company. A spunky little person, with more experience in the motion picture business than any of her employers, Stella chose to go. Everybody was sorry. She was sorry too; but she knew her worth. What neither she nor I knew, until she started to leave the office, was that she had a secret weapon. When she started to leave, she picked the typewriter up off her table and began to stagger through the door with the heavy load in her arms. Only then did I learn that it was her own machine. Where she went, it went. Economy or no economy, she was rehired on the spot.

Many years later, when the Lasky Company had become Paramount and grown to an organization with thousands of employees and, incidentally, owned all its own typewriters, I happened to meet Stella Stray one morning on the Paramount lot, in tears. She was by this time the studio's senior employee, but another wave of so-called efficiency had struck and she had just been dropped again. I told Stella to dry her tears and wait right where she was. It took little more than a few minutes to find the office of the efficiency expert in question and drop into his startled ears a little preachment on the fact that loyalty is a two-way street. I doubt that my father would have used in the pulpit some of the more vigorous expressions I voiced on that occasion, but the sermon had its effect. Stella is still at Paramount, in the forty-sixth year of her loyal, and efficient, service.

4

I still keep in my safe a small red leather-covered notebook, whose ruled pages are now gray with age and frayed at the corners. On them, in pencil, are names and notations, some so faint and smudged that they can hardly be read. They are my first record of the actors and extra players and technicians who were called to or sought us out at the barn to become part of the cast and crew of *The Squaw Man*.

On one page can be made out the name of an eager young extra, with the notation, "$5—O.K.," meaning that we paid him $5 a day and that he was worth it. His telephone is given as West

2376, but you would not find him at that number today. He is identified as "H. E. Roach," but later years made him better known as Hal Roach, director of delightful comedies, founder of the studio that still bears his name, and one of the first motion picture producers to sense the growing importance and value of television.

On another page I come across "Miss Jane Darwell, Heinzeman Hotel, 620 South Grand," who had already progressed in pictures to the eminence of $60 a week. Perhaps that was why we could not use her in *The Squaw Man,* but far greater triumphs lay ahead of her in *The Grapes of Wrath* and countless other portrayals of a sturdy and lovable type of American womanhood. Jane Darwell appeared in a number of my later pictures. When I was casting *The Ten Commandments* in 1955 and sent word to her that there was a part for her if she wanted it, I had a charming, sunny letter in reply, saying how happy and contented she was in a retirement which I, for one, hope is only temporary.

Neither triumph nor tragedy had yet touched the name of Art Accord when I wrote it in my *Squaw Man* notebook and engaged him as one of "Cash Hawkins' crowd" in the ranch scenes. Forgotten today except by film historians, Art Accord went on to become one of the most popular cowboy stars, until, like so many others, he was swept aside when sound came to the screen. He was working in Mexico as a miner when he died in 1931, allegedly a suicide.

Other names and notes loom out of the past as I leaf through the little book: "$5 per day, J. G. Harper, strong old Kentuckian"; "Dick Palace, Indian, hair to shoulders"; "Horses, Mr. W. H. Stratton, $2.50 per horse, $3 per man"; "$25, Miss Helen Carruthers, dresses but no trains"; "Miss Nell Franzler, dark, squaw"; "Packard car, T. M. Hendry, six round trips, San Pedro, $3." It did not take many pages to list everything that needed to be listed. The notebook is fairly thick. Most of the pages are entirely blank.

In the center of the book, leaping from among the blank pages, large bold black handwriting catches the eye. Heavily inked, the words proclaim:

"I confess to the theft of the Orphans' Fund. Jim is innocent. Henry, Earl of Kerhill."

That was the page we photographed for the climax of *The Squaw Man*, the confession that cleared Jim Carston of the crime he had taken upon himself to save a fellow-officer's career. Today it would take several departments of the studio—planning, estimating, sketching, executing, and, I may add, spending—to photograph an "insert" like Lord Kerhill's confession. Things were simpler in 1913. You reached in your pocket for a pad, inked the words, focused the camera on them, cranked, and the shot was made.

Inside the front cover of the notebook are the two addresses that formed the two poles of my Hollywood world. One reads: "Studio—6284 Selma Ave." The other is: "Home. 6136 Lexington." Though Mrs. deMille and Cecilia were still in New York, I did not live alone. My companion was young, faithful, graceful, and, so I was assured by the newspaper advertisement through which I found her, quite tame. She was a gray prairie wolf. I bought her for a scene in *The Squaw Man*. The people, not to mention the horses, around Mr. Stern's barn were perhaps less trustful of her advertised virtues than I was. Because she made them rather uneasy, I kept her at home except when she was working, when she accompanied me to the studio on the end of a leash. 6136 Lexington was never bothered by burglars. Night after night, after the wolf and I had dined on my cooking, I turned her loose in the living room. While I read and as often as not fell asleep in my easy chair, the wolf would pace the four sides of the room, silently, intently, hour after hour through the night. I suppose she slept sometimes; but never while I was wakeful.

So we moved, stars, extras, technicians, director-general, and wolf, toward the first day of shooting—December 29, 1913. It was a clear, sunny day. If it had not been, there would have been no shooting. The history of motion pictures, on the technical side, is largely like the history of any science: a chronicle of the steps by which nature is made to work with man or prevented from working against him. The sun was California's great asset in the making of early films; but it does rain in California at times. Until, later on, we built glass walls and ceilings around our outdoor sets, rain meant that work stopped and cast and crew enjoyed a friendly game of cards or some knitting or chatting or reading, while the payroll kept rolling along. But our first day was a good day. As I look back on it, it was a very good day.

5

I still have the boxy little black camera that Al Gandolfi turned that day. Until sound film made it completely obsolete, we used that camera to shoot at least one scene of every one of my pictures.

Just before the shooting began, we all lined up outside the barn for a still photograph of the entire company. I have a print of that picture on the wall of my office, and next to it a picture of Paramount studio as it is today, so huge that it can only be photographed from the air. As I look at the old picture of the *Squaw Man* company, I can still identify many of those in it. Of those who have slipped out of memory's grasp, there is at least one whom I wish I could identify by name. He was the man who, without knowing it, taught the director-general a lesson that saved the company from ruin.

He had been standing around looking on one day, smoking a cigarette, while Al Gandolfi and I were loading the camera. A bit of the film got twisted. Al tore it off and threw it on the ground. The unknown idler, as I probably thought him to be, picked up the piece of film and touched it with the lighted end of his cigarette. Puff! It was gone, in a vanishing whiff of smoke. Was that how fragile the result of all our work was going to be? Was that how quickly our investment, not to mention the cash we were already taking in from exhibitors, could literally go up in smoke? I made a quick decision and gave Al Gandolfi a startlingly extravagant order. We would shoot two negatives of every scene in the picture. I would leave one at the barn and take one home with me every night. Then, if the barn or my home burned, we would be protected by the other negative.

I was thinking only of possible accident. Since then, as I look over that old picture of the *Squaw Man* company, I wonder if there are in it any of the people who had other thoughts. They were around somewhere, as I soon had reason to discover. Had they been sent or bribed by the Trust? Or were they just disgruntled? I say "they" but I do not even know if there were more than one. If there was only one, he was busy—for he, or they, or someone somewhere, was determined that *The Squaw Man* would never be finished.

That someone first showed his hand, or more accurately his heel, after we had been shooting for some days. Our film was processed in the dark little laboratory next to the barn. One morning, when I went in there, before my eyes had become accustomed to the dim light which was all we could use in the laboratory, my feet scuffled over something that made a rustling sound. I picked it up. When my fingers touched it, I did not need light to tell me what it was. It was our film—it was *The Squaw Man*—unwound, thrown in a heap on the floor, and, as fingers and eyes soon told me, scraped, pitted, disfigured, as if someone had put it on the floor, put his heel on it, and dragged it between heel and floor. It was completely ruined. So would our company have been, if I had not had the extra negative at home.

We went on shooting, and we took extra precautions about the laboratory. I had a bed put in it, and sometimes worked around the clock, taking catnaps at odd hours, partly to speed the production and partly to provide that the inquisitive someone would never be sure when he might have a clear field for another *danse macabre* on our precious film.

Working and sleeping in the laboratory had still other drawbacks, though. The roof leaked. However, I had an umbrella and Mamie Wagner. Mamie was our film cutter. When the rains came, if I was working, Mamie would leave her cutting and hold the umbrella over me. If she was working at her job, I would gallantly return the compliment. Somehow we managed to stay dry enough, by turns anyway, to keep the laboratory work abreast of each day's shooting. No more attempts at sabotage were made upon the film. It was not that our enemies were so easily discouraged. They were only waiting for another and better chance at us.

That came their way not long after I decided to bring Mrs. deMille and Cecilia to Hollywood, early in 1914. When I happened to mention that they were coming, Winifred Kingston, Dustin Farnum's leading lady and later his wife, protested that I certainly wasn't going to bring them to live with a wolf in that house on Lexington, was I? That would not do, she said; and, being a lady of decision, she scouted around and found a house out on Cahuenga Boulevard, which she said was much more suitable for the director-general's wife and child. Winifred was right, of course. The house was little more than a cottage, but it was in lovely open country, in the Cahuenga Pass between Hollywood and the San Fernando Valley.

The day Mrs. deMille and Cecilia arrived at the end of their long train ride from cold and wintry New York, I met them in an open touring car, the back of which I had filled with violets. At five cents a bunch, the violets were an extravagance, but I could not think of anything better than fresh flowers in January to symbolize my welcome and California's to the two new Californians. Five-year-old Cecilia, in her brown fur collar and muff, I remember, took it all with the unexcited dignity which has never deserted her.

The wolf, after playing her part in *The Squaw Man* with distinction, went to a zoo. At the end of her stint in the picture, evidently thinking that an established actress ought to be gracious to the crew, she tried to make friends with one of the workmen, who, however, was not so sure her intentions were honorable. He was plain scared. When the wolf approached him, he picked up the nearest object, a large heavy stick, and hit her aside the head with it. From then on, she developed a chronic shaking of the head which seemed incurable. Others since then have left Hollywood shaking their heads too. Nor was my wolf the last actress that a director might have liked to consign to a zoo.

My wolf was succeeded by a horse. It was possible to drive a car (if one had a car in 1914) over the bumpy, pitted, dirt road which was then Cahuenga Boulevard, but a horse was a much more practical means of transportation between my home and the barn-studio. Every morning Mrs. deMille packed the lunch which I carried slung over my shoulder in a leather pouch, as I rode to work. Every evening the same pouch carried home the precious extra negative to be stored in our attic.

It was a pleasant ride in the freshness of the morning and the cool of the evening on horseback past the vineyards and between the trees and brush which then grew wild in the pass through which thousands of cars now boil hourly on the Hollywood Freeway. It was also a lonely ride. Houses were few and far between. I almost never met anyone on the road—except for the time I almost met death there.

86

I had been warned, but paid no attention to the warning. After the mysterious "someone" found that ruining our negative film had not ruined us, I began to receive anonymous letters, crude threats made up by pasting words cut from newspapers together to convey a very plain message: get out of the motion picture business, fold up your studio, or your life won't be worth much. I treated the messages as I have always been inclined to treat anonymous letters: I threw them away. I did obtain a larger and wickeder-looking revolver than the one I had brought out from New York, and I wore the new and bigger one conspicuously to and from work. I never had occasion to use it, though. "Someone" was too clever for me, or perhaps too careful of his own hide.

He had evidently spied out my movements thoroughly, as well as the lay of the land between the barn and my new home. The trees and brush gave excellent cover. All I knew was that I was riding along homeward in the dusk, when zing! a sharp, whizzing sound passed by my head, followed soon by the crack of a shot from somewhere back in the thick growth beside the road. I turned my horse and drew my gun, ready to shoot. Not a leaf was stirring. The shot had evidently been fired from some distance, by "someone" who knew I was armed, and did not feel disposed to give away his location by another shot, just then. There was nothing for me to do but go on home.

"Someone" tried again, in the same place and same way, a few days later, but this time from a still greater distance and with no better—or should I say no worse?—luck. I have never tried to shoot anybody, to the best of my recollection; but if ever I do get tired of merely shooting pictures and decide to take up a little assassination on the side, I hope I shall be more businesslike about it than that unknown gunman of the Cahuenga Pass. He must have felt terribly frustrated after his two futile attempts at marksmanship. He gave up. I wonder if he is in that photograph on the wall of my office. Well, he deserves to be. He was the first critic of a DeMille picture.

Others took us less seriously. Jesse Lasky tells about his first visit to Hollywood, when he walked briskly up to the clerk in the Hollywood Hotel, announced himself as President of the Jesse L. Lasky Feature Play Company, and asked for directions to the company's studio.

"Never heard of it," was the clerk's laconic reply.

"Our director-general is Cecil B. deMille. Maybe—"

"Never heard of him either.

A less brisk and confident Jesse was walking away when the clerk had a second thought.

"There is a bunch of people making pictures in a barn down on Vine Street. They might know where your company is. Go down the boulevard here to Vine and turn right. You can't miss the barn, on your left."

When Jesse heard "barn," he knew he had found his company.

Local business people took longer to find that the movies were in Hollywood to stay. A few years ago I had a letter from a man in Stockton, California, telling that, as a messenger boy for a Los Angeles store in 1913 or 1914, he had been sent out to the Lasky barn with some cloth we had ordered, and strict instructions not to let the cloth out of his hand until he had our $6 in cash in the other hand. Of course we knew better than to ask any bank for credit; but the bank in Hollywood was still more cautious about movie people than we had imagined. It would not even take our deposits. There was a grocer, though, named C. C. Hall, on Cahuenga Boulevard, with more faith in our infant industry—or perhaps he had seen me riding back and forth and concluded that, if worse came to worst, he could always seize, distrain, and attach my horse. At all events, Hall's grocery was our bank.

Today Alfred Hitchcock and perhaps some other directors have the custom of playing small bits or extra parts in the pictures they direct. Part of the fun of seeing a Hitchcock picture is in spotting that distinguished director in the corner of some crowd scene, buying a newspaper or lighting a cigar or hurrying through the crowd to catch a train. It is fun for Mr. Hitchcock, too. It was not for fun, though, that I appeared as a faro dealer in *The Squaw Man*. It was to save the $3 we would have had to pay someone else. Mr. Hall, the grocer turned amateur banker for our benefit, was a braver man than perhaps he realized. But he never did have to slap a writ on my horse.

Speaking of horses reminds me to correct another "first" for which I have erroneously been given credit. It has been said that I was the first director to provide actors with individual dressing rooms near the sets on which they worked. Credit where credit is due—and, in this case, to Jacob Stern or whoever built his barn. The actors in *The Squaw Man* dressed in the horses' stalls.

6

At last *The Squaw Man* was, in the joyous phrase that no producer says or hears without a sigh of relief, "in the can."

We planned a gala screening for the executives, cast, and crew. Jesse was out from New York. He took the seat of honor, with Mrs. deMille and little Cecilia. Our stars, Dustin Farnum squiring his future bride Winifred Kingston, Monroe Salisbury, Billy Elmer, the Indian girl Red Wing whom I had cast in preference to an experienced actress because I wanted a real Indian to play her part—they were all there, with the rest of the cast, to see themselves in the Lasky Company's first feature play. Our key behind-the-camera men, Oscar Apfel, Fred Kley, Al Gandolfi and Alvin Wyckoff, our secretarial and editing staffs, namely, Stella Stray and Mamie Wagner, were there. So were all the crew and their families. So was the director-general, confident that what he had generally directed would indeed justify the company's policy of feature plays, real drama on the screen. Sam Goldfish, in New York, was awaiting the triumphant telegram.

But the real drama of that evening was not on the screen. It was in the audience which had gathered with such high hopes. The lights in the makeshift projection room dimmed. The title of *The Squaw Man* went on the screen—and promptly skittered off at the top of the screen. The actors appeared, and as promptly climbed out of sight, sometimes leaving their feet at the top of the screen and their heads peeking up from the bottom. The effect was much the same as we see nowadays on television when the vertical tuner is not properly adjusted. *The Squaw Man* was running away from us. We tried again, with the same effect. There was nothing to do but turn up the house lights and send the gaily gathered audience home, amid the kind of subdued, inconsequential, well-meant murmurs that one might hear from the guests if death suddenly struck at a dinner party.

Finally Jesse and I were left alone, with only one unspoken word in both our minds: ruin. Not only ruin for the Jesse L. Lasky Feature Play Company and, perhaps, for the whole idea of feature plays on film. More than that: personal, disastrous, irremediable ruin, quite possibly jail terms, for Jesse, Sam, Arthur Friend, and me—for Sam, remember, had already sold exhibition rights to *The Squaw Man*, sold them for cash which we had used in production, for a picture which persisted in climbing off the screen. We checked the projector; it was in perfect order. We checked the film; nothing wrong that we could see. This was not sabotage. The worst of it was that we could find no reason for the film's uncontrollable skittishness. The message Sam received in New York was one not of triumph but of disaster.

It was Sam who thought of one man who knew more about film than anyone else we knew: Sigmund Lubin, in Philadelphia. He was a man so genial and affable that everyone called him "Pop" Lubin. But he was also a member of the Trust, one of the group that we strongly suspected of wanting and trying to destroy us. It was a risky decision perhaps, but what alternative had we? If our company was already down the drain, there would be small loss in throwing six reels of apparently worthless film in after it. It was decided that I should take the film on to Philadelphia and that Jesse would meet me after attending to some business in San Francisco regarding one of his vaudeville acts. After the fiasco of *The Squaw Man* screening, it seemed prudent that Jesse should give his vaudeville business all the attention it required! If it prospered enough, he might be able to pay off the irate exhibitors —or perhaps a court-imposed fine.

I took a drawing room on the train to Chicago, to keep the second negative of *The Squaw Man*, in its tin boxes, near me all the way; and my revolver was near at hand too. Precious or worthless, nothing else was going to happen to that film until I put it in Pop Lubin's hands. Traveling across the country, I edited the second negative to match the first. Jesse met me in Chicago and glumly we made the last hop to Philadelphia together, not at all certain that it would live up to its name as the City of Brotherly Love.

Cannily, quizzically, Mr. Lubin listened to our tale of woe. Sometimes I can see the wheels going around in another person's head while he is calculating how to react to what I am saying, but Pop Lubin's bland smile was a perfect mask, until he finally said, "Let's look at the film." He turned our jittery masterpiece over to one of his technicians; and we waited.

I think they were the longest fifteen minutes I have ever waited. Then the technician came back. Pop's smile broadened. "There's nothing wrong with your film. We'll fix it."

There was nothing wrong with the film. All that had been wrong was the director-general's Dutch thrift. Sometime during the 18 days of *The Squaw Man's* production, I had come across a bargain: a secondhand, British-made machine for punching the sprocket holes along the side of the negative film. The man who sold it to me may have pointed out that his machine punched 65 sprocket holes per foot of film. If he did, I am sure I nodded wisely. What I had no notion of was the fact that all our other equipment and positive film were sprocketed at 64 holes to the foot. The difference between 1/64th and 1/65th of a foot I will leave to the mathematicians, but it was enough to account for the erratic behavior of our picture. The solution was simplicity itself. It was one of those things anyone should have thought of—anyone, that is, who knew as much about motion picture photography as Lubin knew and as we did not. The Lubin technicians simply pasted a thin strip of film over the edge of our negative, perforated it properly at 64; and the Jesse L. Lasky Feature Play Company was back in business.

Why did Lubin do that kindness to three upstart rivals of the Trust of which he was a part? He could have sealed our ruin by keeping the solution of my blunder to himself. Did he see future business for his own photographic printing company in helping us? Perhaps—though the Trust generally saw no future whatever in feature plays. Looking back on "Pop" Lubin, smiling at us, perhaps laughing at us just a little too, reassuring us, that fateful day in Philadelphia, I think the explanation of his help is a very simple one, but is the one that a cynical view of human nature always looks for last. He was a good man. If we looked for that explanation of human conduct more often, we would be disappointed many times, yes; but we might also find, oftener than we imagine, that it is true.

Anyway, I could have kissed "Pop" Lubin's round, amused, and beaming countenance that day in Philadelphia. Restraining those ardors, however, until we got out of his office, Jesse and I did allow ourselves to do a little dance on the sidewalk; and we ordered champagne at our hotel. *The Squaw Man* had been saved —saved, anyhow, for its greatest ordeal, the New York trade show.

7

In 1914 there were no previews of the kind we have now, when a new picture is "sneaked" into a theater on an ordinary night and run as a surprise before a theoretically average audience, to get their reactions, which they are carefully asked to write on cards provided. I say theoretically because there is one previewer who never misses a preview. He is the man—gallantry forbids me to think it could be a woman—who, no matter what the picture is, no matter how many millions of dollars it cost, no matter what array of talent worked before and behind the camera to bring it to the screen, always gives us the mature fruitage of his critical judgment by writing on his preview card, with simple eloquence, "It stinks." I always look for that card among the hundreds that come in after a preview. When it turns up, as it invariably does, there is a warm glow about it, like meeting an old friend. Age cannot wither, one feels, nor custom stale his infinite monotony. In a rapidly changing world, there is something to be almost grateful for in the fidelity of that previewer who writes of every picture that "it stinks." But he was not around in 1914.

Instead, there were the buyers. Some had already bought *The Squaw Man* on the strength of Sam's persuasion. Others wanted to see the goods before they paid the bill. There were others, too, in that first New York trade show audience, whose opinion would not mean economic life or death, as the buyers' would, but whom I was no less anxious to impress. There was mother. And there was Bill. Mother, I knew, wanted to be proud of her younger son. Bill, like the master of words he always was, had probably prepared alternative sets of phrases, in which brotherly charity blunted the rapier edge of wit in greater or lesser degree, depending upon how bad Cecil's galloping tintypes really turned out to be.

Sam Goldfish was host at the trade show. Jesse and I took seats in the rear of the little theater to watch for the moving of heads, the shifting of bodies, the coughs, the laughter at the wrong places, and the other unconscious signs which are always a more accurate gauge of audience reaction than what the viewers say or write about a picture.

92

This time the actors and titles stayed on the screen where they belonged. The story held. We saw no restlessness or boredom. When the screen went white again and the house lights were turned up, Sam was the center of congratulations. He introduced Jesse and me to his customers, and we received our share of praise. But I was not entirely sure until I looked toward where Bill was sitting with his secretary, a young girl named Anne Bauchens. My learned, brilliant, older brother did not use any of his phrases. He just nodded at me, slowly. Then I knew we had won.

The buyers bought. In those days pictures were sold on what was called a "State's rights" basis, which had nothing to do with Constitutional questions, but meant that the distributor acquired exclusive right to arrange the exhibition of a picture in a given state. *The Squaw Man* was released on February 15, 1914. Two weeks later, only 17 states in the Middle West remained unsold. A week after that, there were only four; and I feel sure that Iowa, Kansas, Missouri, and Nebraska did not long remain deprived of seeing the Lasky Company's first feature play.

Motion picture advertising has never been marked by any excess of shrinking modesty. Before the end of March, the company was taking a full page in *The Moving Picture World* to announce the production of *Brewster's Millions*, calling Jesse Lasky "America's Most Artistic Director," Oscar Apfel "Acknowledged Peer of Directors and Genius of Innovators," and stretching the imagination of anyone who remembered my Broadway career by terming me "Master Playwright, Director and Author of Numerous Dramatic Successes."

The observant will note the absence from that list of one name which surely belonged among those responsible for the company's initial success. I do not know who wrote the advertisement, any more than I know who, seven months later in the same periodical, referred to Sam Goldfish as "head of the Jesse L. Lasky Feature Play Company." These were but tiny clouds, portents of coming storms; but to us in the flush of our first success, the skies looked only clear and bright.

There was jubilation in the barn and at the little cottage on Cahuenga when I returned to Hollywood to plunge into the company's ambitious program of turning out one picture a month. Jesse and Mrs. Lasky were there when the news came that *The*

Squaw Man was sure to gross twice its cost. The four of us, Laskys and deMilles, joined hands and danced around the stove which was the most prominent article of furniture in the Cahuenga cottage. When we sat down to dinner, the family silver gleamed from the tablecloth. It never went back to Simpson's again.

6

Have you ever had to sit still while someone told you the story of a movie that he saw last night? I have. And, though I love movies, that harrowing experience has helped me to make a decision which faces me at this point. I here resolve that I will not tell in this book the story, cast, cost, and technical production history of all the 70 pictures I have produced so far. I can imagine few things less interesting than such a catalogue would be to the general reader, or, for that matter, to me! When a picture of mine is in production, it is important to me to know the exact width and color of the sash worn by that fourth extra in the second row of the crowd over there at the right. When one of my pictures is in release, I am very much interested in what it is doing at the box office in Milan, Manila, or Mankato, Minnesota. But in the long view, as I look back to 1914, the fact that *The Squaw Man* eventually grossed $244,700 means much less, very much less, than the two $1 bills I found on my desk when I arrived at the barn one morning in that year.

Standing by the desk, where she had just put the $2, looking very grim, with her lips set in a thin line of determination, was a girl I had hired some weeks before, just out of high school, to help with the secretarial work. Her name was Gladys Rosson. She had written a note about the $2, reminding me that a week or so previously she had asked me for a $2 raise in her weekly salary. I had refused it or postponed it. I remembered that. What I did not know, she proceeded to inform me, was that she had then gone with the same request to Jesse Lasky, who had expansively granted it. Gladys was in triumph—until she went home and told the story to her mother. Mrs. Rosson was less impressed than Gladys with Gladys' cleverness.

"Mr. deMille refused the raise and then you went and got it from Mr. Lasky without telling Mr. deMille?"

"Yes!"

"Then the first thing tomorrow morning you'll take the $2 and give them to Mr. deMille and tell him what you did!"

And there was Gladys, doing her duty, with much more the air of a stoic martyr than a repentant criminal. That was my first introduction to the Rossons. I have come to think of them that way—as "the Rossons"—because, though there was never a family of more vividly distinct individuals, neither was there ever a family of more close knit unity and loyalty. In time I would come to know them all well: Dick, an able motion picture director until his untimely death; Hal, one of Hollywood's best cameramen; Arthur, the second unit director on all my recent pictures; Helene and "Queenie" (for years no one has called her by her given name of Ethel) whom I never fail to see when I go to New York; and Gladys, standing there by my desk, surrendering her $2, yes, but nothing of her ramrod dignity. This is not the last time that Gladys Rosson's name will appear in these pages. From that day in 1914, she remained with me for 39 years, as secretary and as closest, most trustworthy, most patient and unselfish, most fiercely loyal of friends, until she died. And of course she got her raise back right away, only I made it $4 a week instead of $2.

I have said that Gladys was patient. I am afraid patience is a virtue requisite in those around me: but there is one that I admire still more. That is honesty, including the kind displayed by another employee of the Lasky Company in 1914. I had met a man named Horwitz on the train on my first or second trip across country as director-general. He was intelligent and willing; and those were the days before Hollywood became as closed a shop as it is now—closed all too often to new talent for which seniority regulations leave no room. I offered him a job, and he accepted.

Horwitz was working out very well and I saw the possibility of making him a full-fledged director, when one day he came to me and said he was leaving.

"But why? Don't you like pictures?"

"Yes."

"Don't you like California?"

"Yes."

"Is there any difficulty, are you in any kind of trouble that maybe we could——"

"No, nothing like that at all."

"Then why are you leaving?"

"Well, to tell you the truth, Mr. deMille, I just can't stand you."

There is no answer to that. Horwitz left. I have always had a warm feeling of admiration for him.

It is incidents like those which stand out in memory most sharply; but of course life was not all a tissue of touching or amusing episodes. Hard work and constant expansion went on at and around the barn, where new buildings and roadways were added after we bought the land and the site was no longer Jacob Stern's barnyard, but became the Lasky Studio. Before the end of 1914 we had five directors and five cameramen at work and a stock company of 80 players.

The barn was kept, though. It is still standing, now on the studio lot of Paramount Pictures Corporation, where it was moved when the Lasky lot at Selma and Vine streets was sold. A bank now stands on the busy corner of Selma and Vine, but if the television folk who hurry past there on their way to or from the Brown Derby ever pause long enough at that corner, they can read a bronze plaque on the wall of the bank commemorating *The Squaw Man* and our first studio.

In December, 1956, the old barn itself was officially dedicated as a "registered landmark" by the California State Parks Commission and the Historical Landmarks Committee of Los Angeles County, the first time that any structure or site connected with the motion picture industry had been singled out for that honor. I am glad that Jesse Lasky was still alive then, to be present at the dedication, with Sam Goldwyn, Adolph Zukor, Winifred Kingston, Jane Darwell, Stella Stray, and other pioneers of Hollywood. The speaker representing the Los Angeles County Board of Supervisors, John Anson Ford, said that in the old barn the age-old art of the drama had "found a new and amazing dimension." So had our lives.

2

Our second production, *Brewster's Millions*, directed by Oscar Apfel, taught us fledglings a lesson in showmanship which has been of value to me all my life. As usual, as soon as a finished print was ready, we shipped it to New York for the all-important showing to potential buyers. Sam and Jesse ran it first. Now *Brewster's Millions* was an hilarious comedy. It had been a huge success on the stage. But our *Brewster's Millions* was very obviously a complete dud. There was not a chuckle in it from start to finish. It was too late to do anything about it. The date had been set for the trade showing. It would just have to be shown to the buyers— buyers?—in its pristine, unrelieved dreariness.

Sam, unable to face the agony, left the theater as soon as the showing started and spent his time wandering aimlessly through the streets. Jesse stayed to suffer it through with the stony-faced buyers who would certainly not buy a comedy with no laughs. At length Sam's wanderings brought him back in front of the theater while the last reel was still on. Sam has always been a brave man. He went in, to join Jesse at the funeral of our hopes. The first sound that greeted him when he went through the lobby door was a roar of laughter. This was followed by another, with the steady undercurrent murmur of mirth which meant that the audience was enjoying itself immensely. Sam looked at the screen. Yes, it was *Brewster's Millions*, our *Brewster's Millions*, and it was sweeping the house with gales of fun.

What made the difference? An audience. Emotion is infectious. You never know what a picture will do until it plays before an audience in a well-filled house. Sam and Jesse, watching the picture in executive solitude, of course did not get the impact of *Brewster's Millions*. How many people ever laugh aloud when they are alone? But put them in an audience, the more crowded the better as long as there is at least minimum comfort, and the shared emotion releases their individual emotions.

That is a bit of showmanship psychology which a Hitler, for instance, knew well and used evilly. Winston Churchill knew it when he refused to have the bombed-out House of Commons rebuilt large enough to provide a seat for every member: he wanted, he said, to keep the special feeling which attends great occasions when the House is literally packed. After our experience with *Brewster's Millions*, we learned what every producer learns: never show your picture to one or two or three people if you can help it, if what you are looking for is a genuine, spontaneous reaction.

There have been times when, for one reason or another, I have wanted to get the reaction of some one person to a picture before it was released, perhaps some person whose good opinion would be of value to the picture or whose critical judgment would be of value to me in making possible cuts or re-takes. Unless that person is a professional film maker, accustomed to seeing pictures alone, I always invite him to see it with a group of at least 15 or 20 if possible. Then I get the truth. It is not that such persons would tell me untruths if they saw a picture all alone in a projection room. It is rather that they simply would not see the picture as it was made to be seen unless they saw it with an audience.

Perhaps in telling that I am giving away a trade secret. I do not think so. It is obvious, when you analyze it. Motion pictures are a mass medium. When I go to the Louvre and stand before the "Mona Lisa," other people in the room may be a distraction, not a help to my enjoyment of it. Millions of people have felt, indelibly, the impact of the "Mona Lisa," but she has spoken to each of them individually, almost privately. That is the way painting and some of the other arts speak. But the theater, whether on stage or screen, does not speak at its fullest and highest privately; nor, I might add, does the splendid pageantry of a coronation, or the solemnity of a state funeral, or, for that matter, the World's Series or the Derby. Of them, the audience is a truly necessary part. The motion picture producer or the critic who forgets that, who makes or judges films by no standard but his private, solitary reactions, may satisfy himself—and no one begrudges him that —but he is leaving out an essential element of the medium in which he is working; and that is why those producers so seldom suceed, and why those critics have so little influence.

That is all a rather elaborate way of saying that I make pictures for people. If any aspiring young director or screen writer happens to pick up from this book any ideas which appeal to him, I wish him better fortune than that which greeted a slender young man who came and said he would like to work with me while we were still at the old Lasky lot. I did not talk with him long before seeing in him promise, if not genius. He had had some experience in the industry; he had come out to Universal City as Carl Laemmle's secretary and was soon coping successfully with such brilliant if demanding talent as Erich von Stroheim, then Universal's ace director. I left the young man in my office and went straight to Jesse, to say that we ought to hire him.

"How much is he making?"

"$450 a week. He wants more, and he's worth it."

"We can't do it, Cecil!"

"But, Jesse, this boy is a genius. I can see it. I know it."

"Geniuses we have all we need, Cecil. Tell him no."

So I had to go back to my office, where the young man was waiting, and tell him, "I'm sorry, but we can't use you, Mr. Thalberg."

Louis B. Mayer was less penny-wise. He got the young man for $600 a week and thus gave the first big boost to the brilliant career which was to make Irving Thalberg one of the few producers whose names have outlived their lives. Thalberg died at the age of 37, in 1936; but there is still what Bosley Crowther, the learned critic of *The New York Times,* calls a "lasting cult of Thalberg" in Hollywood.

In an industry choked with "awards," one which is most genuinely valued is the Thalberg Award, voted by the Board of Directors of the Academy of Motion Picture Arts and Sciences, without any of the ballyhoo and political maneuvering that precedes the voting for the better-known "Oscars." The Thalberg Award is not even given every year, but only when the Board of the Academy decides that it is specially merited. I had to say a regretful "no" to young Mr. Thalberg that day in my office in the Lasky studio; but his career and his enduring reputation bear out what I saw in him that day. I think of that now, when I see in my office the small bronze statue of his young head and shoulders: the Thalberg Award which was given me many, many years later, after I had been in Hollywood a long, long time.

100

There were no awards in 1914, however, except human nature's best award, the satisfaction of doing hard work well. After working with Oscar Apfel for some months I felt able to direct a picture all on my own and I decided upon *The Virginian*, a play adapted from Owen Wister's novel, in which Dustin Farnum had starred on the stage ten years before. Perhaps the selection of this vehicle helped Dusty make a decision that was something of a bombshell: he announced that he was leaving the stage for motion pictures permanently. The success of *The Squaw Man* helped too. In the statement announcing his decision, Farnum attributed that success to "the manner in which it was made—the cleverness of direction and the way the whole thing was handled by everyone concerned." Coming from a stage star of Dusty's magnitude, this was a sign of change coming over the theater's attitude toward films.

Although *The Squaw Man* was not the first feature length film, it is not too much to say, as Alva Johnston has said, that "it did revolutionize the industry." A week after Dustin Farnum's statement, we were able to announce that H. B. Warner had signed with the Lasky Company to appear in a film version of his stage success, *The Ghost Breaker*. Motion pictures were beginning to be taken seriously by people to whom serious theater was their very life.

Shooting on *The Virginian*, my first venture in solo direction, began April 14, 1914. The cameraman was our best, Alvin Wyckoff; then and later, critics would give special praise to his work on the many pictures he photographed for me. From the beginning of motion pictures, and still more today, the cameraman does much more than run the camera. Today, in fact, the chief cameraman, or cinematographer as he now prefers to be called, hardly ever touches the camera. That is done by his assistants. He is an artist who paints with light.

In the early days, before the techniques of lighting a scene were so well developed and before color photography had brought its special problems, the cameraman's function was simpler, but even then many a director was indebted to his cameraman's inventiveness and knowledge of what the camera could see and capture. I cannot fail to acknowledge my debt to Alvin Wyckoff and the other cinematographers who have worked with me, skillfully and quite often very patiently, through the years.

One incident in *The Virginian* showed the greater flexibility and effectiveness of motion pictures, as compared with stage technique. The story called for the hanging of two cattle thieves. Good taste, I felt, forbade showing an actual hanging on the screen. On the stage, a playwright might have had another character come on and tell about the hanging in genuinely moving, even heartrending words; but motion pictures had not yet found a voice. In *The Virginian* we photographed, not the hanging of the thieves, but the shadow cast on the ground by their two bodies suspended from their makeshift gallows. The story point was made; and the effect was, if anything, starker, yet certainly much less gruesomely repellent than showing the actual hanging would have been.

A book might be written about the accidents, some tragic, some happy, which sometimes happen during the production of a film. I have in my film vault what I call the "accident film," scenes of some of the untoward events which happened to take place during various productions while the camera was turning. I promise all concerned that the "accident film" will never be released! One such event occurred during *The Virginian*, when Dustin Farnum was supposed to rescue Winifred Kingston from a stagecoach bogged down in the middle of a river. Dusty rode up gallantly, reached into the coach, took a good grip on the fair lady, deftly dragged her forth; and then she lost her balance. Into the river went the leading lady, head over crinolines. The scene was spoiled; Winifred had to be dried out, re-costumed, and re-rescued; but Winifred was a good trouper and held no lasting grudge against her rescuer. She must have forgiven Dusty. She married him later. I have a feeling, though, that he probably did not choose a reminiscent riverbank as the properly romantic spot to ask for her hand.

Dusty's rescues of Winifred in *The Virginian* seemed dogged by a malign fate. Another of them would not have ended so happily if Winifred and Monroe Salisbury had not been such good troupers. In this scene, Winifred and Salisbury were to be sitting on the ground, Dustin was to ride up as usual, draw his gun, and shoot apparently straight at Salisbury. Horror was to be duly registered—until the camera focused on Salisbury's feet, revealing that what Dusty had shot and killed was a menacing rattlesnake, coiled there unknown to Salisbury or Winifred, who must have been very deeply engaged in their conversation.

We had imported from Texas two magnificent rattlers, the Texas variety being much more ominous looking than the friendly little California rattlesnake. Our two Texans had been promptly and thoroughly defanged. I like realism in pictures, but there is a limit. So the precautions were all taken, including the best insurance I could find that the snake would be actually killed by one shot. I had made friends with a cowboy named Frank Hopkins, the best shot I have ever known. He was to stand out of camera range and shoot the snake while the camera shot Dusty firing a blank. We planned to do the scene twice, despatching one snake in each.

But then the Los Angeles zoo heard somehow what we were planning and sent an emissary to me with a perfectly reasonable proposition. Why destroy those two splendid Texan specimens? Why not use them for the close-ups, but in the killing scene use California rattlers, which the zoo would gladly give me in exchange for the Texans? I agreed. The scene was shot perfectly. California rattler number one died for the sake of art, all as scheduled.

Meanwhile, however, California rattler number two had been observing all this and evidently decided that life was more precious than art. The moment the prop man turned him loose, he made straight for the protected refuge afforded by the legs of Monroe Salisbury, who was sitting on the ground with his knees drawn up. Between Salisbury's calves and thighs, snake number two took his stance, and coiled.

"It's all right," I said to Salisbury. "He's been defanged. Don't worry. We'll just wait. He's not dangerous."

Then the white-faced, shaking prop man plucked my sleeve. "He's not defanged, Mr. deMille! The zoo man says they didn't defang him, and neither did I!" He did not say it in a whisper. Everyone on the set heard it.

I looked toward Frank Hopkins, ready with his rifle; but the angle was too dangerous. He could not have hit the snake without hitting Salisbury.

As quietly as I could in the mounting tension, I said, "Monroe—

Winifred—don't move. Sit perfectly still. No one move—no one."

Marvelously, no one did. For minutes we waited, stock still. Then the snake slithered out from his privileged sanctuary. Frank Hopkins' rifle cracked. He never missed. We all breathed again, and went on with *The Virginian.*

"Irritating" is one of the milder words some of my co-workers have applied to me when I insist upon checking and rechecking every detail of a production. Perhaps the ordeal of Monroe Salisbury, shared by all of us in those eternal minutes of waiting for a rattlesnake to make up his mind, had something to do with my resolution never to take anything for granted. The zoo man and the prop man each thought the other had defanged the snakes, or perhaps neither of them thought of it at all. The producer, I learned, has to think of everything. Explanations *post ·mortem* come a little late. Alibis do not mop up spilled milk, and crying over it only increases its dampness. Since *The Virginian,* every detail of a DeMille production has been checked by DeMille; and he is the only one to blame if anything goes wrong.

The critics were kind to *The Virginian.* "Technically perfect," "a picture of the West as it was," "photography . . . smooth and clear" were some of the phrases they used after its release in September, 1914. We agreed with the critics. With a story based on a best-selling novel and successful play, starring the play's leading man, and, if I may say so, fairly well produced and directed, we knew that we had in *The Virginian* a good property, which would add to the company's luster. But we held it back until September, releasing first, in August, what was really my second picture, *The Call of the North,* memorable today perhaps only because it marked the first screen appearance of Robert Edeson and Theodore Roberts, two more established actors in the legitimate theater to succumb to the lure of films.

Theodore Roberts had been a wonderful scene-stealing character actor in the stock company at Elitch's Gardens, Denver, when Mrs. deMille and I had played there some years before. We often took supper with Theodore and Mrs. Roberts, who made the most delicious spaghetti dishes. Alas, though, the bonds of matrimony proved as fragile and delicate as the products of Mrs. Roberts' cookery. A divorce was followed by Theodore's lodging for a year in New York's old Ludlow Street jail, for his refusal or inability to pay alimony. Not unnaturally that experience made New York state seem a rather cold, unfriendly place to Theodore, especially as he had no wish either to go on paying alimony forever or to spend any more time as the state's guest in Ludlow Street. California was in every way more congenial. The loss to the New York stage and to Mrs. Roberts was a gain for Hollywood and the world, for Theodore Roberts was soon established in the new medium as "the grand old man of the screen."

4

It may be that our withholding of *The Virginian* till September was somewhat motivated by another drama that was taking place not on any stage or screen, but in certain offices and around certain luncheon tables in New York. That city was being visited, not for the first or last time, by a tall, thin, rather solemn-looking former telegrapher and correspondence school salesman from Utah: a man with an idea. His name is completely unknown to the public today, but a little sketch he drew on a blotter in one of those New York offices he visited in 1914 is known the world around.

W. W. Hodkinson had started a small picture theater in Ogden, Utah, some years before. His policy was a clean family theater, with clean pictures, for admission to which he was bold enough to charge double the usual price of a ticket, namely, ten cents. It succeeded. Inevitably, being the serious, forward-looking man he was, Hodkinson branched out, became a district manager for the Trust, with territory extending from Colorado to the West Coast, then branched out still farther with his own company distributing pictures throughout the West. He made a success of that too, and asked himself the inevitable question: why only the West? There were 48 states: why not one big distributing organization to guarantee the producers a steady nationwide market and the exhibitors a steady flow of product from all the best producing companies through one channel? That was the idea Hodkinson brought to New York.

When Hodkinson's lanky form stepped off the train, the old, haphazard uneconomic "state's rights" method of marketing films was doomed. By mid-1914, his new distributing company had contracted for the distribution throughout the country of 104 pictures a year. Our company was to provide 30, Adolph Zukor's Famous Players 52, and the remaining 22 were to come from the Bosworth, the Morosco, and other smaller companies. This meant a hasty revision and speed-up of our proudly announced policy of one picture a month: the company announced 28 new pictures for the next Paramount year.

Paramount Pictures Corporation, the Hodkinson distributing company, had been named most casually. On his way to one of the conferences in New York leading to the establishment of his new company, W. W. Hodkinson happened to pass a building called the Paramount apartments. That struck him as a good name. During the conference, remembering the Wasatch range which is one of the scenic glories of Utah, where he had got his start, Hodkinson drew on a desk blotter a picture of a snow-capped mountain; and Paramount had the trademark which it has carried ever since, all around the world.

The first Paramount release was not one of our pictures, but a Famous Players film in which H. B. Warner had starred before coming to us in California. It was billed as *"The Lost Paradise* by Ludwig Fulda and H. C. DeMille." Thus, H. B. Warner's first picture for Paramount was a film version of my father's play, and his last, or what he says will be his last, was my 1956 version of *The Ten Commandments,* for which he came out of retirement to play one of the most moving scenes in the whole picture.*

How far we had come in less than a year was evidenced when David Belasco agreed to sell ten of his plays to the Lasky Company for $100,000 against half the profits we confidently expected to make on them—and did make on all but one. That one made no profit because the film itself was never made. It was *The Darling of the Gods,* which had been a Broadway hit with Blanche Bates and George Arliss; we had signed George Arliss to repeat on the screen his stage success. More than that, we sent to Japan for thousands of dollars worth of authentic and valuable props and costumes, including a samurai sword so precious that when I showed it to Sessue Hayakawa later, he put a piece of paper in his mouth and over his nose before he would lift the sword to examine it, lest even his breath affect the fineness of its edge. But

* The Ten Commandments was H. B. Warner's last film. He died in December, 1958, only a few weeks before Mr. deMille's death. (*Ed.*)

106

it was the story that defeated us. The customs and conflicts of the samurai had been intelligible and moving on the stage, but the executive and sales force of the company concluded that the public at that time would not accept a picture with a Japanese theme.

The Japanese props and gorgeous costumes were fun to have around, though. I still have, in the passageway between my home and office, a handsome palanquin in which, some hundreds of years ago, members of the noble Tokugawa family were cramped and jolted from place to place on the strong shoulders of their bearers. When I walk by it each morning, though, I am reminded of what all novelists and playwrights, and some producers also, should remember: that not every story, however good it may be on paper or on the stage, can be successfully translated to the screen.

I was anxious to get my directorial teeth into the Belasco plays, and one advantage of being director-general was that I could choose my own subject. First, however, in the summer of 1914, I finished *What's His Name*, from George Barr McCutcheon's novel, and *The Man From Home*, from the play by Booth Tarkington and Harry Leon Wilson.

In our dealings with Hodkinson, Belasco, Zukor, and other giants, we were beginning to think and talk in hundreds of thousands of dollars, but back at the corner of Selma and Vine we were still not above pressing members of the family into service when low-cost extras or bit players were needed. Cecilia and later her cousins, Margaret and Agnes deMille, can be glimpsed in some of these early pictures. In *Where The Trail Divides*, directed by James Neill, we needed to show a woman captured by Indians, slung across the back of a horse, and so carried off to her dreadful fate. Someone—it could have been the director-general—remembered that Mrs. deMille had very long beautiful hair which, loosened and trailing down the horse's side, would add a good touch of feminine helplessness and horror; so it was Mrs. deMille, with tresses streaming, who was unceremoniously pitched across the horse and uncomfortably jolted away.

After Cecilia's first or second appearance in a film, with the growing self-consciousness of all her six years, she began to develop the fatal habit of looking straight into the camera. That is the one thing an actor must never do. Paternal patience failing

107

to cure her of the habit, one day I spoke to her about it on the set with a director's sharpness. That night, after telling her mother about it, she added, "I don't understand father. He's not a bit like *that* at home." The implied compliment, from a very independent and forthright little daughter, soothed any regret I may have felt at having to teach her the elementary lesson that when we are making a picture, the picture is all that counts and there is no time or room for hurt feelings.

One of the reviews of *The Man From Home* gave an encouraging sign that I was learning my new trade. W. Stephen Bush, in *The Moving Picture World,* wrote: "It emphasizes in a thoroughly convincing manner that, as a medium of dramatic expression, the film has no metes and bounds. A play in which so much seemed to depend on the dialogue has been adapted for the screen absolutely without loss of any values, either of dramatic action or of characterization."

I was also learning other things besides the specialized art of the silent film. I still keep on my desk and use as a paperweight a small, plain ingot of almost pure silver, one of my graduation prizes from the school of experience. After we took over the film laboratory from Burns and Revier and increased our production to meet Paramount's schedule, we had thousands of feet of film being processed regularly in the large developing and "fixing" tanks. When a tank of the fixing fluid—"hypo" as it was called— had served its purpose, it was simply taken out to the street and poured into the gutter. Of this practice the city authorities soon took a forbidding view. Our hypo was staining their gutters. First they fined us. Well, we still had to dispose of the hypo. We paid the fines and continued to pour the fluid out. Then the guardians of the purity of gutters threatened sterner measures—jail if we did not stop being such a public nuisance. Still, we had to dispose of the useless hypo somehow. Enter a representative of a trucking company, with a proposition.

He would haul away our old hypo and charge us only $5 a load. I opined that that seemed high. He promptly came down to $4, then $3, then $2. His generosity made me suspicious; there was something here that I did not know. I told him I would think it over. The trucking company was so anxious to serve us, however, that their man was back in a day or so with an offer to haul away the hypo free of charge.

"Now," I said, "I know there is something fishy about this. I don't know what you do with the hypo—maybe it's a great cleaning fluid or you use it in paint or distil it for liquor. But I'll make a deal with you. You tell me what it is I don't know about this, how you make your profit out of it, and you can have the hypo if you will split the profit with us, 50-50."

The trucking agent laughed, and explained. In the course of processing film, it was coated with silver. The silver washed off in the hypo tank. The enterprising truckers were making a small fortune extracting the silver from the used hypo, for which motion picture companies were paying them $5 a load just to get rid of it. The ingot on my desk came out of our share of the first silver recovered from our first load of hypo. Evidently the city fathers had been as ignorant as I. Otherwise they could have advertised that in Hollywood the very gutters ran with silver.

In preparing for *The Rose of the Rancho,* and realizing that we would be making other outdoor films, our company leased what was to become known as the Lasky Ranch, several hundred acres in the San Fernando Valley.

There was an old stone house on the Lasky Ranch. I went out there one day while workmen were cleaning it out for us, burning the trash they found in it. In their bonfire I noticed something that looked like parchment, an official document of some kind. Since it was only singed, I fished it out of the fire. It was a copy of the first census of the city of Los Angeles; when I presented it to the city later, I learned that the original had been lost. That first census taker was nothing if not conscientious and objective. He listed the inhabitants by their trades, so many bakers, so many blacksmiths, and so on—"and one idiot." Happy little old Los Angeles. You have changed.

In *The Rose of the Rancho,* Monroe Salisbury gave another demonstration of the courage he had shown when the puzzled rattlesnake took refuge under his knees. In one scene I wanted a water jug shot out of a man's hands, as he held it a few inches over his head. It could have been shown in two camera shots— one of the bullet being fired and another of the jug breaking, as it could have been rigged to break; but I wanted the audience to

109

see the thing really done. It was William Tell all over, but with a live and lethal bullet, not an arrow, aimed near the actor's head. I explained the scene to Monroe Salisbury, and told him that the man shooting at him would be Frank Hopkins, who had killed the snake. Salisbury was willing. He said he knew that, in anything I asked him to do, every possible precaution would be taken for safety—a comforting compliment to the director, but in the circumstances, short of putting the actor behind a thick wall higher than his head, the only precaution I could take was to put the gun in the hand of the best shot I knew. The scene was taken. Frank Hopkins aimed just above Salisbury's head and between his upheld hands, fired, and hit the jug square in the middle. As the shattered pieces of pottery fell about his feet, Salisbury said to me, "Was it all right, Mr. deMille? Or do you want to do it again?" Monroe Salisbury was a professional.

Believability, Belasco realism, was what I was trying to get into this first Belasco play to reach the screen. Monroe Salisbury was willing to risk his life or a shattered hand to help get it. Executives of any film company would certainly applaud him for that. What the front office type would always be less likely to applaud was the other kind of risk which I took, when I re-shot some scenes of *The Rose of the Rancho* just to get on the screen a beautiful antique Spanish sidesaddle which we discovered on one of the old California ranchos while the picture was in production. That sort of thing, you see, costs money; that is what executives do not like about it.

I do not mean that there was any complaint from Jesse or Sam about the sidesaddle; it was not until later that I came in head-on contact with the adding machine mind. I mention the old Spanish saddle—it was beautiful, red velvet trimmed with gold, with a little seat facing sideways and a little platform on which the *señora* could rest her feet as she rode—because that was perhaps my first application of a principle which I have followed consistently ever since, to the dismay sometimes of the front office: I will always consider any amount of money spent on a film well spent if what it buys can be photographed. That may be acting talent, it may be months of costly research in libraries around the world, it may be genuine jewels which will help an actress feel her part better than if she were wearing paste. It may be any-

110

thing: if it can go on the screen and add to the story, it is worth its cost.

I knew that women in the audience would notice and delight in every detail of that antique saddle, just as men, when they saw the jug shot out of Monroe Salisbury's hands, would know that they were seeing a real gun fight, not a piece of trick photography. I did not have David Belasco particularly in mind, but not doubt the jug and saddle, along with some other ingredients, helped produce the comment he made, in his characteristically rich Belasco style, when he saw *The Rose of the Rancho* on the screen.

"It was like a dream," he wrote, "to sit in my theater last night and see my production of *The Rose of the Rancho* unfold in all its beautiful color and with all its dramatic action. You have caught the very shadows of the land of my childhood. My enthusiasm could not be greater. . . . I think it is the most perfect motion picture play I have ever seen." That is a beautifully pure specimen of the Belasco style; but the canny old wizard of the theater would not have gone so far overboard in his praise unless he had really seen something to praise and scented in this flickering new kind of theater the sweet smell of success.

5

For me the most enduringly memorable event of that autumn was the arrival of my brother Bill. After *The Squaw Man,* I had asked him to come to Hollywood. I saw what his writing talent could do for motion pictures, now coming of age as real plays on the screen. A number of my early pictures carry the credit, "Scenario by Cecil B. deMille," but, apart from the early years in New York when I tried my hand at everything in the theater, I did not and do not consider myself a writer. I think better in visual images and dramatic situations rather than in words. Bill had a good visual sense too, as his later career as a director showed, but he was primarily a superb craftsman of language. His taste in drama differed from mine as a cameo maker's differs from that of a painter who loves a big canvas; and a cameo can be as beautiful as a huge mural. But what I hoped for principally from Bill was that he would bring to motion pictures that gift for putting dramatic situations into words which had made him a

111

successful playwright. All this I urged upon him with all the persuasiveness I could command. He said he would think it over.

In his deliberate way, Bill thought it over throughout the spring and summer of 1914, and then decided that he would give it a try. He would come to Hollywood for a couple of months. He stayed for 40 years.

The day of Bill's arrival, we were in the midst of *The Rose of the Rancho,* on location in the San Fernando Valley. Mrs. deMille met Bill's train and told him to hurry and change into old clothes and join me at the Lasky Ranch. In his book, *Hollywood Saga,* Bill has described vividly that first day. He was literally in motion pictures. I made him a cowboy and put him on a strange horse for a wild dash across the line of the camera's eye; remembering that he was more accustomed to the Lambs Club than the Lasky Ranch, however, I saw to it that he had a real cowboy riding on either side of him. In their hot pursuit of whomever they were chasing, the riders happened to overturn some half-hidden beehives; the real cowboys were wearing leather, Bill was not. In case that was not a sufficiently exciting introduction to Bill's new world, I then put him in a ditch with Frank Hopkins, to fire live bullets at a closed door, missing by seconds the actors who had been trying to break it open.

I cannot confess to unbrotherly malice nor claim any wise educational motive for this treatment of Bill on his first day in California. The explanation, as usual, is simpler, if also duller. We were shooting a picture. Bill was there. I knew he was a good rider and good shot. Anyone with as much theater in his blood as Bill had would know that the show must go on. It did. So did he. Bill was a quiet man. They are often the bravest and most dependable.

That was, though, a good introduction to the difference between stage and screen, and Bill's indoctrination advanced rapidly as in the next weeks we went together through all the phases of movie-making, 1914 vintage. It was a heady wine, and Bill was soon caught up in the enthusiasm of it. His good mind was soon aware that one could not just write a play and photograph it. He discovered that the camera had its own language, its own advantages, its own limitations, and that a screenwriter must write

112

in *that* language, always conscious of what the camera cannot do as well as of what it superlatively can do.

It is a pity, in this day of greater specialization, not to say unionization, that few screenwriters and directors can get anything like the general apprenticeship we were all getting in 1914. My office boy at the old Lasky studio was a youngster named Mervyn Le Roy; he is only one of many who became top producers or directors because to their native talent they were able to add experience in all departments of film-making—even if they did not all start literally from the ground, as Bill did in the ditch with Frank Hopkins.

Bill's first film scenario was *Cameo Kirby*. He sat down with the original play soon after his arrival in Hollywood, and two weeks later handed the director, Oscar Apfel, a finished and usable script. I think it is safe to say that William deMille's coming to Hollywood as a full-time screenwriter marked a definite advance in the history of motion pictures, giving a professional status to screenwriting which only someone with Bill's background in the theater could give.

The Rose of the Rancho also marked my first association with another who was to become one of Hollywood's best known writers, Jeanie Macpherson. Jeanie was then an actress, a lovely, petite girl, sensitively feminine but with the high spirits of one descended from a clan whose head could use the noble Scottish title, The Macpherson. She appeared in several of my pictures after *The Rose of the Rancho*, then turned to screenwriting, and stayed on my staff as a writer until her death in 1946. There were misunderstandings between us sometimes; but when for the last time I left the hospital room where Jeanie was dying, I could be glad and grateful that they had all been healed.

My second Belasco picture, *The Girl of the Golden West*, was shot in eight days, something of a record for even a 1914 feature play. Its production history might have been shorter still if the guardian angels had not been alert around Mount Palomar some 90 miles south. We were on location shooting mountain scenes one day and using a big high-wheeled Oldsmobile to get from place to place in a hurry, over the extremely crude mountain roads of San Diego County. Careening down one of them, with mountain on one side and a thousand-foot drop on the other, one

113

of the wheels evidently decided that if we were in that much of a hurry, it would show us what speed was. It went off by itself, daring us to follow. Everyone in the car expected that that awful moment would be crystallized into eternity; but something stopped us at the edge of the road. After that escape from the arms of that other angel who is always waiting for us, we were faced with the problem of how to get director, players, cameraman, and camera down the mountain on three wheels. The old cliff-hanging movie serials were like that. So, we found, is life, sometimes.

The first screenplay of my brother's that I directed was his own *The Warrens of Virginia*. We had many reasons to be sentimental about it. Belasco had produced Bill's stage version with great success. I had played in it. The story itself was based, remotely, on the incident of our grandfather's capture by the enemy during the Civil War. We were determined to do our very best with the picture. Other directors on the Lasky lot were not too happy about the director-general's getting all the best subjects to direct, but that is another story; it was in fact, on both sides, the well-known story of human nature being natural.

By this time, December, 1914, the Lasky Company had become substantial and attractive enough to lure Blanche Sweet away from D. W. Griffith to play Agatha Warren, the feminine lead. James Neill, Mabel Van Buren, Page and House Peters, Raymond Hatton, Lucien Littlefield, and Mildred Harris were some of the other names in *The Warrens of Virginia*, already famous on the stage or to become famous on the screen. Bill's scripts were growing steadily more workmanlike, more cinematic, exemplifying what he was to drill into two generations of writers: "Don't say that the man fell downstairs! Show him falling!"

6

At the same time I was still learning. I could not be satisfied with indoor night scenes that showed California's celebrated sunshine streaming in at the windows. In *The Warrens of Virginia* we hung black velvet outside the windows, and night's cloak was inky indeed. Nor did I feel that realism was helped by the usual practice of bathing the entire set of every scene in uniformly brilliant light. A good part of Belasco's magic on the stage was

114

his marvelous use of lighting effects. Trained in that school, Wilfred Buckland and I decided to experiment, as D. W. Griffith and Billy Bitzer also were doing, with special light effects. What I was after was naturalism: if an actor was sitting beside a lamp, it was crudely unrealistic to show both sides of his face in equal light, so, with some portable spotlights borrowed from the Mason Opera House in downtown Los Angeles, we began to make shadows where shadows would appear in nature.

Buckland, Alvin Wyckoff, and I were very pleased with ourselves as artists, until the first print of *The Warrens of Virginia* reached New York, and a very disturbed Sam Goldfish wired back to ask what we were doing. Didn't we know that if we showed only half an actor's face, the exhibitors would want to pay only half the usual price for the picture?

There are times when the purest Michelangelo is helped by a touch of Machiavelli. Jesse and I wired back to Sam that if the exhibitors did not know Rembrandt lighting when they saw it, so much the worse for them. Sam's reply was jubilant with relief: for *Rembrandt lighting* the exhibitors would pay double!

There are times also when a passion for realism can overshoot the mark. In one of the scenes in this picture, to show the haste of the departing army and the waste of war, we photographed a battlefield strewn with abandoned military equipment, including, standing mute and forlorn, the tripod of a field telegraphy instrument. After the picture was released, the disgusted letters began to come in: how could we be so careless as to leave one of our camera tripods standing there right in the middle of a scene? The movie audience was maturing with the movie industry. It was becoming more critical as well as more appreciative. Those two qualities need not be at odds. In the best critics and the most appreciative audiences, they never are.

As time went on, in my quest for authenticity in films, I developed the habit of sending one of our secretaries, Bessie McGaffey, to the public library to bring me books on costume, architecture, gunnery, or whatever subject I was dealing with in planning a picture. Now, public libraries are most admirable institutions, but they have one irritating custom. They want their books back. When, as often happened, Bessie found it necessary to remind me of that, I would tell her, "Well then, buy a copy of the book and next time we'll have it when we need it." Bessie's office soon became crowded with books, and her time crowded with consulting them in answer to my questions.

That was the birth, I believe, of "Research" as a full-fledged department in a motion picture studio. Now every major studio has its own research department and library, constantly added to, competently staffed, and always busy. One of the key people on my personal staff is the full-time research consultant, who, with scholarly objectivity, must often be a "No"-man to the wilder fancies of producer, director, or writers, in keeping with the verses whose author I do not know, but nevertheless cherish:

> *Cecil B. deMille,*
> *Much against his will,*
> *Was persuaded to keep Moses*
> *Out of the War of the Roses.*

Unlike the research for my pictures, those verses are inaccurate; but they do illustrate one important function of the research consultant. His more important function is to see that what goes *into* a picture is authentic for the time and place of the story.

The compilation of research done for my latest picture, *The Ten Commandments*, was honored by being published in book form by the University of Southern California under the title *Moses and Egypt*. That academic recognition is a deserved tribute to the scholarship, labor and, I may add, patience of my present research consultant, Henry Noerdlinger. It is also, in its way, a memorial to Bessie McGaffey—and to a lonely, misunderstood tripod on a deserted battlefield.

Authenticity for films is not all found in books. Nowadays the special photographic effects department of the studio is a wizard's workshop. Under the directing wand of a master magician like John Fulton or the late Gordon Jennings, upheavals of nature, monsters known only to science fiction, catastrophes to whole cities, horrifying accidents on land or sea or in the air, interplanetary travel, and even, as far as our minds can imagine them, miracles of the divine can be marvelously represented. There were no such departments in 1914. I am not forgetting such works of imaginative genius as Georges Méliès' *Trip to the Moon,* which still looks startlingly good; but in the barn at Vine and Selma, as the critics will readily agree, we had no Méliès. In *The Warrens of Virginia*, for example, the only way we knew how to blow up a wagon train was to blow it up. We rigged the insides of the wagons with bombs, put strong sheets of iron behind the drivers to protect them, fixed the wagons so that the drivers could break the forepart away and drive clear on the two front wheels, and made a good battle scene with nobody hurt.

Nobody hurt then, that is. Unfortunately, a few of the bombs did not go off. After the scene was shot, one man picked up an unexploded bomb and lit the fuse to throw it for sport. The fuse was quicker than his hand. He lost the hand. Another man took one of the unexploded bombs home that evening and, to entertain his wife while she was preparing dinner, told her what that foolish fellow had done—picked up the bomb like this, see, and lit a match and put it to the fuse like this, see? She saw—her husband's hand and half her kitchen blow out into the neighborhood. I have often pondered that incident. In it somewhere there is some truth about human nature. Stupidity? Pathos? Innocence? Ambition, even? Vainglory? In an odd way, love? I have never fathomed human nature, except to realize, as this bomb story shows to perfection, that it can be incredibly unexpected.

Perhaps that is one reason why chance, or what looks like chance, plays so large a part in our lives. One day Jesse Lasky and Al Kaufman, Mr. Zukor's brother-in-law, brought to my office in the barn a stocky but energetic young man whose quick-moving body betokened an equally quick mind and whose ruddy, healthy countenance wore both a shrewd alertness and an infectious Irish grin. They introduced him to me as a lawyer who was handling a real estate transaction for the company; his name was Neil McCarthy.

7

That casual meeting was the beginning of a friendship and a professional association which will last all our lives. Human nature being as unexpected as it is, that is a bold prophecy to make; but I know Neil. At the time we met, he was low man in the legal firm of James, Smith, and McCarthy, with offices in downtown Los Angeles. I liked him from the first; when I had legal business

117

from then on, I gave it to him. He has been my attorney ever since, and much more than an attorney, a partner in many a venture and a friend firm as a rock. If any question comes up tomorrow involving any point of law or just good, sharp, penetrating judgment, I will call Neil. I may have to call four or five times before I reach him. He is now one of Los Angeles' leading lawyers, keeps up a gay and active social life and is one of the best customers the telephone company has for its long distance lines. He has a true Irishman's love for his string of race horses, and is as likely to be out dealing competently with jockeys as with judges when I try to get him on the telephone; but when I do reach him, I will get his whole mind focused on my problem, whatever it may be, and his answer will be quick, piercing, comprehensive, and right. I shall have to tell later on about one piece of bad advice Neil McCarthy gave me; but he did not know me as well then as he does now, and so did not see what I saw at the end of an almost inaccessible box canyon called the Little Tujunga. But that was long ago. Neil goes on, inaccessible himself sometimes, but indestructible.

Another addition to our studio family came over my murmurs of protest, and is still with me. My brother and I had been dividing between us the working time of my secretary, Gladys Rosson. It so happened that Bill was, like many writers, inspired and proficient when he got started writing, but the problem was to start. Throughout his life, if Bill could postpone writing while he attended to such urgent tasks as sorting his pencils, classifying last year's canceled checks, or rearranging the books on his shelves, the writing was postponed. But when he was ready to write, he was ready; and at that moment Gladys Rosson was probably doing something for me. Moreover, Bill's work was increasing as the studio was expanding; in another year he would have a half dozen other writers working under his direction.

One day he came to me and said he thought he needed a full-time secretary and would like to bring out from New York his former secretary, Anne Bauchens, the young girl who had been so thrilled to attend the first New York screening of *The Squaw Man*.

As Bill tells the story, I made some pointed observations on the difference between the Lasky Company and the United States

118

Mint, and when he suggested that Miss Bauchens would probably be willing to come out at a salary of $10 a week, I cut it to $40 a month. I can well believe it. Anyway, Anne came. Bill's quiet persuasiveness was often more than a match for my executive bluster; and I could not deny that he needed a secretary. I daresay that Gladys Rosson was relieved as well, to have only one deMille to cope with instead of two.

After a couple of years as Bill's secretary, Anne Bauchens was graduated to being our film editor, one of the first women to become expert in that highly skilled and important profession. I suppose the average picture goer may wonder, as he sits in the theater waiting for the picture to start, why we take so many feet of film and so much of his time to list all the credits, the names and titles of the technicians who worked on the film he is about to see. Some hundreds of millions of people, at least, have seen Anne Bauchens' name on the screen as film editor. It has meant nothing to them—except to the few who know that gracious, white-haired lady or who know, as we in the business know, how much a film's success or failure is due to the way it is edited.

In the motion picture industry, film editors used to be known as cutters. The present generation of film editors dislikes that term, and they are right, for what the word "cutter" brings to mind is someone with scissors and pastepot. A film editor needs much more than those tools. He needs a well-developed dramatic sense, an ability to think and feel in tune with the director and his grasp of the story as a whole, and a high degree of ingenuity. Why? Because the whole tempo and feeling and even meaning of a scene can be altered by cutting out a few frames of film here or adding a few there, not to mention rearranging the order of the shots. I have seen unedited film, played by good actors, directed by a good director from a well-written script, utterly confusing and even meaningless on the screen, until it had passed through the hands of a skilled editor—one like Annie Bauchens.

"Annie B." has edited every one of my pictures since I made *We Can't Have Everything* in 1918. She will edit every one the Lord gives us time to make in the future. I believe she is the only film editor whose name is written into a producer's contract. There is a reason for that. Like myself, Annie is no longer as young as when she came wide-eyed to the screening of *The Squaw Man*.

I know those economy waves that sweep over studios, and the professional rivalries that smolder and sometimes flare. In every contract I sign to produce a picture one essential clause is that Anne Bauchens will be its editor. That is not sentiment, or at least not only sentiment. She is still the best film editor I know.

8

Gradually then, or quickly, as it seems now when I look back on it, our roots were taking hold. Jesse Lasky was spending more and more time on the Coast, soon to make his home here. With my family and Bill's settled close enough together for frequent going back and forth, our wives good friends, our daughters going to the same school, with Gladys Rosson and her brothers, Jeanie Macpherson, Neil McCarthy, Anne Bauchens and others forging the bonds that only death can break (if death can, which I do not believe), the good pattern of life was taking shape.

And what of Mrs. deMille through all this? I have said that a man cannot write about his wife as he may write about even his dearest friend. But a niece can write about her aunt, and do her justice if the niece writes as felicitously as Agnes deMille does. In Agnes' book, *Dance to the Piper*, I find this paragraph, referring to a slightly later time, but timelessly and perfectly describing my wife, Constance:

> She was ready for all eventualities. I remember one April afternoon began for her with a children's hospital committee meeting that was interrupted by a hysterical summons from across Los Feliz Boulevard because of the drowning of a child in a near-by reservoir. She went to the victim's home, cleaned the house, prepared supper for the brothers and sisters, comforted the mother, bathed and dressed, put in a brisk half-hour hunting flies and ants for her small son's neglected alligator, presided at the dinner table of her own children, sat with them while they studied, and at midnight was found trailing alone around the cellar in a red velvet negligee in search of the special Liebfraumilch which Cecil liked with his late supper. . . . Aunt Constance gave him his dinner every night herself, prepared it and served it no matter what hour he came in, and sat and talked to him until he grew rested enough to sleep.

120

I am grateful to Agnes deMille for remembering that afternoon and evening. To me, there is a lifetime crystallized in her description of it. Until a year or two ago when infirmity relieved my wife of the burdens of others, which she had carried for so many years, and gave me instead the opportunity of caring for her now as she so long took care of me, what Agnes writes in one paragraph was Mrs. deMille's life of every day. If I do not write of her often, it is not only because there are things too private and too dear to write. Another reason is that if I tried to write all Mrs. deMille has done and meant, not only to me but to every life hers has touched, I would not have room to write anything else. But in all I did she has shared, painfully sometimes, I am afraid, but with a victorious loyalty; in all I write, whether I name her or not, she is there.

Agnes deMille's reference to a "small son" introduces another facet of Mrs. deMille's character and an important event of 1914. We adopted a baby boy, named John. After the lean years in New York, were we yet in a position, economically, to adopt a child? That did not matter to Mrs. deMille; nor, I may add, to me. In the course of that untiring helpfulness to others which Agnes has described so well, Mrs. deMille found the baby boy in need of a home. We had a home, small but warm with the security and mother love that every baby needs. The decision was quickly and simply made; and I had a son.

My second Christmas in Hollywood was much happier than my first. The first, I was alone, and greener than a Christmas tree. Christmas, 1914, I had my family, including my new son John, and a position more and more assured. Jesse and I gave out to the studio employees a Christmas bonus, in the form of small bags of gold pieces—a custom we followed until an unsentimental government buried all those golden tokens, so rich in symbolism, at Fort Knox.

And then on New Year's Eve I had what still remains my wildest night in Hollywood. Jesse, Bill, and I had dinner downtown, and topped it off with *café diablo*. The mood was festive, naturally; the "diabolical coffee" was deceptive. The hour grew late. As we rose from the table, we unanimously decided that it would be prudent to stay downtown overnight at the Alexandria Hotel instead of embarking on the long journey to our distant, separate homes. Bill registered at the hotel for us. The next morning I came down to the desk and asked for the bill for Mr. Lasky and William and Cecil deMille. The clerk informed me that no such guests were registered, sir.

"But we must be. We were here overnight. We had rooms number so-and-so and so-and-so and so-and-so."

The clerk checked his room registry and returned to the desk with that air of disdain that only a hotel clerk can assume when he wants to make a guest wish he could go hide behind one of the potted palms in the lobby.

"Sir," he said, "those rooms are registered in the names of Alexander the Great, Julius Caesar, and Napoleon."

Warlike names. We were not thinking about war that night. But a world was, and would for nights and years to come.

7

Months before, in an unheard-of town named Sarajevo, a shot was fired and there was blood on the floor and cushions of a royal motor car. In Vienna, there was new heartbreak for an old Emperor; in Berlin, a younger monarch saw opening before him the vainglorious road at whose end he would be chopping wood instead of carving empires. In St. Petersburg, Slavic blood stirred. In Paris, placards damp with fresh printer's ink and paste called Frenchmen to the tricolor. In Washington, the President, haggard from watching at the bedside of his dying wife, could only say, "Incredible . . . incredible," when he was told that Austria had marched. In London, Sir Edward Grey said that the lights of Europe were going out.

Sir Edward was a true prophet: the resulting darkness would enfold not only Europe and emperors, but millions of ordinary men and women everywhere, and their grandchildren to this day. One of my most prized possessions is a complete set of *The Illustrated London News*, from its first number to its latest. In one of the issues of late summer, 1914, there are photographs of the burial of British and German sailors killed in an early engagement at sea, laid to rest side by side under the flags of both belligerents, with full, punctilious naval honors. To put them beside the pictures that came out of Buchenwald and Dachau, or some

123

that have come still more recently from Hungary or China, is one of the best ways I know to measure the changed world as in one lifetime I have seen it.

But war and the effects of war still seemed remote from us. In November, 1914, Jesse Lasky issued a brisk statement: "No, the war holds no fears for us, we are now preparing for peace, and it is keeping us pretty busy, too."

All unknown to anyone at the time, the war was in fact giving the American motion picture industry the opportunity to take the lead which it has never since lost. Prior to 1914, European films were, by and large, much superior to American ones, with the exception perhaps of some of D. W. Griffith's; and Griffith himself was still learning and feeling his way, as we all were on this side of the water. It was Italian films, like *Cabiria* and *The Last Days of Pompeii*, which gave me my first full conception of the possibilities of great spectacle on the screen, of photographing massive movements, whole battles, whole cities, whole nations almost. Italy kept its commanding lead when the war disorganized or cramped film production in all the other major European countries. Then, when Italy entered the war, our industry was left free and almost alone to spurt ahead; and Griffith had just made *The Birth of a Nation*.

Jesse Lasky and I saw *The Birth of a Nation*, originally titled *The Clansman*, at its Los Angeles opening. Here was a picture that held its audience spellbound through not five or six reels but twelve. Commercially as well as artistically, it was an immense success. It came at just the right time. Our work and that of others including Griffith had broken the ground for feature-length films. A growing audience had been created for them. The Trust's iron grip on the industry had been broken. The precarious "state's rights" method of distribution was being superseded by Paramount's sounder national plan, with its greater assurance of capital to invest in production. And now a very great genius had brought forth the greatest picture that had been made in America up to that time, one of the greatest pictures ever made.

David Wark Griffith was a great genius. His more fervid admirers will consider that an understatement. Some may be surprised that I make it at all, for there was a time when some people were so misguided as to think that one had to be either pro-Griffith or pro-deMille. We were thought to be rivals. In a sense we were, but we were never enemies; and in another sense, Griffith had no rivals. He was the teacher of us all. Not a picture has been made since his time that does not bear some trace of his influence. He did not invent the close-up or some of the other devices with which he has sometimes been credited, but he discovered and he taught everyone else how to use them for more beautiful effect and better storytelling on the screen. Above all, he taught us how to photograph thought, not only by bringing the camera close to a player's eyes, but by such devices, novel and daring in their time, as focusing it on a pair of hands clasped in anguish or on some symbolic object that mirrored what was in the player's mind. He did much to teach the motion picture camera its own special language; and for that I, like every other worker in motion pictures, am his debtor.

Why, then, did Griffith die in relative obscurity and, compared with his great days, relative poverty? Why was not every Griffith picture another *Birth of a Nation?* Why, toward the end of his life, were producers reluctant to engage him to direct a picture? Hollywood is notoriously fickle and forgetful, but Hollywood's forgetfulness, shameful as it was, does not fully answer the questions.

The answer, I think, lies partly in the fact that Griffith had the defects of his qualities. He was a brilliant artist, but a poor businessman. Like many another fine artist of the stage or screen, he did not fully understand the truth of Sir Henry Irving's statement that the theater "must be carried on as a business or it will fail as an art." Griffith could never adapt himself successfully to the commercial necessities of picture making. That is perhaps to the credit of his integrity; but it resulted in depriving the motion picture industry and the world of his talents for the last 16 years of his life.

More basically still, Griffith was not a dramatist. He could take Thomas Dixon's story of *The Clansman* and, through the magic of his direction and camera work, make it into the still thrilling *Birth of a Nation.* But when he followed that with his own original story of *Intolerance,* magnificent in conception and studded with unforgettable scenes, audiences left the theater simply bewildered by his attempt to tell all at once four separate stories, from four

125

widely distant periods of history, linked together only by a common theme, which it took some mental effort to keep in mind, and by the repeated and memorably beautiful shot of Lillian Gish and the cradle "eternally rocking."

I was present too at the Hollywood opening of *Intolerance*, when Griffith in a charming curtain speech diffidently asked the audience to "be kind to my little sun-play." Later audiences, and especially the hard-headed exhibitors, were not kind. Griffith made other pictures that were successes both artistically and commercially; but I have always dated the beginning of his decline with *Intolerance*. Others of his admirers—I say others, because I count myself one—will probably pour vials of wrath upon my head for saying that. But the one secret of success in picture making is sound dramatic construction; and *Intolerance* showed that Griffith did not have that gift. That, more than his lack of business sense, more than his discomfort with talking pictures, more than his sentimentality which seemed outdated after World War I, more than any other explanation advanced by analysts of Griffith's art, was to my mind the main reason why his career ended so sadly.

But David Wark Griffith had other gifts, personal as well as artistic. The last time I talked with Lillian Gish, Griffith had been dead for nearly ten years, but there was still in the voice and eyes of that lovely lady who was perhaps his greatest star a warmth of feeling for him and for his work that any director might well envy. When the history of motion pictures is written a hundred years from now, Griffith will have his honored pages in it. I hope that deMille may have a footnote.

2

But such long, long thoughts were far from our minds in 1915, when, in Jesse Lasky's optimistic phrase, we were preparing for peace and keeping pretty busy too.

Mrs. deMille tells how she and Mrs. Lasky first knew that the company was an assured success. Never, we are told, underestimate the power of a woman, especially in the intuition department. Our wives did not need to consult a balance sheet or anything as prosaic as that. They knew that we had moved into the realm of established big business when they received notice that they could no longer use company cars for their personal shopping. Was this the first tiny breach made by cold-blooded business methods into the more or less haphazard, all-in-the-family way we began? Before long, there would be anguished letters from Wilfred Buckland, protesting that film-making was becoming a factory operation, cramping to his expansive artistic aspirations. But it was inevitable, I suppose, remembering what Sir Henry Irving had to say on the subject.

Our first picture in 1915 was *The Unafraid*, a Balkan romance which introduced Rita Jolivet and Marjorie Daw to the screen. A few weeks after its release, Rita decided to go to Europe. If she saw a very correct, if rather chilling, small advertisement for which the Imperial German Government took space in the New York press, she paid it no more attention than did any of the other distinguished and happy passengers who embarked upon the giant British liner, the *Lusitania*. One was Charles Frohman. When the German torpedo struck, there were evidently life belts enough for some of the women at least. Rita Jolivet had one; and it enabled her to bring back one vignette of the *Lusitania's* story of horror and heroism. She told of Frohman standing on the deck of the sinking ship, the most powerful man in the American theater, powerless now to influence the drama that was sweeping him off the stage of life, but perfectly calm, and comforting her by speaking quietly of death not as something to be feared, but as a great and beautiful adventure.

Like all America, we were shocked by the sinking of the *Lusitania*. I mourned Charles Frohman: he had given me my start in the theater, and it was in one of his companies that I had met my wife. The war was coming closer to us. Jesse Lasky might not have been so optimistic in May as he had been in November.

There are sometimes odd coincidences connected with the titles of motion pictures. *The Unafraid* might well have described Rita Jolivet's later experience on the *Lusitania*. The title of our next picture, *The Captive*, must always have had a bitter meaning for one man who disappeared from Hollywood while it was being made, for he was a captive, as long as he lived, of a dreadful memory. There was a scene in the picture of a detachment of soldiers storming a heavy locked door. They were to splinter the door with live bullets first, then break it down with the butts of their rifles. Like anyone who knows anything about firearms, I have always been scrupulously careful of guns on the set or anywhere else. I gave orders that the soldiers in the scene were to be sure that their rifles were loaded with blank cartridges when they attacked the door. The firing scene was photographed. I called out a reminder to load with blanks for the attack. A glance told me that the men were unloading their guns. Then the cameraman called my attention away with some question. That settled, we went on to the attack.

The soldiers charged the door, battered it with the butts of their guns. Several of the guns discharged their blanks, as planned— and then I saw an expression of surprise come over the face of one of the soldiers. He faltered, and then I saw the neat bullet hole in his forehead, and he fell dead at my feet.

One of the players had neglected to make the change I had ordered from live ammunition to blank. The muzzle of his gun happened to be pointed squarely at the head of another man. And now that man was dead. It was pure accident, of course. No examination of the guns could show which one had killed him, since several of them had discharged their blanks at the same time. No one ever knew, officially, who had carelessly omitted to unload one of the rifles; but there was one of our soldiers who failed to appear for work at the studio again, whom no one ever saw again in Hollywood. The widow of the man who was killed was kept on the studio payroll for many years; but I wonder if her suffering was any greater than that of the man who carried with him to his own grave the memory of having taken, however accidentally, a human life.

People who work with me in pictures sometimes grow restive under what seems to them an unreasonably tyrannical insistence that when I give an order, it must be carried out exactly. They may see in that only the querulousness or vanity of a cantankerous old man; but what I am seeing is the surprised look on a man's face and the small round hole in the middle of his forehead, when an order which I gave, the order to unload all guns, was not carried out.

That was not the only experience I had in those days with a loaded gun. The other one was loaded purposely, with the intention of saving a life, namely, mine. Back in New York there was a man who had been stage manager of one of the plays I had produced, a tall, powerful, capable man whom I shall call John Murphy, since that was not his name. When I came to California, I invited him to come along and do whatever we found that a stage manager did in the making of motion pictures. He declined. Then he began to hear about our success. Perhaps he read in *The Moving Picture World* of our "studios in California . . . occupying three city blocks; a wonderful ranch . . . including twenty thousand acres of land with every imaginable variety of scenery, offices in New York and an immensely valuable association with a most important system of exchanges"; or he might have read in *Photoplay* that "elegance is the quality of Laskyland." Regret at his decision not to come with us must have rankled in his mind, until finally he conceived the idea that he was entitled to some of that "elegance," 25 per cent to be exact.

He began writing me letters, demanding his imaginary 25 per cent. I answered politely; I liked the man, and I have always believed that a soft answer turneth away wrath, though I have had to learn that the wrath of an unbalanced mind is not so easily diverted. Murphy's wasn't, surely: he announced that he was coming out to Hollywood to kill me. I was a very busy man; New York was far away and idle threats, I thought, were cheaper than transcontinental railroad fare. But, one day Gladys Rosson burst into my office with the excited announcement, "Murphy is here. Shall I send for the police?"

"No," I said, "I'll see him."

Gladys always, well, nearly always, followed instructions; but she had a way of obeying orders she did not like which left you in no doubt of her conviction that *such* an order could come only from a soft and senile brain.

"Well," said Gladys—and Gladys' "Well" could always convey an inimitable blend of astonishment, indignation, resignation, and dogged determination to do her duty by her employer even when he was being unusually stupid—"I have already sent for Mr. Fisher."

I had met John Fisher when we were making *The Call of the North*. He was a friend of the author, Stewart Edward White, a fine outdoorsman and a good businessman. He stayed with our

129

studio as a business manager until 1926, and he and I often camped and hunted together.

Before Gladys would admit Murphy to my office, she smuggled in John Fisher with a large and businesslike game rifle and posted him in a closet with the door open just enough to let the business end of the rifle peep through. Then she announced Mr. Murphy.

I stood up to greet him, but his dark gray eyes had the coldness and fixity of the fanatic.

"You know why I've come here," he said.

"I don't care why you've come. I'm glad to see you. Sit down and tell me how you are. How have things been going with you?"

"Never mind that. I've come here to kill you."

Soundlessly the closet door opened just a little wider.

"Well," I said, "I don't think you need to do that, Murphy, because I am not very well anyway."

For the first time a flicker of interest and life came into his eyes, and he said, "Why? What's the matter?"

"Rheumatism," I answered. "I'm just tortured by rheumatism."

All at once his expression changed to one of concern and sympathy.

"You know," he said, "I think I can cure that for you." And then he made the near-fatal move of reaching for his pocket—as I saw behind him the muzzle of John Fisher's rifle leveling and taking a direct bead on Mr. Murphy.

The speed with which I scrambled to get between Murphy and the closet door might have shaken his faith in my rheumatism, if he had not by now substituted mercy for murder as his fixed idea. Out of his pocket he drew a dog-eared envelope and out of the envelope something that looked like a very withered potato, which he handed me with the words of complete assurance, "If you carry that, you'll be all right."

From then on we talked about rheumatism—my rheumatism, his mother's rheumatism, the prevalence of rheumatism, the symptoms, the causes, and the cures of rheumatism, sovereign among which was the literally lifesaving potato I held in my grateful hand, until at length Murphy got around to indicating that he would like to have a job in motion pictures. The only job I had open, I told him, was for a stunt man, someone to jump through a plate glass window, and I thought that was too risky for some-

130

one without stunting experience. But Murphy insisted that he was the man for the jump; and, as it happened, he did it and came through without a scratch.

I wish that I could say that Murphy stayed with me for 20 years and then became production head of one of the major studios; but this one of my gambles on human nature did not turn out as well as some others have done. Poor demented Murphy, absolving poor rheumatic me, took it into his head that Jesse Lasky was the villain cheating him of his imagined 25 per cent. Jesse apparently had little faith in appealing to a would-be assassin's better nature; or perhaps he thought that Murphy had run out of therapeutic potatoes and might prescribe a smaller, harder, quicker-acting pellet, guaranteed to end any disease if administered subcutaneously from a gun. Anyway, the police did have to take Murphy away finally. Gladys Rosson was not an unkind person, but one could detect the slightest sniff of satisfaction when it turned out that we had to have recourse to her advice about Mr. Murphy after all. But then, if I had followed Gladys' first suggestion of calling the police, I would have missed a fascinating experience and one which stood me in good stead in later encounters of the same kind.

I do not mean to imply that I am a particularly brave man. I am not. I have my normal share of fears. But I learned fairly early—perhaps when, as a child, I used to quake with dread at going upstairs in the dark—that the only way to deal with fear is not to deny it but to face the thing you fear. At the very least, the sooner and more squarely you face it, the sooner it will be over—one way or another!—and that is better than living ridden by it. And it is possible to make your fear a friend. The fear of failure, for example, can be a powerful ingredient of success.

Overconfidence, on the other hand, often brings its own revenge. One of the leading exhibitors in Los Angeles in 1915 was Thomas L. Tally. His name deserves to live in film history because his Electric Theatre was the first theater started in America exclusively for motion pictures. He was also, I believe, one of the first exhibitors to install a full orchestra in the pit to accompany the silent picture on the screen, while most others were content with a single pianist. Then as now, as exhibitors all over the United States know, I liked and still like to drop in unannounced at a

131

theater where one of my pictures is playing, to sit in the audience, to see how that particular chance cross section of America is reacting to my work. I also, as exhibitors also know, sometimes have some observations to make on such little matters as focus, sound level, and the like, about which the projectionist in the booth upstairs may tend to get a little careless after running the same picture over and over again for days or weeks on end. Sound level was not a problem in the silent days of 1915; but Mr. Tally's orchestra, I found, was, when following my custom I dropped into his theater one day during his run of *The Warrens of Virginia*.

The house was comfortably filled; the orchestra was fiddling and tootling away with great vigor. Now *The Warrens of Virginia* was a war story, and Mr. Tally or his conductor had arranged a brave score of martial music to go with it. But there is something in motion pictures called cross-cutting, whereby the film director, unlike the novelist or playwright, can keep two threads of action going at precisely the same time by cutting back and forth from one scene to another, timing the length of each cut to get just the effect he wants. This is one of the film's most powerful dramatic devices. Griffith used it marvelously in his pictures; we used it in *The Warrens of Virginia* to contrast a tender love scene in the Warren home with a violent and bloody battle taking place a few miles away. But Mr. Tally's orchestra had been directed to play martial music, and martial music it played, right through the whole action. It was thrilling when the supply train was ambushed and attacked; but the brasses and the drums kept right on loudly blaring and beating away while in the Warrens' quiet drawing-room the Northern officer was declaring, in appropriate pantomime, his gentle ardor for his Southern sweetheart. The effect was a little like that of reciting Mrs. Browning's sonnets in a boiler factory.

I went to Mr. Tally and told him, as politely as I could, that he was ruining my picture. Mr. Tally was polite too, as polite as he could be to a brash and meddling director. He condescended to explain: "Why, Mr. deMille, they don't come to see your pictures. They come to hear my orchestra."

Not very long afterwards another of my pictures was booked into a theater across the street from T. L. Tally's. It played well and drew good audiences. Mr. Tally at the time was running a

132

film that had something to do with the manufacture of coffee. I crossed the street to see how it was doing. The house was practically empty. But the orchestra was playing magnificently.

From my experience with Mr. Tally's orchestra I came to a conclusion which D. W. Griffith had already reached independently: that the producer of a film should provide the musical score to go with it, a score either compiled from existing music or specially composed for the film, and synchronized with each scene appearing on the screen, so that the accompaniment of the pianist or orchestra would help and not hurt the story.

I needed no persuading about the importance of music. In my childhood, mother had often taken Bill and me to the opera in New York, especially the operas of Wagner. Bill would tell me the stories of the operas and play their main themes for me with one finger on the piano, so that I could learn the themes and follow their interplay throughout the opera. I cannot read a note of music, but in working with composers on the musical scores of pictures, I have always remembered and followed Bill's one-finger technique.

Composers have sometimes been surprised when they have brought me pages of fully orchestrated work and I have asked them to sit down and just play their main themes for me with one finger. Perhaps they put it down as another of deMille's irrational demands; but they have usually understood when I explained that often the skill of the musicians and the beauty of the orchestration can make a weak theme seem much better than it is, even to its composer. The producer of a film might be carried away by such virtuosity, until he gets on the scoring stage with a full orchestra and suddenly discovers that the theme he wanted to give strength or pathos to some important scene simply isn't there—because it never was. But if a thematic line can stand the stark test of being played, alone and unadorned, with one finger, it must have a true identity and vitality of its own.

In the days of silent pictures, music was important on the set itself as well as in the theater. Many of the actors, especially those from the stage, found it difficult to play their scenes in the strange, crude surroundings of an early-day studio. Few of them reacted as vigorously as Sir Herbert Beerbohm Tree who, when a director insisted that he must confine his stridings about the stage to the

133

area within camera range, looked contemptuously at the camera, swept his arm imperiously in its direction, and cried, "Take the pesky little thing away!" But for even the least temperamental of actors, there was a vast difference between playing in a darkened theater before an enraptured audience and doing a scene, perhaps four or five times over, in full daylight, with people standing around chewing gum, the prop man tinkering with something, the painter dabbing at something, the carpenter waiting to start hammering again at his boards, and the janitor with an air of oblivious boredom sweeping up the dust a few feet away. To help the actors overcome these drawbacks of the new medium and get into the proper mood for their scenes, we had one or more violinists, and later an organ, to play "mood music."

I did not invent "mood music." Arthur Rosson, who has been in motion pictures longer than I have, tells me that it came first from a happy inspiration his brother Dick had one day in 1910 or thereabouts, at the old Vitagraph Studio in Brooklyn. Florence Reid was having trouble getting the right emotion into a scene, when Dick Rosson picked up a violin and played for her until she was moved to play her scene with the feeling it needed. Among those who saw this—probably the first use of "mood music"—was another young player named Wallace Reid, who thereupon learned to play the viola and picked up a few dollars as an off-camera mood musician to eke out his earnings as an actor in the years before his meteoric rise to stardom.

Mood music was good for the actors, but for the director it could have the same distorting effect as a splendid orchestration of a weak theme. If these lines should be read by any sensitive-souled musician, still hurting because of seeing me with my hands over my ears while his dulcet strains were bathing my actors in the appropriate moods, I hope he will understand why I blotted his artistry out of my hearing. I found that if I let myself be influenced by the mood music, my judgment of the acting was likely to be faulty. Under the spell of the music, I might be deeply moved by the scene, but later, when I ran it on the screen in silence, find it cold and flat. It was not, therefore, a soulless deMille who rudely covered his ears against the seductive melodies of the mood music he had been careful to provide. It was only the cobbler sticking to his last; the director of the picture remem-

134

bering that which he must remember first, last, and always, the one essential of a successful picture—the *story* he is trying to tell.

When I decided that every picture, at least every important picture, should have its own musical score specially composed to help tell its story, my mind turned naturally to the man who had composed much of the music used to accompany the Belasco plays, William Furst. That serious-minded and scholarly gentleman was persuaded to make the venture of coming to Hollywood to compose specifically for films; but his arrival brought him an experience so unnerving that he was tempted to turn and flee back to the civilized East. I was, I fear, unwittingly responsible. One of our company's best directors, George Melford, had asked me to take over one part of a picture he was directing, because he was unable to be at the studio that day for some unforeseen reason. The particular sequence called for a raging blizzard. George Melford had done me the compliment of asking me to direct it, which I appreciated because some of our directors did not take at all kindly to my title and function of director-general: so I resolved to give George the ragingest blizzard ever put on the screen. I ordered extra quantities of the flaked asbestos we used for snow, and extra wind machines to make it rage. The manmade wind howled around our actors. The asbestos snow poured on them, eddied around them, covered them—and kept blowing. I had not counted on nature's help; but we received it abundantly. A good stiff breeze had come up at the same time. When the scene was done and I called "Cut!" I noticed that our blizzard had developed a rage all its own and was filling the Hollywood sky.

That was the moment of William Furst's arrival. After the hot, dusty drive out from Los Angeles, he had found the Lasky lot at Selma and Vine, bowered in orange and pepper trees; and, suddenly, snow everywhere, snow in the air, snow on the buildings and the street, snow on the trees and California's famous year-round flowers, snow on Mr. Furst. He had expected Hollywood to be a topsy-turvy sort of place, but none of the warnings of his eastern friends had prepared him for a blizzard out of the clear blue summer sky. But he stayed, to make his fine contribution to film music; and it was not long before Victor Herbert and other established music masters of the day were composing for the once despised movies.

135

Perhaps there was another appropriate coincidence in the title of my next picture, *The Wild Goose Chase*. Certainly the front-office executives have often thought, I fear, that some of my ideas and plans for pictures are very wild geese indeed; it takes the returns from the box office to convince the front office that what look like geese are sometimes very downy swans. There was no complaint about *The Wild Goose Chase*, however, because it set a record which neither I nor the front office's fondest dreams will ever equal: I made it in seven days for $9,000, including the salary of its star, Ina Claire, making her first screen appearance after many stage successes in New York and London.

Sometimes nowadays when I ask Paramount for budgets of millions, I think of *The Wild Goose Chase;* I do not mention it in these latter-day negotiations, however. Perhaps there is a lesson about hurried schedules and cheese-paring budgets in the fact that when I once met Ina Claire years later at a party given by Hedda Hopper, she had completely forgotten that there had ever been a film called *The Wild Goose Chase*. So has everyone else.

A genial and beloved American humorist, however, never forgot his first screen appearance in my next picture, *The Arab*. In that adaptation of Edgar Selwyn's play about love in the desert, among such colorfully-named characters as Jamil, Abdullah, Meshur, Turkish Governor, and Mysterious Messenger, was one prosaically identified only as "the American tourist." Irvin S. Cobb happened to be in Los Angeles and to pay a visit to the studio when we were shooting *The Arab*. In the delightfully haphazard way of 1915, we persuaded him to play the American tourist. He received no screen credit, but years afterward, when he launched upon a whole new career as an actor, he still gave me credit for his screen debut. I am not sure that "debut," which makes one think of willowy young girls in white, is quite the right word to apply to Irvin Cobb's rotund, rather pear-shaped appearance in *The Arab;* but I think he'd like it.

Irvin S. Cobb is best remembered as a writer, one of the outstanding American humorists of the generation that followed Mark Twain. Casting him in *The Arab* was rather in the nature of a lark for both of us, and for the audience. Soon after that, I had a hand in giving a start to another career in films which was also slow to mature, but more enduring.

We bought a play, *Chimmie Fadden*, by E. W. Townsend, the story of a Bowery tough and his emergence into the plushy grandeur of Fifth Avenue. My mother, who had seen the play, wrote me that there was only one actor who could play the part of Chimmie. I must get him. He had never been in films, but I would be sorry if I did not cast him in this one. Mother's judgment of talent was considerably better than her business judgment.

As she had urged, I sent for Victor Moore and gave him his first screen role as Chimmie Fadden. I am sure he was the main reason why Peter Milne, the critic of *The Motion Picture News*, wrote of that film as "a delightful picture" and went on to say that "Victor Moore distinctly lives in the title part, he performs sincerely, without a touch of affectation, and performs all the incidental tricks that have been assigned him by the author with a power that will call for rounds of admiring laughter." The rounds of laughter were so satisfying that the same year we produced a sequel, *Chimmie Fadden Out West*, of which *The New York Times* said significantly that "it proves conclusively that a picture may be funny without a single Chaplin trick . . . its humor is the humor of character and situations that arise logically."

Those two critiques of Victor Moore's first two pictures contain the best possible summary of his art and a profound understanding of humor as distinct from slapstick. *The Times* comment is a little unfair to Charlie Chaplin. Chaplin was a great comedian, and his art was not a matter of "tricks." I detest his political views, and I am sorry that he has allowed politics and personal bitterness to influence his work adversely; but of his great talent there can be no question. When Chaplin used slapstick, it was never a mere trick; it was always integrally related to the character he was playing and always helped to reveal and win sympathy for that character. But Chaplin's humor was always essentially humor of character rather than of situation. *The Times* was right in saying that Victor Moore could do both equally well.

The reader may tire of my insisting again that the one essential ingredient of a successful picture is the story. Victor Moore was always completely *in* the story. We played the Chimmie Fadden pictures deliberately without any slapstick. By subordinating him-

137

self to the story, by accepting the direction that ruled out all camera-catching "tricks" for the sake of "the humor of . . . situations that arise logically," Victor Moore achieved the artistry that made him such a wonderful Vice-President Throttlebottom in *Of Thee I Sing,* from which he came back to Hollywood and the series of successful roles, too recent and too memorable to need mentioning.

After *Chimmie Fadden Out West,* my brother directed Victor Moore in *The Clown.* Bill always said that the reason Victor decided to leave Hollywood then and return to the stage was that after a most realistic drowning scene in *The Clown* it was discovered that the cameraman had become so excited by Victor's drowning that he had forgotten to turn the camera. When told that he had to descend into the deep and rescue the rather hefty lady again, according to Bill, Victor said, "You know, Bill, the more I see of pictures the better I like the theater."

Be that as it may, Victor did go back to the stage; but our friendship has been lifelong. I was the one to whom he chose to make an announcement more important than any starring contract. I still have the postcard he sent me in November, 1917: "Tell all my friends I am the father of the most wonderfull baby girl. Much cuter than Pickford or Clark. Best regards. Victor Moore." Victor's spelling (like my own in its unrevised version) may leave something to be desired—but then, is there anything much more "wonder-full" than a new baby girl?

I really must not try to find coincidences in all our picture titles, but I cannot help saying that *Kindling* did move as fast as flame in a new fire, for I finished it in 17 days; and it did kindle gratifyingly warm comments from the critics as "one of the best samples of the Lasky school of motion picture art." It was my first picture with a young man who had only recently matriculated in "the Lasky school" by making his first motion picture appearance in *The Fighting Hope* directed by George Melford; but his ruggedly handsome and expressive face was well known on Broadway, and we shall meet him again in other and bigger pictures. His name was Thomas Meighan.

Actually, titles were the occasion for more worry and woolgathering than philosophic reflections on their deeper meanings, as we scurried to fill our quota of films for Paramount distribution,

138

especially after our company, Famous Players, and the Bosworth company signed a new contract with Paramount in April, 1915, committing our product for the next 25 years. We were often in the position of having to announce a picture without having any idea what it would be. For years, when we found ourselves in that position, we would tell the distributor to put *Her Great Sacrifice* down on the list as the next Lasky epic; and then, when we caught our breath and got our bearings, a hasty telegram would inform the cynically waiting advertising department that *Her Great Sacrifice* had been withdrawn and to substitute *Chimmie Fadden* or *Kindling* or whatever it might be.

4

There was no doubt, though, what the title would be for the first film of the star whose engagement was announced to me by a telegram that Fred Kley brought out to me on the *Chimmie Fadden* set one fine day in May, 1915. Fred was excited. The telegram in his hand seemed to quiver with excitement. Back in New York, Jesse and Sam had achieved the impossible; they had signed Geraldine Farrar to come to Hollywood and appear in movies. The nationwide movie audience would see her in the same role in which opera-goers had thrilled at hearing her at the Metropolitan and practically every other great opera house in the world—*Carmen.*

The Moving Picture World wrote that "next to the entry of Belasco into the domain of films . . . the resolution of this marvelously gifted young woman to employ her talents . . . in the films is the greatest step in advancing the dignity of the motion picture." That was probably true. It was certainly pleasant to realize that it was our company which had brought both Belasco and Farrar to motion pictures. But even the long and fulsome announcement in *The Moving Picture World* did not do justice to Geraldine Farrar and what her coming to Hollywood meant.

Today television can create a "personality" overnight. One may recall, for example, with whatever emotions one deems appropriate, Elvis Presley's first appearance on Ed Sullivan's television program. In the yesterday before television, radio, with the help of a certain amount of press agentry, had much the same power; one has heard tell that some of Frank Sinatra's early admirers were not without some help from the publicity department, in the way of coaching on when and how to swoon. This is in no disparagement of Mr. Sinatra, who has developed into a very good actor, or Mr. Presley, whom I know and whom I have always found to be, off stage, an attractive, modest, unassuming, pleasant young man. I myself have some reason to know what it means to be the victim of one's own press agents. But Geraldine Farrar, 40 years and more ago, without benefit of radio, television, or films, had achieved a height of acclaim which I do not believe has been equaled in my lifetime by any theatrical figure except Maude Adams and Mary Pickford.

She had a good press, of course; but the Farrar personality was not synthetic. It was magic. She was adulated, one might almost say adored, by people of all ages and kinds. Princes of Europe were at her feet. American teen-agers swarmed around her whenever she appeared, copied her style, gloried in being nicknamed "Gerry-flappers." And Miss Farrar, be it remembered, was not a practitioner of the croon or the rock-and-roll; her work was in that highly specialized area of the theater, supposedly of very limited appeal, grand opera. Both professionally and popularly, she was at the top of her splendid career when she agreed to come to Hollywood for us.

Such a prize jewel deserved a worthy setting, Sam and Jesse thought rightly; and they proceeded to create it for Miss Farrar. In addition to the largest salary we had ever paid a star, her contract included provision of a private railway car for her journeys between the coasts, a two-story house in Hollywood staffed with butler, cook, and maid, a limousine and chauffeur, a private bungalow at the studio equipped with grand piano as well as other amenities, an augmented orchestra on the set for mood music worthy of the reigning queen of the opera, living expenses for the star and her entourage, billing as *Miss* Geraldine Farrar, and, Jesse added, "our best director." Carpet, presumably red, was laid from the train to Miss Farrar's automobile when she arrived at the old Santa Fe depot in Los Angeles; the mayor was on hand to welcome her; children strewed flowers in her path. Perhaps the greatest inducement, however, was the promise that she would first appear before our cameras in her favorite role of *Carmen.*

140

There was some consternation when I decided that she would not.

By then I had had enough experience directing actors from the stage to know that there is a great difference between stage technique and film technique. There is still no better preparation for acting in films than a sound and thorough training on the stage, but the best stage actor still has things to learn and unlearn when he comes before a camera; and that, I felt, was particularly true of one coming from grand opera, where the tradition is to over-act and where the glorious music can carry or cover a certain amount of less than glorious acting if necessary. Our cameras were silent. The first step, I told the disturbed executives, was to forget that Miss Farrar had had any connection with opera.

On the stage, an actor is trained to project himself, his character, his actions and thoughts, to an audience the nearest of whom is 30 feet away from him. To be effective, his projection must reach and grip the people sitting in the last row of the top gallery. They must be moved by voice and gesture. They cannot see the actor's eyes. But the camera can, ruthlessly, infallibly. You cannot lie to a camera. That is in part what I mean by the motion picture's ability to photograph thought. Until an actor learns to use his eyes and the slightest flickering change of facial expression to project what is in the mind of the character he is playing, the motion picture audience will not believe him; and they will be, as usual, right.

When directing an actor new from the stage, I had learned, it is wise to put all his big close-ups at the end of the shooting schedule, giving him time to adapt himself to camera technique and the special requirements of film acting, before bringing the merciless eye of the camera within five feet of the windows of his soul. But even that precaution, I felt, might not be sufficient to protect the risk of letting Geraldine Farrar learn a new art and hazard her reputation by appearing first in *Carmen*.

"If we make *Carmen* first," I told my doleful colleagues, "we will have to throw half of it out. We have another property, *Maria Rosa*, a Spanish love story, not unlike *Carmen* in its setting. Let's let Miss Farrar cut her motion picture teeth on that, and then make *Carmen*, and she will give you a good performance in it. You can hold up the release of *Maria Rosa*." Executive faces bright-

141

ened as light dawned. "Release *Carmen* first, as you have announced," I went on, "and it will have all the values of the experience Miss Farrar will have gained in *Maria Rosa*, which you can bring out afterward."

"Let's," said Jesse; and it was agreed.

But how would Miss Farrar take to this change? How, indeed, would she take to the whole new world of motion pictures? Opera stars are reputed to be notoriously temperamental. They have tempestuous tantrums. They do not endanger their precious vocal cords by screaming. But they throw things. They break things. They sulk. They stalk from one dudgeon to another, each higher than the last. Firmly believing that myth, we were prepared for the worst. The director-general steeled himself to cope with the imperious diva, to do battle, if necessary, worthy of a Wagnerian hero. But Geraldine was not in Hollywood an hour before she exploded the myth and won everyone's heart, including the director-general's.

When Jesse Lasky escorted her from the train to her new house, showed her through it from room to flower-filled room, introduced her to the servants, and prepared to take his leave, he said to her, in his most courtly way, "Mr. deMille would like to see you tomorrow, after you've rested, of course, from your trip."

"Oh," she said, "just give me a few minutes to change and I'll go and see him now."

That was typical of the way Geraldine fitted in. It never varied. She was always gracious, always co-operative, always worked hard, was always ready to do whatever the exigencies of the strange new world of Hollywood demanded of her. A strikingly beautiful woman, she had the warmth and laughter and down-to-earthiness, and a total lack of airs or affectations, without which beauty is only mere beauty. She might be billed as *Miss* Farrar, but it was not long before everyone on the lot was calling her Gerry.

In casting the male lead of *Maria Rosa*, I took the risk of putting a new and comparatively untried talent in to play opposite Geraldine Farrar. When Jesse and I had gone to see *The Birth of a Nation*, I had noticed in it a young man playing a very small part as a blacksmith. He stayed in my mind. He was handsome and clean-cut; he knew how to behave in front of a camera, making

142

even his brief appearance memorable. His name, I made it my business to discover, was Wallace Reid. He had had a few years' experience in films, but in parts so small that he welcomed the extra dollars he could make playing mood music for the big stars. I sent for him, and our conversation confirmed my belief that he was star material himself. I felt, as I have often felt since about stars and stories, that the public would like what I liked in Wally Reid; and I backed my judgment by giving him the lead in *Maria Rosa*, his first starring role.

I have not always been right in my estimate of players. Whenever I see the tremendous magnetism of Clark Gable on the screen and think of his enduring and unchallenged popularity, I shrink a little inside myself, remembering that I once declared pontifically that that young man did not have what it takes for a successful career in films. And Clark Gable is not the only one about whom I have been wrong. But I was right about Wallace Reid.

Because *Maria Rosa* was withheld from release according to our plan, the public saw him first as a star in *Carmen*. From then on his rise was steady, until the terrible shock of his death shattered the public's image of him and almost shattered Hollywood. The public learned of the narcotic addiction which hastened Wally Reid to the grave at the age of 30. The public never knew the heroic efforts he made to break himself of the addiction. The public is quick to judge; but I prefer to remember the brave determination in what Wallace Reid said to me just before he entered the sanitarium where he died: "I'll either come out cured or I won't come out."

We profited by making *Maria Rosa* first. I learned more, I think, than our star did. Geraldine, I found, had a talent for screen acting as natural, and so as capable of cultivation, as her vocal talent. As I always do, I tried to help her bring out her own best performance, rather than force upon her arbitrarily my concept of her role. What I learned was more technical. We were photographing under such strong lights that, to our horror when we screened the "rushes," Geraldine's lovely gray eyes were washed out completely; her pupils had contracted to invisible dots, and she looked at her screen lovers and at the audience with staring, solidly white eyeballs—a disquieting vision to any lover, and fatal as far as the audience was concerned. The strong lights also performed marvels of dental surgery; when our actors flashed their most beaming smiles, they showed up on the screen as completely toothless grins, which are not helpful to creating an atmosphere of romance either. We solved these problems by hanging large curtains of black velvet behind the camera, on which Geraldine could focus her eyes restfully enough to keep the pupils from disappearing, and by cross-lighting which gave our players back their teeth.

Alvin Wyckoff, the cameraman on most of my early pictures, loved strong light. He was a skillful cameraman and on most camera angles and effects we agreed completely, but it was a struggle to convince him that there are shadows in nature and that mingled light and shade can be more beautiful than glare. When Alvin got the point, he got it strong. He coined a word to describe me: I was the director who liked everything "contrasty." When that reputation spread among the cameramen, of course, I had another struggle to make it clear that contrast of light and shadow meant what you naturally see with normal eyes if you look out your window in the late afternoon when the long shadows of the trees fall across your lawn, and not the solid pools of Stygian black in the middle of a brightly-lighted scene which some cameramen began to create in order to please this director who wanted it all "contrasty."

Screenwriting had its problems too, we were learning. My brother wrote the scenarios for both *Maria Rosa* and *Carmen*. His only major problem with *Maria Rosa* was that, in the stage play on which we based it, the character we called "Andres, a vintner" had been killed before the action of the play began. The drama of the play was in Maria Rosa's gradual discovery that the man she was now about to marry was the murderer of Andres, her first husband and great love. Since it seemed rather wasteful of Wallace Reid's potential talents to have him dead and out of sight from the beginning to the end of the picture, Bill thoughtfully changed all that. Instead of having Andres killed before the story started, he put him in prison, from which, of course, he escaped in time to come on the screen and achieve love's triumph in the expected happy ending.

There was no happiness on the Lasky lot, however, the day Jesse and I had to summon Bill to let him in on a discovery we had just made about *Carmen*. Bill was well along on the *Carmen* script, working chiefly from the libretto of the opera by Georges Bizet. We broke it to him as gently as we could: we had found out that the opera was copyrighted, and the copyright owners were demanding a price which might have been reasonable if they had thrown in the Louvre and a few thousand front-feet along the Champs Élysées. Fortunately for us, Bizet had borrowed *his* Carmen from a story by Prosper Mérimée; and the Mérimée book was at our disposal. Some of the characters and some of the situations were different in book and opera, but Carmen was Carmen in both; and it was Geraldine Farrar as Carmen that the public, we hoped, was avidly awaiting. Bill was equal to the challenge. He delivered a good script, based on Mérimée, and I do not believe anyone knew the difference, except perhaps the heirs or assigns of Monsieur Bizet.

When *Carmen* was completed, I was given much credit for the masterly direction of two scenes in particular, the bull fight and the knock-down tussle between Carmen and another girl in the cigarette factory. I have never deserved credit less. In both scenes my masterly direction was almost confined to saying "Action" and "Cut" at the appropriate moments.

For the bullfight I had engaged a professional matador to double for that fine character actor, Pedro de Cordoba, playing Escamillo. The bull, however, was the more professional of the two. He caught my matador with his feet badly placed, and the next thing we knew the bullfighter was spinning through the air and landing hard squarely in front of the bull. The bull lowered his head to gore the man to death. We were helpless. But nature, which is benign at times, had helped by giving that bull, out of all the thousands of bulls born in his generation, a pair of horns set unusually wide apart. Instead of cruelly piercing the prone body of the matador, the horns gently cradled him and lifted him into the air in their embrace; and when the bull recovered from his surprise, the bullfighter had had time to land again, far enough away for safety. The camera caught it all. Masterly indeed.

In the original story of *Carmen*, there is some first-act bickering among the girls in the cigarette factory. We decided that it would help establish the lusty, passionate character of Carmen if we expanded the argument into a full-blown brawl. I selected Jeanie Macpherson to play Frasquita, the cigarette girl who would tangle

145

with Carmen. Jeanie was a daughter of Scotland's warrior clans. Geraldine Farrar's father was an Irish-American baseball player. Jeanie was game for anything, and, as I have said, Geraldine needed little direction. I expected a good fight. I called "Action!"; and I got it. We had rehearsed a very convincing bout, but I noticed that something was not quite according to the rehearsal. Geraldine's first haymaker had knocked Jeanie's wig askew. Jeanie was much too good a trouper to stop before she heard the director's "Cut!" She merely put up one hand to hold her wig in place and went after Geraldine with the other. Geraldine, too excited to notice that anything was wrong, with her mind only on giving the scene all the realism she knew I wanted, waded in, and the two hot-blooded Spanish cigarette girls did their Scots and Irish ancestors proud, rampaging back and forth across the set, with Jeanie frantically holding on to her wig with one hand and vainly trying to defend herself with the other. Jeanie and I were perhaps the only two people on the set who knew that her gyrations had one object: to keep the wig from flying off in the middle of the scene. But it photographed, as Jeanie knew it would, as if Jeanie, terrorized, were desperately trying to protect her head from Carmen's furious assault; and it made Geraldine look like a one-woman whirlwind. Masterly indeed: that is the way a real master of direction establishes character—if he is lucky enough to have a Jeanie Macpherson on the other side of the camera, with a nimble brain under a wayward wig.

Geraldine told me later that when she returned to the Metropolitan to sing *Carmen* again, she conspired with one of the chorus girls to include the fight in the opera, to the astonishment of the rest of the cast and the delight of the audience. Since then it has become a traditional part of every *Carmen*, I am told.

Many, many years later, I received an invitation which would flatter any director in the world. Through indirect channels, I was discreetly asked if I would care to direct a production of *Aïda* at what is probably the most celebrated opera house on earth, La Scala in Milan. I felt, however, that after my two immortal contributions to that art form—my conducting the orchestra for *Martha* when Rudy Berliner was taken ill and my masterly direction of the fight in *Carmen*—it would be more discreet on my part to rest upon those laurels and spare the historic La Scala a performance which might not have turned out as well as those.

Two weeks after we finished *Carmen*, we started Geraldine Farrar's third picture, *Temptation*, the first work of Hector Turnbull, the drama critic of the New York *Tribune* whom, with his sister Margaret, William deMille had enticed to Hollywood to form the beginning of a full-fledged writers' department in our studio. Like *Maria Rosa*, *Temptation* also was shelved until after the release of *Carmen*. Our judgment there was good, for the critics declared *Temptation* to be "adequate" and "acceptable," but "conventional to a degree," though one critic, Oscar Cooper in *The Moving Picture World*, did note that "nothing has been allowed to interfere with the full expression of Miss Farrar's personality." Our cautious decision to withhold *Maria Rosa*, however, was somewhat deflated when it was finally released and *The New York Times* casually said that it was "as good if not better than *Carmen*."

5

It may have been around this time that Jesse came into my office one day, bubbling with the news which our wives had long since discovered in their own mysterious feminine way. The balance sheets left no doubt now. The company was a success, a very great success. When Jesse was enthusiastic, he bubbled like a just opened bottle of champagne.

"Think what it means, Cecil," he said. "Now we can do all the things we planned to do. Remember how we wanted to go to the South Seas? Before long, we'll be able to go there—or hunt in Alaska, or fish down in Florida, or lie on the beach in Hawaii, or anything, anywhere. Let's make an agreement. Let's work for three more years and then retire! We can do it, Cecil!"

"That's fine," I said, "but you won't stick to it."

"Oh yes, I will. Three more years. That's all we need. Then quit and enjoy ourselves."

"Will you sign a paper to that effect, Jesse?"

'Put it in writing. Write it down now. I'll sign it."

I glanced at the calendar and the clock and wrote out a formal statement that Jesse L. Lasky and Cecil B. deMille agreed that exactly three years from that date and hour they would retire from the motion picture business and go off adventure-bent. Jesse signed with a flourish.

I have a habit of keeping little pieces of paper; and three years to the minute later I knocked at the door of Jesse's office. By then his power and prestige in the industry had grown beyond the most effervescent dreams of three years before. He was in the middle of a conference, and by that time any conference was a high-level conference. Just a little impatiently, he asked me if I couldn't wait.

"No," I said, "this can't wait, Jesse. It's too important."

I laid the little piece of paper on his desk.

"Come on," I said. "I'm ready."

Jesse silently read our mutual agreement to retire, first with a frown of puzzlement, then read it again with a frown closer to annoyance. He had completely forgotten it. With the other men sitting around his office in ill-concealed impatience, he was in no mood to be reminded of it.

"Very funny," he said, with a notable lack of either enthusiasm or enjoyment, "very funny"; and went right back to his conference. I closed the door behind me, gently.

Then and there, like Kipling's Diego Valdez, we were "sold . . . to bondage of great deeds."

If we had retired then, our pursuit of gentlemanly ease would probably have lasted, I would guess, about two months. I know now that I will never retire, until I am retired by the Director who controls all our entrances and exits on this stage of life. I have thought about retiring; I did even try it once, but it was no use. Creation is a wine that, once tasted, leaves an ever unsatisfied thirst for more. I hope to die working—and working on something better than I have ever done before.

I do not think, though, that I shall ever work harder than I did as 1915 drew to its close. Crises are an old story in the motion picture industry. Economic crises are solved by the front office according to an invariable rule of thumb: fire as many people as you can, beginning with those who can least afford to lose their jobs. Artistic crises call for somewhat less rough-and-ready handling. We met one, not the first or last, in the fall of 1915. As director-general, it was my job to solve it, which I did by doing what my brother Bill describes as "something which no other director, even partially sane, would have attempted."

Hector Turnbull had written another scenario, *The Cheat*, so far superior to his first, *Temptation*, that to this day film historians, especially in Europe, regard *The Cheat* as a landmark in the development of the cinema. It was a rather daring theme for its time, the story of a society woman who gambled away Red Cross funds entrusted to her, borrowed $10,000 from a wealthy Japanese in consideration of a promise which was plainly if delicately hinted, then tried to repay her debt in cash instead of keeping her promise. At this point the Japanese branded her on the shoulder with the mark he used to identify all his possessions. The woman's husband shot the Japanese and was saved from imprisonment only when his repentant wife bared her branded shoulder in open court. Told that baldly, the story sounds melodramatic if not lurid. That is why I resolved to direct its acting with great restraint; and I had two highly accomplished artists in the leading roles, Fannie Ward as the woman and Sessue Hayakawa as the Japanese. I put *The Cheat* into production on October 20, 1915.

Six days later, another picture was started, *The Golden Chance*, by Jeanie Macpherson, but it very soon ran into trouble. I forget what the trouble was. My brother recalls it was the director; Jesse Lasky's recollection of the whole incident is totally different; but my job as director-general was to act as medicine man, not judge. I just remember it as trouble, serious because if *The Golden Chance* did not meet its announced release date, it would mean a loss to the company in both money and prestige. There was nothing to do but what aroused Bill's hint about my sanity: I would direct both pictures at the same time.

I had another reason, which I think was really the most compelling one, for attempting what to the best of my knowledge no director had ever done before or since. Some of the other directors at the studio were complaining that they were overworked. I could not think of a better answer to that complaint than for the director-general to make two pictures at once.

From 9 o'clock in the morning until 5 in the afternoon, I directed *The Cheat*. Then Gladys Rosson served me dinner on my desk and I lay down to rest until 8 P.M., when it was time to meet and direct the fresh-as-a-daisy cast and crew of *The Golden*

Chance until their quitting time at or about 2 A.M. Often I slept the few remaining hours in my office. When I went home, Mrs. deMille was waiting up for me, as always. Both pictures were finished on schedule. According to *The Moving Picture World*, I then took a three days' vacation.

The Cheat was the first motion picture to be later made into a stage play. It was also Sessue Hayakawa's first giant stride on the road that made him within two years the peer of such contemporary bright stars as Douglas Fairbanks, William S. Hart, and Mary Pickford. Legend has it that Sessue Hayakawa was a poor gardener when I discovered him and made him a star overnight. The truth of the matter is at once more prosaic and more plausible. Sessue, a highly educated gentleman of exquisite taste, had played in a few pictures, but was not getting much work when I engaged him for the lead in *The Cheat*. After that, he had all the work he could handle for several years. Now a whole new generation has seen in *The Bridge Over the River Kwai* the same authority and dignity and polished artistry of which the world had its first real glimpse in his performance in *The Cheat*.

If Sessue Hayakawa's career had its real beginning in *The Cheat*, another film career came to a sad ending in *The Golden Chance*. I will not mention the actress' name. She was a very good actress, with a record of stage successes on two continents, a beautiful woman, a prize feather in the Lasky Company's cap when Jesse signed her to play in that film. But, in the whispered phrase our fathers used to describe her particular weakness, she "drank." I think that phrase, by the way, is misleading. Many people drink, jovially, temperately, in the spirit and with the good effects recommended by the Psalmist and by St. Paul to Timothy. The tragedy of alcoholics is not that they drink, but that they *cannot* drink. Realization of that is the first step toward their cure. But our actress did not realize it, and patience and advice apparently did not help. One night she appeared on the set so much the worse for indulgence that I knew I had to decide between her feelings and the picture.

If I am ever ruthless, and I am sometimes, it will usually be found, I think, that I am ruthless for the sake of a work into which I and hundreds of other people have put time, money, thought, labor, the stuff of their very lives, which I will not see jeopardized

150

by the negligence or carelessness of any one individual. I made my choice that night on the set of *The Golden Chance*. I escorted the actress to the door of the set and told her she was through. That had never been done in Hollywood before, as far as I know. It meant re-shooting part of the picture, giving another actress the golden chance lost by the one who stumbled off the stage into the dark. I would do it again; but I am glad I have never had to do it again.

Having my own full share of them, I hope that I am not hard on human weaknesses. Many years later, there was an actor in Hollywood whom no casting director would touch because of the escapades which regularly began with a bottle and as regularly ended in police court and the headlines. I had never even met him; but I sent for him and said, "I have a part for you in my next picture. It is a part that fits you. You have the ability to play it. This picture is costing several million dollars, and it has a long shooting schedule. You can have the part if you give me your word you won't take a drink until your work is finished." He got the part. He did not let me down. Nor was that the only occasion of its kind in the years that I have been in Hollywood. Perhaps the other side of ruthlessness is knowing when you can give another human being a golden chance.

I had a similar understanding with one of the most popular male stars of, well, let us say between twenty and forty years ago. While a picture was shooting, he stayed scrupulously cold sober. The day the shooting ended, he was straight off on a quiet and unobtrusive but gigantic bender. This pattern was as regular as a clock, and it worked very well until after finishing one picture we found that certain scenes had to be re-taken. I sent an informal posse out to comb the bars. They found him, unshaven, disheveled, a bit fuddled, but ready to go back to work. As it happened, the scenes to be re-taken called for our hero to appear unshaven, disheveled, and a bit fuddled. We got a capital performance.

There is a well-meant expression of good wishes which I never use and which always makes me slightly uncomfortable when I hear it. That is the saying, "Good luck!" It is not that I am superstitious about it. On the contrary, it is rather that I do not much believe in "luck." I think there is something deeper at work in the ordering of human events. I could not be Henry DeMille's son without believing in a Divine Providence, and I have had too many experiences of it in my own life to let me doubt it. The cynical may ask where Divine Providence is when things happen which they would call "unlucky." It is there, in the heart of those things too; and its purpose in them is often, I believe, to reveal and strengthen character. I saw that revealed one evening in September, 1915, when Jesse Lasky and I were in New York and, when we came out from dinner, noticed the downtown sky alight with one of the most spectacular fires in the city's history.

Curious, we made our way down to 26th Street and found that the blaze was leaping up from the now totally destroyed studio and offices of the Famous Players company. We stood watching, and my eye happened to light on a little man, with his hands in the pockets of his overcoat, standing absolutely still in the excited, milling crowd.

"Look at that man," I said to Jesse. "He hasn't moved a muscle since we have been here. He has something to do with this fire. I don't know what, but I am sure of it."

Jesse looked. "You're right," he said. "That's Adolph Zukor."

I did not know then that not even the muscles of Adolph Zukor's eyes were moving: they were fixed on one spot on the wall of an upper story of his building, where a wall safe containing the fragile negatives of his company's unreleased films hung precariously, licked by flame. More than the safe hung there. On its clamps holding it to the wall and on its manufacturer's assurance that it was fireproof hung Adolph Zukor's past—the 27 years of struggle since he had landed at Castle Garden, an immigrant boy from Hungary—and his future, now a question mark written in ashes and evanescent smoke.

I had never met Adolph Zukor. Jesse took me over and introduced me. I said the futile things that are all one can say to a man standing in the dust of his life's work. There were tears in his eyes, not caused by the smoke.

He looked away from the ruin long enough to say, "Thank you. We'll build a better one."

That was my first contact with the steel and iron, the indomitable bravery and driving determination, in that little man. He is little in nothing but his physical stature, and even that has still the tough stamina he gave it in his youth as an amateur boxer who could hold his own with professionals of the ring. In his ambitions and dreams, his shrewd judgment, his showmanship, his generalship, Adolph Zukor has had no peer in the history of motion pictures.

That was my first contact with Adolph Zukor. It would not be my last.* There would come a time when he would put his two clenched fists together and, slowly separating them, say to me, "Cecil, I can break you like that." There would come a time, the only time I ever saw Adolph Zukor show a weakness, when perhaps some words of mine helped him fight his way out of a business disaster more devastating than the fire on 26th Street, and a time when he alone among the New York executives of Paramount would back one of my most cherished dreams, which was *The Ten Commandments.* The respect I have for him is shared by an entire industry, whose easy-going ways put most people in it on a first name basis five minutes after they have met, but in which no one, including a septuagenarian like me, ever calls this man anything but "Mr. Zukor."

* The last was on January 23, 1959, when Adolph Zukor was a pallbearer at Mr. deMille's funeral. There were no honorary pallbearers: Mr. Zukor, in his 87th year, personally performed this last service for his friend. (*Ed.*)

8

I AM an "ex-victim of Zukor's voracity," according to Bosley Crowther. If that were strictly true, I could only report that the ex-victim is feeling very well, thank you, and feeling nothing but respect, tinged with affection, for his supposed devourer. We had our battles, Mr. Zukor and I, which may be touched upon in their proper place; and I have witnessed from the sidelines other and more decisive battles in which Mr. Zukor was a doughty participant and usually the victor. The detailed and definitive economic history of the motion picture industry remains to be written. I make no apology for not attempting to write it here.* Necessarily I have been in and out of various companies, holding companies, subsidiary companies, and other corporate combinations; but I have always been more interested in making pictures than in making deals.

Still, some of the bloodless battles of the board rooms and stockholders' meetings were not without their elements of high drama, and sometimes of comedy and tragedy.

Mr. Zukor was never entirely happy with the terms of the releasing arrangement with Paramount. Neither was Sam Goldfish.

* For the reader specially interested in the economic structure and development of the motion picture industry, one of the most succinct and clear descriptions of that complex business is in Ralph Cassady, Jr., "Impact of the Paramount Decision on Motion Picture Distribution and Price Making," *Southern California Law Review*, Feb., 1958. (*Ed.*)

Both those titans felt that we would all be in a stronger position to deal with the Paramount distributing organization if our two companies, Famous Players and Lasky, merged. Mr. Zukor thought and thought, as is his way; Sam and Jesse and Arthur Friend cogitated the pros and cons; the bankers gave their advice.

While I was in Hollywood making pictures, my associates in New York kept me informed. The telegrams and letters I still have from those early months of 1916 read something like an old-fashioned cliff-hanging serial: the merger was going forward, the merger was off, conversations were being resumed, until finally Sam wired me on June 28th, "Merger with Famous Players completed . . . all very enthusiastic . . . ," and Jesse wired the next day, "We all are very much pleased and congratulate the new director-general of the Famous Players-Lasky Corporation."

But already a tiny discord had made itself heard in that harmonious chorus. It had been agreed that the presidency of the new company should go to Mr. Zukor and the first vice-presidency to an officer of the former Lasky Company. But which officer? Both Jesse and Sam felt entitled to that recognition; but there was, obviously, only one first vice-presidency. Through no wish of my own, it fell into my lap to decide between them.

I sympathized with Sam's position. For three years he had been slaving successfully at the unglamorous job of selling the pictures directed by Cecil B. deMille and presented to the public by Jesse L. Lasky. He and all the world read in the trade press about the "Lasky elegance" and about "DeMille as the foremost photo-dramatic producer in the world." Even if those lush phrases came from his own publicity department, Sam could not help feeling that his light was being hidden under a bushel, however elegant. Nor was this presumptuous vanity on his part. Sam knew his worth. So did I, and I did not hesitate to tell him so; but I was hardly prepared for his telegram construing what I had said to him as an agreement with his claim to the contested office, declaring ominously that he did not "propose to give Jesse his way on this," and requesting "please wire me straight message how you will vote on this proposition."

With my two friends thus squared off, and myself in the middle, I was not in a comfortable position. I was also on the set all day every day directing Mae Murray and Theodore Roberts in *The*

155

Dream Girl, which was more to my taste than anyone's dreams of where his name should appear on a new corporation's letterhead. I slept on Sam's telegram, and the next day wired him, "If the election of First Vice President is a reward of merit purely then I consider that I am entitled to it!" Of course I had no intention of claiming it, but I thought it might wholesomely deflate the sails of both men-of-war if they thought another dreadnaught was coming into the fray.

Then I went on to say in the same telegram, "I believe the First Vice Presidency is offered to the Lasky Company because of the merit and efficiency of the company and not because of the value of any one member and that therefore the position should go to the President of this company and Jesse as such will have my vote. We entered into this deal as a unit and should continue as such . . . with a solid front and in the same ratio of positions as now exists."

In the final merger, Jesse was made first vice-president, and Sam chairman of the board. It seemed a solution worthy of Solomon. I have letters from Jesse saying how co-operative Sam was. In one, he writes that Sam "is now as easy to work with as you yourself"—a comparison which some who have worked with me might consider somewhat less than complimentary to Sam.

Meanwhile, Mr. Zukor's thoughts, on his long walks from the Battery to Central Park and back downtown again, were vaulting far beyond our little family tiffs. He quietly began buying Paramount stock; and then, one day in June, when W. W. Hodkinson, President of Paramount, called to order what he thought was a routine stockholders' meeting, he found himself being promptly voted out of office and Hiram Abrams, Mr. Zukor's nominee, voted in. Jesse, representing our company's holdings of Paramount stock, supported this move. Soon two smaller producing companies, the Morosco Company and Hobart Bosworth's Pallas Pictures, joined us. Soon Mr. Zukor himself became President of Paramount as well as of Famous Players-Lasky. Soon he would begin buying theaters, many theaters, uniting the three great divisions of the industry—production, distribution, and exhibition—under one control.

That, I suppose, is what Bosley Crowther means by "Zukor's voracity." Mr. Zukor enjoys power. Who does not, if he is honest enough with himself to admit it? But there was much more than

156

power-hunger involved in the building of Adolph Zukor's Paramount empire. Of the three great divisions of the motion picture industry, production is the creative part. It is what is done in the studios and put on film that people pay to see. But people cannot see the product of the studios unless it is brought to them by the distributor and put on the screen of their local theater by the exhibitor. As the middleman, whoever controls distribution can control the creative element of the industry by the simple dictate, "Make what I say, or I won't handle it." Moreover, if production is tied by rigid financial terms to distribution, as we were tied to our contract with Paramount, production can be crippled as producing costs rise and the return from distribution remains fixed. By gaining control of the distributing company, Mr. Zukor liberated production from a squeeze which might have developed into a death-grip. In the terms that interest me most, that meant more creative freedom and better pictures.

I therefore gave my approval to the various negotiations, throughout which Jesse Lasky faithfully represented my interests, the chief of which were, as I wired him, "I to remain in complete authority of whatever studio am connected with and that I may not be moved from California without consent." I wanted to make pictures, and to make them in Hollywood. When the mergers were finally merged all around, I wired Jesse, "I have just been elected president of Morosco Company and vice-president of Bosworth Company, so I am filled with honor and have lost a good day's work."

2

When I was not increasing the profits of the Western Union and Postal Telegraph companies, I managed a good many days' work on three pictures which the critics liked. The critics had not yet discovered what a bad director I am.

The Trail of the Lonesome Pine was based on the popular novel by John Fox, Jr., and the play by Eugene Walter. It was said that novelist and playwright went to see the picture together. On their way out of the theater, Eugene Walter is supposed to have remarked, "Well, at least DeMille kept the pine tree."

"No," said John Fox, Jr., sadly. "It was a redwood."

Authors and readers alike often complain that motion pictures

157

distort or destroy the books on which they are based. Sometimes the complaint is justified. There is in human nature a sort of itch to make what we fondly think are improvements in another man's work once we get our hands on it. More often, though, I believe, that complaint arises from a misunderstanding of the film medium and of the audience for which motion pictures are made. The novelist uses words, with all their economy and all their allusive power. In one sentence, he can portray a character and reveal a lifetime. But we cannot photograph that sentence: it may be necessary to write into a film scenario a whole sequence, which was not in the novel at all, to convey to our mass audience a background of character or an element of plot essential to the story. The disappointed comment, "That wasn't in the book," may be an unconscious tribute to both the novelist and the screenwriter.

The Heart of Nora Flynn was praised particularly for its lighting effects. "An automobile charging along a dark street, with only the lights and the reflection of the street lamps on the pavement visible" seems commonplace now, but it was deemed worthy of special mention in *The Motion Picture News* at the time; and, if my memory serves me, it was in this picture that we first used a very tiny light, cupped in Elliott Dexter's hand, to give a realistic effect when he lighted a cigarette. The title role was played by the lovely Marie Doro, who had the largest and most beautiful eyes I have ever seen. As sometimes happens in nature, she paid for them; she was nearly blind. That took nothing away from her loveliness, however, as Elliott Dexter, her leading man in *The Heart of Nora Flynn*, would be the first to agree. They were later married.

I have already mentioned *The Dream Girl*, the third of my pictures in 1916. Apart from the fact that it was the only picture in which I directed Mae Murray, I cannot see any reason for ever mentioning it again, though the critics were kind to it too.

It was taking longer to make pictures, though. As against the 13 I had directed in 1915, there would be only 4 in all in 1916. Thereafter I would never make more than 5 in any one year. That number now sounds stupendous, considering that my latest film, *The Ten Commandments*, was alone five years in the making. But even in 1916 the reduction of the schedule from 13 to 4 left time for more careful preparation and more finished production;

and it also left some time for personal life and for planting deeper roots in that California from which I insisted that I could not be moved "without consent."

My brother and I had finally prevailed upon our mother to move to California. Even after she had agreed to our persuasion, however, she almost did not come; or so at least she wanted us to believe. Her reluctance to budge from New York was part of a little game mother and I played for years. She was always worried about money. She would never "haggle" with tradesmen, it will be remembered. She was never stingy; if anything, she was rather lavish, whether it made good business sense or not. But the early years, before father's success, had left their mark. By now, happily, Bill and I were able to give mother everything she needed; but she was always worried that, again, times might suddenly turn hard and she would not have enough, so she always asked for more than she needed. The game, as I have called it, developed an invariable pattern. If Mother said she needed $100 for something that could not possibly cost more than $50, I would offer her $75. Then she would reason with me, with flights of logic that would astonish Aristotle. She always won, of course; and she thoroughly enjoyed her victories, proving to her complete satisfaction that she was so much better at business than her now prosperous son.

So it was with her move to California. I sent her a check rather smaller than the extravagant sum she said she needed to cross the continent. An indignant letter came back. She could not possibly come. The check, incidentally, did not come back. Mother knew how the game always ended. It took several more letters. I was unshakable. Mother stood firm. When she came at last, it was on her own terms.

Mother was nothing if not independent. I bought her a house on Argyle Avenue in Hollywood. She liked it; but she promptly rented in addition an apartment away off in Long Beach, where she could hide away and write without interference from solicitous sons. Mother was not one to retire, even though that was now financially possible. She started writing scenarios and, surprisingly, our company bought some of them. They were not very good scenarios; the director-general, as I recall it, was not consulted about their purchase. One of them, curiously, was entitled

159

Unconquered. I had completely forgotten it when I gave the same title to a picture I produced 30 years later, until someone called it to my attention in a list, compiled by *The Film Daily*, of more than 20,000 titles that have been used for films.

As with the apartment, so with the automobile. Mother had had an electric car in New York. In Hollywood I provided her with a respectable little vehicle. It was soon traded in on a huge and ancient Packard. One day when I was driving in downtown Los Angeles, I was stopped a block or so away from a traffic jam. It was impossible to get through. Now, 40 years ago, considering the size of Los Angeles and the number of motor cars on the streets, to create a traffic jam of those proportions took some doing. But it was a feat not beyond mother. When I walked up to see what was causing the delay, there she sat, swathed in her beloved and voluminous veils, at the wheel of her Packard, in the middle of an intersection, calmly maintaining, against all comers, including the municipal police force and a swelling number of very annoyed citizens, that she had the right of way and that justice must be upheld. Any mere man who had walked up and admitted kinship with this Boadicea in her chariot would have been torn limb from limb. I prudently and quietly walked away. Knowing mother, I knew she would get home all right. She did.

Life with mother was always adventurous. She was a prime prospect for any scheme for making a fortune overnight; and, once her imagination was fired, she disdained to "haggle" about any obstacles or other practical considerations. She had a mysterious and expectant air one day when I went to her house and noticed on the table a small flowerpot containing one rather puny leaf. Did I know what that was? It looked like cactus. It was cactus, but couldn't I see that it was *spineless* cactus? Mother was about to become richer than Hetty Green, not to mention revolutionizing the economy of a continent, by introducing spineless cactus into Australia as cattle fodder. She nursed the lonely leaf for some two years. It never grew, but it never put out any disillusioning spines either. The Australian cattle industry, I understand, survived without it.

There was one soundly lucrative business proposition, however, which mother turned down. Her reputation as a play broker, her very real skill at bringing playwrights and producers together,

160

had evidently preceded or followed her to California, for she was approached one day by a wealthy and socially prominent young lady who had a creative idea which, she felt, needed just the delicately diplomatic handling which the well-known Mrs. H. C. de-Mille could give it. The young lady had decided that she wanted to have a child. She had selected the father. There were only two points to be negotiated: she did not want to get married and she required an introduction to the prospective father, whom she knew only by sight. Therefore she needed an agent. Mother was never shocked; mother was always understanding and firmly gentle, but this was one time that opportunity knocked at her door unheeded. She declined the commission. Come to think of it, I wonder what form the customary agent's percentage might have taken.

Mother told that story with a mixture of indignation and amusement. It is easy to recount the amusing things, harder to express the fact that my mother was one of the strongest and most wise and understanding women I have ever known. Until she died, I consulted her always about my work, about my most personal affairs; and she never failed to understand. I must turn again to Agnes deMille's *Dance to the Piper* for a description of mother in those last years of her life. Agnes is writing of mother taking dinner with me:

> She talked to him about all his work. She would sit opposite him at dinner decked in the extraordinary collection of laces and beads and flowers with which she covered her beautiful gray curls and talk to him sometimes very sternly. He always listened . . . at the praise or condemnation of his mother, his heart jumped. She remained critical, hard to please, and enormously proud of her extraordinary son.

Until she died . . . that was October 8, 1923. We had her with us in Hollywood for seven years. They were good years; I am glad that they were good to her. Up until the very end, almost, we played our little money game. It was our little game that told me mother was dying. She came to me one day and asked for a few hundred dollars for what she described rather vaguely as medical expenses. I thought it was the game again, and made the answering gambit. Mother did not play up as usual. Tears came into her

161

eyes. She had to tell me then. She was not playing our game. She had learned that she had cancer.

We called her "Bebe." The only person I ever hear speaking of mother by that name now is my daughter Cecilia; and the way she says it, the warmth and softness in her voice, are perhaps the fittest memorial my mother could have. So fragile, so enduring, is the memory of those we have loved.

In 1916, too, Mrs. deMille and I acquired the house which has been our home ever since. We had moved from the little cottage on Cahuenga to a house on Hollywood Boulevard. Then came an opportunity to buy a place, with ground around it for the gardens Mrs. deMille loves, in the area then known as Laughlin Park, across Los Feliz Boulevard from the hills of Griffith Park and almost due south of the Griffith Observatory, where earnest watchers of the skies pursue the study of those spaces which have always fascinated me and which men may soon explore. The house next door was later occupied by Charlie Chaplin. Later still, I was able to buy it and connect the two houses by a covered walk, using the Chaplin house for my offices and library and its upper story as a guest house for the relatives and friends we have often loved to have with us, but who overflowed our own fairly modest dwelling space. When the narrow winding roads in Laughlin Park were given names, some of them were called after people who lived on them: the street around the corner, where my neighbor W. E. Cummings lives, was called Cummings Drive, our street was named DeMille Drive, and so on.

For more than forty years, 2000 DeMille Drive has been a home of quiet simplicity and loveliness, thanks to the lady who presides over it, and, since I joined the two houses, 2010 DeMille Drive, next door, has been a place where I can browse and project films and work, undisturbed except by the occasional and not unwelcome invasion of assorted children, grandchildren, and now great-grandchildren and their friends—and where Gladys Rosson, Russel Treacy, Ella King Adams, Rose Finegan, Florence Cole, Joan Brooskin, Grace MacLean, Carol Bogden, Shirley Arnett, and others of my office staff through the years have done so much of the work for which I have received the credit.

There is only one bone of contention between Mrs. deMille and me regarding our home; and Mrs. deMille has all the other members of the family on her side. Mrs. deMille is a woman of excellent taste, and her taste is reflected in any place where she lives. But I like rocking chairs, and I have an old one in our living room. I have it there, that is, except when Mrs. deMille periodically decides that it must go. Then it goes. It is never thrown away or chopped up for firewood, though. I always find it. Then it comes back, incongruous, utterly out of harmony with all the rest of the furniture, I admit all that; but it is a very comfortable rocker. Mrs. deMille, as the reader must well know by now, is a very patient woman. Living with me for more than 50 years, after all, is an unequaled training for sainthood.

Keeping the same house for four decades must be something of a record in Los Angeles. We have never been lured by Beverly Hills, Bel Air, or other places which have become much more fashionable than Laughlin Park. Since I came to California in 1913, I have never lived anywhere but in Hollywood. There I have done my work. There I hope to die; and my last earthly home is waiting for me there, in Hollywood Cemetery.

3

If I have not yet made that final move, however, I attribute it largely to another purchase I made in 1916, which, it is not too much to say, has kept me alive. I call it Paradise. Like my father at Echo Lake, like my mother with her apartment at Long Beach, I wanted a place where I could get away, away from the city, away from the studio, away from telephones and all the demands of the daily routine. I wanted a retreat, where I could recharge the batteries of energy my work was needing more and more.

I could see what constant driving work was doing to Jesse Lasky. Again and again, his letters to me from New York apologized for being all business. The old bubbling Jesse would often peep out in a handwritten postscript or in a nostalgic reminiscence of the days when we were poor enough to have time to go camping together in the Maine woods, but this sentence from the end of one of Jesse's letters was more typical of their tenor: "I started out to write a personal letter and not a business one but as you see—I have become a machine—and there isn't anything else in my life except business." When he wrote that, Jesse was planning a short vacation in the wild "Nippigon Regions of Canada" which, he said, "will mean my salvation—at least will preserve what little soul I have left." Jesse had a great deal of soul, and of heart, left until he died. I was in no doubt of that. But I was resolved that I would not become a machine. A film director can never afford to become a machine; and machines miss all the joy of life. Yet, even though Fred Kley and Milton Hoffman were relieving me of most of the routine studio management, setting me freer to concentrate on creative work, I could not leave the studio for more than a week end or so at a time. I would have to find my "Nippigon Regions" nearer home. So I found Paradise; but almost did not get it.

California land, away from the cities, was comparatively cheap at the time. I noticed an advertisement that a fairly good-sized tract, up in the Little Tujunga Canyon about 25 miles from Hollywood, was for sale. I asked Neil McCarthy to go up and have a look at it; Mrs. deMille and Cecilia and I would drive up and meet him there. We met him on his way back.

"You might as well turn around," Neil said. "You wouldn't want it."

I happen to be curious and persistent sometimes; and we had driven 20 miles or so already anyway. "Tell me about it," I asked Neil. "What's the matter with it?"

"Well, there's nothing there but sage bushes. It's the wildest, most terrible place you ever saw in your life. You couldn't grow a crop there."

"Go on," I said. "Tell me more."

"It's all rocks and mountains all around. The only way you can get in is this little narrow canyon here. It's an impossible place. You could never subdivide it. You could never do anything with it."

There was a little stream running through the canyon near where our cars had met. "Does this stream run through it?" I asked.

"Yes," Neil said, "the stream goes through it, but you can't get water power out of that."

"It's completely surrounded by mountains? The only way in is through this narrow canyon? It's really wild country?"

"Yes, it's terrible," Neil said, making ready to go to his car and head back to the city.

"Go back and buy it," I said. "It's exactly what I want."

164

That was the only bad advice I can ever remember being given by Neil McCarthy. Even he would admit it now, I think.

Except for some necessary building, I have kept that tract of land named Paradise exactly as it was when I first saw it. From time to time, I have been able to add to it, acquiring adjacent pieces of land when they went on the market. My new neighbors, remote though they were, did not all welcome a stranger. There was one old gentleman, whose land I had to skirt on my way into the canyon, who used to sit on his porch with a shotgun across his knees, just waiting for me accidentally to trespass and give him the chance for a homicide which he considered, of course, entirely justifiable. Eventually, however, Paradise grew to embrace the whole end of what in California we call a box canyon, surrounded by the mountains of the Angeles National Forest, and with only the one narrow point of ingress which Neil thought was one of the place's worst drawbacks. Across the road that begins at that point I later placed the huge iron gates used in *The King of Kings;* and there have been very few keys to those gates ever made.

To step through those gates is to step back 200 years in California history. The only timber ever cut at Paradise is along the fire trails I have cut through the mountains, helped at times by such rare and hardy guests as may feel up to joining in that climbing and chopping. Forest fire is always a hazard in California, and especially for anyone who is caught in a box canyon if fire leaps across its mouth. The fire trails, which we keep clear of growth, are meant to help firefighters maneuver in the otherwise thickly wooded hills and, unless the wind is too strong, to keep the fire from spreading. There was a ruinous fire at Paradise in 1919, when only the stream running through it and the heroic efforts of a skilled band of Mexican Indian firefighters, fighting for their very lives, were able to save anything.

I allow no shooting at Paradise, with either gun or camera. All rules have their exceptions, of course. We do kill rattlesnakes there; and I have permitted a very few friends, the most recent being Yul Brynner, to take some photographs. Otherwise the place is a sanctuary for the animals as well as for me. Deer, foxes, even an occasional mountain lion, and all the small and secret creatures of the California forest seem to know that they are safe there. It

165

took me more than 30 years to convince the deer that the unant-
lered, hairless biped who comes there on week ends is their friend,
but now, though still aquiver for the first false, sudden move, they
will eat apples out of my hand; and there is a fox who takes breakfast with me on the porch every morning when I am there. I hope
they miss me as much as I miss them on the week ends when I
cannot get to Paradise.

Whenever I can, which, alas, is seldom oftener than twice a
month or so and never when I am in actual production of a picture, I go there late on Thursday afternoon and stay until Saturday afternoon. There is a telephone at Paradise now, but no one
ever calls me unless on the most urgent of business. If I take work
with me, it is usually only reading; that is why I have to return
to Hollywood on Saturday, to do my really heavy homework at
DeMille Drive before I am due at the studio on Monday morning.
My work at Paradise is re-creation—I put a hyphen in the word
because that is what it literally is: there, from nature, from hard
physical exercise, from solitude or from the company of a very
few, very close friends, kindred spirits, and, I like to think, from
some communion with the Spirit of all things, who seems somehow closer when one is close to the elements of earth and wood
and water and to the creatures whose lives pulse with nature's
own rhythm of the seasons and the sun and the dark, I can draw
upon resources that are literally life-giving, re-creating. But for
that Paradise, I would almost certainly be in the other one (or
elsewhere) by now; and, if I ever reach the other Paradise, I shall
probably be as surprised as anyone to find myself there, but I do
not expect it to seem altogether strange, for I have had a little
foretaste of it here.

It would be wholly false, however, to think of Paradise (either
one, I feel sure) as an oppressively solemn place. Certainly my
ranch is not. I used to entertain there, in years gone by, more
than I do now. We made a swimming-pool on the place, simply
by damming the brook that runs through it so that it is filled with
running water, always clear and always cold; and one of my most
vivid memories of the ranch is of looking out my window early
one morning and seeing the slight figure of Leopold Stokowski,
topped by his luxuriant bush of beautiful silver hair, gingerly
dipping his toe into the icy water of the pool. He had evidently

not been warned how cold it was. Other guests, who have experienced the pool, tell newcomers to pay no attention to their host when he is foolhardy enough to dive in head first. The only way to manage it, they say, is to walk in at the shallow end and stand still until you are completely numb with cold. Then you can swim, because by that time your body has lost all sensation and, like fair Charlotte in the old song, you can freeze to death in complete comfort. They exaggerate, the tellers of that tale, but not much; I do admit the water is bracing.

From the entertaining which I used to do at Paradise has grown one of the customs which I follow now even when I am there alone. It has been cited as one of the clearest proofs of DeMille's megalomania. From my mother I learned, even when we were poorest, to set as good a table as possible and to make festive the principal meal of the day, however scanty it might be, a high symbol of the reunion of family and friends. At Paradise, after a day of hiking or wood-chopping, it certainly did not seem the thing to come to the dinner table in khaki. Business suits are dull; we were there to get away from business for a while. Yet dinner jackets seemed at least equally out of place in those rustic surroundings. I know better than to make rules of dress for the ladies, God bless them, but it was suggested to male guests that they bring black trousers, and they would find in their closets at the ranch wearing apparel for the upper half of their manly forms— silk Russian blouses and cummerbunds, in a variety of colors. Very seldom a guest jibbed at donning his blouse. H. G. Wells was one who did, when Charlie Chaplin brought him to Paradise for a week end. After his visit, he gave me one of his books, inscribed "To Cecil B. deMille, an artist—in living." Weighted with his responsibility as an historian, I suppose he could not bring himself to call me an artist in anything else, especially perhaps in the matter of Russian blouses.

But those who braved the unaccustomed blouse not only made a colorful dinner party: they also found that the Russian blouse is one of the most graceful and comfortable garments ever devised. That is why I still wear it to dinner at Paradise even when I am alone; and I wear a cloak from my stone cottage to the dining room because they are some distance apart and the evenings are cool in the mountains of California. I also carry a revolver because I am as likely to meet a rattlesnake in the middle of the narrow path as I am a hungry deer or a friendly fox. It seems a pity to demolish legend with such sober and practical facts, especially a legend which has earned a more or less honest penny for two generations of imaginative journalists; but really, if I were inclined to indulge in delusions of grandeur, I think I should be able to find grander ways of doing so than any of those journalists have so far attributed to me.

It is the same with the puttees. As long ago as 1915, the press was writing about puttees as one of the "chief factors" of my "working garb." This has now become standard in descriptions of DeMille the eccentrically dressed director. When we were shooting the early pictures on the Lasky ranch and at other rugged locations, I began wearing leather boots or leggings as a protection against snakes, scorpions, cactus, or poison oak. I found that good boots or leggings also gave support to the legs, so I continued to wear them at the studio when directing a picture required me often to be on my feet for twelve hours or more a day. A director's work will suffer if he has to be bothered by tired ankles. That is the simple explanation of the boots. But I suppose that "puttees," with its exotic overtones of Tommy Atkins defending the Empire amid the perils of jungle warfare, has a more romantic sound.

I do not deny that I enjoy "dressing up." I like costume and really well-staged ceremony; I think something bright and heart-lifting went out of human life when in the nineteenth century everyone, with the exception of soldiers and sailors and the clergy, judges, and professors on occasion, began to dress all alike and as drably as possible. There is probably a deep psychological significance in this; but I still leave that to the experts and just confess unblushingly that, on the rare occasions when I have to wear academic dress or a uniform of some kind or even my American Legion cap or Shriner's fez, I rather like it. So, I believe, do most people, if they would or could admit it. There is a Champion Driver, or a Walter Mitty, hidden in most of us, under the layers of conformity. If we cannot let him appear, we can at least gratify him vicariously by going to the movies.

168

4

Perhaps that is one reason why I chose, for my final picture of 1916, the story of Joan of Arc, against the misgivings of some who adhered to the dogma that "people won't come to see costume pictures." *Gone With the Wind* and *The Ten Commandments* had not yet exploded that dogma and established the sounder principle, in which I have always believed, that people will always come to see good pictures, whether the actors are dressed in togas or tuxedos. Costumes will not draw or hold an audience if the story is badly constructed or badly played; but costumes will not hurt, and they may enhance, a good story well told. *Joan the Woman* was not an outstanding success financially, but it was not by any means the "costly . . . flop" which one film historian has called it. It cost $302,976.26 and grossed $605,731.30. The difference between those two figures, of course, does not represent anything like clear profit, as the distributors' and exhibitors' large share, as well as advertising and other expenses incurred after the completion of the negative, must always be deducted from gross receipts. But, *Joan the Woman* was, as Jesse Lasky puts it, "passably profitable."

More important than its financial return, however, was the fact that this was my first big historical picture. It was the beginning of a pattern which I have followed in many pictures since: a pattern which has been very widely misunderstood.

I expect that I shall never live down the word "spectacle." For years now, the press has been dutifully and monotonously calling every new DeMille picture a DeMille spectacle. There is nothing wrong with spectacle in its place. Many historical events, many natural cataclysms, are spectacular. The motion picture screen is an unequaled medium for portraying them; and David Wark Griffith and I were among the first, in America at least, to bring the screen to its full potential in that respect. But spectacle alone does not and never will make a good picture or a successful one. The most spectacular action or photographic effects will not carry a weak or poorly constructed story.

The audience is interested in people, not masses of anonymous people, but individuals whom they can love or hate, in whose fortunes they can feel personally involved. When my grandson Jody was six or seven years old, he used to sit beside me some-

169

times when I screened pictures at my home; and invariably, when a character came on the screen, Jody would ask me, "Is he good or is he bad, Grandfather?" That basic point settled, Jody could sit back and follow the story as a conflict of good and evil personified in the good men and the bad men; and his emotions were invested in wanting the good to win. If a battle raged across the screen, if a gigantic earthquake toppled tall cities, the spectacle was exciting, to be sure, but what held Jody and gave the spectacle meaning was whether the hero's side was winning the battle or whether the villain was being swallowed up by the quaking earth. There is a good deal of Jody in every audience, I think. I know there is in me. Which do we read in the newspaper with greater absorption and involvement, the story of a flood taking thousands of lives in the interior of China or the story of a single miner trapped in a cave-in, an individual man whose name we know and whose family we can visualize and suffer with? To us reading about it, the flood in China is spectacle; the single miner's fate, enlisting our own hopes and fears, is story.

If there is a DeMille formula for the historical pictures that began with *Joan the Woman,* it is a very simple one: to tell an absorbing personal story against a background of great historical events. The story gives to the historical events a more vivid meaning than most of the audience will have found in their history textbooks. The historical background gives an added dimension of significance to the personal story, as well as an opportunity to utilize the camera's full range for spectacle. But it is the story that counts most. The dramatic construction of the story is the steel framework that holds up the building. Everything else— spectacle, stars, special effects, costume, music, and all the rest— are essentially trimmings.

I like spectacle. I like to paint on a big canvas. I like it when the critics say I do it well. But I spend much more time working on dramatic construction than I do planning spectacular effects. The audience does not analyze these elements in a picture, but I must, or the audience will not come to see my pictures. And they do come. I am afraid that those critics who see only "another DeMille spectacle" do not analyze very deeply either. Perhaps that is why some critics' opinion of the public goes lower and lower every time I make a successful picture.

170

Jeanie Macpherson, who wrote the screenplay of *Joan the Woman,* chose that title because she wanted to emphasize the humanity of Joan of Arc rather than project the conventional, and so frequently false, image of a saint. We portrayed Joan as a strong peasant girl, with a sense of humor and human sympathy, ever faithful to her Voices, but tempted and fearful too—a woman of flesh and blood, whose heroism was as much in her victory over herself as in her victory over the English. That is what real saints are like, I think.

Our treatment of the theme, perhaps especially our characterization of some churchmen as the villains they were, caused flutterings of resentment in some religious circles. We were simply 39 years ahead of Pope Pius XII's declaration that in a film dealing with the Church it may well be "necessary to present faults and failings of ecclesiastical persons, in their character and perhaps even in the exercise of their office." More surprising was the criticism voiced by Alexander Woollcott, who praised *Joan the Woman* as "among the finest things the motion picture has achieved thus far," but said that the title role should have been played by a more ethereal type of actress, "Mae Marsh, perhaps," instead of the one whom I selected as the obvious choice for the part: Geraldine Farrar.

As often happens with critics, no one seems to have mentioned what I see now as the greatest dramatic fault in *Joan the Woman.* At the beginning and end of the film we had scenes of the trench warfare then actually raging in France, with Wallace Reid playing an English soldier named Eric Trent in both the modern prologue and epilogue and in the main story of Joan of Arc. It was an interesting idea, with its hint of reincarnation which appealed particularly to Jeanie Macpherson. I have used historical flashbacks in a number of other pictures. But experience has taught me that if you put an audience back into the fifteenth century, or any other distant time, and then at the end snap them back to the present with modern scenes, you are likely to lose the emotional impact of the main story. The audience may think it was just a dream. They will certainly be forcibly made aware that it happened a long, long time ago. Its actuality, which is the heart of drama, is weakened if not destroyed.

The struggles of Joan of Arc were actual enough to those who

171

took part in our re-creation of them. Fine performances were given by Wallace Reid as the young English soldier, Raymond Hatton as the King of France, Hobart Bosworth as La Hire, Theodore Roberts as Cauchon, Tully Marshall as "a fanatical monk," and by Charles Clary, James Neill, Lillian Leighton, Marjorie Daw, Billy Elmer, and others in smaller roles. Our company of cowboy extras made quite passable medieval soldiers, even if the director had to keep a sharp eye, and sometimes give a sharper reminder, on the fact that chewing gum was not in general use in fifteenth century France. But the heroine of the production, as well as of the story, was Geraldine Farrar.

Our personal relationship was not as close as it had been during the making of her first pictures. She had not yet forgiven me for refusing to allow her new husband, Lou Tellegen, to direct pictures for our company. He had directed one. Jesse, Sam, and I had screened it together, and we all knew it was a dismal failure. Tellegen was a handsome Frenchman who had been Sarah Bernhardt's leading man; but, like some other actors who have tried, he could not direct. Sam and Jesse unanimously elected me to break the unpleasant tidings to him and Geraldine.

When I went to Geraldine's house, Tellegen was there. I could see him through the front doorway, lying on a couch from which he did not move during my interview with Geraldine. I did not get very far through the doorway. Geraldine, evidently warned, met me with the air of a lioness defending her young or an angel guarding the portal with a flaming sword. She was magnificent, but I was firm. Lou Tellegen had ruined one picture. We could not afford to let him ruin any more. Both Geraldine and I have some small gift of forceful speech when aroused. All through our conversation, the subject of it lay blandly on his couch, in full sight and hearing, letting Geraldine defend him.

They had been married four months when Geraldine began work in *Joan the Woman*. Though it was to be seven more years before the marriage she worked hard to save finally ended in divorce, perhaps she was already discovering the kind of man she had married. Perhaps that is why, rather puzzled by a change in her, I wrote to Jesse Lasky in July, 1916, that Geraldine seemed "to have lost a little something of the great spark of genius that animated her last year. Although she is tremendously enthused

172

over the story and says it is the greatest work of her life, at the same time, that little spark seems missing. She may get it as we go on in the work."

She did, splendidly; and, whatever the reason for her temporary loss of it, it is typical of Gerry that, although in her memoirs honesty compelled her to tell the shameful and humiliating truth about Tellegen, her last words about him are words of charity: "May those tormented ashes rest in peace."

I think she has forgiven me now. In fact, we have met several times in the years between, most cordially, when concert tours brought Geraldine to Los Angeles and Mrs. deMille would invite her to dine with us at our home. But even in the summer of 1916, when there was the little but noticeable personal coolness between us, it never affected her wholehearted devotion to her work.

I had a suit of silver armor made for her, lighter than the iron worn by the men, but it was still so heavy, especially when she carried her great sword and banner, that she had to be lifted onto her horse. She never complained. She spent days in a water-filled ditch. I was afraid of the effect that might have on her voice; but I was the only one who got laryngitis. She was in the thick of the battles. When we filmed the great battle of Les Tourelles on the Lasky ranch, with every director in the company, including my brother Bill, George Melford, and a youngster named Donald Crisp, in the scene in costume, each responsible for the direction of a group of soldiers, I posted specially skilled riders to surround Geraldine Farrar and protect her from being unhorsed or injured; but it was a real battle none the less. I had seen to that too—by offering a bonus to the English Army if Joan of Arc was captured and a bonus to the French if she was not. Once her horse ran away with her, but fortunately it ran in the direction of a young man whose riding skill and bravery might not have been expected from one who had spent his sheltered childhood in an Episcopal rectory. His name was Jack Holt. In some of the scenes calling for extraordinary horsemanship, Pansy Perry doubled for Geraldine Farrar; but Geraldine took her share of the rough scenes as well as of the magnificent and moving coronation scene and the mystical and tender personal scenes, and she put her whole soul into them all.

Our medieval cowboys would have died for her, gladly, I believe. One of the most difficult stunts a player can be asked to do is to fall, rather than jump, from a height. It looks easy; but at the moment of going over, self-preservation whispers and, unless the player makes the tremendous effort to keep his muscles relaxed, what the audience sees is not a deadweight fall, but a more or less skillful jump. For that reason, our first take of a scene in which wounded soldiers were supposed to fall from high parapets was most unconvincing. Back they came the next day, ready to practice falling like corpses until they had it right, rather than disappoint the star and the director. One evening, after one of the riders assigned to guard Geraldine had failed to keep her helmet from getting knocked off in a melee, he was tossed in a blanket by his fellows for his carelessness. When the picture was finished, the cowboys staged a rodeo in Griffith Park in Geraldine's honor and presented her with a pony, which must have seemed an appropriately gentle gift after her weeks on Joan of Arc's caparisoned charger.

The climax of the picture, of course, was the burning of Joan at the stake. It was a real stake, with fire as real as that which had consumed the young body of the real Joan in the public square of Rouen in 1431. Obviously it was constructed so that Geraldine Farrar would not be burned, but it was still acutely uncomfortable and not entirely without danger. Agnes deMille, who was at the studio that day, writes that I "stood at the stake for hours trying out smoke." I probably did; a director should never ask a player to do anything he is afraid or unwilling to do himself.

It must have been after I had tried it out myself that I called into service what may well have been Hollywood's first stand-in. Gladys Rosson was shorter than Geraldine Farrar, but she was a girl and with much the same brunette hair and complexion as the star, so I called Gladys away from her desk and burned her at the stake while we were setting up the scene in preparation for Miss Farrar and the camera. But when the camera turned, it was Geraldine Farrar who stood amid the smoke and flame until the very end of the scene, when, of course, a dummy was substituted for the actual burning of Joan's body. Geraldine wrote later that it was a "truly terrifying" experience; but she did not weaken for a second until, standing aside after her part was over, she saw the dummy being burned where she had stood a short time before. Then she had to go to her dressing room and be sick. That was how thoroughly she had put herself into her role.

Joan the Woman was the first picture in which I used color photography. It was used only for certain scenes, not throughout the film. Color was still very much in the experimental stage, as it had been for some years. Most of the color used in American productions at the time was applied to the film by the laborious method of painting it on by hand, using a brush consisting of one single hair, or by a process which depended for its results on attaching special lenses with revolving color screens to the projection machine. I was no expert in these technical mysteries, nor am I now, so I shall not attempt to describe them in detail. However, I had seen multicolor lithographing done in New York, and I wondered if some such mechanical means might not be devised to print color on the film, more quickly and cheaply and more durably than the processes then in use. The great advantage that amateurs have over experts is that the experts always see mountainously insuperable obstacles of which the amateur is blissfully ignorant. The amateur sees only the result he wants to get; and if he drives hard enough, he may often get it.

In addition to Alvin Wyckoff, we had in the Lasky studio laboratory two who were experts, Max Handschiegl and Loren Taylor. The color process developed first for *Joan the Woman* was advertised as the Wyckoff process, referred to in publicity as the DeMille-Wyckoff process, and later widely known as the Handschiegl process. It was in fact the work of several minds, including one amateur's, and the name of Loren Taylor should be remembered among them. Loren Taylor had come to the Lasky studio in 1915 after having tried his hand at such varied occupations as bandleader and newspaper editor. Those were the days when one could make a place in the industry for an inventive, creative mind, from whatever improbable background it came. Except in the areas of writing and acting, that is not generally true today. The front offices are not adventurous; the unions are entrenched. If a Loren Taylor came to me today, I might be able to get him a job in the studio mail room. Yet the industry in all its branches needs and always will need the infusion of fresh talent; and talent is not created either by executive timidity or by union security

175

clauses. That might be borne in mind by any who wonder why tired audiences sometimes find that movies are not necessarily better than ever.

5

While we were burning Joan of Arc at the stake, another and more explosive fire was growing in the New York offices. Mr. Zukor, as I have said, had been made president of Famous Players-Lasky and Sam Goldfish chairman of the board of directors, of whom I was one. In the ordinary course of American business, the chairmanship of the board is a lofty and dignified position. The chairman may sometimes have his name listed above that of the president. He often exerts great influence in the company's affairs. But he does not usually take an active part in the company's day-to-day operations. Like the British monarch, he reigns; but he is decidedly not expected to rule. If there was ever a man unfitted by temperament to be a British monarch, that man was Sam. He kept right on functioning as general manager, as he had done so superbly in our original company. Sam could not do otherwise. His great ability and his unbounded energy have destined him throughout life to be a man of decision and action. But in the president's chair of the new company was another man, a little older and quieter, but in his way no less able and certainly no less determined and accustomed to rule. Clashes between the two were inevitable, and not infrequent.

The conflict came to a head immediately after Jesse Lasky's return from his vacation in Canada in August, 1916. Adolph Zukor informed Jesse that either Sam must leave the company or Mr. Zukor would. He left it for Jesse to decide. It is a sign of Jesse's strength and balance that he kept his own counsel until he had made his decision. He did not write to me about the matter until the middle of September. His letter is important and revealing enough to quote at some length:

> When Zukor gave us his ultimatum, I did not agree with him but rather took issue with him and supported Sam. . . . Zukor insisted that we must choose between Sam and himself. Before coming to an absolute decision as to where I would stand in the matter, I determined to study Zukor. . . . The result of my constant study was more than satisfactory. It was gratifying. First he

176

is an all around better businessman—has better foresight—is a better financier and has a broader and bigger grasp of the picture business . . . he is considered the biggest man in the motion picture industry and . . . his reputation for honesty and integrity is remarkable. . . . We once thought he was vacillating and changed his views too often. I find that is not the case. He only changes his views when he finds that the position he has taken is not sound and then he has the courage to change his mind, and stands by his new convictions no matter in what light he might be placing himself. To sum it all up I feel that we couldn't have a better man than Zukor as president of our new corporation. Incidentally Arthur and I work 100 per cent more efficiently with Zukor. . . .

Sam resigned yesterday and I am particularly glad that we did not have to call upon you to cast a vote. There was no need to bring the matter in front of the Board of Directors as I told Sam frankly that I would support Zukor and that being the case—there being 6 Lasky directors and 6 Famous directors—my vote would give Zukor the majority. As a matter of fact, every director in the organization except you, whom we tried to keep out of the controversy, was determined to support Zukor.

I was pained by this first breach in our triumvirate. I was glad that the other parties to the quarrel did keep me "out of the controversy." That was part of the same consideration Jesse, Sam, and Mr. Zukor had all shown me at the formation of the new company, when they had offered me a contract guaranteed for five years, while making no such provision for themselves.

I thought that we might keep our old partnership together, and save Sam's undoubted value to the company, if he would come to Hollywood permanently, away from the inter-office warfare in New York, and join me in the production end of the business. Sam, however, preferred to strike out on his own. How right he was in that decision is an indelible part of the history of Hollywood.

He formed a partnership with Edgar Selwyn and, combining syllables from each of their surnames, called the new company the Goldwyn Pictures Corporation. Later he changed his own name to Goldwyn; and it is as Samuel Goldwyn, brilliant, shrewd, irrepressible, energetic, not always predictable but always strong, a master in every phase of the motion picture business, that the world now knows and history will remember him. What the world and much of Hollywood do not know is that Sam Goldwyn is also one of the most generous men alive.

Of all the things that have been said about me I value among the highest what Sam Goldwyn wrote seven years later: "To me deMille was a true friend, and the memory of his truth and loyalty illumines one of the bitterest chapters of my life."

That bitterness was long in healing. Through the years Sam and Jesse met sometimes at industry functions and exchanged formal compliments, for they respected each other's ability, but it was not until 1958 that our triumvirate came together again as we had been in 1913. It seems right to vault across the years between and tell that story here.

In 1957 Jesse Lasky rejoined me at Paramount to begin work on a picture which he said "I want to make more than I have ever wanted to make any picture. . . . I'd name the picture *The Big Brass Band* and dedicate it to the nine million kids who spend their spare time practicing on their instruments instead of running with juvenile gangs, making music instead of mischief." At the same time Jesse was being harassed by the Bureau of Internal Revenue over a disputed tax matter. Our government seems to operate sometimes on the curious theory that the way to increase revenue is to ruin those who produce it. To settle the matter even partially and temporarily and to free his mind for the big project he had in work, Jesse needed a large sum of money right away. I talked with one or two of Jesse's friends; and then I called Sam Goldwyn and asked if he would join in helping.

There was silence at the other end of the wire for a few seconds, then Sam said, "Let me think about it, Cecil. I'll call you tomorrow."

The next day Sam telephoned. "I'll do it," he said.

Early in January, 1958, I brought Jesse and Sam together, the first time in more than 40 years that they had met as friends.

On Monday, January 13, Jesse Lasky, buoyant and bubbling as ever, free of his immediate financial worry, his way clear to proceed with the picture he wanted so much to make, his old friendship with Sam restored, went to Beverly Hills to make a speech at a luncheon. On his way to his car, in the parking lot of the hotel, he collapsed and died.

178

Jesse was the first of the three of us to go. He and I had often talked about death, sometimes seriously, sometimes lightly as when we wondered aloud which of us would read the other's name in large black headlines in the newspaper. When my turn comes, one of the things I shall look back upon most gratefully is the part I had in restoring, only days before Jesse's unexpected death, the comradeship among the three of us that began in 1913 and seemed in 1916 to be irrevocably broken.

The remainder of the latter year was given over largely to preparing for the release of *Joan the Woman*, which had its world première at the 44th Street Theatre, New York, on Christmas Eve. In the language of the motion picture industry, the publicity and advertising campaign, preparing the way for a film, is called by the horrid term "exploitation." I do not know how that term started in the industry. I know, of course, that it is used innocently, almost as a technical term. But, whenever I hear it, I keep remembering its meaning in the English language, as distinct from the language of the motion picture industry; and if Joan of Arc knew English, I would expect her scattered ashes to come together long enough to smite with the legendary sword of Charles Martel whoever wrote our publicity about the "careful exploitation" of her life story. I battle regularly with the publicity department when they begin to talk about "exploiting" any of my pictures; I do not want to have to answer to Moses for "exploiting" the Ten Commandments! But, language aside, an important film deserves proper presentation, which is a service to the public as well as to the producer. For *Joan the Woman* we planned and executed such a presentation, not only in the newspapers and film magazines, but by the public exhibition of costumes and properties used in the picture, which may perhaps have been the first time that such displays were so used.

Part of the preparation involved also coping with the censors. Not to anticipate what I shall have to say later about the genuinely serious problem of art and morality, I shall reveal now only the one single safe prediction which can be made about censors: that if you are dealing with 28 different boards of censorship, you may be fairly sure that they will suggest 28 different scenes or lines which they think should be cut out of your work. A lady member of one censorship board objected strongly to Joan's saying the line, "Lord God, why hast Thou forsaken me?" A saint like Joan, the lady said, could never utter such a cry of seeming despair. Fortunately there was a clergyman on the same board, who quietly pointed out that Jesus had uttered the same cry from the Cross. The lady censor had apparently not heard of that, but she admitted that the precedent was convincing. If the clergyman on the board had had a wedding to perform or a bad cold in the head that day, the people of that community might have been protected from those words, which the Saviour on Calvary did not disdain, but which an ignorant lady censor considered unsuitable for repetition in *her* bailiwick. So much, for the present, for censorship.

6

Toward the end of 1916 I received the opportunity to help what was to become one of the brightest careers in motion pictures, that of Mary Pickford. We had not met since appearing together on the stage in *The Warrens of Virginia*. Mary Pickford had since become one of the main assets which Mr. Zukor brought to the merger of Famous Players with our company; but Mary was not happy with the merger. Her personal relationship with Mr. Zukor had been almost that of a father and daughter. Now, since the merger and the advent of Jesse and Sam to positions of executive power, she felt oppressed by the sense of being part of a machine rather than a family. She too had some serious clashes with Sam. Added to her professional discontent was the growing unhappiness of her marriage to Owen Moore. Her last two pictures had been failures: *Less than the Dust* lived up to its name, and *Pride of the Clan* was an opus of which neither Mary nor anyone in the Famous Players-Lasky clan could be proud. Mary's mother and her doctor both felt it urgently necessary that she get away from New York and Owen Moore. Mr. Zukor asked me if I would direct her in two pictures to be made in Hollywood.

I agreed very readily. Then developed the first hitch. For the films she had made in New York, Mr. Zukor had given Mary the privilege of selecting the writer of her scenarios, approving the scripts, and in other ways exercising an authority which belongs strictly to the producer and director. When I received word that she would expect the same rights when she came to Hollywood,

I put my foot down firmly. I liked Mary, I knew her ability as an actress, and I respected her writer, Frances Marion. But I would not be moved from the principle that it is the producer-director's job to produce and direct. If he divides that authority with anyone else, the result is almost certain to be a bad picture. The director of a symphony orchestra does not allow the French horns to improvise flourishes of their own *ad lib*. A commanding general does not allow the supply corps to decide all by itself when and where to deliver the needed material. I have never allowed script approval or any other such major authority to anyone who works in any of my pictures. It fell to Mr. Zukor to explain this to Mary and persuade her to send me a most docile telegram, abdicating her previous privileges and placing herself unreservedly at my direction. Mary yielded; but she came to Hollywood fearing that her older brother in *The Warrens of Virginia* had become an ogre.

The second hitch related to the subjects of Mary Pickford's two pictures with me. With the attention of all the world focused on the European war, I had in mind a vivid war story, laid in Belgium, not propaganda of any kind, but a gripping human story painted, as I like to paint, against the broad canvas of gripping world events.

The New York executives wanted a western.

As late as January, 1917, they still had their minds fixed on the German and Austrian market; they were still apparently "preparing for peace." Their telegrams were so imploring that I gave in, rather against my own judgment, and my first picture with Mary Pickford was *A Romance of the Redwoods,* a story of the vigilantes.

Mary's fans were given something of a shock when, at the climax of the film, the hero's life was spared by the vigilantes so that he could marry Mary, all because she was seen knitting baby clothes. To her vast and adoring audience, Mary Pickford was the image of innocent girlhood. It was shocking enough that the famous Pickford curls had been shorn. Baby clothes, and especially premarital baby clothes, decidedly did not fit the image. When the vigilantes were safely out of the way, however, it was revealed that they were really doll clothes; and all was saved.

Though terrified of me at first, Mary was not difficult to work

181

with. If she resented not having her own way all the time, she did not show it. Mary is a good trouper. In the foreword I wrote a few years ago for her memoirs, *Sunshine and Shadow*, I said that "there is another word for being a good trouper, a word that show business would think too grand to use. That word is dedication." Mary Pickford is a dedicated person, one of those who sees goals steadily and aims for them unswervingly. It is a tribute to her, rather than the reverse, to record that, though she lived up to her promise to me completely throughout the making of our two pictures together, she immediately afterward returned to her resolve to have her own writer, Frances Marion, and her chosen director, Marshall Neilan. And from there she went on to the pinnacle which, as I have said, has been occupied in my lifetime by only two other stars—Maude Adams on the stage and Geraldine Farrar in opera.

By the time we finished *A Romance of the Redwoods*, in March, 1917, even the New York executives were ready for my Belgian story, *The Little American*, Mary Pickford's second picture with me. This too, for the times and the star, was strongly mature provender—the story of an American girl in Belgium to do relief work, meeting her German-American fiancé, now an officer of a brutal invading army. But the critic of *The Moving Picture World* termed it "superior in theme and craftsmanship to any of the previous Pickford pictures." The German officer was played by the young man who had fortuitously saved Geraldine Farrar by stopping her runaway horse: this was one of Jack Holt's first major starring roles. Others whose names later became world-famous could look back on *The Little American* as one of their first steppingstones. I gave a small bit part in it to a handsome youngster named Ramon Novarro and another to a player less classically handsome but no less talented, even if in the picture he surprisingly showed a severe case of camera fright at first, Wallace Beery. One of the extra players was Sam Wood, who as a director in later years was less known to the public than those who continued their career as actors, but whom until his death Hollywood respected both as a director and as one of the staunchest fighters against the inroads of communism in the motion picture industry. There also was a little boy whom television viewers can see now week after week, in somewhat larger size, as Sergeant

Friday's more talkative partner in the pursuit of evil-doers: Ben Alexander.

For the scene of the sinking of the *Lusitania*, we built almost an entire deck of an ocean liner and mechanically tipped it so that the passengers were seen actually slipping into the water. I believe that this had not been done in films before. It pained Mary Pickford's thrifty soul to wear a $400 dress splashing around in the waters of San Pedro harbor; I think the ruination of the dress pained her more than her immersion in the chilling waters, for she took the dousing with the same good will that marked her wholehearted devotion to her job and to taking my direction, in keeping with her promise.

No one can claim to have made Mary Pickford the great star she became. Adolph Zukor nurtured her early career with both great showmanship and fatherly tact. D. W. Griffith taught her much, as he taught all who worked with him. I was fortunately able to give her career a needed lift at a time when both her professional and her personal life were at an unhappy ebb. Mary has touchingly paid due tribute to her mother's influence. But it was her own talent and her own strength that made and kept her unchallenged as "America's sweetheart."

The Little American was timely, as I had known months before it would be. On April 2, 1917, President Wilson went before Congress to ask for the declaration that a state of war existed between the United States and the Imperial German Government. A patient people rallied, with the terrible determination that only such a people have; and we were at war.

9

Today's dispatches from Cape Canaveral make those April days of 1917 seem very far away and almost pathetically naïve. Two weeks after war was declared, I offered the city of Los Angeles, on behalf of the Famous Players-Lasky studio, 75 men, with a machine gun, rifles, and ammunition! Amusing now, that item, but we were in earnest then. For some months, since the President's call for "preparedness," motion picture workers from several studios had formed a company of the Coast Artillery Reserve, under the command of Captain T. E. Duncan and Lieutenant Walter Long. Now our studio was designated a recruiting station for a Home Guard unit, of which I was made captain; my brother Bill was top sergeant.

At first we drilled in civilian clothes, with brooms supplementing the property department's supply of rifles. When we were at length outfitted with uniforms and proper arms, our company was sworn into the California militia, the colors were ceremoniously presented to us by Mary Pickford and proudly borne by Color Sergeant Wallace Reid. That ceremony, vibrant at once with patriotism, beauty, and reasonably warlike panoply, was marred for me when, in the midst of my stirring speech, I noticed my brother, standing stiffly at attention but making the most ludicrous and horrid faces at me. I finished the speech, with somewhat less than total concentration on my patriotic theme; but I did not have Bill court-martialed when I learned afterwards that his facial contortions were not really signs of disrespect for his captain. They were defensive maneuvers: Bill was undergoing aerial attack by a tremendous blue-bottle fly, which he was trying to blow or scare away rather than besmirch the honor of the company by lifting a hand to swat it.

The Home Guard was the subject of many jokes; but of the 105 men who went into the regular army after their rudimentary training in our company, every one became a commissioned or noncommissioned officer. Our studio employees subscribed heavily to the Liberty Loans, as aroused Americans were doing everywhere throughout the country. We paid full salary to the dependents of every family man who went from our employ into the armed services. I resolve to exchange my neat Home Guard captain's uniform for the battle-dress of the regular army as soon as I was free of commitments I had already made, on which the work of the studio and the employment of many of our workers depended.

In the early months of World War I, however, battles within the motion picture industry still seemed closer to us than battles on the other side of the Atlantic Ocean. The exhibitors now began to gird themselves. From Mitchell Mark in New York to T. L. Tally in Los Angeles, exhibitors throughout the country began protesting the high cost of film rentals. They have been doing so ever since; but in 1917 some of the most powerful among them decided to combine and enter first the distribution field and later that of production, making pictures and leasing them to themselves at lower rentals than the Zukor companies or their competitors could charge. That was the theory on which the First National Exhibitors' Circuit was organized.

From our point of view, we had to charge the exhibitors increasingly higher film rental because of the increase in our costs, especially as the star system grew. Mary Pickford, for example, was commanding a salary of $10,000 a week; and Mary was not the only star in the Famous Players-Lasky firmament able to demand compensation a far cry from the $250 a week with which we had lured Dustin Farnum from the stage less than four years before. The producing companies faced competition among themselves not only in selling their product, but in bidding for the stars they needed, or thought they needed, to make that product. When the exhibitors, under the First National banner, entered the production field, the result, of course, was to increase the bargaining power of the stars: here was another bidder, to boost what the much-coveted star could demand.

When First National offered Mary Pickford $1,050,000 for three pictures, I concurred heartily in Mr. Zukor's decision not to try to match it. Mary went to First National. A few months later she joined with Charlie Chaplin, Douglas Fairbanks, and D. W. Griffith in organizing the United Artists Corporation, which was the stars' contribution to the industry's civil war: since stars were apparently the kingpins in the situation, why, they thought, should they not produce and market themselves? It was the organization of United Artists which gave rise to the famous remark attributed to Richard Rowland, the head of Metro, one of the producing companies which later merged with Goldwyn and Mayer to become the lion of the industry, M-G-M. "So," said Mr. Rowland when he heard that the stars had invaded the production field, "the lunatics have taken charge of the asylum."

Mr. Rowland's remark was not a kindly one perhaps; but it has been applicable more than once in the history of the motion picture industry, and not only to the stars. It has been applicable any time that any segment of the industry has acted on the delusion that it alone is all-important. The end product of all our industry— the intangible, fleeting images on the screen of the neighborhood theater, fragilely freighted with drama, comedy, great music, laughter and tears, heartache and heart-lift—is the work of all who labored to bring it there, from the author of the original idea to the projectionist in the booth. When anyone in that long chain of collaboration begins to think that he is the all-important factor, whether it is a star who begins to believe what the publicity department says about him, or a director who wastes hours of time and thousands of dollars and reels of film because he comes on the set ill-prepared, not knowing what he wants, or a union which feels the muscles of its bargaining power and uses them recklessly, the picture, the industry, and the public suffer.

Believing in 1917, as I still do, that the story a film has to tell is the one all-important element in it, I believed then, and still do, that great pictures can be made without "name" stars. Perhaps I

186

am harking back to the stock companies in the theater of my father's time, but for years I have dreamed of assembling a group of competent players, using them interchangeably in a whole series of pictures in which a player might find himself the leading man in one film and the butler in the next, stressing story and good performance of *all* the roles rather than the glamour of one or two big "names." I think the public would accept that type of production, if it were well done, and that it would build up a public confidence in the company producing such pictures, which would be sounder both artistically and economically than the star system. I have never been able to carry out that idea, though. The industry, having created the star system, is now saddled with it; and executives feel that star names are box office insurance. I have often given leading roles to relatively unknown players; but then, lo and behold, they not only became stars, but sometimes in their own estimation became suns around which the universe must revolve!

That is by no means true of all the stars with whom I have worked, of course. The greatest have often been the most conscientious and reliable workmen; and I have no compliment in my vocabulary higher than to call anyone a good workman.

2

Such was Geraldine Farrar when she returned to Hollywood in the summer of 1917 to make the last two pictures under our contract with her, *The Woman God Forgot* and *The Devil Stone*. In both I cast Wallace Reid again as her leading man and other veterans of *Joan The Woman* in supporting roles. Though I have never had the "DeMille Stock Company" of my dreams on a permanent basis, I have, whenever possible, followed the practice of giving parts to actors and actresses who have worked competently and congenially with me in earlier pictures. Some have appeared in almost every one of my pictures for 20 or 30 years or more. Whenever I am casting a picture, I give the casting director a list of these older players and instructions to find them and see if they want work. They credit me with loyalty for doing that, but it is not entirely a matter of sentiment. I know their work. They know my ways. In many of my later pictures, you can see famous stars of years gone by, giving to small parts the same artistry they gave to

187

leading roles a generation or more ago. They are good workmen; I like to think that they are also good friends.

So it was that two lifelong friends played their first roles for me in *The Woman God Forgot,* Theodore Kosloff as an Aztec warrior and Julia Faye as a maiden-in-waiting upon Geraldine Farrar who played Montezuma's daughter.

A native of Russia, trained at the Imperial School of Ballet in Moscow, Theodore Kosloff had danced with Nijinsky and the other great artists of the Ballet Russe, until the opportunity came to organize his own troupe and take it on tour through this country. When he came to Hollywood with Jesse Lasky's recommendation, there was a happy coincidence: Theodore decided that he liked California enough to stay and open a ballet school, and I decided that his vibrant personality and forceful style could add a desirably barbaric note to the part of Guatemoc ". . . whom men call the Tiger," in our story of the conflict between Montezuma and the Spanish invaders under Cortes. Fortunately *The Woman God Forgot* was a silent picture, for Theodore never lost his strong Russian accent and never mastered the illogical intricacies of English; but he appeared or directed the choreography in many of my pictures thereafter and shared a number of personal adventures with me. He remained my friend until the day in 1956 when I stood at the head of his coffin in the little converted frame dwelling which serves as a Russian Orthodox chapel in Los Angeles, while the long and somberly magnificent Orthodox liturgy committed his soul to God and transformed the densely crowded little chapel into a cathedral of that Russia which was once, and will be again, I hope, a land of faith and prayer.

Julia Faye is still one of my best workmen and closest friends. She has been in almost every one of my pictures since 1917. Ordinarily I might consider it ungallant to refer to the calendar in the presence of a lady, but Julia Faye is truly one of those to whom the calendar is absolutely meaningless. Her hair is gray now, but she sparkles with the same bright vivacity that impressed me when Wallace Reid introduced her to me in 1917. Again I am not speaking as a loyal old friend, but objectively. Julia still impresses people the same way. There are 40 years between 1917 and 1957, but in February, 1957, I had the following telegram from Father Francis J. Matthews, director of the Catholic Radio and Television

Apostolate in St. Louis, where Julia went to make a personal appearance at the opening of *The Ten Commandments:* "Miss Faye was thoroughly gracious and entertaining and a real trouper. . . . I do not believe that we could have had a finer person for our première. . . . I can only say that Miss Faye is 'magnificent'." She is. Calendars become obsolete. Julia doesn't.

While I have often been accused of tampering with history, the critics have strangely overlooked their opportunity to charge me with altering geography, as we did in *The Woman God Forgot.* The big scene in the picture is the battle between Aztecs and Spaniards up and down the sides of the temple-pyramid or teocalli. Today the special effects department would be very helpful. Having none in 1917, we found a hill of approximately the same size as the Aztec teocalli and simply covered it with the exterior walls and stairways of the pyramid, thus making a good solid set for our warriors to clamber up and tumble down as the tides of battle surged.

The New York Times called the fighting "unusually realistic." *The Exhibitors' Trade Review* said "Mr. DeMille has gotten more out of his extra people than the majority of directors could." That was one result of treating extra players as players, not just extras. No matter how large a mass of people there are in a scene, if the director regards each individual as an individual and lets each one know and feel that a real performance is expected of him, that director will get a real performance. Oftentimes, in a scene of battle or other vigorous crowd action, the players will be so intent on giving a good performance that inevitably there will be accidents and injuries more or less serious. There were some in *The Woman God Forgot:* anticipating that there might be, I had a doctor, with an ambulance and stretchers, near the teocalli set. Fortunately none of the injuries was really serious: what was injured most was the director's temper and his regard for human nature when some of the spectators, whom I have always welcomed on my sets, burst into the most hilarious laughter as some of the players fell from the pyramid and had to be carried to where the doctor could examine them. They might have been killed, but to some of the visitors it was all uproariously funny. I made a brief but pointed speech to those visitors, in English plain enough for an Aztec to comprehend.

I still welcome guests on my sets; but I expect them to behave as human beings, if not as ladies and gentlemen. Let me add that bad manners and callous stupidity are not a monopoly of any social or economic class. The two rudest guests I have ever had on a set, I believe, bore a name which places them very close to one of the few remaining royal thrones. After bearing with their bad manners for a while, I did not tell the electrician to put some large and opaque equipment directly in front of where they were sitting; but I did not reprimand him either. Most visitors to the set are well-behaved, possibly because they have heard tales of a terrible-tempered director who likes to have intelligence in front of the camera and silence behind it, but mainly, I think, because most people are fundamentally decent.

"Quite piffling" was one critic's estimate of *The Devil Stone,* which was based on an original story by my mother and Leighton Osmun. This was Geraldine Farrar's last picture with us, and the only one of my mother's stories that I have produced on the screen.

In my working scripts of *The Woman God Forgot* and *The Devil Stone* appear certain new pages: color sheets, as we called them, indicating which scenes and titles should "go amber," "go pink," "go special firelight," and so on. We were experimenting with the new color process, very cautiously, however. Alvin Wyckoff and I declared in a published statement that "color photography, in the sense of absolutely faithful reproduction of natural colors, . . . can never be used universally in motion pictures." Forty years after, that prophecy still holds, though I would not now make so flat and final a declaration as "can never." For certain types of pictures, including the type that I make, the vastly improved color processes of today provide an almost essential ingredient. Color, as we have it now, enhances the story values of such films and has an almost measurable effect on the box office. But it is still true that other types of films are more effective in black-and-white.

The same critic who called *The Devil Stone* "piffling" said that my next picture, *The Whispering Chorus,* was "the quintessence of morbidness." I hope that he has lived so see some of the screen's more recent offerings. *The Whispering Chorus,* written by Jeanie Macpherson from a story by Perley Poore Sheehan, was in fact one of the first, if not the first, of the films that have come to be called "psychological." The conflict in it is in the souls of the characters rather than in forces external to them. It is the story of a man condemned to death for his own murder. To escape the consequences of thefts from the office where he works, John Tremble, played by Raymond Hatton, runs away, finds a corpse in a river, mutilates it to make it unidentifiable, puts his clothes on it, with his papers in the pockets, and, years later, his own face now disfigured from a waterfront brawl, is arrested and convicted of murdering John Tremble. No one will believe his true account of the affair except his wife, now happily remarried and expecting a child, who will be illegitimate if she acknowledges that Tremble is still alive. For the child's sake, she yields to her old lawyer's advice that, even if the condemned man is Tremble, he will surely be convicted of murdering the man whose body he dressed in his own clothes. Tremble himself, moved at last by love for his wife, lets her believe that he is guilty and goes to his death after writing out a confession that "the law is vindicated—I killed John Tremble."

The Whispering Chorus was "supposed to be a non-star production," Randolph Bartlett wrote in *Photoplay Magazine*, "but Raymond Hatton is the unmistakable star, in as brilliant a character study as the films have ever produced." Kathlyn Williams played his wife, and Elliott Dexter her second husband.

In addition to Raymond Hatton's remarkable performance, this film was noteworthy because of the "chorus of faces" which gave the film its name. To show the thoughts struggling in the troubled mind of John Tremble, we faded in and out, around his figure on the screen, various faces, kindly, sullen, tempting, laughing, accusing, encouraging, as if they were speaking to him what he himself was thinking. This was for its time an outstanding feat of photography. It was done by double or multiple exposure of the film. For the final appearance of all the faces together in the condemned man's cell, there had to be as many exposures as there were faces, accomplished with all the carefulness and precision which such treatment of film demanded.

In the making of most motion pictures, there is some incident which seems funny in retrospect but does not at all seem so when it happens. To portray John Tremble's degradation during his years as a fugitive, Jeanie Macpherson had written a scene of his being lured into a low dive in Shanghai in the course of a rather wild celebration of the Chinese New Year. A Chinese New Year meant crowds and fireworks, of course. We transformed one side of Selma Avenue into an approximation of a Shanghai thoroughfare, with elaborate fireworks strung all along the block, and we assembled a suitable number of Chinese extras to throng the street.

For such an important and expensive scene, I called for a thorough rehearsal. I gave what I thought were explicit instructions that the scene was to be played in rehearsal exactly as it would be before the camera, with the one exception that, obviously, no one should touch the costly fireworks. The Chinese extras' desire to please was characteristic of that gentle race which I do not think even Mao Tse-tung's methods will radically change; but their knowledge of English was limited. The one Chinese extra who had been instructed to set off the fireworks evidently thought that when I wanted a full rehearsal, I wanted a really full one. With not a camera even focused, much less turning, he touched off the single fuse, and Selma Avenue in broad daylight was treated to a pyrotechnical display which was matched only by the director's verbal fireworks. Despite his lack of English, there must have been something in my tones which conveyed to that unfortunate Chinese that I was annoyed. He took off through a hole in the fence. I did not note his direction, but I assume that he was headed toward a fast boat for China.

3

Too, there are often incidents which seem small and insignificant when they happen, but which cast long shadows or long rays of light, as the case may be. One such, casting both light and shadows into future years, occurred in 1917; and it seems better to follow at least some of its sequels through the years as a connected story even though that means some departure from strict chronology.

It was in 1917 that, for one of the films being made at our studio, as I recall it, we had need of an airplane and so engaged a young flier named Al Wilson and his monoplane to work for us. A curious director-general went to look it over. Al let me sit in the cockpit and fiddle with the controls, but we did not leave the ground. I had never flown. A plane was still as much a novelty to me, almost, as when, while still in New York, I had gone to watch the end of someone's historic flight down the Hudson River valley from Albany—an event so marvelous that crowds gathered, the river boats whistled their loud encouragement, and one Catskill Mountain farmer fired two shots at the strange huge bird flying over his land.

I was interested in the new contraption as Al Wilson demonstrated it to me. Having seen the horseless carriage refute my schoolboy prophecy of its uselessness, I felt that aviation would have a future, militarily and commercially as well as for sport; it occurred to me particularly that airborne cameras could make a decided contribution to motion pictures. But when I climbed out of Al Wilson's monoplane and thanked him for his courtesy, I had no thought that the clouds and I would ever be much closer together personally than we were then.

It took a major disappointment to bring us together. As I had resolved when America entered the war, I applied for a commission in the army as soon as I was free enough to do so. The army was polite but not enthusiastic. I was too old, they said. I was chagrined; but I do not give up easily. I remember making a special trip to Fort Sill in Oklahoma to talk with the commanding general there about my ambition to fight for my country; but the general was as firm as his subordinates had been.

"There's just one thing," he said. "We need fliers so badly that if you will learn to fly, we'll commission you if you're aged ninety."

"Then I will learn to fly," I said to him.

"All right. You learn to fly well enough to satisfy Colonel Harvey Burwell at Rockwell Field, San Diego, and you'll get your commission."

I did not then know Harvey Burwell, the young cavalry officer who had transferred to army aviation as soon as it was organized, had been brevetted from lieutenant to lieutenant colonel in one jump, and put in command of Rockwell Field at the age of 28; but I told the general that I would put myself under his instruction as soon as I got back to California.

"There's one more thing," the general said as I turned to leave

193

his office. "We don't have enough planes to let you use one to learn on. You'll have to find your own plane."

Soon after my return home, I heard that there was a plane standing in a field in the near-by coastal town of Venice, California. The owner had gone home to Montana on business. While there, he had died from injuries after being kicked by a horse. Aviation was literally that close to the horse-and-buggy days in 1917. I asked Neil McCarthy to go down to Venice with Al Wilson and inspect the plane. Neil had never been near such an object before, but he walked all around it and looked inside the cockpit and listened to Al Wilson's description of it as a Curtiss JN-40 with an O.X.5 motor; and then Neil made a proposition which I think should go down in the history of American business.

"Take me up in it," he said to Al Wilson, "and if it flies all right, we'll buy it."

When I related that story many years later at a Civil Air Patrol dinner, with Neil McCarthy present, I told the audience that they could plainly see why I have respected Neil as a shrewd trader all these years. He made no commitment to buy if the plane did not fly all right, if it drowned him in the Pacific Ocean or crashed him on top of the Santa Monica mountains.

It flew all right. We bought it. I reported to Lieutenant Colonel Burwell, who assigned another young flier named Tony Lynch to instruct me along with Al Wilson, and I began my lessons at a field near Venice, later known as Clover Field, and now the mainland terminus for regular flights to Catalina Island as well as home base for many private planes.

I had another motive, in addition to the patriotic one, for wanting to learn to fly. That was fear. All my life I had had an unreasoning dread of heights. Before I flew, whenever I thought of flying I was appalled with terror at the idea of going up in the sky and looking down with nothing but thousands of feet of air between me and the earth below. That was something to be conquered, as I had once conquered my dread of going upstairs in the dark.

In one way, flying was really very easy in those days. There were only two instruments to watch, a fuel gauge in the plane and an altimeter on your wrist: with those, you could tell how high you were and how long you might stay there. There were no parachutes. Your first serious mistake was, as a rule, your last. Practic-

194

ing night flying with Tony Lynch, we came down once through a barbed wire fence and another time through a eucalyptus tree, landing the fuselage, with the wings left in the leafy branches some little way behind us. I came through these instructions without a scratch, without so much as a speck of dust in my eye.

There was one other instrument, if such it can be called: the monkey wrench which the instructor always had with him in the rear seat while the pupil was at the controls in front. That emergency tool never had to be used during my lessons, however. Its function was to knock the pupil unconscious if his teacher saw him beginning to make a mistake which might kill them both.

I soon came to enjoy flying. Once fear is conquered, there is an expansive sense of freedom in being at the controls of a plane. I do not know if the pilots of the great airliners of today feel it, but it was certainly there in the little open cockpits of 40 years ago. I began to enjoy it—with all the nonchalance of the amateur. Once, when I was sitting in the rear seat, with Tony Lynch at the controls, I felt sufficiently at home in the skies to undo my safety belt to put something in my pocket. Tony chose that moment to loop the loop. The instant I noticed his intention, I rammed my hand against his back with a smash that he must have felt for days afterward, to push him forward over the "stick" so that he could not pull it back to go into his loop. Otherwise I would have made, literally, a solo flight, a very speedy plummet earthward all alone. There is a saying about the kinds of people the Lord has to take special care of, which I shall not repeat here; but I am afraid I kept Him busy.

Incredibly, some of my friends were willing to fly with me. William deMille and Jesse Lasky both found their first flights with me so unforgettable that they have given acounts of them to posterity in their memoirs; but the passenger whose first venture into the empyrean I remember best was Julia Faye. We were not long airborne, over the city of Venice, when a sudden fog came in from the ocean, enveloping us completely. Julia enjoyed it hugely: all the sense of mystery and solitude and isolation from the earth that flying through fog or clouds can give. I put the plane through its paces, hoping the fog would go away as quickly as it had come. It didn't. I put the plane through some more exercises, this time with one eye on the fuel gauge. The fog was still thick when I decided that I would have to land through it. Of course I had no idea where we were, other than up. Gingerly I nosed down through the fog, far enough to find that we were just over the roller-coaster on the Venice amusement pier. I did my quickest pull-up on record to avoid taking a ride on the roller-coaster. I tried again, heading toward where I knew the field was in relation to the pier, but I was much too short: again the roller-coaster loomed up out of the fog, and again I climbed sharper and faster than before. All the while, behind me, Julia was clapping her hands with thrilled delight. She thought I had planned a special treat for her, an aerial roller-coaster ride. She did not realize how close she had come to her last thrill, before I finally sighted the field.

One who never flew with me, but who followed my exploration of the skies with deep and touching concern, was Adolph Zukor. When he was in California, I used to see him standing at the edge of the flying field, looking up, thinking of the many thousands of dollars invested in the picture I was directing, watching its director demonstrate how birdlike, not to say bird-brained, he was in the air. He would stand there patiently until I came down and the studio's investment was safe for another day. Then he would go home, looking reprieved.

I have no evidence that reports of my prowess in the air were communicated to the German General Staff by any of the spies who, we thought in those days, were everywhere. I should like to think that the Kaiser's abdication and the decision to sign an armistice were hastened by the word, whispered through chancellery and camp, that the Champion Driver was about to get his wings. All I can soberly report, however, is that just before I was ready to qualify for my commission, the war ended.

I was disappointed in my resolve to be a soldier of the sky; but out of the frustrated preparation for it I gained a lifelong friendship with Harvey Burwell, a lifelong interest in aviation, a fascinating if somewhat fantastic adventure in the business world, and perhaps an opportunity to make a very small contribution to the story of man's age-old dream of wings.

We were eased into aviation as a business almost accidentally. Flying was still such a novelty that going out to the field to watch the planes take off and land was a sort of public entertainment.

196

When we would land, brave souls among the spectators, first a few, then many, would come over to Al Wilson and offer him $5 or $10 just to take them up in the air for a few minutes. I told him to go ahead, using my plane and dividing with me whatever money he took in from such flights. The fistfuls of currency Al brought to me every evening grew larger and larger. Then one day a businessman came to the field in a state of urgent commotion. He had to get to Bakersfield in a great hurry. Would we fly him up there? Al Wilson took him up, landing in a bean field because there was no place else to land; the businessman kept his appointment and was delivered safely back to Los Angeles. There is no record of the farmer's reactions when our Jenny, as the JN-40's were called, rolled across his bean field; but I began to see greater possibilities in commercial aviation.

4

The result was the Mercury Aviation Company, organized early in 1919 and put into full operation in May of that year, the first commercial airline in the United States to offer regular passenger service between cities. In 1914, there had been a line in Florida, carrying one passenger at a time between Tampa and St. Petersburg, a distance of 21 miles; but the Florida line was frankly a temporary experiment, which terminated at the end of its appointed three months' time. The Mercury Aviation Company was intended and organized and launched as a permanent business enterprise, serving all the principal cities between San Diego and San Francisco. If our hopes of permanence were not entirely fulfilled, that takes no credit away from those who had faith enough to join me in founding America's first commercial airline. I was president and chairman of the board; George H. Flebbe, a good businessman and the husband of one of our best writers, Beulah Marie Dix, was vice-president; Neil McCarthy was secretary and treasurer. We engaged a number of young fliers demobilized from the army— William S. Kenyon, David E. Thompson, Wayne Alles, and later others—to work with Al Wilson as pilots and technicians.

An airline needs more than one Jenny. First we heard of another which had been wrecked in Canada, killing its owner. We bought the wreckage from his widow and pasted it together somehow. After the war's end, we were able to acquire other types of planes.

We had four when the company began to operate, and we more than doubled that number within a few months.

An airline also needs ground as well as air. There were, of course, no airports as we know them today. The army had three fields in California—at San Diego, Riverside, and Sacramento. We established our own fields at what are now the built-up and busy corners of Melrose Avenue and Fairfax Boulevard and Wilshire and La Cienega Boulevards in Los Angeles; later we added a field in Pasadena. In 1953, when I attended a luncheon at the splendid new western home office of the Prudential Insurance Company on Wilshire Boulevard, one of the officers of the company, wishing to show me graphically how that booming business district had developed, pointed to a picture on his wall and said that that bare space of land was Wilshire Boulevard only thirty-some years before. "Yes," I said, "that's my field, and those people in the picture are gathered to watch the delivery of our first all-metal plane, a German Junker, flown across country for us by a young man named Eddie Rickenbacker."

When we held an Air Memorial Day at the DeMille Field in May, 1919, a Colonel H. H. Arnold was listed in the program as the War Department's representative for the occasion. When he became the famous General "Hap" Arnold of World War II, he remembered and spoke to me about the days when the only places army planes could land in the Los Angeles area were the DeMille Fields. Another youngster who took part in one of the demonstrations on that Memorial Day is listed as "Lt. Doolittle;" but perhaps the experience he was gaining in and around the DeMille Fields, which he frequently visited, was of some value in the exploits of General Jimmy Doolittle in the Pacific Theatre of war in the 1940's.

The first commercial flight between Los Angeles and San Francisco was made on June 12, 1919, when Al Wilson piloted William W. McKeighan to a convention being held in Oakland. They stopped overnight in Fresno and reached San Francisco, after seven hours and twenty-one minutes of actual flying time, on the afternoon of Friday the 13th. One of California's State Senators had planned to make the flight; but the Senator weighed 250 pounds. We were willing to flout superstition, but not the law of gravity.

198

The Champion Driver, of course, gave a touch of showmanship to the promotion of the science of aviation. I helped Sid Grauman open his Million Dollar Theatre in downtown Los Angeles by circling low over the top of the building, seeing how close I could come to its tall flagpole. Sid Grauman opened the doors; a few inches of error, and I would have opened the roof and literally brought down the house.

That feat of stupidity was matched by an inspiration I had the day we arranged to fly a group of prominent Los Angeles businessmen down to the Coronado Hotel, near San Diego, for lunch and back to their Los Angeles offices in time for their afternoon's work. The idea was to convince them that flying saved time and was also comfortable and safe: as one of our newspaper advertisements put it, they could "avoid the dangers of auto and railroad travel" by using our "Aero Passenger Service, Safe, Reasonable, Quick." As I was leaving my office to meet the picked five influential business leaders for their first air jaunt, it occurred to me that one final touch of psychology was needed to allay any fears that might linger in their hearts even after reading our advertisements. I personally would show them how to be nonchalant in mid-air. I picked up the nearest book at hand in my office and dashed to the field where our giant six-passenger cabin plane was waiting for its important cargo.

As soon as we were airborne, I settled back and opened my book to read as comfortably and casually as if I had been in my own living room. After a few minutes to let the impression register, I looked up at my nearest fellow passengers, with a smile that, I believed, spoke volumes for the comfort and security of air travel and silently challenged them not to agree. They said little, but, out of their long and solemn faces, their eyes were riveted on the book I had hurriedly snatched from my desk. Only then did I look at its title. It was called *The Broken Wing*.

As a matter of history, the Mercury Aviation Company carried thousands of passengers without a single injury to any of them, except, as the company's eloquent brochure put it, "injuries to the feelings of many who, having once got up in the air, wanted to stay there longer than their contract called for." The same brochure went even further in its discourse on the safety and benefits of flight. "Aerotherapy," it said, "has come into existence," citing

199

the "medical experiments of great significance . . . made by noted local pathologists and physicians . . . as to the increase in the total volume of blood, in metabolism, lung ventilation, blood pressure and arterial tone, expansibility of the heart, and hemoglobin."

The Society for the Prevention of Cruelty to Animals had evidently not heard of the benefits of "aerotherapy" when it learned that we were planning to fly a pony to the Santa Barbara horse show. An officer of the Society rushed to our field to protest that this would be extreme cruelty because the noise would hurt the pony's ears. I replied that it had never hurt my ears. Refraining from any comparison between me and a horse, the zealous officer demanded that if we flew the animal we must tightly stuff its ears with cotton. Anyone who has ever flown with a cold in the head need not be told why I refused to subject the pony to that real cruelty. The impasse was broken only by the arrival of the Mayor of Los Angeles, who came out to watch the take-off of the first horse to fly since the legendary days of Pegasus. His Honor decreed that the pony might fly, without ear-stuffing. The least concerned of the principals in this drama was the pony, who turned out to be a natural born aviator.

That was a stunt, of course. So was the flying of a prize Holstein calf from the ranch of the former heavyweight boxing champion, Jim Jeffries, to the Los Angeles Live Stock Show. So was the scattering of hundreds of miniature blue bonnets from the air over Los Angeles by Billie Rhodes, an actress appearing in a picture which the reader will not be surprised to learn was entitled *The Blue Bonnet*. But even the stunts served a serious and useful purpose. They kept aviation prominently in the public mind, in a way that our more lasting but less spectacular accomplishments, such as the safe transport of regular passengers or the thorough instruction given in the Mercury School of Aeronautics, could not.

I believe that *The Los Angeles Examiner* exaggerated a bit when in 1920 it congratulated me for "enormously expanding the commercial use of aircraft." The Mercury Aviation Company's contribution was not enormous; but it was real, and it did help.

It would be accurate to say that the Mercury Company helped, more or less, all phases of aviation except the Mercury Company. Another industry which it surely helped is the one that manufactures red ink. Commercial aviation was still a highly speculative

200

business at best. With my work in motion pictures, I did not have time to give the Mercury Company my full attention. Even if I had, I am not the world's most efficient business executive. I have fairly good business judgment, but as an administrator I tend either to get so involved in details that the administration slows down or, on other occasions, to imitate Admiral Farragut in Mobile Bay, damning the torpedoes and going ahead toward the goal I want to reach, without sufficient attention to what I may call the supply lines. I wanted the Mercury Company to help establish commercial aviation in the United States and help make people air-minded. I also wanted it to make money. In the actual circumstances, we found that it could not do both.

For a brief and rosy period, it looked as though Mexico might be the Mercury Company's salvation, but I am afraid that our Mexican adventure appealed to me more as a dramatist than a businessman. First, in an endeavor to interest the Mexican government in buying some of the new all-metal planes from us, George Flebbe, "Tommy" Thompson, and C. V. Pickup, another of our pilots, flew one of them to Mexico to show it off. Trusting souls, they left it insufficiently guarded, not for long, but long enough to have it stolen by a small but brave band of revolutionaries. The rebels' bravery was not equaled by their aeronautical skill. They promptly crashed the plane. The incident may have caused a little coolness between our representatives and their official hosts, but it did not affect the salesmanship of Messrs. Flebbe and Thompson. They came home with one of our aircraft missing indeed, but with a permit to start a passenger airline between Mexico City and Popocatepetl and with such glowing accounts of Mexico as a market that we formed a new company, the Mercury Export Corporation, to handle the volume of trade we expected to have with our good neighbor to the south.

Since I could not give time to still another company, John Fisher, representing me, was made head of the export corporation, and our team of Flebbe and Thompson was off to New York to secure agencies for the merchandise for which, we believed, all Mexico was panting.

It fell to me to break the news of this venture to our stockholders. I am very sure that none of them expected a dividend check to flutter out of my letter, but they could not be more sur-

201

prised by the announcements that did leap out at them. The board of directors had decided, I wrote, "that it would be very wise to dispose of our field and equipment" since, in view of the rapid obsolescence of airplanes, "it would be necessary to purchase additional ships" and "the success which we have met in flying does not justify this expenditure at this time." With that last understatement I am sure that every stockholder was in full accord.

But, I went on, "we have reached this decision without the regret we might otherwise feel because we will be permitted from now on to concentrate all of our energies on the Export Business where apparently large profits are to be made." In earnest of these great expectations, I informed the astonished shareholders, "Mr. Flebbe and Mr. Thompson went to New York . . . and there secured agencies and established credits with concerns manufacturing a great variety of articles ranging from submarine chasers and machine guns to socks and underwear."

The stockholders reacted precisely as I, older and wiser now, would react if I received such a communication in today's mail. They did not question our financial honesty, to be sure, but one of them wrote wistfully, "I understood that I was associating myself with practical men . . ."

I had come to a personal crossroads of decision. The protesting stockholders had invested their money at my request and recommendation. My belief in the future of commercial aviation was unshaken. So apparently was that of the stockholders; what shook them was the sudden switch from wings to "socks and underwear." In my mind, the export business, however grand the prospective profits seemed, was essentially a stopgap: in my letter to the stockholders I had definitely said that we would keep "the Mercury Aviation Company alive until such time as it is deemed advisable to again undertake commercial flying." But to do this, I realized now, would mean that I would have to give up motion pictures and devote all my time to recouping the addled fortunes of the aviation company. Pictures had become my life. I knew I could make successful pictures; I could not deny the statement of one stockholder that "we have had no evidence of conspicuous success in . . . administration of the Mercury Aviation Company."

I personally bought back the shares of the protesting stockholders, so that they lost nothing. The Mercury Export Corporation died unlamented. The Mercury Aviation Company sold its equipment to the Rogers Airport, across the street from our field, and went out of business in September, 1921. In less than two and a half years, it had made its small but valid mark in American aviation. It had cost me much, but given me much more, for what I gained was in the intangible but more enduring currency of knowledge, experience, friendships, and the satisfaction of having served a cause whose present-day achievement has justified our early faith. When men like Captain Eddie Rickenbacker and General Carl Spaatz joined LeRoy Prinz in sponsoring me for membership in the Wings Club, composed of aviation pioneers, in 1956, I felt rather like a sparrow among eagles, but by that time perhaps even the disappointed stockholders would not have blackballed me, for by that time the Mercury Aviation Company's contribution could be seen in true perspective; and it was not a thing of which to be ashamed.

I kept one plane, a little Spad, for my own use, but I had to give up flying that as I found that I had less and less time to keep my pilot-hand in practice. For years, though, I kept the little Spad, shorn of its wings, in my garage and I used to go down and walk around it and look at it and, I confess, pat it with my hand; for it *was* alive—with memories. The last time I was at the controls of a plane was in 1934, when I was flying home from a motion picture tour with Paul Mantz, and that intrepid pilot casually asked me to fly the plane while he went back to take a nap. Nowadays, when I cross the continent or the ocean in the comfort of an airliner, the courteous flight officers sometimes invite me up to the front to show me their modern equipment. I am careful not to touch anything, though; I'm afraid I would feel lost without my altimeter on my wrist, and at present speeds we would have passed the point of no return before I found the fuel gauge among the bewildering array of instruments and indicators which we did not have in 1918.

One last, or anyway latest, link with aviation was forged in 1955 when Secretary Harold E. Talbott asked me to design the uniforms to be worn by the cadets at the new Air Force Academy in Colorado. I was in the very middle of making *The Ten Commandments*. Several of my associates urged me to decline the Secretary's request. They said no one could ever satisfy the varying tastes and notions of the officials, military and civilian, who would have to pass on the uniform designs. However, I have never refused a request from the government when I could possibly fulfill it. Harold Talbott had been a friend of mine, a good friend, for years. I also have some definite ideas on military uniforms: they should be handsome and attractive, but thoroughly masculine, and that is not a combination always easy to achieve in designing them. Finally, it was for an Air Force Academy that the request had been made, and my interest in aviation and my delight that we were now to have a West Point of the Air would have moved me to accept the invitation if nothing else had.

The press jumped for joy—not, I hasten to say, at Secretary Talbott's selection of me, but at the opportunity to have some fun with it. The Winston-Salem *Journal's* comment was typical of many: "Don't be surprised if the cadets at the new Air Force Academy appear in Egyptian helmets and Roman breastplates, and bear crusader shields and oriental swords. Their uniforms are going to be designed by Cecil B. DeMille." The columnist Bugs Baer revealed that "foreign agents are trying to find out how many straps Cecil will use on his puttees."

Then, as will be recalled, Harold Talbott was succeeded as Air Force Secretary by Donald A. Quarles. I have another settled policy concerning government service: whenever I undertake a job for the government and my superior is changed, I submit my resignation immediately to the new man so that, if he wishes, he can start with a clean slate and a new team of his own choice. Secretary Quarles acknowledged my letter of resignation with cautious courtesy. Perhaps he had been reading the newspapers' hilarious forebodings. When he visited me in Hollywood a short time later, however, he asked me to go on with the project as I had been doing under his predecessor.

I was fortunate in having on my staff at the time two highly competent artists, Arnold Friberg and John Jensen, both of whom had been in the army, Ralph Jester, who had been a lieutenant colonel and was now doing some costume sketches for *The Ten Commandments,* and my associate producer, Henry Wilcoxon, a former naval gunnery officer who, in addition to his other talents, has a fine conception of design and the eye and hand of an artist.

204

I asked all four of these skilled men to form a committee to help me with suggestions and sketches. The final designs were mainly the work of Henry Wilcoxon and John Jensen; the Western Costume Company co-operated ably by making up specimen uniforms following our designs.

When the job was finally done, Secretary Quarles invited Henry Wilcoxon, John Jensen, and me to luncheon at the Pentagon, where we were surprised to find assembled a group of high Defense Department officials, including General Nathan F. Twining, and to receive the department's Exceptional Service Award. It brought me back full circle to 1917, to the first Jennies, the first airfields in Los Angeles, and the Mercury Company's brief but eventful and not inglorious history, when the citation accompanying my Award stated that "Mr. DeMille's deep devotion to the cause of aviation reaches back to the first World War." This was high commendation from the highest source; but I think the reward that pleased me most was the report from Major General James E. Briggs, the Academy Superintendent, that when lantern slides of the new uniforms were shown to the first cadets at Colorado Springs, they were not only applauded but actually cheered by the future Arnolds, Doolittles, Spaatzes, Twinings, and Burwells who will wear them in their years of preparing to defend their country in the air.

5

To bring that aviation story to full circle, I have skipped over the years since 1918, to which I must now return. The reader will remember that there was a war on. Unable to get into it actively, I had to content myself with the Home Guard and the civilian efforts which were open to the stay-at-homes.

One of those efforts gave me what was perhaps my second most embarrassing moment in Hollywood. It was at a big rally for the Red Cross or a similar relief activity, at which I was the speaker. In the audience was my small daughter Cecilia, aged nine, who had just earned $50 by appearing in a picture. I must have been unusually eloquent, for as soon as I ended my speech by asking the audience to give and give generously, Cecilia was the first on her feet, tears streaming down her small cheeks at the plight of the war sufferers, to pledge her whole $50 to the cause. Of course it looked as though I had staged the touching scene, planting my tender child in the audience as a shill. Knowing Hollywood, I could imagine what the cynics were imagining—me slipping Cecilia the money before the meeting, and giving her her cue when to stand up, and be sure to cry. I apologize now to Cecilia if I showed any annoyed embarrassment at her spontaneous generosity. To her credit, she bravely parted with her $50 anyway.

I had still not given up the hope of getting to France somehow. If I was considered too old to fight on the ground and still too inexperienced to fly, I thought I had found an opportunity to serve in another way when the Secretary of War, Newton D. Baker, asked me for suggestions on how the motion picture industry might increase its co-operation in the war effort. As I talked with men who came back from France wounded, there was one theme to which they all recurred: the boredom they experienced, waiting out their rest periods behind the lines. A popular chronicler of the war, Captain Ian Hay Beith, told me that in his opinion the deciding factor in winning the war would be the success or failure to overcome the boredom of troops left with little or nothing to do between their spells in the front-line trenches. It occurred to me that motion pictures would help, if there was some way of bringing them right up behind the second-line trenches and to other places where the men were resting.

I had been experimenting with a portable dynamo, to produce electrical current for filming at night in out-of-the-way places where there were no power lines. On the same principle, I built a unit consisting of a smaller but sufficiently powerful dynamo, a projection machine, portable screen, and a tent with its walls darkened to be perfectly opaque, all compact enough to be fitted on a specially constructed automobile chassis. When I was satisfied that it would work, I wrote to Jesse Lasky proposing "to have two of these machines made at my own expense, take them to France, and start a regular portable motion picture circuit for the benefit and amusement of the men" and to arrange, "should the machines prove successful, for an enlargement of the proposition to say fifty or sixty machines which would very nearly take care of the entire French front." I asked Jesse to put the proposal to Mr. Zukor, together with my request for two sets of all the Famous Players-Lasky pictures, one set with English and one with French titles, for exhibition to the American, British, and French armies in the war zone.

Jesse was doubtful. Mr. Zukor was not. They were not lacking in patriotism, but their final word was that "there were many reasons why you should not go." I could not go without being released from my production commitments to the company; so I did not go. The care taken to provide our troops and men at sea in World War II with the latest motion pictures and radio programs proved the soundness of the idea and the value of good entertainment for morale.

The New York office was, however, willing to let me make a war picture in 1918: *Till I Come Back to You,* starring Bryant Washburn and Florence Vidor. We took the title from the Belgian King Albert's pledge to his people, and we were considered daring for making that heroic monarch one of the characters in the picture, played by Winter Hall. When I met the young Prince Albert of Belgium in 1955, I confessed to having portrayed his grandfather on the screen without bothering to obtain the King's consent; but, with royal courtesy, the young man did not mind.

What seemed that it might be another opportunity for more active service came when the War Department again approached me, this time to make a motion picture record of the activities of the Army Air Corps. Here at last was something I could do, but I knew that I could do it well only in the same way that I make my own films: by forming my own unit, with all the phases of the operation under my authority, to make a really complete film record of all the Air Corps activity both in France and in this country. As I wrote to Jesse, "I am very willing and anxious to go out and fight in any rank or place the Government may be able to use me," but if the War Department wanted me to go as a motion picture expert without giving me enough authority to do a good job in my own special field, "I would not leave—at least until I can be placed in the fighting forces." The matter was still hanging fire when I wrote that letter to Jesse on October 16, 1918. This time Mr. Zukor and Jesse were willing to let me go, even at the very moment when the influenza epidemic was closing theaters all over the United States and costing our company a round million dollars in lost revenues. And then, the armistice was signed on November 11.

I have snubbed chronology again in order to round out a chapter that might be called "The Champion Driver Six Thousand Miles Behind the Lines." I was still making pictures, five in all in 1918, including *Till I Come Back to You* and a new version of *The Squaw Man* written by Beulah Marie Dix, with Elliott Dexter playing the role that Dustin Farnum had created for the screen five years before.

The other three films I produced in 1918 were the start of a cycle which, according to the French film historians, Bardeche and Brasillach, caused motion pictures to withdraw "from the realm of art for several years." Such an achievement surely merits treatment by itself in another chapter. MM. Bardeche and Brasillach also credit me with having originated sex appeal. I should have thought that that commodity originated in the Garden of Eden; but who am I to dispute MM. Bardeche and Brasillach?

10

"DISGUSTING DEBAUCHERY . . . most immoral episodes."

"It at least shows that the photoplay is breaking away from the marshmallow school of the drama."

"Classy . . . but rough in spots."

"A splendid story . . . faultlessly produced, carrying a powerful sermon."

Thus four different critics in their reviews of the same picture: *Old Wives for New,* released in May, 1918.

That film and some of its immediate successors have cast a long shadow. I shall never forget a large civic dinner in Pittsburgh in 1947 and the puzzled looks on the faces of some of Pennsylvania's most distinguished citizens when they picked up and curiously examined the souvenirs which a press agent with more energy than good taste had put at their places. The souvenirs were miniature bathtubs.

Essentially, *Old Wives for New* is the story of the damage which a lazy and slovenly wife can do to her marriage. Sylvia Ashton, as Sophy Murdock, the wife, was wonderfully disgusting; it is not every actress who would take such a part or play it as realistically as she did. The first scene of the husband, Elliott Dexter, trying to shave in the messily littered bathroom of the Murdock home, was successfully designed to establish the character and habits of his wife and to foreshadow the plausible, if not excusable, reason why he was attracted to the neat, trim, fastidious, and altogether lovely "other woman," played by Florence Vidor. That was the first DeMille bathroom scene. Like every other scene of any consequence in any of my pictures, its simple purpose was to help tell the story. If it or the picture as a whole had any other purpose, it was not to suggest to husbands that they should get rid of slovenly wives, but to suggest to both wives and husbands that marriages, though proverbially made in heaven, are woven on earth of many strands, among which such elementary things as cleanliness and good housekeeping can be of great importance.

But out of that beginning in *Old Wives for New* has grown one of the hardiest of the DeMille legends: the notion, fostered, I confess, by such press agents as the one in Pittsburgh, that my fame as a director rests upon the imperishable distinction of having photographed a large number of different kinds of bathtubs.

Personally, I think better of the human race than to believe that it pays good money into the box office for what it could see as well in a wholesale plumber's catalogue; but legend dies hard. Mrs. deMille tells of the time she gave a tea in our home for the ladies of a certain very worthy religious organization. Two of the ladies confessed to our maid their cherished secret yearning: *could* they have a glimpse of Mr. deMille's bathroom? They were terribly disappointed. It was just a plain, comfortable, standard American bathroom, without a square inch of onyx or ermine, without even a tap over the tub for rose water or milk.

I do not shy away at all from the fact that bathtubs and bathrooms have appeared in many of my pictures; and if the modern American bathroom is a clean and comfortable part of the modern American home, my pictures may have had something to do with that wholesome development. I can almost remember when indoor sanitation was something of a novelty. I can remember very well our family bathroom in New York some 70 years ago— a dark, cramped space with its tin tub boxed in wood, and under it a little closet for the dustpans, cloths, and brushes, a playground for the revels of a large convention of cockroaches. That is not a pretty sentence. It was not a pretty place, though it was no different from the bathrooms of our friends and was, I suppose, luxurious compared to those of the very poor. I did not like it

210

as a child. When I had the opportunity to show on the screen that this room could be bright and clean and comfortable, I took it.

In *Old Wives for New* there is a subplot concerning an elderly roué, played by Theodore Roberts, and some of his lady friends of easy virtue, one of whom, portrayed by Julia Faye, shoots and kills him when she finds him in the arms of another. While this subplot was integral and necessary to the main construction of the story, it was, I imagine, the reason why a few of the critics and censors condemned the picture.

What surprised me more than that, however, was that it scared the New York executives; and here I must reveal something which will deprive me, perhaps, of some of the credit which historians of the school of MM. Bardeche and Brasillach have given me for debasing the art of the film and which friendlier observers have given me for foreseeing, if not helping to create, postwar social trends.

The fact is that I made *Old Wives for New* only after repeated urging from the New York office; and behind that lies a history of company politics which, as far as I know, has never been told.

We had two scenario departments, one in Hollywood under my brother Bill, the other in New York under Hector Turnbull who it will be remembered, Bill had brought into the industry and who married Jesse Lasky's sister Blanche after her divorce from Sam Goldwyn. I shall refer to the two offices simply as "Hollywood" and "New York." I steadily supported my brother's policies, and Jesse no less firmly backed the views and methods of his sister and brother-in-law. It will be gathered that there were differences.

With increasingly expensive players under contract and all other costs rising, New York quite naturally wanted speedy production. Hollywood was no less interested in making money, but it held to the belief that a well-constructed picture might conceivably make more money than a poor one thrown together hurriedly. New York complained that Hollywood wasted weeks of time revising scenarios and story treatments sent out from New York. Hollywood retorted that the material suggested by New York was sometimes so lacking in dramatic values and construction that it would be a greater waste to put it before the cameras. I knew perfectly well, as I have said, that Bill deMille was sometimes a slow worker; but he had one of the best dramatic minds I knew, and that was more important in my estimation than speed.

New York also believed, and did not fail to remind us on occasion, that it was closer to the public pulse than we were. As early as January, 1917, Jesse sent me a memorandum signed by Carl H. Pierce of the New York publicity department, which merits quotation: "What the public demands today is modern stuff with plenty of clothes, rich sets, and action. Nothing prior to the Civil War should be filmed, until such time as the artists among our audiences shall comprise more than the present 10 per cent." In another and lengthier report from the New York scenario department, there were so many references to New York as the "home office" that I was moved to write to Jesse: "While there is no question in anybody's mind that the New York office is the seat of government, there is considerable doubt in our minds that it is the seat of great literary and dramatic discernment."

Taking compassion on the reader, I skip the other exchanges of compliments between New York and Hollywood that year, until Jesse wrote me in December: "We are holding *Old Wives for New* which we paid $6500 for until we get some word from you as to whether or not you think you can make a picture out of it. Personally, I would like to see you become commercial to the extent of agreeing to produce this novel. It will do twice as much business as *The Woman God Forgot* or *The Devil Stone*. . . . However, you need not feel obligated to do it, as we will have no trouble in getting it produced here."

Three weeks later, Jesse resumed the theme: "Remember that we are holding *Old Wives for New* until you decide whether or not you want to produce it. I am strongly of the opinion that you should get away from the spectacle stuff for one or two pictures and try to do modern stories of great human interest."

So I did.

The reader may, if he chooses, consider that my original sin. He may write down, sadly or smugly as suits his mood, the date on which I bade a last good-by to integrity and art. I wish that integrity and art and life were as simple as they are made by pundits like MM. Bardeche and Brasillach (whom, incidentally, I cite so often only because their work happens to be near at hand at the moment: a visit to any sizable public library will enable anyone to

212

find the same things said about me by various other film historians whose earnestness is to be commended even if they frequently do not know what they are talking about).

Certainly any director would rather produce only subjects of his own choosing. He would also like to have an unlimited, unquestioned budget. He might like to make 57 takes of each scene, and pictures 40 reels long. He may often feel that art would be served if "New York" were blown off the map. If he happens to be the Champion Driver, of course he would love to make only big historical pictures: "costume stuff," Mr. Pierce's memorandum called them, quoting an exhibitor in Des Moines. If a director is willful enough, he may insist upon having his own way in all matters all the time, regardless of cost or public taste or the viewpoints of his associates, who might just conceivably know more about some aspects of motion pictures than he does. And then he will not be a director for very long, as some very good directors have found, to their own sorrow and the public's loss.

The theater, in whatever form—stage, screen, radio, television—is a mass medium. If there is no audience, there is no theater. Eric Gill has defined art as making well whatever needs to be made. The thing that needs to be made in a theater is a play or film that will fill the theater. The art of the theater, therefore, to fulfill its purpose, must be popular. To be sure, there is a place for the specialized little theater, the experimental film, educational radio, documentary television, and so on: but these are not theater, or they are different kinds of theater from that of the mass audience, as different as Kipling is from Keats, though both used the same English language and both made well the kinds of poetry that they set out to make. To produce films for one's own pleasure or for the admiration of a small, like-minded coterie is an honorable occupation, as long as the producer is not using up other people's money under false pretenses. To produce films for the entertainment of the people is no less honorable. To deny either of those propositions is simply stupid snobbery.

My profession is making motion pictures for popular entertainment. Because I believe in the value of that profession, I have never felt it demeaning to adapt myself to the requirements of success in it, any more than a baker or a brain surgeon feels degraded or frustrated by the requirements and limitations imposed

213

on him by his job. If the baker were seized by an artistic impulse to frost his cakes with glittering ground glass, if the brain surgeon thought it original to operate with a claw hammer, I do not think we would hear much praise of their incorruptible integrity; I think we would send quickly for strait jackets. It is no less insane for a purveyor of popular entertainment to insist upon giving the people what the people do not want.

So he must know what they do want. He may have a good instinct for that. I think I have. But I am also ready to listen and, if occasion warrants, yield to the viewpoints of others. I wrote to Jesse Lasky, while the scenario struggle was going on between New York and Hollywood, "You are quite right in saying that we do not always have first-hand information on the trend of public thought excepting as expressed here on the Coast."

New York wanted "modern stuff with plenty of clothes, rich sets, and action." All right, I'd give it to them; and I would give it as good a job of dramatic construction, direction, photography, and all the rest as I would have given the stories of Charlotte Corday or Morgan the buccaneer or any of the other "costume stuff" and "spectacle stuff" which sent shivers through New York whenever I broached it that year. The result was *Old Wives for New*. When New York saw it, it was such strong stuff that they were scared.

I was told indeed that there was opposition in New York, from Mr. Zukor himself, to releasing it at all. I had an unanswerable answer to that, however. I took a print of the picture to a theater in a small town near Los Angeles late one afternoon and asked the manager to put it on his screen, no announcement, no rental either, I just wanted to see how it would play. It had not been playing long when people began to get up and go out to telephone their friends to hurry down to see it. Husbands particularly, I was told, telephoned wives to come down: let supper go, but come down and see *Old Wives for New*. When the screening was finished, there was so much new audience in the theater that the manager had to screen it again. He was still screening it well after midnight. When I reported that to New York, opposition crumbled.

There was one small sequel to the scenario struggle between the Coasts. I took the script of one of our pictures and asked Gladys Rosson to copy it word for word in longhand, put another title on it, and send it to her sister in New York with instructions to submit it to the scenario department as an original screenplay. She did. In due course Gladys's sister got the manuscript back, with the notation that it was quite unusable for pictures.

Even I did not know how much talent we had lurking in the Hollywood studio. One day I needed a stenographer. There was none available, but it was thought prudent not to offer excuses to the director-general when what he wanted was not an alibi but an amanuensis, so someone sent Grover Jones in to me. Grover was a former sign painter, then employed at the studio as a kind of assistant to all the assistants. He knew nothing of shorthand; but while I dictated he made an impressive assortment of straight and wavy lines and pothooks and prayed that his memory would hold out. It must have done so, for Grover Jones stayed on to become eventually a good screen writer; he worked with Courtney Riley Cooper on the first treatment of my production of *The Plainsman* in 1935.

I believe it was Grover also who originated the saying that everyone believes himself capable of doing two jobs: his own and being a writer. I would add a third: motion picture producer. Everyone without exception knows how to make movies, better than ever. I was visited once, not long ago, by a physician and a young pianist, with an idea for a film. This was not to be a Hollywood movie. It was to be an entirely new concept in film-making. I must be a slow learner, for I do not remember all the details of this revolutionary concept, although my enthusiastic visitors instructed me patiently about it until past 3 A.M. I wonder what they would have thought of me if I had told them I was planning to perform an appendectomy or a concerto.

On such occasions one may be reminded of a priceless line in William deMille's script of my next 1918 picture, *We Can't Have Everything*. Some of the scenes are laid in a motion picture studio, and for one of them Bill wrote this description: "Director starts to go crazy (not too much here, as he has to go much crazier before the scene is over)."

The director in *We Can't Have Everything* was played by Tully Marshall. He said later, "It was a sort of composite. Partly Mr. DeMille and partly D. W. Griffith. I didn't tell anyone what I in-

215

tended doing and when the time came I could see Mr. DeMille smiling covertly. But I went on as unconcernedly as if I had no thought of caricaturing anyone." The question remains in my mind to this day whether it was Griffith or I that Tully Marshall's clever mimicry resembled more as the director went crazier and crazier; I can guess which.

The biggest and most exciting scene in this film is one that I cut out of the scenario. The novel by Rupert Hughes on which my brother based his screenplay contained a spectacular fire in a motion picture studio. As Jesse had written me, "Our policy for 1918 is a simple and clear one. We will hold down expenses everywhere." I rather reluctantly agreed to Bill's suggestion that we could save a great deal of money by eliminating the fire and making its story point in some other less costly, though less interesting, way. Then one late April afternoon, as I was returning with members of the cast from some location shooting in Griffith Park, we noticed smoke rising into the sky from somewhere off to the southwest.

"That looks as though it might be close to the studio," I said, and ordered the driver to get down there as fast as he could. It was very close indeed, I found: our studio itself was going up in flames. Bill was already on the scene. Our minds had a single thought. We would get our "fire stuff" after all.

Cameras were set up. Players leaped into costumes. Grand old Theodore Roberts agreed to be photographed coming out of a burning dressing room, on my assurance that he would not catch fire and, if he did, we would extinguish the flames when he came out. All the players were magnificent. Only the fire department was puzzled. The firemen had never seen the victims of a conflagration enjoying it so much before. After they had finally put out the blaze, they did not wait around long enough to see me start another little fire in the ruins, in order to get close-ups.

The damage was around $100,000, all because a little wire had apparently got crossed in our color laboratory and ignited a rack of film; but the end result was a new three-story concrete building —this one with automatic sprinklers.

2

On Christmas and my birthday and other such days that friends remember, I am likely to receive a telegram of good wishes, always cleverly and warmly worded, and signed "Youngfellow." If there happens to be a new secretary receiving the mail and messages that day—and by new I mean someone who has not been with me more than five years or so—she is likely to say, "Youngfellow? Youngfellow? I don't believe Mr. deMille knows any Mr. Youngfellow. And I wish people would sign their full names, especially strangers! How can Mr. deMille acknowledge a telegram signed like this, and with no address?" Then I have to explain that the wire is not from a strange and inconsiderate man named Mr. Youngfellow, but from one of the most famous and glamorous first ladies of the screen: for Gloria Swanson has never forgotten that nearly 40 years ago I used to call her "young fellow," and the nickname so struck her fancy that she has been playfully reminding me of it ever since.

I do not see Gloria often now, but when I do I never fail to marvel at the way she has kept the beauty and the young vitality she had when I cast her in *Don't Change Your Husband* in 1918. The generation that has seen her only in *Sunset Boulevard* may have caught a glimpse of it, but only a glimpse because in *Sunset Boulevard* she was playing an older woman desperately trying to stay young and vital. One must see her off the screen to realize that Gloria hardly needs to try. She is another of those who ought to use special calendars, without years or months printed on them and with each page marked only "today."

Gloria Swanson's name always figures prominently in any list of the players whom I am supposed to have made into stars. There will be no such list in this book, for such a list is necessarily misleading. It perpetuates the legend of the all-powerful producer or director, a kind of Svengali of the cinema, spotting a beautiful face behind a lunch counter or in a crowd of merry youngsters coming out of a high school, and overnight, through some magical power, putting that face's owner on the pinnacle of stardom and her name ablaze on thousands of marquees across the land. Some few producers have tried that, frequently with sad results when audiences discovered that the breathtaking, heart-stopping face had emotional power about equal to that of a damp dishcloth, or a flat and irritating voice, or an intelligence to make one marvel how it had ever managed the transition from kindergarten to the first grade. The most beautiful woman I have ever met in Hollywood dashed

217

any star-making hopes I may have had for her when she proudly summed up her brief career by telling me, "Whatever I have did, I have did good."

The worst effect of the legend of stardom overnight has been in the lives of uncounted numbers of young girls who have come to Hollywood hoping to be "discovered." Few have any experience in acting. Many are quite pretty, but they are coming to a place where there is a surfeit of prettiness. They stand little or no chance of getting inside the gate of a studio, and less of being seen there or anywhere by a producer. They are fortunate if their fate in Hollywood is no worse than bitter disappointment; many of their pathetic stories have had more tragic endings. The motion picture industry has tried in various ways to discourage these vain hopes. Mrs. deMille and others founded the Hollywood Studio Club as a means of giving wholesome and congenial surroundings to some of these young women; but, for all its splendid work, such provision as the Studio Club can make does not begin to meet the problem.

But still they come, and try all manner of expedients to get themselves noticed. There was the girl who, all unknown to me, clocked my movements between my home and the studio and then, one night as I was driving home, placed herself and what appeared to be an injured little dog in the street where the beam of my car's headlights would fall on them. Naturally I stopped to offer first aid to the little dog. That girl's method of attracting attention was at least so ingenious that I did give her a part in a picture. I hope that telling this story will not cause Hollywood traffic to be snarled by wistful-looking maidens kneeling over anguished-looking dogs. It should not; because that young lady, pretty and inventive though she was, did not go on to great stardom. If I ever published a list of the stars I am supposed to have created, it would be salutary to publish alongside it the much longer list of players whose careers I have tried to help, but who never made stardom because they did not have the one essential ingredient: sufficient talent.

And then there are the young ladies, and some not so young, who are prepared to give their all in exchange for a part in a picture. But the director doesn't want their all. All he wants is a good performance on the screen.

Acting is hard work. It takes talent to begin with, but that beginning is not the end. Acting is an art that must be learned and practiced as diligently as a concert violinist learns and practices his art. It demands discipline and sacrifice. When you have all these qualities, you have the potential makings of a good actor or actress—provided you have also that indefinable something which I call authority, that inner power to project yourself, not overbearingly or overwhelmingly, but with an assurance that speaks silently of inner reserves of power. One of the best signs of that authority is restraint. A great actor, like a great orator, never gives the impression that he is using all his emotional power. He gives just enough for what the role or scene demands, but he leaves the audience with the unconscious conviction that he has still more to draw upon, an untapped depth of which he remains the master. The minute an actor reaches the extreme of any emotion, he becomes weak; he has nothing more to give. He should let the audience take up the emotion where he leaves it, and let them carry it the rest of the way.

The amateur may think that to show that quality of authority he needs some flamboyant opportunity like Henry V's speech to his army or Richelieu's "I launch the curse of Rome!" The professional knows that authority can be shown as well in a shrug of the shoulders. As a young man in New York, trying to learn something about the theater, I saw it most memorably in Sir Henry Irving, in the scene in The Bells in which all Irving did was continue dropping coals in a stove, without any show of emotion, while he was being told that a murder he had committed was on the verge of being solved. As a director in Hollywood, I saw authority, as well as beauty, in Gloria Swanson when I first noticed her, simply leaning against a door in a Mack Sennett comedy.

Gloria was, of course, very young then, but I saw the future that she could have in pictures if her career was properly handled. I could name stars, some of them very competent artists, who have ruined their careers or at least suffered serious setbacks because early success has gone to their heads, or a kind of greedy overconfidence or misjudgment of their own talents has led them to take on roles for which they were not suited. I have seen this so often that it has become almost an axiom with me that the last person capable of judging what roles an actor should play is, with some

219

few exceptions, the actor himself. William S. Hart's place in motion picture history is secure, but it was shaken when he insisted upon departing from his unequaled portrayals of the steely bad man turned good in the end, to playing a wholesome character, full of sweetness and light, named Singer Jim McKee, a cowboy whose pure soul loved to express itself in song. Many actors who can be magnificently hateful villains always want to play Little Bo-Peep. But Gloria Swanson suffered from no such illusions. I never told her, until after her first few successes under my direction, why I was handling her career in a certain way; but she was intelligent enough to know and patient enough to wait.

I kept her, so to speak, under wraps. If a pun may be permitted, they were gorgeous wraps, designed by Alpharelta Hoffman and later by Mitchell Leisen, and worn in settings of Wilfred Buckland's best creation. Nothing was spared to bring out all the glamour that was Gloria. But I did not star her. She received the same billing as any other member of the cast; she also received, and was contented with, a relatively small salary. I knew what would happen; and it did. The public, not I, made Gloria Swanson a star. Exhibitors began to demand that she be given star treatment. Some people began to think that DeMille was doddering, to have this obviously stellar property and not build it up with the usual publicity for all it was worth, or, as is the way of publicity men, a little more. There were some, I believe, who said that Swanson was all that was saving DeMille. But the plan worked, with Gloria's perfect co-operation.

When the time came, when Gloria had a solid grounding in dramatic roles, when by its own power her image had been fixed in the mind of a public that wanted more and more of her, I said to her, in effect, "Now, young fellow, go and be a star. You don't need me any more." But Gloria chose to remain under my direction for six pictures in all, before going on to become the reigning "queen of the movies," as she was deservedly called in the 1920's. When Billy Wilder was casting *Sunset Boulevard* in 1950, he could not have made a better selection, historically, artistically, or sentimentally, than to choose Gloria Swanson to play the silent movie queen; and I am glad to have appeared in *Sunset Boulevard* in a supporting role to the "young fellow" who had been such a good workman for me at the beginning of her great career.

220

Gloria Swanson's second picture with me was *For Better For Worse*, adapted by William deMille from a story by Edgar Selwyn. It is the story of the love of two men, a doctor played by Elliott Dexter and a soldier played by Tom Forman, for the same woman, who, of course, was Gloria. If *For Better For Worse* is remembered at all today, it is probably lumped together with the other DeMille marriage-and-divorce pictures of that era; but it had another serious and purposeful theme, at once timely and daring for a film released only five months after the signing of the armistice that ended World War I.

Only those of us who lived through that period remember the strong, sometimes violent, feeling that the American people had about "slackers," men who did not join or try to join the armed forces. The total mobilization through the Selective Service, with which we became familiar in World War II, was not operative during World War I. A man who was not drafted was under considerable pressure to enlist; if he did not, he was fortunate if the only reprisal of his neighbors was to pin a white feather, the emblem of cowardice, on his coat. The doctor in *For Better For Worse* declines a commission in the army medical corps because he is the only doctor available to take charge of a children's hospital in his home town. The story brings out dramatically that the man who stayed home was not necessarily a coward or a slacker: it may have taken more courage to stay and do a needed work at home than to go to the fighting front.

Before even starting production on this film, I asked Jesse Lasky to try to obtain for me the motion picture rights to a work by one of the most eminent playwrights in the English-speaking theater: Sir James M. Barrie's *The Admirable Crichton*. This was a bold venture, especially since none of us knew Barrie and the negotiations had to be conducted by cable between New York and England. How would the celebrated master of gentle and fragile whimsy feel about turning one of his most successful plays over to a group of probably brash and brassy American movie-makers? Sir James was willing, however. In January, 1919, Jesse wired me that the deal had been closed. I immediately gave the play to Jeanie Macpherson, to start on the scenario. Everyone was delighted—until I sent a tremor through the New York office by suggesting that I wanted to change the title of Barrie's play from *The Admirable Crichton* to *Male and Female*.

I had taken alarm when both a letter and a telegram from Jesse referred to the play as "Admiral Crichton." I knew that of course Jesse had not made this mistake, but I said to myself that if Jesse's experienced secretary and the Postal Telegraph company could make it, the public certainly would. They would think the picture was about some unheard-of naval officer, probably "war stuff" or "costume stuff" or anything but what it was: the amusing and touching story of how a butler's natural leadership asserted itself when the noble family he served was shipwrecked on an island in the South Seas. We first thought of changing the title to "The Spell," but I settled upon *Male and Female* as best expressing the elemental situation of the story, when the primitive necessities of life on a desert island knocked out the class distinctions between lords and butlers, ladies and maids, and left them all merely men and women.

From the anguish in New York, however, one would have thought that I had proposed to set up a hot-dog stand on Lincoln's tomb. Jesse wrote me that "practically the whole office objects to the title chosen for Crichton . . . we are making great progress in negotiating with Barrie through Alf Hayman for all of Barrie's plays, and they fear he would be offended if we changed the title of his play. . . . I think the New York office is right . . . it really isn't right or proper to change the title of a Barrie play."

I persisted, though, and left it to poor Jesse to bear the news to Sir James Barrie in London, when he went over to show the author our version of his play. When Jesse explained, with many hems and haws, that I had changed the title to *Male and Female*, Barrie thrust out his hand to shake Jesse's and exclaimed, "Capital! I wish I'd thought of that myself!" In spite of my vandalism, perhaps in part because of it, Alf Hayman's delicate negotiations were not upset: Sir James gladly sold to our company the motion picture rights to all his plays and to any plays or novels that he might write in the future, surely a high mark of confidence from an impressive source.

In addition to Gloria Swanson as Lady Mary, the cast of *Male and Female* included the familiar names of Theodore Roberts, Raymond Hatton, Julia Faye, and others who had worked with me before; but there were also some newcomers. One was a little black-haired, hazel-eyed beauty, still in her teens, Lila Lee, who played Twenny, the maid. Another was a child named Wesley Barry, to become famous later in adolescent roles more wholesome and, I think, more representative of American youth than some we have seen lately spreading terror through blackboard jungles.

Still another was a young girl I had noticed, without being overwhelmingly impressed, in some of Hal Roach's comedies. But when I saw her one evening at dinner in a restaurant, it occurred to me that there might be more behind those big dark eyes and cupid's-bow mouth than a steady diet of comedy roles had brought out. Then and there I asked Bebe Daniels if she wanted to work for me. More honorable than some in those cutthroat days, she said that she could not because she was under contract to Mr. Roach. More than a year later, however, she came to see me, all dressed up in her mother's clothes to make her look mature enough for dramatic roles, and I gave her a small part in *Male and Female*.

In later years, Bebe Daniels was to play a role in life greater than any Hollywood could offer her on the screen. All through World War II, she and her husband, Ben Lyon, stayed in London, sharing the dangers and privations of the British people, contributing to British morale, and being two of the best unofficial ambassadors the American people have ever had. When Derek Bond interviewed me on the B.B.C. television in London in 1957, he could not have brought on the program anyone better fitted to introduce me to the British audience, or anyone I could have been more glad to see, than Bebe Daniels.

I must have been exceptionally fortunate in choosing the times and places for dining out while we were preparing for *Male and Female*. Another evening, at the old Ship Cafe, Jeanie Macpherson introduced me to a young man who, she said, was a talented costume designer. On Jeanie's word, I engaged Mitchell Leisen to design the lavish costumes for the Babylonian flashback scene; I feel sure that the superlative quality of Mitch's work may have been one reason why Sir James Barrie neither exploded nor fainted when he saw the Babylonian embellishment added to his play. I kept Mitchell Leisen with me as costume and set designer, art director, and assistant director until he became a director in his

223

own right—one of the best in the profession for originality and taste in mounting his productions.

Of course, the director-general could not individually know every one of the hundreds of people who work on a production. It was not until nearly 40 years later that I learned the identity of a youngster who was earning some $12 a week doing advertising sketches for *Male and Female*. I remembered how good the sketches were. They should have been good, for they were among the first work done in Hollywood by one of Hollywood's very few authentically creative geniuses, Walt Disney.

Originally we had planned to cast Elliott Dexter as Crichton, the admirable butler, but he became seriously ill, thus giving Thomas Meighan the opportunity for one of his most successful roles and also for what must have been one of his most unforgettable adventures. There is a scene in which Crichton, as admirably skilled with bow and arrow as with the more customary tools of a butler's profession, saves the life of Lady Mary by killing a ferocious leopard and then, very male indeed, drapes the dead beast across his shoulders while playing a love scene with the grateful Mary. The safe and easy and usual way to make that scene, of course, would be to use a stuffed leopard; but, no matter how clever the taxidermist or the cameraman, a stuffed animal never looks like anything but a stuffed animal. I wanted more realism. I happened to hear that at the Selig Zoo there was a leopard which the Selig people were going to destroy because it had killed a man. I promptly got in touch with its keepers, who were glad enough to postpone the execution and let me have the animal on my promise that I would have it killed just before we used its corpse over Tommy Meighan's shoulders.

When the leopard was delivered and I saw it pacing its cage with passion and pride and sinewy grace, I said, "That animal is too beautiful to be killed."

I was greeted by the chorus I have heard so often: "But, Mr. deMille, you can't——"

Not unnaturally, Tommy Meighan's was one of the leading voices in that choir of negative thinking.

"Don't worry," I said. "There will be no danger. We'll chloroform him."

"But, Mr. deMille——"

"Yes, we can—if you will just go down to the drugstore and buy enough chloroform, in quarts or gallons or whatever the biggest containers it comes in, and soak some big cloths in it and put them around the cage and soak some big sponges in it and put them in the cage. I guarantee that you will have a sleeping, harmless leopard that will still be and look like a real leopard."

After these ministrations, the leopard was indeed sleeping as sweetly as a lamb when Tommy hoisted its limp and languid form around his shoulders and began the scene which the script described: "He comes a step nearer; and gripping her wrist tightly, whispers, low and tensely: 'I know I have paid through lives and lives, but I loved you then and I love you now.' For a breathless second, she looks up into his face (hold this); then, the *answering light* that he has been waiting for, suddenly drenches her eyes, and Crichton, bending, sweeps her into his arms."

But the sleeping leopard began to dream. In that sleep of chloroform, what dreams may come to a man-killing leopard, I cannot say, but the leopard also began to talk in his sleep. First cozy sighs and purrings, then low, contented growls, then, as the drama of his dream progressed, more ominous snarls and snorts issued from the head that was nuzzling close to Tommy Meighan's ear.

If *Male and Female* had not been a silent picture, the microphone would have picked up lines that Jeanie Macpherson never wrote.

"I know I have paid through lives and lives—Mr. deMille, the damn thing is waking up!—but I loved you then and—get me out of this, I tell you he's coming to!"

If, as I have said, an actor needs the quality of authority, a director needs it still more. I kept giving Tommy and Gloria my firmest and blandest assurances that everything was all right; and they trouped through the scene to the finish. It took the leopard another day to sleep it off. After that, he was one of the gentlest, meekest, most friendly and approachable animals I have ever known, so admirable in fact that we named him, naturally, Crichton.

At the time Elliott Dexter became ill, my brother William, who was now directing as well as writing, had scheduled several pictures for Dexter which could not now be made. As one result of this major shift in Bill's plans, I took over from him an idea on

225

which he had been working and produced it under the title, *Why Change Your Wife*. Bill's story was about an exceedingly prim and proper wife, "whose virtues are her only vices," and whose efforts to impose her tastes and perfectionism upon her husband cause her to lose him to another, more attractive woman, until at last the wife learns that being virtuous does not mean being dowdy and that being cultured is not inconsistent with being human. Gloria Swanson was as successful as the plain young matron in the first reels as in the changed character of a gay and femininely appealing wife at the end. As the other woman, Bebe Daniels had her first big dramatic role and she divided the acting honors equally with Gloria. Thomas Meighan was the husband shuttled between the two, rather helplessly it might seem; but I daresay it did not occur to the men in the audience to pity him for being fought over by Gloria Swanson and Bebe Daniels.

4

Fighting of another kind, with combatants less pretty than Gloria and Bebe but no less determined, was going on elsewhere in the motion picture industry. Adolph Zukor was kept busy through 1920 issuing statements denying that he was trying to destroy the exhibitors or establish a monopoly. He also felt constrained to deny that Wall Street was dominating our company. That was true enough, but not because Wall Street did not have a good try at it. The expansion of the previous few years, new studios, more and more theaters, the acquisition of the Charles Frohman company, and the steadily rising costs of production, all created a need of money or credit; and credit meant the entry of bankers on the scene. Jesse wired me jubilantly when Kuhn, Loeb, & Company extended a very substantial line of credit to our company; but soon thereafter the bankers extended another line into our midst, this one of supervision, if not control, over how the money was being spent.

This supervision took tangible shape in the person of a gentleman who, said Messrs. Kuhn, Loeb, & Company, would bring efficiency and economy into our wild and wonderful operations if we would give him authority to cut and trim, to watch the pennies and pare the cheese. Jesse, optimistic as ever, wrote me in January, 1920, that the new man was "a real addition to the company and works splendidly with Mr. Zukor." My comment on him to Jesse, the next month, was hopeful but more cautious: "I tried to have a good talk with him. He came up to my house for dinner, but I think he is a pretty cold fish. However, I have no doubt that he is great for the business and I hope he makes us all a lot of money. I am pretty well into my next picture, etc."

The man lasted, surprisingly, nearly two years; but in September, 1921, I was writing to Jesse, "I was very glad indeed to get your letter and to note that he has resigned." So, by that time, was Jesse; and so especially was Mr. Zukor, who had hastened the resignation by one of his famous and potent ultimatums.

I have mentioned this incident not to pillory a well-meaning and, in his own way, an able man, but to point out one instance of a recurring phenomenon in the motion picture industry: the entry into it, frequently with fanfares, always with a serious, well-intentioned "Now let's be businesslike about this" attitude, of gentlemen who know all about banking or engineering or some other field of business and nothing whatever about the business of artistic creation. Our guardian's strictures on the number of words we used in telegrams and his fiat about how much, and not a penny more, we should pay for story properties were only typical of innumerable other similar efficiency experts. I once entertained on one of my sets a group of executives from a large automobile company, whose comment after watching the shooting of a scene was, "This would be a lot better if you could eliminate all the confusion," as if drama could be delivered and emotion engineered on an assembly line.

I myself once innocently brought into a studio one of the most brilliant minds I have ever known, a man trained to high military command, and asked him to study our operations and plot out a work schedule that would make for greater efficiency. He did, with such precision that if we had tried to follow it, most of the day would have been taken up with synchronizing our watches to make sure that we were starting and finishing each task on time.

The efficiency expert I remember best was one who came to take charge of one of the major studios with so much promise and publicity that the industry gave him a dinner of welcome to Hollywood. All the studio heads were there, all a little more anxious than they would admit about the competition that they would get from this much-heralded new broom that was about to sweep *his* studio clean of all the inefficiency and waste in which the rest of us were wallowing. At the end of the dinner, he stood up to speak. Everyone leaned forward expectantly.

"Gentlemen," he said, "I have studied this industry and I have come to the conclusion that there is one thing wrong with motion pictures. It's the voices of the actors."

You could almost hear the sigh of relief as the studio heads settled back to relax. No one heard the rest of the gentleman's speech, however, because each was busy with his own thoughts about which of that studio's assets he could get his hands on when the reforming expert ran it into bankruptcy.

While Sir Henry Irving was right in saying that the theater must be run as a business or it will fail as an art, it is also literally true that there is no business like show business. There is no other business that deals in so many unpredictable intangibles. If you are manufacturing tractors or breakfast food, you can be reasonably sure that your budget and production schedule will not be upset by anything but acts of God, strikes, war, fire, flood, or civil commotion. But when you are making a picture, will it be weeks or months before the writers turn out a satisfactory screenplay? Will any given scene have to be shot once or ten times before it is right? Will the irreplaceable star come down with appendicitis halfway through? Will a scene that moved you to tears on the set strike the preview audience as so funny that you will have to shoot something else to take its place and re-edit the whole picture around it? The novice coming into our industry, whatever his experience elsewhere, is never prepared for such eventualities as these; he never realizes that what looks to him like waste of time and money may make the difference between a picture that people will want to see and a picture that will play briefly to half-empty houses. The producer-director is always the despair of the bookkeeper; but what devastates creative work is when the bookkeeping mentality takes hold on those who control the fiscal sinews of production.

5

It was time, in 1920, to negotiate a new contract with Famous Players-Lasky. The date was not lost upon our competitors.

United Artists offered me $300,000 per picture. First National, in their particular anxiety to hurt Mr. Zukor, offered me $1,000,000 per picture; I can only assume that this meant $1,000,000 gross, including the cost of the picture, but even that would have netted me more than double the United Artists offer for each picture. Famous Players-Lasky offered me $260,000 a year; I was making about three pictures a year at the time.

Pointing out that the company had been paying Douglas Fairbanks and Mary Miles Minter twice what was offered me, and Mary Pickford three times as much, when their pictures were not earning as much as mine, I wired Jesse Lasky, "I hope I do not have to assure you of my loyalty to the organization and of my intention of remaining with it . . . but I do believe that I should share somewhat more in the success of my . . . thirty-seven pictures with but two that were not successes. . . . Having avowed my intention and desire to remain with the company I want to let the matter rest with you and Mr. Zukor and feel sure I can abide by your decision. I know of no other way to show where my heart is."

It took some little time to arrive at a contract giving me $6,500 a week as advance against a gross budget of $290,000 per picture. The crowning touch was Mr. Zukor's published statement, when the contract was signed, that "Mr. DeMille . . . had the entire industry to choose from, and after thorough investigation, made as a businessman as well as a director, selected Famous Players-Lasky Corporation."

I shall not burden the reader with so much mathematics again if I can help it; but it may have become clear why, in the same year of 1920, I judged it wise to form a company of my own. I felt that the day might be coming when an independent company might be a useful entity for me to have around. Cecil B. DeMille Productions was formed in 1920 as a partnership, with Mrs. de-Mille, Neil McCarthy, and Ella King Adams, Mrs. deMille's youthful and brilliant stepmother who was also my script reader, as my partners. The company was incorporated, under the same name, in 1923.

The reader may wonder about my personal relationships with Jesse and Mr. Zukor through all this. They were basically unchanged. My friends drove a hard bargain. They knew I would not leave the company that I had helped to found. They took advantage of that knowledge. But it was not a personal advantage. They acted, according to their view of the matter, for the good of the company, and, I have no doubt, in a spirit that they considered fair to me. In the first years, when Famous Players-Lasky was a fledgling, they had treated me generously. They still had the abilities which earned my respect. If, under the pressure of his heavy responsibilities and the looming shadow of the bankers, Jesse was becoming sometimes more businesslike than brotherly, the old affectionately bubbling Jesse was only submerged, not lost, and he rose to the surface when we met.

A much more severe strain on our relationship was only a few years away; but our friendship eventually weathered even that. When you like most of a person, it is better to forget, if you can, the parts that you don't like. You sleep better; and you have more time for making pictures if you do not waste it in making enemies.

Still, there may have been another of those coincidences in the title of my next picture, *Something To Think About*. By the beginning of 1920, Elliott Dexter was well enough to appear again, though slightly lamed after his illness, and Jeanie Macpherson wrote the scenario around a lame man's frustrated and embittered but finally victorious search for love. Monte Blue played Dexter's rival for the affections of Gloria Swanson; and Elliott and Gloria were led to the happy ending of their story by a little child who is now a vigorous and efficient assistant director at Paramount, Mickey Moore. *Something To Think About* was the first of my pictures on which Alvin Wyckoff shared camera credit with Karl Struss, a cameraman whose brilliant mastery of black-and-white cinematography was, I have always believed, one of the factors in keeping the place that black-and-white still holds in American motion pictures.

This was also the first of my pictures to embody a religious theme: it is the faith of Elliott Dexter's housekeeper, played by Claire McDowell, which keeps him from despair, and it is her inspired wisdom and her prayer that win through in the end to reconciliation and deep love. That, no doubt, is why the critic of *The New York Mail* said that the picture "suffers from too much psychology." It seems to be part of the constitution of some critics to dislike having something to think about.

230

Forbidden Fruit, which followed *Something To Think About,* was a rather slighter story with a Cinderella theme. My principal production in 1920 was *The Affairs of Anatol,* based on, or it would be more accurate to say suggested by, the play by Arthur Schnitzler.

I could not complain of the New York office's generosity in making talent available to me: the cast of *The Affairs of Anatol* included Wallace Reid, Elliott Dexter, Gloria Swanson, Wanda Hawley, Theodore Roberts, Theodore Kosloff, Raymond Hatton, Agnes Ayres, Monte Blue, and Bebe Daniels, the latter playing "Satan Synne, the wickedest woman in New York." Four writers collaborated on the script—Jeanie Macpherson, Beulah Marie Dix, Lorna Moon, and Elmer Harris; and Jesse Lasky sent out from New York Paul Iribe, one of the best art directors I have ever had, who remained with me for several years. One of the bit players was the lady who deserves more credit than I do for inventing sex appeal—Elinor Glyn, the priestess and prophetess of "It," whom Jesse Lasky had brought from England to write a screenplay which he hoped would outdo her sensational novel, *Three Weeks.* Madame Glyn, as she liked to be called, happened to be at the studio and condescended to join Lady Parker, the wife of Sir Gilbert Parker, at a bridge table in *The Affairs of Anatol.*

The literary world brushed me again at the same time, when I had the distinction of being accused of plagiarism by Somerset Maugham. Maugham was also among the English authors whom Jesse had garnered to write for Famous Players-Lasky. Hearing some studio gossip that I was using in *The Affairs of Anatol* a story that he had told to Jesse and me, he wired Jesse a dignified protest naming witnesses; but when the facts were laid before him, it was not difficult to convince that superb literary craftsman that I had been working on this particular film for many weeks before his arrival in Hollywood and that there was only the remotest superficial resemblance between his story and ours.

In the Christmas, 1920, number of *The Motion Picture News,* I am quoted as saying: "Barely six years ago I made fourteen pictures in a single year. . . . Today, working just as hard or harder, I find that I can only turn out three pictures in the same length of time. But the three pictures that I make today draw more patronage than the entire fourteen of six years ago. It is not beyond the

231

bounds of reason to say that the picture of the future may take a year or more to produce." Bringing my own prophecy closer to ful-fillment, I made only two pictures in 1921, *Fool's Paradise* and *Saturday Night*. I must add that the New York office approved an upward revision of my budgets, though not without a memoran-dum from the executive and finance committees containing a plea which will ring familiarly in the ear of every producer and director in Hollywood: "Take every means in your power to cut costs of your productions without hurting their quality!"

Neither cost nor quality was spared for the Halloween swim-ming party in *Saturday Night*. Since this was another Cinderella story, Claire West used a lavish hand in designing the bathing suits and fancy dress costumes to make the scene a wonderland to the eyes of the heroine as well as the audience. Julia Faye's bath-ing suit was made of big squares of patent leather, shining and sparkling in the light of the lanterns hung around the set. During the scene I noticed one of the extra players, a handsome young man, holding Julia stock still in the pool with her back to the camera, while the other players cavorted gaily in the water. At the end of the scene Julia, with the man's coat around her shoul-ders, brought him over to me and said, "I wish you'd thank this boy for what he did. He not only saved the scene; he saved me from an awful embarrassment. My patent leather suit came apart when it hit the water, and the top came off!"

I thanked the young man and congratulated him on his pres-ence of mind in protecting Julia and playing into the action of the scene so that I could still use it, whereas a less quick-witted player might have spoiled the scene by yelling, "Stop the camera! Miss Faye has lost her bathing suit!" I used that resourceful and chival-rous young man in later pictures, and I was not surprised when he achieved his present fame as the resourceful and chivalrous hero of the Hopalong Cassidy movies; his name, he told me, was William Boyd.

6

Early in 1922, I made my first trip to Europe, accompanied by Paul Iribe and my Japanese valet, Yamabe. The acute illness which hit me in Paris at the end of the trip has rather obliterated my memory of the more usual things one does on one's first grand tour, but there are two incidents that stand out vividly, perhaps because of their very different settings.

On January 22, in Rome, Paul Iribe and I arrayed ourselves in the very formal clothes we had had made especially for the occasion and set out across the Eternal City for our scheduled audience with Pope Benedict XV. We expected the audience to be a duly solemn and impressive event, but we were not prepared for the rather distraught and wondering reception we were given when we presented ourselves at the bronze doors of the Vatican. The Vatican's manners are always impeccable, but there was an unmistakable air of "What are you two doing here?" on the part of the Swiss Guards and Monsignori who met us. We could not understand it: we were properly introduced, we were dressed according to the strictest protocol, we were on time. Then only did we learn that in fact we were not on time: the Pope had died that day. In the bustle of traveling, we had not kept up with the news; and indeed the Roman newspapers were of little use to an innocent abroad whose education had not included Italian. It was not until 1957 that I could pay my belated respects to Pope Benedict, when I admired the splendid statue of him in St. Peter's.

The other incident, in Paris, involved a visit to an establishment as different from the Vatican as could be imagined. In the best tourist tradition, Paul and I went to dinner one evening, at Maxim's, of course. In Paris at that time there were certain ladies, beautiful, exquisitely gowned, highly cultivated and supremely dignified, who dined alone at Maxim's or other restaurants of the same class, with an eye to making what we may call a temporary acquaintance with any visiting gentleman who came up to their fairly exacting standards. There may still be such ladies in Paris, but the last time I was at Maxim's I was surrounded by my daughter and secretary, and hence unable, even if I had felt inclined, to pursue any sociological surveys. In 1922, however, I evidently passed inspection, for I found myself talking with a very beautiful young lady, who spoke perfect English and who, after a proper interval of conversation, invited me to her apartment.

I accepted the invitation and, excusing myself to an understanding Paul, escorted the young lady home. She may have thought it odd that this American kept his overcoat on; but, with the fatalism of her profession, she made no comment on that oddity, and she proceeded to undress.

"No, no," I said, "I don't want that. I just want to talk with you." An American bank note of reasonable size made its appearance and, as discreetly, disappeared. She put on a dressing gown and we talked. She was as intelligent, witty, and sensible as only a Frenchwoman can be. I was interested, and expressed interest, in her work, the how and especially the why of it. She smiled, stood up, went to another door of the room where she had received me, and opened the door. Through the doorway I saw a modest dining room, and her husband and small children having supper. She introduced me to her little family. I sat down with them and enjoyed the perfectly apparent atmosphere of understanding, affection, and domestic warmth that reigned among them all. On one side of the door she was obviously a devoted wife and mother. Her profession was something totally apart. If I put that scene in a motion picture, it would hardly be believed. I wonder myself if it could happen anywhere but in Paris.

Like all who visit Paris, I lost my heart to that city. I also nearly lost my life there. My medical history belongs in my doctor's office, not here: I shall spare the reader most of the details which I found harrowing enough when an acute rheumatic fever attacked, as it seemed, my whole skeleton and put me to bed in the Hotel Ritz, under the care of a French physician whose hopes for me were so dismal that he felt free to make notes with his fountain pen on my bare and swollen leg. I suppose he thought that was the handiest place to file his memoranda of the case for a few days, after which the undertaker could erase them.

Since waiting for death can be a very boring business, I passed the time by letting my nurses dress up in the elaborate gowns, furs, and precious jewels that the Paris shops, more optimistic than my doctor, wanted me to buy for use in pictures and for my own jewel collection. The nurses enjoyed being mannequins for a change, discarding their starched uniforms for more attractive garb. When that palled, I told them to let in anyone who might want to see me; and for some days I was diverted by the strangest procession of anonymous Frenchmen and Frenchwomen who stood at the foot of my bed, shook their heads, clucked their tongues, and made what I can only hope were sympathetic observations on the dying American.

My illness gave me two of the finest demonstrations of friendship and loyal devotion that I have ever experienced in a long life. One was from my valet, Yamabe. In view of the purchases we planned to make in Europe, I had brought with me a very large amount of money. Much of it was still unused when I was taken ill; much was represented by the costly jewels I had already bought. I told Yamabe that I might be going to die and that I was entrusting to him the money and jewels because I knew that he would deliver them faithfully to Mrs. deMille. From that moment, Yamabe never left my room. He sat on the floor, just inside the door, silent and unobtrusive, but every moment watching me, watching everyone who came in the room, watching the places where I had told him the money and jewels were kept. To Yamabe they would have represented a fabulous fortune, but I knew that they were as safe with him as if they were already in Mrs. deMille's hands.

The other instance of extraordinary friendship and loyalty came from my old flying instructor, Colonel Harvey Burwell. He was then with the army of occupation in Germany and, as soon as he heard I was ill, flew from Coblenz to Paris, stayed as long as he could, came back as often as he could, and took charge of me like a combination of a mother and a commanding general. I was completely helpless, unable to move enough to do anything for myself. When I protested at Harvey's insistence on doing personal services for me that it was bad enough to have to let trained nurses do, he said, "C. B., I'd rather do these things for you than shake hands with a lot of people I know!"

Harvey Burwell's visits to Paris, however, rather roused the suspicions of his commanding officer. After all, sitting up with a sick friend seemed a pretty threadbare excuse for extended leave to visit the city most noted for gaiety and romance. The general decided to come and have a look for himself at this allegedly sick friend. Instead of being perturbed, Harvey was delighted to bring him along, as I was to see him, as anyone interested in aviation would be to meet the prophetic, if ill-starred, exponent of airpower, General Billy Mitchell.

I was to meet him again on and off through the years, whenever we were in the same vicinity. He sometimes visited me at my home in Hollywood; and one of those times was more tragic than our first meeting at my supposed deathbed. Immediately after General Mitchell was convicted by the court-martial, Harvey Burwell brought him to my home; and, depressed though we all were by that martyrdom of the one general who foresaw what airpower would mean to national defense, we made a pact that at all costs the three of us would keep Billy Mitchell's vision alive and do all in our power to advance the cause of aviation.

As the reader will have guessed by this time, I did not die in Paris in 1922. Thanks more to Harvey Burwell's generalship than to the doctor's memoranda on my leg. I was able to be moved on a stretcher, hoisted aboard an Atlantic liner, and brought home. The voyage was made pleasant for me by the presence on board of my old friend Victor Herbert, who gave up much of his time to visiting me in my cabin and reliving the days when he used to play his compositions for me at the Lambs Club in New York and I was, I believe, his first audience for some of the tunes that America is still humming.

On my arrival in New York, I had my first experience of a union jurisdictional dispute, when the dockmen, reasoning that in my condition I was obviously either luggage or cargo, refused to let the ambulance attendants carry my stretcher off the ship. As the argument over the privilege of carrying my immobile frame waxed hotter, the disputants became so engrossed in it that its innocent object, the stretcher with me on it, got dropped with a resounding and excruciating thud at the top of the gangplank. Perhaps that treatment helped loosen the grip of the disease, for after reaching Hollywood I was soon able to walk and gradually to use my arms and hands again.

Anyway, I was glad to be home; but not so glad to find that, though I was getting better, Hollywood was sick and many of the public were getting sick of Hollywood.

11

THE ARBUCKLE SCANDAL had broken before I left for Europe, when Famous Players-Lasky's leading comedian, the immensely popular Roscoe Arbuckle, was indicted for manslaughter following the death of a pretty young actress named Virginia Rappe. Five months later, one of our company's leading directors, William Desmond Taylor, was found murdered in his Los Angeles home, in circumstances which involved the names of such well-known stars as Mabel Normand and Mary Miles Minter and gave the press its opportunity to ring the changes on all manner of rumors about drink, dope, blackmail, and indescribable orgies.

If the reader expects me either to whitewash the Hollywood of the early 1920's or to make any new and spicy revelations about it, he will be disappointed. I averted at least two other public scandals, which involved no crimes but would have blackened several names as prominent as those of Arbuckle or Taylor if I had not been able to convince two vindictive husbands that it was in their own interests to behave as if they were gentlemen. But I see no reason for recounting their unproven charges simply because they lived in Hollywood, California, rather than in Hartford, Connecticut, or Hattiesburg, Mississippi.

There was a sickness in Hollywood, but it was a sickness that infected the whole postwar world. I am neither excusing nor accusing. There was throughout the world a crumbling of standards, aggravated in America, I have always believed, by the Eighteenth Amendment and the Volstead Act, by which government attempted to regulate the personal habits of individuals and succeeded only in teaching many of them disrespect for all law. But the germ of that sickness was older than Prohibition, older than World War I. Theologians call it original sin.

If someone in Hartford became addicted to narcotics, it was a grievous trial to his family and friends. If a wife in Hattiesburg was unfaithful to her husband, he might take a vengeance which would perhaps be given an inch or two of newspaper space outside Forrest County. But anything that happened in Hollywood was magnified far beyond the family concerned or the industry or the local community. That was inevitable. Hollywood had built its big names, and anything they did was news. It was more titillating news if its mongers could hint that, beneath what smoke appeared, there was a fire of corruption consuming Hollywood's very vitals.

I believe that the only time I figured publicly in that connection was when I received the news from a little town in the South that Cecil B. deMille had married Louise Glaum, a popular and lovely film star of the time; the news did not trouble to mention how I had disposed of Mrs. deMille in order to effect these startling nuptials. Investigation brought out the fact that, one dull afternoon, some young people in the back room of a drugstore had decided to wile away the time with a mock wedding. One of the boys said, "I'll be Cecil B. deMille"; one of the girls said, "I'll be Louise Glaum"; and a sharp-eared customer happened into the store in time to overhear the mock marriage vows exchanged in the back room.

Some people will believe anything. Another time, I happened to hear that the Indians living on Tiburón Island off the west coast of Mexico were suffering from dire poverty and privation. As I sometimes cruised in those waters in my yacht, the *Seaward*, I stocked the boat with blankets, warm clothing, and other supplies for the relief of the Tiburón Islanders. But, as the story circulated in Mexico, it was that Cecil B. deMille and a party of friends were on their way to Tiburón with machine guns, to engage in the sport of hunting and shooting Indians!

With the very real Arbuckle and Taylor affairs as a basis, how-

238

ever, much of the press, many pulpits and organizations, and a goodly part of the public went into full cry. It would have been useless to point out that, then as now, the overwhelming majority of the thousands who work in the motion picture industry were sober, hardworking men and women, devoted to their families, and as moral as any comparable cross section of America. That is never news. What the press screamed and the pulpits thundered was the lurid conception of Hollywood as a citadel of sin, and the entire motion picture industry was tarred with a brush wielded in broad strokes by righteously indignant but none too discriminating hands.

It was necessary for the industry to do something. It has become a cliché for film historians to say that of course the industry had to do something, to protect its investments. Certainly that was a consideration; but it was not the whole story. It was necessary to do something in fairness to the public and to the workers in the industry itself, including the accused. Trial and condemnation by public clamor have never been the best way of assuring justice.

The day Fatty Arbuckle was acquitted of the charge of manslaughter, I was besieged by reporters demanding to know what we were going to do with the unreleased Arbuckle pictures the company had been holding back during his trials. I wired Jesse Lasky for a clarification of company policy. His answer was prompt and forthright: "We will release Arbuckle pictures immediately, bringing no pressure one way or another on exhibitors, leaving reception of pictures up to American public. Arbuckle having been acquitted of any crime, it would be grave injustice and unfair to him for us to take any other position."

Other counsels prevailed eventually; the Arbuckle pictures were not released. The company lost money by shelving them. It could have lost much more if the public had not only rejected the Arbuckle films but boycotted Famous Players-Lasky for releasing them. But Jesse was willing to take that risk, in the interest of fair play—fair play toward a man who, whether technically guilty or innocent of manslaughter, had certainly done the industry a grave disservice by his conduct.

A far greater danger than financial loss was the hysteria that sought to punish individual offenders by putting the entire product of the industry into the strait jacket of government censorship.

I want to make very clear the difference between censorship of a film before its release and any lawful action which may be taken by governmental agencies or private groups after a picture has been released. If a motion picture is obscene within the meaning of the law, the authorities certainly should take action against it by due process. If a motion picture offends the principles or the sensibilities of any private group, they have every right to publish their opinion of it and urge their members to stay away from it. That is part of their liberty. But the right to produce without prior censorship is part of ours. A policeman or a self-appointed guardian of public morals may sincerely believe that righteousness would be served if he could censor all films before they were released. But grant him that power, and he can just as logically apply it to plays before they are staged, books before they are bound, newspaper copy before it is printed, speeches before they are delivered; and with that power he can extend his definition of the field of righteousness to include political, economic, scientific, or religious views, in all of which the standard of what he likes or dislikes then becomes the standard of what the public may or may not see or hear or read. In the film industry's opposition to external censorship there is more than a question of artistic freedom, important though that is. When we fight censorship of our product, what we are ultimately defending is every person's right to freedom of speech.

Yet the problem of morality in films remains. Despite the fact that the most successful pictures of all time have been films to which anyone could take his children without having to brainwash them afterward, there will always be a few producers who mistakenly believe that dirt will necessarily turn out to be pay dirt. Censorship is not the answer, for the same reason that decapitation is not the recommended remedy for a headache. It is the industry's job to police itself, subject to the ultimate court of public opinion.

The American motion picture industry was well aware of this long before the scandals of the 1920's. Adolph Zukor, with his characteristic statesmanship, was one of the first to sense the industry's need for self-regulation in this respect. As early as February, 1917, Jesse Lasky addressed a letter to each of the directors employed by our company, informing them that they were expected to adhere as much as possible to the standards of the National Board of Review, a non-governmental, non-profit organization of public-spirited citizens interested in better films. Our company, Jesse explained, "although it has never tolerated anything but the best in pictures, is taking this means of assuring itself in the future that the moral tone of our pictures will be such as will meet the demand for clean pictures."

It was this same statesmanship which induced the heads of all the major companies, in December, 1921, to invite Will H. Hays to become President of the Motion Picture Producers and Distributors of America. They reached high. Will Hays was Postmaster General in the Cabinet of President Harding. But their goal was high: their letter, asking Hays to "induce the President of the United States to relieve you from your present high duties," expressed their realization of "the necessity for attaining and maintaining the highest possible standard of motion picture film production." This was not only a matter of the content of films. The industry needed self-regulation in some of its business practices; it needed a unified approach to problems of taxation, international trade, and its other relations with our own and foreign governments; and, as the same letter put it, it needed "proper representation before the people of this country so that its position, at all times, may be presented in an unbiased and unprejudiced manner." Will Hays brought to these tasks the unbounded energy, skill, and dedication which served the industry with great distinction and great success, until his retirement in 1945, when he was succeeded by Eric Johnston as President of what is now called the Motion Picture Association of America.

I met Will Hays for the first time when he came to Hollywood in July, 1922. I introduced him at a mass meeting of our studio employees. Later he came with Jesse Lasky to Paradise, where we had a long talk about the industry's problems and the immense job that lay before the man chosen to lead us to their solution. Will Hays was a slight, wiry man, sharp-featured, quick in his movements and incisive in his thought. The way he made a telephone call was typical of the way he tackled everything: he is the only man I have ever known who did not take the first minute or two of a telephone conversation for assorted "Hello's," "How are you's," and "I'm fine's," but went straight to the point of whatever he

241

wanted to discuss. He and I remained close friends until his death in 1954.

Through all the excitements of those hectic days, Mrs. deMille kept to the unruffled tenor of her way, making our home a refuge from the strain of the crises that rocked Hollywood, while still finding time for her persistent good works in the community. She was never found wanting when called upon to rise to any occasion, and never lowered by a hair's breadth the standards of her Adams heritage. When Jesse Lasky asked me if I could give a party for a hundred guests—industry leaders, stars, and delegates to a Paramount distribution meeting—I was able to wire back: "Constance and I will be delighted to entertain you all at our house on Thursday evening. . . . If it meets with your views we will make it a dry party."

The same year, Mrs. deMille opened our home to two others who appealed to her and to me infinitely more than all the celebrities and all the dear friends who have enjoyed Mrs. deMille's hospitality for longer or shorter periods. These two came to stay. One was a dark and beautiful little girl, a Canadian war orphan. The other was a baby boy, who was found in Neil McCarthy's car; and it seemed to Mrs. deMille and me providential that if Cecilia was to have a sister, John should have a brother, and so our two children became four. The little girl, Katherine, has carried the name deMille on for another generation in motion pictures as a talented actress. The baby boy, Richard, is following in my father's and my brother's footsteps as a scholar. But, best of all, our four children, Cecilia, John, Katherine, and Richard, have given Mrs. deMille and me twelve grandchildren and two great-grandchildren. The youngest grandchild, Richard's son, not only carries on the family name but is burdened with two initials that he will have to live up to or live down, for that innocent infant is named Cecil B. deMille.

2

Having told of my venture into the business world with the Mercury Aviation Company, I turn now to what may somewhat restore my reputation as a solid citizen in the estimation of any business-minded reader. In 1922 I became a banker, being elected a vice-president of the newly organized Federal Trust and Savings

242

Bank of Hollywood. Since the banks were becoming more and more interested in motion pictures, I thought it would be a good idea to have a foot in their camp; and a new bank in Hollywood apparently thought it would be good to have a motion picture man among its officers. Times had changed since we had had to do our banking at Hall's grocery store.

Through this new venture began my business association and lifelong friendship with the Italian immigrant's son of whom a President of the United States was to say: "In my opinion A. P. Giannini has done more to build California through his great bank and his personal efforts than any other Californian." There is hardly a town, hardly a neighborhood, in California where, if you want to see the monument of Amadeo Peter Giannini, you need do no more than look about you: you will see a branch of the Bank of America. My part in that great and typically American success story was very small indeed, for A. P. Giannini was already, as his biographer calls him, a "giant in the West" when I first met him; but my association with him was to me important and valuable enough for me to depart once more from strict chronology and tell some incidents of it as a connected whole.

The business of banking, especially in the days when A. P. Giannini was building his empire, was even more complicated, in its corporate aspects, than the motion picture business. I can well understand it if any reader is not entirely clear in his mind about the various motion picture companies; and I have mentioned only a few of the nearly 20 that were affiliated in one way or another with Famous Players-Lasky. If I were to give here the kind of account of my banking experience that I might have to give, say, to the Federal Reserve Board, the reader would surely echo what Mr. Zukor said to me once in a moment of vexation: "Cecil, the trouble with you is that you are too many bank presidents!"

Actually, I was president of only one bank, the Culver City Commercial and Savings Bank, in 1925, and that bank was owned by the Ameri-Commercial Corporation, which was a holding company for the Bank of America and the Commercial National Trust and Savings Bank. That will give the reader an idea of why I am mercifully not going into detail. Behind all those corporate names and many more was the one name that counted: Giannini. In 1923, I became a vice-president of the Commercial National Bank

243

of Los Angeles and chairman of its advisory board on motion picture loans. The other offices I held later on in banking all stemmed from that. So did some adventures.

One day Sam Goldwyn, still carving his way to success but still far from having a firm foothold on that pinnacle, came to see me. He had an idea for a picture. That was about all he had. To produce it, he needed $200,000. His request for a loan had been turned down by a number of the soundest bankers. It was a big loan, bigger than any that had yet come across my new desk in the Cherokee Avenue branch of the Commercial Bank. In the Giannini empire, it was expected that requests for unusually large loans would be submitted to headquarters in San Francisco. But I knew Sam; and I approved the loan. Then I took the first train north.

A. P. Giannini was a hearty man, with a big voice and a warm, expansive manner. His greeting to me boomed through his new office building on Powell Street, San Francisco.

"C. B.! Glad to see you! You haven't seen the new building! Come on, let me show you around it!"

I tried to interrupt. "There's something I want to talk to you about, A. P."

"Never mind! Talk business later. Come and see these offices."

I tried several times to interrupt, but there was no stanching A. P.'s enthusiasm for the new building. I saw every corner and cranny of it before he finally shepherded me back to his own office and said, "Now what was it you wanted to talk about, C. B.?"

"It's about the Goldwyn loan——"

"Yes, I looked at it. No good, C. B. He has no assets."

"I made the loan, A. P."

"What's that?"

"I okayed the loan of $200,000 to Sam Goldwyn, A. P."

A. P. let out a roar for "Jim!"; and we were joined by his first lieutenant, the cool and cautious James A. Bacigalupi.

A. P. began to explain. "You remember that request from Goldwyn that was going the rounds, Jim."

"Yes," said Bacigalupi. "Not a good risk. He has no assets."

"C. B. made the loan, Jim."

I could see cold fury rising behind Jim's steely eyes. I thought it was now or never to make my stand.

"Just a minute," I said. "You gentlemen made me vice-president of a bank and chairman of the motion picture loan committee. Why? Did you want me for window-dressing? I'm not very good at that. If that is all you want me for, you can have my resignation. If you want me because I know something about motion picture values, that you don't know, then I've got to have full authority to pass on motion picture loans. You say Sam Goldwyn has no assets. You're right. He hasn't. He has no assets, except talent, which is the only asset worth anything in the motion picture business. I made that loan on talent and on character, and that is the basis every motion picture loan is going to be made on while I am chairman of the committee of the Commercial National Bank. Now, gentlemen, do I have the authority? Or do I resign?"

Mr. Bacigalupi stalked out. When he was out of earshot, A. P. gave me a long look. "It's all right, C. B.," he said. "But don't do it too often!"

If my memory serves me, the only motion picture loan that defaulted while I was chairman of that advisory board was a small loan made by A. P. Giannini—without asking me about it.

I made another small but surely rare contribution to banking history when, a month after becoming president of the Culver City bank, I reduced the interest on all existing and pending loans from 8 to 7 per cent. I do not recall any reactions from San Francisco to that gesture. Perhaps the gentlemen up there were too busy crying over spilled interest; or perhaps they agreed with my statement that "money offered at generous terms yields far better profits in the long run than the immediate high return which carries in its wake the danger of lost friendship."

The friendship of the banking community, at all events, was manifested in a singular way when I returned from a trip to Europe in 1931. I was hardly off the ship when I received a pressing invitation from a group of New York bankers who wanted to honor me with a small and intimate luncheon. I felt very set up about it. How civil of them, I thought, to pay this nice compliment to a fellow banker just back from his travels. The luncheon was held. The conversation was interesting and urbane. My hosts listened attentively to my comments on the situation in Europe. When the time came for us to part, they did have a little matter of business, which would not take more than a moment if I could spare it.

245

There was to be a stockholders' meeting of the Transamerica Corporation and the management, headed by Elisha Walker and James Bacigalupi, would be obliged if I would just sign the usual proxy in the routine way, allowing them to vote my shares in that great Giannini-founded holding company. Of course I would. I had no intention of traveling to Wilmington, Delaware, to attend the meeting; I knew that A. P. Giannini had put Walker and Bacigalupi at the head of Transamerica. That was good enough for me. A slip of blue paper, printed with the customary proxy form, was produced; and I signed.

As soon as I reached California, one of the first persons who wanted to see me was A. P. Giannini. He had a tale to tell and an appeal to make. While he had been in Europe for his health, the Walker group had made changes in Transamerica's policies which he considered disastrous; and Bacigalupi had gone over to Walker. A. P. had hurried back from Europe to put up a fight for control of the corporation. Would I give him my proxy?

I had to tell him then about the intimate luncheon in New York and the slip of blue paper. "But," I said, "I'll make it good. I have appreciated your confidence. I won't go back on my word to Walker, but I will buy as many more shares of Transamerica as I have now and give you the proxy for them, and that will at least offset the proxy I have given Walker." A. P. Giannini won overwhelmingly. I had comparatively very few of the more than 20,-000,000 shares outstanding, but it was a small chance to repay the friendship of a great and good man; and A. P. Giannini never forgot it.

One of the pleasant privileges of being a banker in the 1920's was to have one's name on legal tender. The banks in those days issued currency, and the officers signed it. In 1926 the Commercial National Bank issued four hundred $10 and $20 bills, bearing my signature. As they were unusual and made good conversation pieces, I bought and kept a number of them—until one day Mrs. deMille needed some shopping money, and she knew where I kept the little oblong green emblems of my vanity. I have one now, which stays in the wallet that I always keep on my person.

I have not been active in banking for many years, except as a depositor and, on occasion, a borrower; but I like to think that the space my desk occupied in the Commercial National Bank was

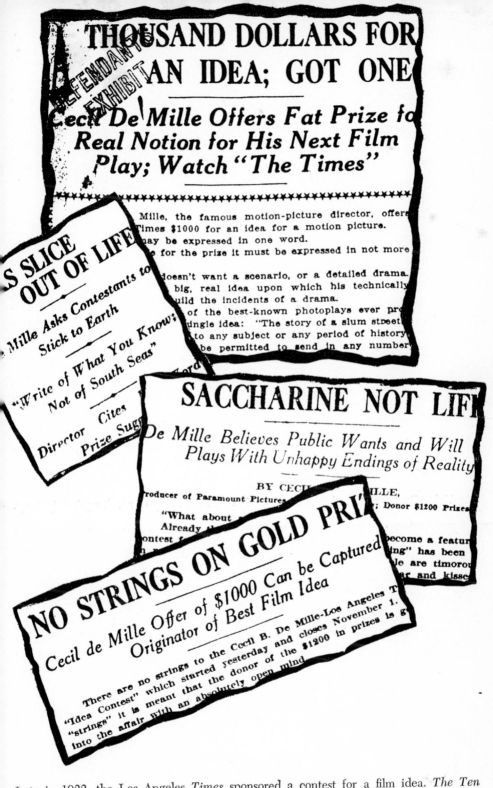

Late in 1922, the Los Angeles *Times* sponsored a contest for a film idea. *The Ten Commandments* produced the following year was the result.

Theodore Roberts as Moses can be seen high above the crowd in orgy from the prologue of the 1923 production of *The Ten Commandments*.

The Volga Boatman starred William Boyd in this 1926 study of revolt against tyranny.

The King of Kings (1927).

H. B. Warner's reverent and memorable portrayal in *The King of Kings*.

David Wark Griffith was the teacher of us all.

In Russia: with Mrs. deMille outside the home of Tolstoy.

On our Russian trip in 1931 the Military Police were usually nearby as here before the Opera House, Moscow.

Like the mountain retreat, Paradise, the *Seaward* provided a welcome respite from production pressures. It was turned over to the U. S. Navy during World War II.

Reginald Denny and Roland Young in *Madam Satan* with Kay Johnson in the title role.

Charles Laughton's Nero dominating a scene of Roman opulence in *The Sign of the Cross* (1932).

A radiantly beautiful Loretta Young matched Henry Wilcoxon's virile Richard the Lion Heart in *The Crusades*, which was as popular in the Moslem world as in America and Europe.

The Plainsman with Helen Burgess, James Ellison and Edgar Deering supporting Jean Arthur and Gary Cooper began in 1937 a series of pictures presenting important epochs in American history.

The 1939 production of *Union Pacific* climaxed by a painstaking recreation of the Golden Spike ceremony.

Not the least important of my awards was this "Golden Ear of Corn"
presented by my grandson, Jody Harper, on behalf of the National
Association of Popcorn Manufacturers—though the idea could have
originated with a number of critics.

Ray Milland, Paulette Goddard and John Wayne were our stars in *Reap the Wild Wind* (1942).

The giant squid contributed to the outstanding box office success of *Reap the Wild Wind*.

Lt. Clement B. Asbury on "Bill of Rights" Day in 1945 after my address from the steps of the Sub-Treasury Building in New York. With me is Barney Balaban, President of Paramount. I have never forgotten that quiet demonstration of his friendship when he came to stand beside me when friends were few.

With Frank Freeman, Neil McCarthy, Adolph Zukor, and Louis B. Mayer, March, 1952.

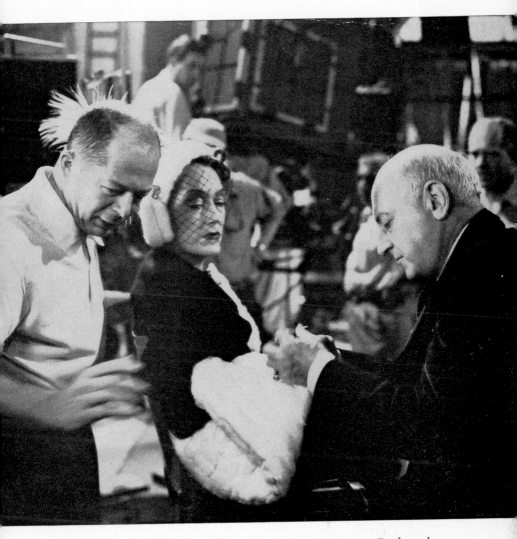

Billy Wilder directing Gloria Swanson and me in *Sunset Boulevard*, 1949.

A case of the picture being worth
a thousand words. Dan Groesbeck's
sketch for *Samson and Delilah*.

Hedy Lamarr as Delilah with Victor Mature as the blind Samson.

Words cannot adequately describe the loyalty of Gladys
Rosson, my secretary for 39
years; shown here during
filming of *The Greatest Show
On Earth* in 1951.

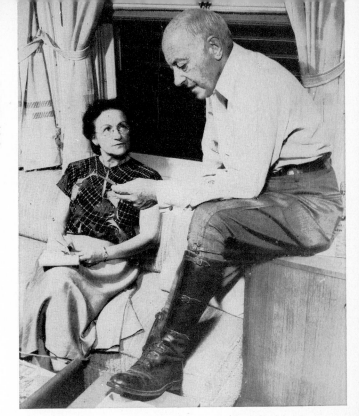

Viewing a featured performer on location for *The Greatest Show On
Earth* at Appleton, Wisconsin.

California Registered Landmark No. 554. Our barn where *The Squaw Man* was made in 1913 now stands at Paramount. With minor alterations it has been used in many pictures. Sam Goldwyn, Jesse Lasky, Adolph Zukor, Leo Carillo, and Frank Freeman at the dedication.

An Academy Award Oscar in 1953 for *The Greatest Show On Earth,* and the Thalberg Memorial Award, a highly prized recognition from the motion picture industry . . . presented by my good friend the perennially popular Bob Hope.

An exception to the rule of no shooting at my ranch is this picture by Yul Brynner.

My office at 2010 DeMille Drive.

not altogether wasted and that the policy I established with the Goldwyn loan has been of benefit both to motion pictures and to banking.

3

It is an interesting pastime to speculate on the pictures that might have been made but were not. One I suggested to Jesse Lasky in 1922 was a production of *Romeo and Juliet* with Rudolph Valentino as Romeo, Leatrice Joy as Juliet, Wallace Reid as Mercutio, Theodore Kosloff as Tybalt, Conrad Nagel as Paris, and Theodore Roberts as Capulet. Jesse's telegram in reply was a frantic veto, and he wrote me the same day that if necessary, he "would jump on a train and come across the continent and try and lock you up rather than let you make such a terrible mistake." Jesse was right; the public had to wait for Sir Laurence Olivier before being ready for Shakespeare on the screen.

Jesse was also right about another film, which was made, but about which I wrote him that "it is a very stupid, uninteresting picture, with not a moment of reality, and it bores one throughout. . . . There are some of the most beautiful shots of Arabs riding that I have ever seen, but I saw so many Arabs riding for so long that I would take little naps and wake up to find them still riding." I offered to bet Jesse $50 that the picture would be a failure. He did not take the bet; but the public agreed with him rather than with me about *The Sheik.*

There was complete agreement between us on the subject of my first picture of 1922, however. Jesse was even able to get the executive committee in New York to increase my budget for *Manslaughter,* written by Jeanie Macpherson from Alice Duer Miller's novel about an irresponsible, speed-crazy girl sent to prison by a district attorney who loved her. Leatrice Joy and Thomas Meighan played those two leading roles.

To get the authentic prison atmosphere into her script, Jeanie Macpherson went to Detroit, stole a fur piece by prearrangement from a friend of hers, was arrested with the goods on her, and sent to jail. Apart from Jeanie's obliging friend, the only person in Detroit who knew the circumstances was one police official. Fortunately he was around when Jeanie came to the conclusion that

247

three days in the Detroit lockup had given her all the atmosphere she needed.

A willingness to risk an incomparably greater sacrifice for the success of the picture was shown by a stunt man named Leo Noemus. In naming him, I salute all the stunt men who have risked life and limb in my pictures. I cannot say that all the players I have ever known deserved medals for courage; but Leo Noemus was certainly one of bravest. His job in *Manslaughter* was to ride a motorcycle when it was hit at high speed by a powerful roadster driven by Leatrice Joy. There was no fake photography about it: he had to be hit and thrown. Immediately before the shot, he called me over to him. All he said was, "If anything happens, remember my wife," and all I said, all one could or needed to say to a man of such calm courage, was, "She'll be all right." With that, he made the scene, and came out of it undamaged.

Manslaughter was a success with everyone who saw it, I believe, except for one lady who marched up to the box office and demanded her money back. The exhibitor, surprised at this reaction to a picture which was playing well, asked the lady why. "False pretenses, that's why," she said. "You advertise a picture called 'Man's Laughter,' and I certainly didn't find anything to laugh at in this one!"

The 1920's were the era of, among other phenomena, the flapper. With her bobbed hair, her short skirts and rolled stockings, her preference for the athletic Charleston over the sedate waltz, she became as much an obsession to the pointers-with-alarm as Hollywood itself. I confess to an old-fashioned belief that bare legs belong in the boudoir or on the beach, not in a business office, and my taste in feminine beauty has never run toward mouths or fingernails that look as though they have been in an accident with an explosive catsup bottle; but I did feel that the flapper was a maligned and plucky little person. Youth always revolts; it would not be worth its salt if it didn't. For my second picture in 1922, therefore, I decided to come to the defense of the flapper with *Adam's Rib*, an original story by Jeanie Macpherson, in which a typical modern teen-ager, apparently as light in her head as on her toes, shows the courage, intelligence, and devotion needed to save her parents' marriage. The flashback to prehistoric times also

248

enabled her to show that bare legs, short skirts, and feminine resourcefulness were nothing new.

The critics unanimously deplored *Adam's Rib*. Since I make my
pictures for people rather than for critics, I had already decided
to let the people choose the subject of the film that would follow
this production.

4

At the time there was a young man named Barrett Kiesling
working in the studio publicity department, occasionally helping
my press representative, Al Wilkie. When Al Wilkie was transferred to another job, I appointed Barrett Kiesling to handle publicity for the DeMille unit and gave him his first assignment: to
get the idea for my next picture from the public, by means of a
contest. Kiesling took hold of this with the assurance and skill that
marked his next ten years with me as my press representative. He
arranged with *The Los Angeles Times* to sponsor the contest; the
Times assigned Hallett Abend as special editor for it. First prize,
for the best idea for a picture, was to be $1000, with lesser prizes
making up another $1000. Since this was the first time a producer
had invited the public to advise him in this manner, other papers
picked it up as a news story, and what began as a local contest
finally brought in many thousands of letters from almost everywhere in the world.

The letters came from men and women of every station, creed,
and trade. They ranged in subject matter from the most sacred to
the most profane, and in value from the most ridiculous to the
sublime. I was struck by the number that suggested a religious
theme; and there was one that, for both subject matter and power
of expression, kept surviving every winnowing process devised by
the editors and kept coming back again and again to my mind. It
was not from a professional writer. It was from a manufacturer of
lubricating oil in Lansing, Michigan. His name was F. C. Nelson,
and this is the beginning of the one page he wrote: "You cannot
break the Ten Commandments—they will break you."

Here was an idea, bigger than any I had attempted to put on
the screen. Here was a theme that stirred and challenged in me
the heritage of being Henry DeMille's son; a theme that bright-
ened memories of his reading the Bible aloud to us and teaching

249

his sons that the laws of God are not mere laws, but are the Law.

We found that seven other contestants had suggested the Ten Commandments as a theme. None of them had submitted a usable story, but I was so filled with the grandeur and value of the theme that I was sure a story would be found or made. Instead of dividing the first prize, as the contest rules provided, I awarded $1000 to each of the eight persons who had given me the subject and the title of my next picture: *The Ten Commandments.*

I do not know what the New York executives thought would be in the picture, for I did not know myself when I announced it, but Jesse Lasky wired me on November 11, 1922, "Have succeeded arousing considerable enthusiasm in minds of Zukor and Kent over Commandments idea." Sidney R. Kent was manager of sales; enthusiasm in that department was essential. When Jesse himself was enthusiastic, there was no better missionary for an idea. With that support from New York, I was much encouraged.

After considering the possibility of constructing *The Ten Commandments* as a series of episodes, each to be written by a different author, I decided against that. Few, if any, episodic pictures have ever succeeded: the audience's instinct is, rightly, for dramatic unity of construction. The only writer who worked with me on this film was Jeanie Macpherson.

When the names of the winners of the contest were published, one of them, Harry J. Bradt of Los Angeles, announced that he was turning his $1000 prize over to the Children's Hospital for the endowment of a bed to be known as The Ten Commandments bed. That generous act prompted a letter which I received not long afterward from a man who said that he was writing by lantern light "in a solitary bunk house" at Calabasas, California, suggesting that I follow the example of Mr. Bradt and turn over *The Ten Commandments* "with all its proceeds" to charity. I had to have Gladys Rosson reply, on December 2, 1922, that "Mr. DeMille is sorry to say that your suggestion really could not be carried out, as he expects to spend $1,000,000 on his production of *The Ten Commandments,* and it would ruin any firm in the world to give that amount away." The man in Calabasas had added a postscript to his laboriously written letter: "I am just wondering what is going to become of this scrap of paper is it going to be cast into the waste basket." I am wondering if that man is still alive and if he will ever know that I still have his letter and that, when I made the 1956 version of *The Ten Commandments*, I was then in a position to follow his suggestion and turn my share of its earnings over to an irrevocable trust for charitable, religious, and educational purposes.*

I am also wondering if the New York executives had any idea, in December, 1922, that I was expecting "to spend one million dollars" on *The Ten Commandments* (1923).** I made no secret of it, as Gladys Rosson's letter to our Calabasas correspondent shows; but events were to prove that New York's enthusiasm diminished as costs increased.

The Ten Commandments (1923), as we finally developed it, is a modern story with a Biblical prologue. The prologue, following the Book of Exodus, shows the liberation of the Hebrews from Egypt under the leadership of Moses, their trek across the desert to Sinai, and the giving of the Commandments. The modern story is of two brothers, one of whom keeps the Commandments while the other breaks them all and is in the end himself broken by his defiance of the Law. Retribution comes upon him not as a vengeful visitation of an arbitrary God: rather it grows inevitably out of his own acts, for the moral law is as much a part of the structure of the universe as the law of gravity. His mother is killed, for example, in the collapse of a church because he violated the Commandment, "Thou shalt not steal," by cheating when he built the church of faulty materials.

The cast included Theodore Roberts as Moses, Estelle Taylor as his sister Miriam, Charles de Roche as the Pharaoh Rameses, Julia Faye as the Pharaoh's wife, Terrence Moore as their first-born son, James Neill as Aaron, Lawson Butt, Clarence Burton, and Noble Johnson in other Biblical roles; and in the modern story Richard Dix and Rod La Rocque played the brothers, Edythe Chapman their mother, Leatrice Joy and Nita Naldi the feminine leads, with Robert Edeson, Charles Ogle, and Agnes Ayres in supporting parts.

When we were assembling the battery of cameramen needed for

---

* Mr. DeMille also made over to the same charitable trust all the proceeds of this autobiography. (*Ed.*)
** Where there is any possibility of confusion regarding the 1923 and 1956 versions of *The Ten Commandments* in Mr. DeMille's text, the respective year of release has been added in parentheses. (*Ed.*)

251

a picture of this size, the then relatively young Technicolor company approached me with a proposition both interesting and fair. For the big scenes of the Biblical prologue, would I let them set up a camera alongside mine, to shoot the scenes in color? If I liked the result, I could buy it. If I did not like it, the experiment would cost us nothing and they would give me the film to burn. I agreed, and Ray Rennahan, still one of Hollywood's best cameramen, was assigned to do the color photography. The resulting film was so good that his name should be listed with those of Bert Glennon, Edward Curtis, Peverell Marley, A. J. Stout, and J. F. Westerberg, who did the main black-and-white photography on *The Ten Commandments*. Pev Marley is another of the veterans who worked with me on both the 1923 and the 1956 versions of *The Ten Commandments*, as well as many of my other pictures.

The great scenes of the Exodus and the crossing of the Red Sea were shot on the sand dunes at Guadalupe, near Santa Maria, California. We set up a veritable tent city and compound for the 2500 people and 3000 animals engaged for these scenes. It seems unbelievable that the credits on the film list only one assistant director, Cullen B. Tate, as helping me with the direction of that mass of people, but "Hezzie" Tate was something of an army in himself; and in those days everyone did a little of everything. When not acting as the Pharaoh's wife, Julia Faye plied needles and pins, helping to design and make Estelle Taylor's costume. For my breakfast on several mornings I enjoyed fish caught in a near-by stream by Theodore Roberts before he donned his beard and costume to be Moses.

For one day, though, a good many of the people in our camp went hungry. We had brought from Los Angeles several hundred Orthodox Jews because we believed rightly that, both in appearance and in their deep feeling of the significance of the Exodus, they would give the best possible performance as the Children of Israel. But on the first fateful day the dinner provided by our commissary department consisted of ham. I sent posthaste to Los Angeles for people competent to set up a strictly kosher kitchen to take care of our Orthodox extra players from then on.

These Orthodox Jews were an example to all the rest of us, not only in their fidelity to their laws but in the way they played their parts. They *were* the Children of Israel. This was their Exodus,

252

their liberation. They needed no direction from me to let their voices rise in ancient song and their wonderfully expressive faces shine with the holy light of freedom as they followed Moses toward the Promised Land.

If, a thousand years from now, archaeologists happen to dig beneath the sands of Guadalupe, I hope that they will not rush into print with the amazing news that Egyptian civilization, far from being confined to the valley of the Nile, extended all the way to the Pacific Coast of North America. The sphinxes they will find were buried there when we had finished with them and dismantled our huge set of the gates of Pharaoh's city. Pharaoh almost had to get along without sphinxes, however. They were made in Los Angeles and transported by truck to Guadalupe; but no one had thought to measure the clearances of the bridges along the route. There were some anxious moments when our majestic and mysterious sphinxes were ignominiously halted by a bridge too low for them to pass under. No one lost his head, though, except the sphinxes, who were decapitated long enough to pass under the bridge and then had their heads restored for the remainder of their progress.

It is no reflection on those in charge of our transportation to say that that contretemps would not have occurred if Roy Burns had been managing the unit. But I did not meet Roy Burns until I arrived at the Guadalupe location. He was a waiter, assigned to my table. It did not take more than a day to convince me that he was capable of bigger jobs. What convinced me was the perfect way he did the job he had. I never had to ask him for anything. He always anticipated me: as soon as I thought of anything I wanted, Roy was putting it in front of me. After the location, I brought him back to Hollywood as a property man. He stayed with me for 29 years, holding finally the responsible job of production manager, keeping a sentimental and loyal heart under a gruff, tough exterior, still knowing and anticipating whatever I wanted done, and seeing that it was done. He rode herd on everyone including me, until ill health forced him to retire from my staff after *The Greatest Show on Earth.*

The Ten Commandments owed much to another Roy, Roy Pomeroy of the special effects department. I hope it is not irreverent to say that the waters of the Red Sea had been parted only once before in history, and that when I gave Roy Pomeroy the assignment of doing it again, I was almost literally asking for a miracle. But it was done. I do not intend to tell exactly how it was done, in either version of *The Ten Commandments*. A full description, such as the confidential one that was filed with the Academy of Motion Picture Arts and Sciences after *The Ten Commandments* (1956), would be too long and technical, and anything less would not do justice to the marvelous ingenuity of the men who made possible the impressive spectacle—for once I will use that word because it is the only right one—of the mighty waters parting and standing in boiling walls as the Children of Israel passed over, then coming together again to destroy the Pharaoh's pursuing army.

And there is another reason why I think that some of the work of the special effects department should be kept confidential. It is the same reason why a lover, writing a sonnet to his beloved, does not go into the details of digestion and circulation which give her the rose-petal skin whose loveliness prompts his pen to song. Like every other part of a motion picture production, the special effects are subordinate and contributory to the story. Their value depends strictly upon the impression they give of reality. To many minds, especially those of a cynical turn, that impression is destroyed, and the all-important story values weakened, if too much of the inner workings of production are revealed. The best answer to some questions about special effects is the one given by a quick-witted member of my staff when a college student asked us to settle an argument among his classmates: did Gary Cooper and Paulette Goddard, in our production of *Unconquered*, really go over a real waterfall in a canoe? He replied, in effect: "We are gratified by your interest in this question. The answer is: your eyes did not deceive you."

I may say, however, that the crossing of the Red Sea did require the construction of certain posts and wires along the seashore at Guadalupe, to serve as guidelines for the Israelites so that their line of march would not stray outside the area which the special effects department needed to have circumscribed for its later work. In order that these fences would not cast shadows where they would be seen on the film, the scene had to be shot precisely at high noon. At 11:45, I was on an elevated platform with one of

254

the cameras, the Children of Israel were massed and expectant at their starting point, the Orthodox Jews among them in an exalted state of fervent emotion, the musicians were tuned and ready to begin the "Largo" from the *New World Symphony* for mood music to accompany the surge of liberated humanity into the hands of God. Everyone was keyed to his highest pitch. It was one of those moments that gives a director his greatest thrill of creative power and achievement—and his greatest anxiety lest one slip on his part, one second of inattention or indecision, cause him to lose his grip on the whole situation and weaken the invisible bond that exists between his will and every single one of the thousands of individuals in the scene.

And then I noticed that the sand over which the Israelites were to march looked exactly like what it was, a strip of sand along the seashore, not the bottom of a sea.

Second by second, the sun was approaching its zenith. Once it passed the meridian, the scene, the day, would have been ruined. I called out an offer of a reward, I forget whether it was $100 or $500, to anyone who could come up with an idea of how to save the scene; but in the agonizing silence no one spoke. Then, looking out at the ocean, only a few hundred feet away, I saw a bed of kelp floating near the shore. That was it! Calling out for everyone to follow me, I was off the platform and wading into the surf, coming back with armfuls of kelp to strew between the lines of posts, whose shadows were growing shorter and shorter.

From Theodore Roberts to the latest and lowliest of the production crew, there was a wild rush into the ocean by everyone on the location. Stars, cameramen, musicians, the thousands of extras, everyone plunged in to bring back and spread the kelp. In less than ten minutes the long path between the fences looked as it should, as the bottom of a sea would look if the water were suddenly lifted up in walls on either side. Back on the platform, I blew the whistle that signaled "Action!" The musicians began those first three familiar, haunting notes of Dvořák's "Largo." The first of the Children of Israel moved forward, their faces lifted, tears streaming down their cheeks. I looked at my watch and at the sun. It was exactly noon.

The other big location scene, the pursuit of the Israelites by Pharaoh's chariots, was shot at Muroc Dry Lake, now a testing ground for our country's faster chariots of the sky. For this we had two groups of expert horsemen, cowboys with motion picture experience from Hollywood and a contingent of artillerymen from the regular army, lent us by their commanding general in San Francisco. They mixed rather less amicably than oil and water. I confess that my sympathies were with the soldiers, especially after a delegation of the Hollywood cowboys came to me to protest that it was too dangerous for them to drive down a fairly steep hill where I wanted to get a shot of them descending into the Red Sea. While they were protesting, my teen-age daughter Cecilia happened to ride over the brow of the hill in question. I called out to her, "Ciddy! Come here," and without a second's hesitation she galloped down the hill in full sight of the fearful cowpunchers. That shamed them into making the scene I wanted, but they were more terrified of the artillerymen than they were of me or my daughter.

They had reason. The tough army men held the Hollywood horsemen in supreme contempt, and they planned to show their superiority in the biggest scene of the chariot charge. Word got around that the artillerymen intended to ride down the Hollywood cowboys more thoroughly than the ancient Egyptians would have ridden down the Israelites if they had overtaken them. That word did not reach me, however, until the scene was being shot and I saw that a good many of the chariots with drivers from Hollywood did not come into it at all. Literally scared stiff, they refused to get into the melee with the artillerymen and neither pleas nor objurgations from the capable Hosea Steelman, who handled the "horse stuff" in many of my pictures, could move them. No Pharaoh ever used stronger language than they heard from me after the scene was over, but they preferred being verbally skinned alive to what they feared the cannoneers would do to them at close quarters.

5

It was not the mounts of the timid cowpunchers, however, but two other horses which brought production of *The Ten Commandments* to a sudden, grinding halt halfway through. As I have said, actors and audiences alike instinctively react to real quality in the properties used in a film. With that in mind, I had sent

Hosea Steelman to Missouri to buy the two finest horses he could find to draw the Pharaoh's chariot. He came back with two of the most magnificent animals I have ever seen, coal-black, perfectly matched, entirely fit for the chariot of the god-king of Egypt. He paid $2,500 for them.

A month before we had even started shooting, Mr. Zukor had wired Jesse Lasky, on one of Jesse's visits to the studio, "I am very much concerned over Cecil DeMille's *The Ten Commandments* as I note the cost already scheduled so far runs over seven hundred thousand. This is a big sum to undertake to put into a picture without being absolutely sure in advance that it will be a success." Mr. Zukor had a point. It was a big sum, and he had to explain big sums to the bankers. Jesse tried to reassure him, and I wired him, "I fully realize the responsibility of the enormous sum of money I am spending. . . . and as an evidence of my appreciation and of my faith in this picture, I hereby waive the guarantee under my contract on this picture, other than the regular weekly payments. . . . I believe it will be the biggest picture ever made, not only from the standpoint of spectacle but from the standpoint of humanness, dramatic power, and the great good it will do." Mr. Zukor replied that he was "very pleased . . . appreciate your expression regarding guarantee . . . you have our co-operation one hundred percent."

But when the costs mounted to $800,000, to $900,000, to $1,000,-000, uneasiness returned to the New York office. The bill for the Pharaoh's two black horses was the proverbial straw. Horses could be had in Hollywood for a couple of hundred dollars; and I had pany's secretary, Elek J. Ludvigh, a good, practical lawyer whom paid ten times that for a pair. The principal objector was the com-Mr. Zukor trusted and who convinced him that this wild and irresponsible director three thousand miles away was ruining the company. Jesse Lasky was torn between his affection for me and what he conceived to be the interests of the company and his New York associates, toward whom he believed and honestly told me he thought my attitude was unreasonable and unjust. Mr. Ludvigh was despatched to California, his normally stern-looking face set in sterner lines and his dark Napoleon beard bristling, to put a curb on my extravagance. I sent Neil McCarthy to New York to counteract, if possible, the influences working on Mr. Zukor—and perhaps to convince him that they were really a very fine pair of horses.

Neil reported to me that Mr. Zukor was beyond any convincing from us. The bankers were eying him as coldly as only bankers can. He wanted nothing but some way out of the disaster into which he was certain I was plunging the company.

"Very well," I said to Neil. "Ask him if he will sell me the picture for one million dollars."

I did not have $1,000,000, or even what present-day television commercials would call a low, low down payment on such a sum. But I had faith in *The Ten Commandments,* and confidence that with it I could raise the money and pay it back.

Neil hurried back to California to help me raise it. Joseph M. Schenk and Jules Brulatour, who knew motion pictures and knew me, each promised $250,000. Then Neil went to see A. P. Giannini.

Not unnaturally, Mr. Giannini asked for a financial statement of Cecil B. DeMille Productions and time to consider it.

"There is no time," Neil told him. "Mr. deMille needs a half million dollars today to close the deal and go on with the production."

"You say it's a good picture?"

"It's good."

"He can have the loan."

The speed with which we had raised the $1,000,000 surprised New York even more than it surprised us. But Mr. Zukor had made a deal, orally and tentatively at least, and he would have gone through with it, I believe, if one of the company's top Hollywood executives, Frank Garbutt, had not said a word of caution over the long distance telephone, "Don't sell what you haven't seen." With the knowledge that there was $1,000,000 in cash ready to buy *The Ten Commandments,* Mr. Zukor was able to appease the bankers. I had no wish to insist upon closing a deal which would have meant rupture with the Famous Players-Lasky company. Production went on under the same banner. Its final cost was $1,475,836.93. Its gross receipts were $4,168,798.38.

But such a strain had been placed upon a business relationship that it would not stand the next major crisis.

258

6

The really important question to ask about a motion picture is not "What did it cost?", but "What is it worth?"; and the real worth of a picture cannot be measured in money alone. As soon as *The Ten Commandments* was completed, I screened it for Jesse Lasky and Sid Kent. The next day Kent wired Mr. Zukor: "We could not wire you before because we were unable to put our real feelings into such words as would express what we felt. *The Ten Commandments* is not a motion picture. It is bigger than all the motion pictures that have been made. . . . it plays on the emotion in a manner that I have never felt or witnessed before. . . . it will compensate you for all the agony you went through this summer . . . and will do more good than all the combined pulpits of the country. . . . If you didn't make a dollar out of it I still know you wouldn't exchange it for anything else that you have had in your business life. . . ."

I had had my own share of agony that summer. But there is a Lutheran pastor in California and a Benedictine nun in Minnesota who attribute their vocations to having seen *The Ten Commandments* more than 30 years ago, and they are only two among many, in all walks of life, who testified that to them this film had been not a moving picture, but an experience that moved their souls. That is what a picture can be worth; and that is why some pictures are worth making, whatever they cost—including the agony that they always cost.

Adolph Zukor was and is a man who understands that. After he saw *The Ten Commandments*, there was nothing he would not do to give it the finest possible presentation. We opened it at Sid Grauman's Egyptian Theatre in Hollywood on December 4, 1923, and at the George M. Cohan Theatre in New York on December 21. I still have and treasure the sincerely eloquent telegrams sent me by Mr. Zukor, Jesse Lasky, and Sid Kent; and at the New York opening, Elek Ludvigh said to me that the $2500 horses were the best single thing in the picture!

But perhaps the most touching message was the telegram I received on Christmas Eve, 1923: "I congratulate you, dear Cecil, on your wonderful achievement in *The Ten Commandments*. I'm proud of the little boy I used to bring candy to at Echo Lake, whose father was one of the most brilliant men that ever lived and

259

the sweetness of whose mother I shall never forget. The DeMille family are all tucked away in my heart. A Merry Christmas to you and your dear ones. David Belasco."

There was a sweet little old lady in Alabama who liked *The Ten Commandments* too, so much so that she decided to claim the authorship of it and sue me for plagiarism. Charges of plagiarism against motion picture companies were so common in those days that it would be boring to list all those that were leveled against me, but this one was the most interesting and the one that came nearest to succeeding.

The little old lady claimed that in 1918 she had sent Famous Players-Lasky a synopsis of a story based on the Ten Commandments, which I had brazenly used five years later without giving her either credit or payment. She displayed to the court her copy of the synopsis. Beyond question, it was the story that I had used. Sympathy for the alleged victim of a rapacious Yankee movie company ran high in the South; I have heard that at one showing of the film the dear little lady stood at the door of the theater graciously accepting congratulations on her masterpiece.

But there was one bit of phrasing in her synopsis which kept striking a false but familiar note in my mind every time I read it. It was a small error, a matter of one or two words out of place. I was sure that I had seen it somewhere else, though of course I had never seen the lady's synopsis before. Then I or someone remembered: the same error had appeared in a lengthy synopsis-review of *The Ten Commandments* written by Hallett Abend of the Los Angeles *Times* before the picture was released. Barrett Kiesling remembered that Hallett Abend had been a little annoyed by having to see the picture in a totally darkened theater instead of in a projection room where he might have had a small light to make his notes; and the tiny error written in the dark had crept into his copy, which we had used in a very limited edition before getting out our final synopsis for publicity purposes. Somehow the little old lady had got her hands on the Abend review and laboriously copied it out as her prime exhibit.

A call to the *Times* brought the disheartening news that, with the trial in progress or about to begin, Hallett Abend was on a hunting trip in mountain country so inaccessible that it would have taken days on horseback to reach him. An airplane was sent for him, however, and he was rushed to Atlanta in time to take the stand. It was a strong point for our side, but still not absolutely conclusive: it was conceivable that we might have made the lady's 1918 synopsis available to Hallett Abend to refresh his memory of what he saw in the dark theater.

The clinching point in our case was the result of some brilliant detective work by Neil McCarthy. He had the sweet little lady's copy of the synopsis examined by paper experts, who reported themselves ready to swear that the paper it was written on could not have been in the United States in 1918, because it was manufactured by a German process and was not available in this country until some time after the end of World War I. With that the lady's case collapsed.

When amateur writers today send manuscripts to motion picture studios and promptly get them back unopened, accompanied by a letter from the legal department which the hopeful authors must think cold and heartless, they should remember the sweet little lady in Alabama and the hundreds of others who have tried to get a share of wealth and glory by charging the studios with plagiarism. Some of the charges are probably sincerely made: it is entirely possible for two authors, thousands of miles apart, to think of the same dramatic situation or to write a story about a character named Bill Swivens. (If there is anywhere in the world a real person named Bill Swivens, I hasten to assure him that I have never heard of him!) Other charges of plagiarism are made with the calculated hope that, however farfetched the charge may be, the producing company will settle the case with a money grant in order to avoid the bother and expense of defending the suit in court. This is simply a refined form of blackmail. To protect themselves against both these forms of harassment, the major studios have all adopted the rule of never reading an unsolicited manuscript unless it comes from an established author or through a recognized literary agent.

I have had to hurt the feelings of good people in countless cities throughout the world when they have sent or brought or tried to telephone to me stories which they are sure would make colossal movies and I have refused even to touch the manuscript or continue the conversation; but I am as much bound by the studio rule as the boys in the mail room. Its purpose is not to quash budding

261

talent, but to protect ourselves from sweet little old ladies with an eye for loot. Budding talent will bloom if it is real talent. The route for it to take is through publication: if a story is good enough to get printed in a national magazine or in book form by a well-known publisher, it will be read by the story department of every studio and if it is suitable for the type of film a studio wants to make at that time, it will be bought on fair terms. There is no shortcut.

The same rule protects others as well as the motion picture companies. Within the past year or two, another good lady did manage to get through to me in a letter a synopsis of a story written, she said, by her fine old father who had had this inspiration and written it down but circulated it only among a relatively few chosen friends. Now his daughter was giving me the opportunity to give it to the world on the screen. I replied that it was a very good story indeed, that I had thought so ever since Henry Van Dyke wrote and published it nearly 60 years ago.

7

The three pictures I made after *The Ten Commandments* (1923) need not detain us long. They were comparatively low-budget modern stories, according to the understanding I had with the company that between the big stories I wanted to make I would produce smaller commercial pictures for a lower financial outlay and, it was hoped, quicker returns.

Triumph, with Leatrice Joy and Rod La Rocque in the leads, brought to the screen a Hungarian actor who in many of my later films fulfilled the promise I saw in him, Victor Varconi; and there was a small part in it for a young girl who was beginning to show her great gift for comedy with a wistful appeal all her own, ZaSu Pitts.

Feet of Clay was a somewhat more ambitious production, with its plot resolved by a sequence in which Rod La Rocque and Vera Reynolds are shown being turned back from the shadowy borderland of Eternity to finish and rectify their prematurely ended lives on earth. Again Roy Pomeroy managed the technical effects skillfully, on sets designed by Norman Bel Geddes.

My last film in 1924 was *The Golden Bed*, in which a veteran and a comparative newcomer to films gave characteristically good portrayals, Henry B. Walthall as the head of an aristocratic but impoverished southern family and Warner Baxter as a highly-polished ne'er-do-well. The big scene was the candy ball, in which the whole set was constructed and decorated with candy and Theodore Kosloff staged a ballet with the dancers dressed as different kinds of candy or wearing costumes made of actual candy. As always with such scenes in my pictures, the candy ball was put in to make an important story point: it was a wife's glittering revenge on the lofty matrons of the town who snubbed her for marrying a candy manufacturer, and it was so costly that it broke her husband and sent him to prison.

When I was making *The Greatest Show on Earth* in 1951, a mature and dignified woman walked up to me on the set and, if any bystanders heard her introduce herself, I can only hope that they supplied the capital letters and quotation marks which spoken English cannot express, for what they and I heard was the lady saying, "Mr. deMille, you probably don't remember me, but I was a harlot in your golden bed."

All through 1924, discussions and negotiations went on about the subject of my next big picture. One I wanted very much to make, and still do, was a story around the theme of unity, the unity of all mankind and the unity of man with nature and with God. I have never yet found a suitable story that would adequately portray this theme, but in my search for it I have had some disappointments that were not without their lighter aspects. In April, 1924, I spent many hours discussing this theme with a certain author, but, after he went away from the conference and returned with his ideas written down on paper, I had to report to Jesse Lasky: "He still seems to have no other idea than the Life of Lincoln, plus a gathering in Heaven in walls of gold of Moses, Buddha, Christ, Mohammed and Lincoln. What happens at this celestial meeting, he does not state."

There were, however, some very earthly meetings going on that year, in which a prophet might have discerned the forecast shadows of some coming events. In July, D. W. Griffith left United Artists and signed with Paramount for three films. In early November, there was no DeMille picture listed in Paramount's semi-annual announcement of forthcoming productions; that, however, may be explained by the fact that negotiations to buy Marie

263

Corelli's *Sorrows of Satan* for me were not quite completed the week the announcement was made. On November 18, Thomas H. Ince's attorney approached me privately with the information that the Ince Studio in Culver City was too large for their company and could be purchased reasonably. At 5:30 the following morning, Tom Ince died with shocking suddenness. I immediately wired Jesse Lasky in code about my conversation with the attorney, "for such action as you may deem advisable although it seems a little brutal to mention it at this time." Jesse asked for further information, but, as events turned out, Famous Players-Lasky did not buy the Ince Studio, which was left in and on Mrs. Ince's hands until another buyer was ready to take it.

I made plans to sail for Europe soon after New Year's Day, to begin work there on *The Sorrows of Satan*. On December 2, Mr. Zukor asked Jesse to open discussions with me relative to a possible readjustment of my contract, substituting as my share from my pictures 50 per cent of the profit, if any, instead of the existing sliding scale of percentages based on the gross receipts, and suggesting what I regarded as severe and unwise restrictions on my keeping competent players under contract and an efficient production staff together between pictures. That this was in the nature of an ultimatum was made clear when Sidney Kent wired me from New York on December 18: "It is not your advance we object to as much as the added expense caused by your separate unit from which we feel you get no return commensurate with the expense it costs us. Mr. Zukor feels that this must be taken off our backs. . . . Zukor's letter must be the general basis upon which we meet. . . . Appreciate position you placed in by sailing without definite plans . . . but if you would not be interested in any proposal after you reached here, very likely you would not desire sail anyway. Kindest and best regards."

All these strands were coming together when Mrs. deMille, Jeanie Macpherson and her mother, Julia Faye and her mother, Mitch Leisen, Pev Marley, and I took the train from Los Angeles at the end of December, on our way to Europe.

We did not sail. After meeting with Mr. Zukor, Jesse Lasky, and Sid Kent, I began the year of 1925 as one of the unemployed. I will not burden the reader with a detailed account of the proposals and counter-proposals upon which we could not agree. There is no

264

doubt in my mind that those three gentlemen believed they were acting in fairness to the company and to me, as firmly as I believed that the only way I could make good pictures was the way I had been making them. But my long life has had few bitterer moments than when one of those gentlemen said to me, and the other two heard it in unprotesting silence: "Cecil, you have never been one of us."

There was a little sequel to these events, of which I kept some small brown souvenirs in a bowl at Paradise until an autumn evening in 1952, when I finally put the last of them in the fire. One of the New York executives had been quite ill, and during his convalescence I invited him to come out and spend a month on the *Seaward* and at Paradise, fishing and resting, regaining his strength. When he was ready to go back to New York, he said to me, "C. B., I wish there was some way I could repay you for the wonderful time you have given me, but what can anyone do for you? You have everything. But is there anything in the world I could do for you?"

"Yes," I said, "there is. When I was a little boy in New York, there used to be Italian chestnut vendors on the street corners in the wintertime. The chestnuts cost a nickel a bag. They roasted them right there and sold them hot out of the roaster, and you'd hold the bag to keep your hands warm while you ate the chestnuts. I haven't had any in years. Will you send me some?"

He was delighted. "C. B., you'll have the biggest bag of the finest chestnuts in the world."

They came, and they were fine.

Then in the early part of 1925, I had to spend several weeks in New York arranging to get out of the ranks of the unemployed. When I returned to Hollywood, I asked Gladys Rosson how things had been going in my absence.

"Everything very well," she said, "except for one thing that came in, that I don't understand."

"What was that?"

"This," Gladys said, handing me a piece of paper, "— this bill that came to you, for chestnuts."

12

". . . A man by the name of Milbank in New York and this is his first venture in the picture business."

The vagueness of that phrase, in a report made to me by John Fisher on the availability and assets of the Ince Studio, was not surprising. Jeremiah Milbank is one of the most modest men alive; it was not until I knew him well personally that I came to know the quality of his mind and heart. There is a persistent myth that capitalists never think of anything but capital, except when they divert their minds by thinking of dividends. I have known a certain number of very rich men who were scamps, and a larger number who were just dullards; but two of the finest men I have ever known, with the largest minds and the highest ideals, were also men of great financial power. One of them is Jeremiah Milbank.

What John Fisher reported to me about him was that he had taken over a distribution contract which the Ince Company had had with W. W. Hodkinson. It is a commentary on the impermanence of fame and power that, less than ten years after W. W. Hodkinson had been dethroned from the pinnacle of Paramount, John Fisher spelled his name "Holkinson." What interested me most about the report, though, was that the man named Milbank had formed a new film distributing company, Producers Distribut-

266

ing Corporation, which would need pictures to distribute as much as I needed outlets for the pictures I hoped still to make.

After Famous Players-Lasky canceled my contract on January 9, 1925, and I canceled our sailing to Europe the next day, I stayed in New York but kept the telegraph wires to Hollywood crackling. Mrs. Ince agreed to sell the Ince Studio to Cecil B. DeMille Productions for $500,000. Then I invited Mr. Milbank to stop in at my hotel one evening on his way from his Wall Street office to his home uptown.

I told him of my situation, my plans and hopes; but it was not until I told him of what was still an impossible dream that he became interested enough to consider putting up the very large sum of money that I needed. Sometime, I told this practical man of business and finance, I wanted to make a film on the life of Christ. I wanted simply to take the four Gospels and tell the story of Jesus of Nazareth, as He appeared to those around Him, a figure no less human than divine, to tell that story in a way that might bring millions of people throughout the world to know Him better, might bring many to know Him for the first time. I spoke too about my other plans for other productions, but the only thing that moved Jeremiah Milbank to put his resources behind me was that first mention of *The King of Kings* and the good that it could do. That is the kind of man Jeremiah Milbank is.

In the mundane sphere beloved by corporation lawyers, the result of our meeting was the Cinema Corporation of America, organized as a holding company to own all the stock of Producers Distributing Corporation and all the stock of a new subsidiary called Cecil B. DeMille Pictures Corporation and to distribute not only my films but any others we could bring into the fold. The Cinema Corporation of America was owned in equal shares by Mr. Milbank's Realty and Securities Company and by me.

The voluminous documents, signed by the parties of the first, second, and several other parts, meant one thing to me: I had a place to work and financial backing to make the pictures I wanted to make. The Ince Studio was renamed the DeMille Studio. The Los Angeles branch of Producers Distributing Corporation mustered a crowd of 200 to meet me at my homecoming on February 27; a crowd ten times that size was gathered on the lawn in front of the studio when I went there the same day. Joseph Schenk, representing the producers' association, made an address of welcome, many of the Culver City merchants closed their stores for an hour in honor of the event, and I thought it was a particularly happy omen when a little girl of Oriental descent stepped forward to present me with an American flag. Altogether it was a homecoming very different from what it might have been.

It was a wrench, moving from the corner of Vine and Selma where the Lasky lot had grown up around Jacob Stern's old barn and turned an orange grove into the capital of an industrial empire; but Jesse lived up to what he referred to in one of his letters to me at the time as "the friendly spirit which you splendidly set forth . . . and which you may be sure I will do everything possible to maintain." My agreement to disagree with Famous Players-Lasky permitted me to take with me certain studio equipment and certain personnel, so I was surrounded in the new DeMille Studio with the familiar faces of good workmen, some of whom are still with me.

In fact, the first person I see now at the beginning of each business day has been with me since the days of the DeMille Studio. Every morning when Russel Treacy, now my business manager, walks over from his office at 2010 DeMille Drive to join me at my breakfast table in my home next door, bringing me the business news of the day and his good advice about it, we are adding another day to the association that began when he first came to the DeMille Studio as assistant to the business manager in 1926.

For my first picture made at the DeMille Studio, *The Road to Yesterday*, I engaged two players who had never worked with me, Joseph Schildkraut and Jetta Goudal. William Boyd played a virile young minister and Trixie Friganza a comical aunt whose constant talk about reincarnation laid the groundwork for an historical flashback showing the same characters in seventeenth century England. Vera Reynolds portrayed a very modern miss, and among her flapper friends, who were incredulously amused at the thought of her marrying a minister, was a pretty youngster who was later to receive more revealing fame, Sally Rand. That later fame, I fear, has given the public an extremely erroneous idea of Sally Rand. She is an intelligent and serious-minded person; I still hear from her occasionally, and her letters are always thoughtful and wise.

268

Joseph Schildkraut, bringing to the screen not only his striking good looks but the polished artistry acquired from his experience on the European stage, played in several of my later pictures. Jetta Goudal did not. She was a good actress, but our professional temperaments did not exactly blend. When she learned that I did not intend to use her services again, she sued me.

The judge considerately consented to hear the case in my office. He first questioned Miss Goudal. Was Mr. deMille a bad director, had he ever been violent or abusive toward the plaintiff? Oh, not at all. He was an excellent director and a perfect gentleman. The judge then turned to me. Miss Goudal now, was she in my opinion a competent actress? Oh, yes, one of the best. Did I just dislike her then? No, I did not dislike her at all. She was a fine person, and a particular friend of my daughter's. This was just a difference of opinion about some money due or not due. Jetta and I kept exchanging compliments and the judge kept getting more and more puzzled by such unusual litigants; but he finally decided in Jetta's favor. Perhaps the defendant had been too good a witness for the plaintiff. Incidentally, Jetta is still a good friend of Cecilia's. When Mrs. deMille and I celebrated our golden wedding in 1952, we had to limit the guests to a number our house could hold, but Jetta Goudal was one we particularly wanted to have with us.

I have never understood why professional or business differences need necessarily affect friendships. My continued good personal relations with Adolph Zukor and Jesse Lasky proved the point, for they felt the same way. If their attitude after our business break was unimpeachably correct, however, the same could not be said about some in lower echelons of their organization.

After the release of *The Road to Yesterday* as my first independent production, Famous Players-Lasky held one of its huge sales conventions to announce its coming product to the trade. Featured on the program was a short film about the company's activities, in which Ford Sterling acted as a master of ceremonies showing Marshall Neilan, in the garb of a returning prodigal son, all the wonderful things that the company was achieving and planning. In the course of their tour, they came to an empty chair marked "DeMille" and bearing a funeral wreath.

"What ever became of him?" Neilan asked.

Sterling answered, "Oh, he's gone down the road to yesterday."

One of the exhibitors in the audience, Al Harston, jumped up and cried, "That's too dirty! Take it out!" *Motion Picture Today,* an influential trade paper, editorialized: "What could be viler? Just imagine Sidney Kent and Adolph Zukor sanctioning and okaying a gratuitous insult like this to the one man who had made them and their organization possible."

Ten days later, Marshall Neilan had a letter in *Motion Picture Today,* taking full responsibility for "the sequence . . . conceived by myself and made by myself. . . . neither Mr. Zukor, Mr. Lasky nor Mr. Kent saw the trailer before it was shown at the convention"; but it was, said Neilan, "just clean kidding."

The kidding was less clean when an employee of the Lasky Studio took it upon himself to inform the federal authorities that I had been cheating on my income tax. The charge was false, of course, but it could have been an embarrassing nuisance if Jesse Lasky had not reacted with indignation and taken steps to set the matter straight.

Jesse's personal attitude toward me, after the dust of the business break had settled, could not be better shown than by the telegram he sent me in December, 1925: "They are celebrating the twelfth anniversary of the founding of the Lasky Company . . . tonight and have dedicated the evening to me. I don't feel very good about being put in the limelight and taking a lot of credit that properly belongs to you. You may be sure if I get a chance to talk that I won't forget you and will do my best to pay you the tribute you deserve. I don't know why I am wiring this except that when an occasion of this kind arises I miss your presence more than I can tell you. Best regards always. Jesse."

2

An electric bulb gave William Boyd his first starring role. Walking along Fifth Avenue in New York one day, I noticed in a shop window a cut-out sign advertising the Mazda lamp. It was a picture of a group of people, all with their heads bowed except one whose face was lifted toward the light. It reminded me of mankind's long struggle for freedom, led by the few who dared to raise their heads out of the shadows of oppression; and it gave me the idea for my next picture, *The Volga Boatman,* in which William Boyd played the peasant leader, Feodor. The title of the film came, of course, from the surging Russian song made popular in those days by the magnificent voice of Chaliapin.

If *The Volga Boatman* were made today, I would be anticipating a summons from the Un-American Activities Committee. In 1925, most of us were more naïve politically. Prohibition seemed a more burning political issue than Communism. Not that *The Volga Boatman* was communistic in either its inspiration or its effect; but we were still close enough in history to the tyranny of the Czars to look upon their overthrow with at least guarded optimism, and to the average American at that time Russian Communism had not yet been revealed as a tyranny far worse than that which it replaced.

The Volga Boatman gave good opportunities to Elinor Fair, Robert Edeson, Victor Varconi, and Theodore Kosloff, and to Julia Faye what was one of the best roles of her entire career, as Mariusha, a gypsy girl. Smaller parts were played by a number of exiled Russian princes and officers who had come to Hollywood—handsome men of aristocratic bearing. Theodore Kosloff told me that in the old Russia a prince was anyone who was head man of a small village; but the punctilious bowing and saluting that took place when the cast assembled on the set each day rivaled the ceremonious protocol of the vanished court of the Czar.

The critics, for once, almost unanimously liked *The Volga Boatman*. Robert E. Sherwood, writing in the old *Life* magazine, called it "the best picture that Cecil B. DeMille has made," with "visual beauty in abundance, and that strange vibrant strength that is evident in all the DeMille pictures." The New York *Telegram* spoke of the "nice Lubitschean direction of a naughty scene where sensual faces register the successive stages in a suggested undressing of a princess."

That scene caused a little difficulty with some censors. You must not, they said, show the undressing of the princess. But in fact we had not shown it. The story point of the scene is that the princess, protected from the revolutionaries by their leader, Feodor, is captured with him by the Imperial Army, whose commander gives his officers permission to "pay them in kind for what they do to our women" and only discovers, after the officers have begun to disport themselves with the princess, that she is in fact

271

his fiancee. The scene is focused on the faces of the officers: the princess is not seen at all. But the acting and, if I may modestly say so, the direction must have been so good that some censors apparently thought they had witnessed an actual disrobing.

I had a similar reaction when I screened *The Ten Commandments* (1956) for a large group of Methodist bishops. After the screening, the wife of one of the bishops said that she had liked the picture very much, except for the part in which she had seen a Hebrew slave struck with an ax by an Egyptian overseer. There is no such scene in the picture. The bishop's wife had seen the overseer hurl the ax. She had seen the slave fall mortally wounded. Her imagination had supplied the intervening shot, which of course we would not put on the screen. As I have said before, the audience is an integral part of the total experience of a film; and good acting and direction always leave something for the audience to contribute to that experience.

Two new co-workers joined me at this period, one destined to become one of the few people who are world-famous by their surnames alone, the other to be respected and beloved in the smaller world of Hollywood until his death in 1953. The first was a young man, still in his late 'teens then, whom I made it a point to meet after seeing the designs he made for the Music Box Revue in New York. I brought him to Hollywood and to the DeMille Studio. His first name is Gilbert, but he is better known by the phrase that appeared among the credits for *The Volga Boatman*, "Costumes by Adrian."

The other was Gordon Jennings, a big, athletic, but soft-spoken and almost diffident man, the best special effects expert I have ever been privileged to work with. A director could say to Gordon Jennings that he wanted a volcano to obliterate a city teeming with people or Niagara Falls to roll back and expose a dry cliff. A few weeks later Gordon would come around and say, "Well, you might as well come and look at this. I've spent a lot of money and it's probably not what you want, but, well, come and see it anyway"; and the effect would be so realistically perfect that the director himself could hardly believe it. One of the hardest assignments I have ever had was to pronounce the eulogy at Gordon Jennings' funeral, after he died suddenly on a golf course, in the open air he loved, on a bright California winter day. I doubted that I could finish what I had to say about him without breaking down, for he was one of those friends, rare enough in anyone's lifetime, whose passing leaves one's world somehow different and diminished.

In addition to the pictures I directed myself, the DeMille Studio produced many others, some of which I supervised. In 1926 my brother William terminated his contract with Famous Players-Lasky and joined our staff of directors.

Expansion was the order of the day. I can see now that it was overexpansion; I have already commented on my abilities or lack of them as an administrator. The business of Producers Distributing Corporation was managed by F. C. Munro and John C. Flinn in New York; but I was responsible for the Culver City studio. We merged with some other independent studios, under the general management of William Sistrom. We put up new buildings at the DeMille studio. We even put in a radio station so that I could keep in touch with the studio when I was sailing the coastal waters in the *Seaward*; and we also bought two clipper ships, the *Bohemia* and the *Indiana*, which were undoubtedly seaworthy when they were launched in 1875, but were probably not very realizable assets after they served their purpose for us in a picture.

The Producers Distributing Corporation acquired theaters in various parts of the country; and the Cinema Corporation of America consummated a deal with the B. F. Keith Corporation whereby, in exchange for Cinema stock, our pictures were assured of favorable release terms in the far-flung chain of Keith theaters. This also brought onto the Cinema Corporation's board of directors the patriarchal and powerful Edward F. Albee, head of the Keith company, and his doughty lieutenant, J. J. Murdock.

We were out to challenge the mighty majors, Famous Players-Lasky, First National, and Metro-Goldwyn-Mayer, which had lost Goldwyn but kept his name as it does to this day. In an advertisement in 30 leading newspapers in June, 1925, I had said: "I will back to the limit any movement to protect the independent producer and exhibitor from being crushed out of existence." But expansion of production, talent, and grounds and buildings, not to mention clipper ships, meant expansion of financing, too. Eventually the need of additional outside capital brought about a merger with—or I might better call it a submerging in—the Pathé Exchange, and brought again into the picture the bankers, in this case Blair & Company and the Chase National Bank.

Every motion picture producer who has had to depend upon outside capital has probably collided with the point of view, perfectly understandable but none the less vexing at times, that whoever pays the piper should have something to say about the tune. The fault in that proverb is that sometimes those who are paying the piper do not know very much about tunes, and might be better advised either to trust the piper or get themselves a new one.

So there were budget troubles again, on which in May, 1926, I expressed myself to F. C. Munro, president of Producers Distributing Corporation in words which I would have signed in 1913 and which I would sign today: "I can assure you no one is more interested in profits than I am but I have firm conviction there is only one way in which to get profits and that is by making good pictures. I have been through . . . years of this discussion without a losing year to my organization and with the policy of increasing the budget when I believed I had a big piece of property. There would have been no *Ten Commandments, Covered Wagon, Big Parade, Stella Dallas, Sea Beast, Behind the Front* and a dozen others I might name had a policy of sticking to a budget been adhered to when the producer saw he had a big subject and a big production in the making. In every instance the money expended on these pictures was a deliberately planned increase on account of the strength of the subject."

3

In approaching the one production which would have justified all the travails of the DeMille Studio even if we had done nothing else there, however, I had one asset of incalculable value: the confidence of the "man by the name of Milbank." To this day Jeremiah Milbank has not taken a penny of profit from *The King of Kings*: all his share in its continuing earnings goes to make and distribute new prints of it, principally for use by churches and missionaries.* It took me many years to get Jeremiah

* Mr. deMille's share of the earnings of *The King of Kings* has also been devoted entirely to charity. (*Ed.*)

274

Milbank's permission to reveal that, but I think I would have revealed it here even against his wish, for every one of the 800,000,000 people who have seen *The King of Kings* should know how much they owe to him.

Jeremiah Milbank's confidence was not shared by all the wise-acres in the motion picture industry, however. Every time I have proposed making a Biblical picture, there have been those who were certain that I was heading for disaster—and now I was proposing to put on the screen the figure of Christ Himself? The church people would be up in arms at the irreverence of the very idea. The people who were indifferent to religion would be monumentally indifferent to a picture in which, presumably, sanctimonious characters would walk around in long robes. So I was told.

There was some truth in it. I knew that there would be in the audience religious people fearful of how a subject dear and sacred to them would be treated, and people who were skeptics and had come to scoff, and people who were cynics and had come to witness deMille's disaster. I decided to jolt them all out of their preconceptions with an opening scene that none of them would be expecting: a lavish party in the luxurious home of a woman of Magdala, and that beautiful courtesan surrounded by the leering, sensual faces of her admirers who taunt her because one of their number, young Judas, has evidently found the company of some wandering carpenter more interesting than hers. When Mary Magdalene, goaded to jealous fury, calls for her chariot to take her to this Nazarene carpenter who has bewitched her favorite suitor, the people in the audience have forgotten their precon-ceptions: they want to see what happens when Mary, Judas, and the Carpenter meet.

But what they see is a crowd of poor people outside a fisher-man's house, and a curly-haired little boy hopping around telling everyone who will listen that the Man who is inside the house has healed his lameness, and he can walk and run and play. Then they see a little girl, blind, groping her way through the crowd. The boy, Mark, leads her to the house. The crowd is so thick that he has to lift her through the window: and she finds the other Mary, the Man's mother, who takes her to her son. Still we see only the child, lifting her sightless eyes, begging for light. Only

275

then appears a dim form, then gradually a face: and we see the Christ first through the eyes of the blind child.

There was only one man, I felt, who could portray the Christ, with all the virility and all the tenderness, with all the authority yet all the restraint, with all the compassion and all the strength, and with the touch of gentle humor and enjoyment of small simple things and human love of friends and divine love of His enemies, that the Man of Nazareth had. It was literally a superhuman assignment that I gave to the actor I chose for the part, H. B. Warner. How perfectly he fulfilled it has never been better told than by a minister who said to him many years later: "I saw you in *The King of Kings* when I was a child, and now, every time I speak of Jesus, it is your face I see."

H. B. Warner perfectly understood the conception of Christ that I wanted to portray. All my life I have wondered how many people have been turned away from Christianity by the effeminate, sanctimonious, machine-made Christs of second-rate so-called art, which used to be thought good enough for Sunday schools. This Man of Nazareth was a man, with a body hard enough to stand 40 days of fasting and long journeys on foot and nights of sleepless prayer, a man with a mind sharp as a razor and balanced as a precision scale, whose ranging thought measured the kingdoms of the world and their glory, yet noticed things like lilies of the field and how they grow or mother hens and how they keep their chicks warm under their wings, a man who had only compassion for those sinners for whom most men have only contempt, and who kept His anger and biting scorn only for hypocrites and those who made a racket of religion. There could well have been a note of admiration in the proud official voice of Pilate when he said of Him, "Behold the Man!"

That was the Man whom H. B. Warner portrayed to such perfection; and two incidents on the set stay vividly in my memory as indications of that fine actor's understanding of his role. One was the scene in which Christ drives the money-changers out of the Temple. The slightest trace of overacting would have ruined it. It was H. B. Warner who suggested to me how the scene should be played. He simply picked up a leather thong and wrapped one end of it around his hand, but with such authority that it was entirely believable when the money-changers fled in confusion from a Christ whose anger was the more terrible because so perfectly controlled.

The other scene was shot in the garden of my home in Laughlin Park, a scene in which a little girl, with childlike naturalness, comes to the Carpenter to have Him mend her broken doll. He took a twig from an olive tree, and healed the doll's broken leg with the same infinite tenderness that He healed broken bodies and broken hearts.

There is, in fact, not a single bad performance in *The King of Kings*. Dorothy Cumming as Mary the Mother, Jacqueline Logan as Mary Magdalene, Ernest Torrance as great, impetuous, fickle, loyal Peter, Joseph Striker as John, Joseph Schildkraut as Judas, his father Rudolph Schildkraut as Caiaphas, Victor Varconi as Pilate, Montagu Love as the Roman centurion, Josephine Norman and Julia Faye as Mary and Martha of Bethany, William Boyd as Simon of Cyrene, all the players down to little Mickey Moore as the boy Mark and Muriel MacCormac as the blind child, gave to their parts not only finished artistry but the understanding which made *The King of Kings* for them, as well as for the audience, more than a motion picture.

In making a picture on even so sublime a theme, however, there occur incidents not without a touch of the ridiculous, or at least the amusing. In 1926, I was already beginning the practice, which is invariable with me now, of having on my production staff one or more artists to make sketches of every scene, every shot, every costume, every important prop. The budget balancers may deem this an extravagance. Actually it makes for great saving of time, which in a production means money also, because it completely eliminates the misunderstandings which can arise when one depends upon words alone for the description of anything. If a director says he wants a fence on the set, one set decorator may have a mental image of a white picket fence, another of a redwood fence, another of a New England stone fence, and so on: if everybody can look at a sketch of the fence as the director wants it, the mental images, and the tempers of all concerned, will be in harmony. That explanation is by way of introducing one of the artists who worked with me on *The King of Kings* and many of my other pictures until his death—Dan Sayre Groesbeck. He was enthusiastic about the story of *The King of Kings* when I told it to him, so enthusiastic that he went straight to the research department and asked Bessie McGaffey if she could supply him with a synopsis of the four Gospels! Bessie rose to the occasion and turned out a summary of Matthew, Mark, Luke, and John, which I am sure will never be considered for inclusion in the canon of Scripture, but which satisfied Dan. It apparently did not occur to him to read the Gospels themselves: in the movie business, he must have thought, you never read anything if you can get it painlessly synopsized.

Dan Groesbeck's reluctance to read words, however, was more than compensated by his great gift for form and color. He always knew what I wanted and he could capture character and drama in a few strokes of his brush, while his finished drawings, like the marvelous series he made while traveling through China, are worthy of a museum.

While Dan Groesbeck, Anton Grot, Edward Jewel, Julian Harrison, and Harold Miles were turning out the large number of sketches we needed, and Adrian, Gwen Wakeling, and Earl Luick were designing the costumes for *The King of Kings*, Jeanie Macpherson and I worked on the script, with assistance from Denison Clift, Clifford Howard, and Jack Jungmeyer.* But we almost did not have a script when, after spending some days on the *Seaward* putting it in final form, I ordered the skipper to turn homeward, where the principal players and production heads were waiting for a first reading. Gladys Rosson had been typing the script on deck, and was sorting it, finished and neatly piled on her typing table—without a paperweight. When the *Seaward* changed course, the sea breeze was just right to lift the pages of the script and scatter them over the broad bosom of the Pacific Ocean. All hands were called to action stations, and we managed to retrieve the

* It takes nothing away from the work of Jeanie Macpherson and Mr. deMille's other good writers through the years to point out what Mr. deMille fails to mention: the amount of work he always did himself in the actual writing of his scripts, in most cases without taking screen credit for it. Going through the impressive collection of his original shooting scripts, one finds hardly a page without changes —which were improvements—made in Mr. deMille's handwriting; and in some places there is page after page in Mr. deMille's penciled hand, added to the typed script. This evidence is not so apparent in the neater typescripts of his more recent films; but for them it can be found in the voluminous notes of the story conferences in which Mr. deMille spent hours of each day with his writers while a script was in preparation. (*Ed.*)

soaked pages with harpoons and boat hooks and to dry them out in time for the reading.

Throughout the production of *The King of Kings,* we had the benefit of advice from Bruce Barton and his father, the Reverend William E. Barton, the Reverend George Reid Andrews of the Federal Council of Churches, and Father Daniel A. Lord, S.J. This was the beginning of my lifelong friendship with Bruce Barton and Father Lord. Bruce Barton went on to Congress, and his experience in those legislative halls prompted the advice which helped save me from embarking on a political career a decade later. Father Lord and I did not always see eye to eye on artistic matters, but I never lost my admiration and love for that devoted, manly, brilliant Jesuit, whose quality of soul was never better manifested than when he was dying of cancer and I ventured to ask him if, out of that soul-searching experience, he would write for the benefit of others a little statement that I could use in my work as an officer of the American Cancer Society. He complied, with the utterly calm courage which had its unfailing source not in this world.

One of my brightest memories of the making of *The King of Kings* is of Father Lord celebrating Mass in the open air soon after sunrise every morning while we were on location on Catalina Island. It was like a continued benediction on our work, which began on the first day of shooting with a short service of prayer participated in by representatives of the Protestant, Catholic, Jewish, Buddhist, and Moslem faiths.

I could wish that my memory of that opening service had not been marred by the disappointment expressed by some of those representatives of organized religion when they found that there was not a huge crowd in attendance. There were present only those directly concerned in the making of the picture. Remembering the red-bearded minister of my Pompton childhood, I did not think prayer needed an audience, but only the Presence promised to any two or three gathered together in His Name.

All through the production, every effort was made to maintain the spirit of reverence of the opening day. No one but the director spoke to H. B. Warner when he was in costume, unless it was absolutely necessary. He was veiled or transported in a closed car when he went between the set and his dressing room or, when we were on location, his tent, where he took his meals alone. Into the contract of every player were written clauses ensuring their exemplary conduct away from the studio as well as on the set. I doubt that those clauses were strictly needed in most cases, for the players were imbued with the spirit of what they were doing; but that some precaution was necessary was proved when H. B. Warner found himself followed from the studio to his home every evening by a mysterious automobile. Investigation revealed the occupants of the car to be men who were vainly hoping to catch the portrayer of the Christ in some indiscretion, for the purposes of some gutter journalism or blackmail.

One of the high moments in the making of *The King of Kings* was brought back to me only a few years ago when I had a telephone call from a small town in the deep South. A strong woman's voice at the other end of the wire said, "I am a preacher. I'd have nothing to do with the sin that you're in in Hollywood. I've never seen a moving picture and I never will. But someone told me that you made a picture called *The King of Kings* and that when you were making it, you let loose some doves and they went straight by themselves to fly around the Cross of the Saviour. I just want to hear from your lips whether that's true or not."

"Yes," I said. "It's true."

"That's all I wanted to know. Good-by."

It was true, and it was a moving experience to us who saw it.

But the highest moment of the production—perhaps the highest moment of my life—was on Christmas Eve, 1926.

We had just finished filming the scene of the Crucifixion. There were hundreds in the scene, the faithful little group of John and Mary and the other women at the foot of the Cross, the good and the bad thief, the Roman centurion and his hard-bitten legionaries, the scribes and Pharisees come to mock, the motley crowd come to gape at the spectacle of three men in their agony on three crosses on a little hill. They were actors and actresses and Hollywood extras, all kinds of men and women, some inspired by what they had seen and done that day, others to whom, like the Roman legionaries themselves, it was just another day's work. They were tired. They were anxious to get home to their families for Christmas Eve. But when the final "Cut!" was called and they started to drift or hurry toward the exits of the stage, I spoke to them.

280

"Just a minute, if you please, ladies and gentlemen," I said.

The straggling eddy of humanity halted, turned, and I could see plain on many faces the unspoken question, "What does the old fool want *now?*"

"It is Christmas Eve," I said, "the birthday of the Saviour, and we have just finished reproducing the scene of His death. I want you, if you will, to think about that for just five minutes. I am going to ask the organist to play. I am going to ask you to think. If you are in the habit of praying, you may want to pray. If not, just think, about what we have seen here, or about your mothers or your homes and those dear to you, or about whatever is the best and highest in life for you."

The organ played. There was a little movement, that grew general, back from the doors of the stage, toward the three crosses on the deserted Calvary. First one, then others here and there, dropped to their knees. A few made the sign of the Cross. Most just stood, in total silence; but there were tears in eyes and on faces that had long forgotten the gift of tears.

When the five minutes were up, I said, "That's all, ladies and gentlemen. Thank you. Good night, and happy Christmas." The stage emptied, without a sound; and I too went home to Christmas with my family.

4

We opened *The King of Kings* at the Gaiety Theatre in New York on April 19, 1927, and at Grauman's Chinese Theatre in Hollywood on May 18. Its statistical history can be summed up in the fact that it has been playing steadily somewhere in the world, I believe without a day's interruption, ever since. I have quoted 800,000,000 as the number of people who have seen it, but that can be only a minimum guess, because there is no count of the television audiences of recent years, and when a Protestant or Catholic missionary takes a print of it into jungles where the people have never seen a film before, or when, to give but one example, Madame Chiang Kai-shek sent an emissary to me to ask for a print to screen in prisoner-of-war camps during the Korean conflict, one does not expect the operator in such circumstances to count the house. It is enough to say, again as simple fact, that probably more people have been told the story of Jesus of Nazareth through *The King of Kings* than through any other single work, except the Bible itself.

Incredibly, in spite of excellent reviews, endorsement by religious leaders of all the major faiths, and immediate and sustained public acceptance, still more in spite of or because of its theme, *The King of Kings* met with some bitter opposition. It was easy enough to ignore the vociferousness of some tiny but militant atheist societies. What was harder to comprehend and cope with was the organized opposition of certain Jewish groups to this filmed history of the greatest Jew who ever lived.

Certainly one can understand and sympathize with the sensitivity of Jews to the lie that the Jewish people as a whole were responsible for the death of Jesus. Well aware of that, and of the awful consequences which have followed historically from the propagation of that lie, we went to great lengths in *The King of Kings* to show that the Jewish people of Jesus' time followed and heard Him gladly, that His death came at the hands of a few unrepresentative, corrupt religious leaders and the cowardly and callous Roman government. Still, the opposition to the picture mounted, in some places to disheartening and alarming proportions.

I am not going into a detailed account of how the story of Jesus of Nazareth was banned from the screens of certain American cities. The painful documentation is in my files. Some day, when men learn to discuss religious prejudice dispassionately, some historian of motion pictures or of American folkways may publish it. I will not. I will content myself here with quoting Rabbi Alexander Lyons of the Eighth Avenue Temple in Brooklyn, New York, that *The King of Kings* was "reverent, instructive and inspiring. It should make the Jew more nobly and proudly Jewish, the Christian more emulous of the character of Jesus." Rabbi Lyons was only one of numerous rabbis and leading Jews who did not feel as some of their co-religionists did about the film.

But I wish that Rudolph Schildkraut had lived to hear the story which a German Lutheran pastor told Joseph Schildkraut and me on July 30, 1957. Rudolph Schildkraut was, in my opinion, perhaps the finest character actor ever to appear in motion pictures. He was as fine a man as he was an actor. His son Joseph once said to me about him, "He smiled, and the sun rose." The Schildkrauts were Jewish. They suffered for playing the roles of Caiaphas and Judas in *The King of Kings*. They had taken the roles as artists, with no thought of credal prejudice, and they played them superbly. Then they were caught in the wash of opposition to the film, and condemned by some of their fellow Jews as traitors. Rudolph Schildkraut came to me, stunned but not embittered, and took my hand and said to me, "I understand what this means, but I'm not sorry about it."

The story that I wish Rudolph Schildkraut had lived to hear was told to his son and me by Pastor H. E. Wallner. As a young man in Danzig in 1928, he went to see *The King of Kings* because he was a fan of Joseph Schildkraut's. He was so moved by the picture that he decided to devote his life to the ministry of the Lutheran Church. He had a parish in Prague when Hitler marched on Czechoslovakia. In his congregation was a doctor, a Jewish convert to Christianity, who was promptly thrown into a concentration camp, where his example and encouragement to the other prisoners to die bravely, with faith in their hearts, so angered the Gestapo officers that they beat him with an iron rod until one of his arms was so smashed that it had to be amputated. But they could not silence him. Then one Gestapo officer beat the doctor's head against a stone wall until the blood was streaming down his face, then took out a mirror and held it in front of him, saying, "Take a look at yourself. Now you look like your Jewish Christ." The doctor raised up the one hand he had left and with his last dying breath said, "Lord, never in my life have I received such honor—to resemble You."

That night the Gestapo officer went to Pastor Wallner. He was haunted, he said, by what he had done and by the doctor's dying words. Could Pastor Wallner help him, free him from the terrible burden of his guilt? They prayed together; and the Pastor said to the Gestapo officer, "Perhaps God let you kill that good man to bring you to the foot of the Cross, where you can help others." The officer went back to his duties, but through Pastor Wallner and the Czech underground he assisted the escape of hundreds of Jews.

The pastor told his story very simply. He ended it by saying, "If it were not for *The King of Kings*, I would not be a Lutheran pastor, and three hundred fifty Jewish children would have died in the ditches."

And Joseph Schildkraut said: "To hear that after all these years —one knows why one did it, suddenly."

A book could be written on *The King of Kings* alone, based on the letters that still keep coming to me about it, 30 years after its release. The stories in those letters are not all as dramatic as Pastor Wallner's, but many of them tell a hidden drama of the soul, such as this one written by a Frenchwoman in 1953: "This letter will reach you almost thirty years late. . . . One day, in a little theatre in Auteuil, I saw your film, *The King of Kings*. . . . Jesus had always been a lifeless concept, a mere word. Now He revealed Himself to me; I saw him alive, the source of all truth. . . . Ever since that day, like all others who have faith, I have struggled to become His champion; and this struggle has become the end and the joy of my life."

That Frenchwoman was a young girl, with life before her. Another woman, an American, was dying and knew it when she persuaded the theater manager to let her be brought on a stretcher to see *The King of Kings,* and when it was over, she said, "You have changed what must happen soon from a terror to a glorious anticipation."

In Mexico, when the churches were closed by government edict, people went to see *The King of Kings* and knelt in the theater to offer the prayers they could not say in church. From Egypt came reports of a mother walking with her children 20 miles to see the film, and of people, Christian and Moslem alike, going up to the screen to kiss the place where Jesus' feet had walked. During World War II, a doctor whom I knew, then with the American Army in the Far East, wrote me about the effect of screening *The King of Kings* for boys who watched it, sitting on the ground or on empty oil drums, in the rain, and then next day went out to die.

If I felt that this film was my work, it would be intolerably vain and presumptuous to quote such stories from the hundreds like them that I could quote. But all we did in *The King of Kings,* all I have striven to do in any of my Biblical pictures, was to translate into another medium, the medium of sight and sound, the words of the Bible.

If the story of our budget troubles and corporate maneuver-

284

ings has been as boring to the reader as it is to me, it may relieve him to know that one of those corporations, the Cinema Corporation of America, has been kept in existence for the purpose of continuing the distribution of *The King of Kings;* and there are more prints of it in circulation now than when it was first released in 1927. There can be a corporation with a soul, you see—when its soul is "a man by the name of Milbank."

Though the story of *The King of Kings* was obviously not my work, there were, astonishingly, some who considered that it was theirs! There was a rash of claims of plagiarism, the most publicized being that of an actress named Valeska Suratt. When she sued me for $1,000,000, I made this statement to the press: "I was always under the impression that Matthew, Mark, Luke, and John wrote the accepted version of the life of Christ. If Miss Suratt wrote it the record should be changed." In all cases, the judge agreed that the record need not be changed.

A more serious brush with the law was recalled many years later when I had to fill in forms for the Federal Bureau of Investigation in connection with my appointment as chief consultant on motion pictures to the United States Information Agency. My secretary automatically typed in "No" as answer to the question, "Have you ever been arrested?" I had to remind her of the day in 1927 when the Los Angeles *Evening Express* came out with a headline four inches high reading, "CECIL B. DEMILLE FACES JULIAN CASE USURY CHARGE."

No reader of the esteemed *Express* could have been more surprised than I. No guardian of the law could have been more civil than the police officers who arrested me for usury. They politely telephoned and asked when it would be convenient for me to be arrested. Consulting my schedule, we fixed upon a mutually agreeable time, and I was duly docketed. When the fact was brought out that I had indeed, with Louis B. Mayer and others, unwisely invested in the floundering Julian Petroleum Corporation, but had never loaned it any money, not to mention never collecting 20 per cent interest from it as charged, the public prosecutor graciously granted that he had been misinformed.

The kidnaping which I did commit in 1927 never came to the attention of the law, however. I was traveling from Chicago to Los Angeles on the Santa Fe Chief with John C. Flinn, vice-president of the Producers Distributing Corporation, when suddenly my companion was taken very gravely ill. There was no doctor on the train, but the conductor wired ahead to Marceline, Missouri, a town through which the Chief usually appeared only as a speeding streak; and there, when the train halted, was Dr. P. L. Patrick, with the engine of his new Chevrolet still running, beside the track. When Dr. Patrick saw how ill John was, he went right to work and did not notice that the train was moving until it had passed far beyond the suburbs of Marceline.

He saw that John was sick enough to need constant attention for several days. But what about the Chevrolet with the key still in it? What about his patients at home? What, last but not least of his worries, about Mrs. Patrick, who might not interpret the Hippocratic Oath to include gallivanting to Hollywood with two movie moguls?

I am not sure whether I was charming or ruthless, but by the time we reached Kansas City, it was arranged for a garage to pick up the Chevrolet, and a telegram was sent to Mrs. Patrick, which we all hoped she would receive with the patience that distinguishes doctors' wives. As the train sped on through wheatfields, mountains, and desert, Dr. Patrick saved John Flinn's life.

In gratitude, we kept the doctor in Hollywood for four days. We made sure that he went everywhere and saw everything, including the Hollywood first run of *The King of Kings*. And then he went back to Marceline and to being the devoted, hard working country doctor he had been before he was kidnaped.

Though innocent of plagiarism and usury, and with a happy doctor safely restored from kidnaping, I did have occasion to see the inside of a penal institution one evening when I arrived home in time to find a suspicious character lurking around the outside of my house, evidently looking for a good place to break and enter. Knowing that the Laughlin Park watchman, who has some police powers, would be making his rounds soon, I engaged the would-be burglar in a casual chat until the watchman came along. Then I had to accompany suspect and guard downtown, as the complaining witness. While the desk officer greeted the suspect as an old friend, since he had been released from durance only that morning, I took the chance to telephone Mrs. deMille, to explain why I was late for dinner. She returned to the dining room and

286

in her calm way told our guests, as if it were a regular occurrence, that Cecil was in the Lincoln Heights jail, but that he would be getting out soon.

5

It seems not at all inappropriate that my next picture should have been about life in a reformatory. *The Godless Girl* is the story of a militant atheist club in an American high school and of a pitched battle between the youthful atheists and the rest of the students, in which a child is killed, resulting in the sentencing of the leaders of both student groups to an institution for juvenile delinquents. The "godless girl" of the title, played by Lina Basquette, is of course redeemed in the final reel. It was considered by some a shocking and brutal picture, but it only reflected all too faithfully the shocking and brutal conditions in some reformatories at the time, for it was based upon exhaustive research. The idea of the picture was welcomed by some of the most zealous workers in the prison reform movement as a contribution to their cause. Prison conditions have improved, I understand; but what seems most dated to me now about *The Godless Girl* is the high school atheist club. More youngsters of today are more indifferent about God than belligerent toward Him. I wonder which is the more godless of those two attitudes.

When I visited the Soviet Union in 1931, I found *The Godless Girl* a most popular feature on Russian screens and myself almost something like a national hero for having produced it. I could not understand this. The story, after all, is that of a girl's redemption by gaining faith in God, which did not seem to me quite the sort of thing that the communist masters of the Russian people would particularly welcome. It was not until near the end of my trip that someone enlightened me. The Russians simply did not screen the last redeeming reel, but played the rest of the picture as a document of American police brutality and the glorious spreading of atheism among American youth.

But something was happening in Hollywood which made *The Godless Girl* almost outdated before it was released. The screen began to speak.

Looking back, it may seem surprising that the producing companies so long resisted the inevitable coming of sound films. True, the early experiments of synchronizing the action of the film with some kind of talking-machine had not been technically perfect and had not caught the public fancy as anything other than a novelty. But when a method was developed of putting a sound track on the film itself, only Warner Brothers and William Fox were ready to take the plunge into a new era. The method had been shown to be practicable as early as 1924. The historic night of the première of Warners' *The Jazz Singer,* in which Al Jolson spoke and sang, was October 5, 1927. But it was not until the following year that the major companies accepted sound to the extent of announcing cautiously that a certain minor percentage of their product would henceforth be "talkies."

The reasons, I think, were twofold. One was the opposition, on artistic grounds, of some who thought that sound was simply alien to the whole technique of motion pictures which had been created out of the necessity to tell a story to the eye alone, with the help of a minimum number of printed subtitles. There are still some who hold this view. The other reason was cost. To bring in sound meant huge new expenditures, both in the studios and in the theaters, and the scrapping of much of the existing studio equipment. All this would be enormous waste if, after the novelty wore off, the public preferred their screens to be silent.

But the public was not long in letting their preference be known. Sound came to stay.

The Godless Girl was caught in the middle of the transition. Some feet of sound track were added to the film before its general release, but it is still classified as a silent film, the last silent picture I made.

I was, of course, in no position financially to take a major part in the decisions which led to the industry-wide change to sound. The purse strings of the DeMille Studio were held in New York, so tightly that occasionally my own small company, DeMille Productions, had to meet the studio payroll when the advances due from New York did not reach us in time. We were working that close to the financial edge, which gives point to some testimony I gave in telling this history to the United States Board of Tax Appeals some years later: "When banks came into pictures, trouble came in with them. When we operated on picture money, there was joy in the industry; when we operated on Wall Street money, there was grief in the industry."

The trouble in 1928 was that I did not have enough "picture money" to be completely independent and make only the kind of pictures I wanted to make. I never have had, as a producer, that complete financial independence. It was not until after my return to Paramount that I obtained, not without occasional struggle, a measure of budgetary leeway sufficient to let me carry out my own ideas more or less freely. The holders of the purse strings in 1928 did not have either the understanding of picture making or the confidence in me which have made my present association with Paramount both pleasant, in the main, and profitable to Paramount as well as to me.

Jeremiah Milbank had confidence in me, but he was not in a position to act alone either at the time. J. J. Murdock, representing the Keith-Albee-Orpheum interests, knew vaudeville and theater management as well as anyone in the world, but his ideas of motion picture production may be judged from his saying once that surely there was somewhere in the United States someone who could have played a certain part for $8,000 less than we paid the actress we had cast in the role. It did not occur to him that it might have cost $10,000 to find that talented unknown.

The bankers' part in our affairs is beautifully vignetted in one of Bill Sistrom's witty, if despairing, letters of 1928: "About this time an elderly and very charming old gentleman associated with Blair and Company came out. He saw *His Country* and cried without shame, so I liked him. Then came a hard sort of individual from the Chase Securities. He didn't say much, but seemed to think the whole business was silly and ought not to be permitted. I think he wired to New York, but the nice old gentleman probably didn't, because there was none of his influence there."

When news reached me that Joseph P. Kennedy was interested in taking hold of the Pathé and Keith-Albee-Orpheum companies, I welcomed it. The future Ambassador to the Court of St. James' was a successful Boston banker who had entered the motion picture business as president and chairman of the Film Booking Offices of America in 1926. His credit and reputation were strong. He brought financial shoring to our parent companies in New York, which gave him control of Pathé and K-A-O by the summer of 1928.

Meanwhile, however, I had been reconsidering my own position. Two years before, Harvey Burwell, with the freedom of the good friend he was, had written out what he called a "personnel rating" of me, analyzing some 40 qualities on the basis of percentage points. He gave me 100 per cent only in "singleness of purpose," "magnetism," "mental capacity," and "emotional intellect," whatever they may be, but some of his remaining estimates were as follows: administrative ability, 50 per cent; decision, 40 per cent; tact, 25 per cent; organization zeal, 0 per cent; analysis of routine, 0 per cent. Harvey took a rather roundabout mathematical way of saying that I belong behind a camera, not an executive's desk.

I knew that, even without Harvey's mathematics. Less than a year after my break with Famous Players-Lasky, I offered Jesse Lasky the presidency of Cecil B. DeMille Productions. He preferred staying where he was, and I had to retain the executive position I had assumed in the hope of building the DeMille Company to a point where it could independently finance and produce its own pictures. This was not happening under the tie-up with New York financiers; and my chosen work, directing, was suffering both from restrictive outside control and from the mass of administrative detail involved in my being head of a studio. When Joseph P. Kennedy brought his strength to the Pathé organization, I decided ultimately that it would be better for DeMille Productions to sell its Pathé stock, at a very handsome profit, and for me to form another connection free at least from the uncongenial burden of studio administration.

That other door opened to me in another part of Culver City. On August 2, 1928, I signed a contract to make three pictures for Metro-Goldwyn-Mayer. My personal staff came with me, including Mitch Leisen who designed the interior of the spacious and attractive bungalow which M-G-M built for the DeMille unit. When, in September, I turned over the keys to my old office to Bill Sistrom, my letter of transmittal was significantly addressed to him at "Pathé Studios, Culver City, Calif.": the DeMille Studio was no more. Since then, I have been offered the chief executive

290

job at more than one major studio, including Paramount. I have always declined with thanks.

6

Sometimes I am asked where the ideas for motion picture plots come from. The only answer is that they can come from anywhere. In my experience, I have never had the joy of being presented by any writer with a fully developed script ready to shoot. More often, the idea comes as a tiny germ, perhaps a single dramatic situation, perhaps less even than that, and then comes the labor of developing out of it an articulated plot. My first picture at M-G-M, which was also my first "all-talking" picture, was born when I read a small item in a Newark, New Jersey, newspaper, telling of a prisoner under sentence of death, who was married a few days before his execution. The thought occurred to me: what if he had been reprieved then? What would be his emotions and his wife's, what would their future lives be, especially if the marriage had been one based on some legal convenience rather than on love and shared interests?

The result was *Dynamite,* the story of a spoiled rich girl whose grandfather's will provides that she must be married by a certain date or forfeit her inheritance. The playboy she wants to marry is not yet divorced. The executors of the will are adamant. The girl reads of a condemned convict, a burly, rough-hewn miner, offering his body for medical research in hopes of getting money enough to keep his little sister out of an orphanage. With the help of a friendly judge, the girl gets into the prison and pays the condemned man to marry her the day before his doom. Next morning, minutes before the execution, the real murderer confesses. From that situation, the strangely-matched couple have to work out their destiny.

To play the miner and the girl, I brought from the legitimate stage a rugged, red-haired actor named Charles Bickford and the lovely Kay Johnson whose beautiful performance in *The Silver Cord* had shown me what talent she could bring to the new medium of talking pictures. In addition to his ten years of experience on the stage, Charles Bickford had another qualification for playing the burly miner. His strong physique was partly due to his having been in the navy when President Theodore Roosevelt sent the fleet around the world. I do not know how much of the world Charlie Bickford saw from his particular station in the fleet on that famous voyage, but my picture was improved by his experience as a coal-passer aboardship. Conrad Nagel, another young veteran of both stage and screen, was the not yet divorced playboy who dies a hero's death in a mine disaster in the last reel; Julia Faye was his mercenary wife. Among Kay Johnson's giddy friends was a youngster who had gone to school with my daughter Cecilia and who is still one of my best friends in Hollywood, Joel McCrea.

The new intoxication with sound in 1929 made it almost compulsory for a motion picture to have a theme song. We engaged Dorothy Parker to write the lyrics of one for *Dynamite*. That cleverly astringent poetess was rather annoyed when I changed a few of her words, but the public liked and remembered "Oh, How Am I To Know?" They must also have liked the pleasant, dark young man we cast as a Mexican prisoner to strum the tune and sing the words of that theme song in a near-by cell while the condemned man and the girl are being married and the sound of hammers building the gallows can be heard outside. The young singer's part was too small to get his name on the list of the cast, but the public has a way of eventually bringing into deserved prominence anyone as talented as Russ Columbo.

To leaf through my shooting script of *Dynamite* is to see at a glance what sound had done to films. The dialogue, typed in red, is the outstanding feature of each page; and some of the dialogue in the first reels seems, nearly 30 years later, painfully bright and brittle, as if we were dinning into the audience what good playwrights we were, now that they could hear as well as see.

That in fact is what the early sound films were: photographed stage plays. Every writer on that era in motion pictures has told of the sudden eclipse of silent stars whose voices did not register well through the pitiless microphone; but the greatest effect of the coming of sound was upon the film technique of storytelling, and there too the microphone was the innocent villain.

That little round instrument had no judgment. It picked up not only the dialogue, more or less brilliant, composed by the writers and spoken by the players who flocked to Hollywood from New York when the screen began to speak. It picked up every sound.

292

We learned soon enough to insulate the studio stages. But there in the middle of the stage was the camera, grinding away. The only way to eliminate the noise of the camera seemed to be to imprison it in a glass cage, where, like a good child, it could see and be seen but not be heard. But neither could it be moved. Faced toward the set, it could photograph what was in front of it. What with new writers and actors accustomed to the legitimate stage and a camera as immobile as an audience in a legitimate theater, moving pictures ceased to move.

They ceased to move, that is, until one day the word went around M-G-M that there was a madman loose on the set of *Dynamite*. I wanted the camera to follow an actor up a flight of stairs. I told the cameraman to take his machine out of its little glass prison and bring it close to the stairway.

"But, Mr. deMille—the noise!"

"Never mind the noise," I said. "Send to the property department and get some bed blankets. Wrap them around the camera and that will deaden the noise."

It was tried, and the sound engineer shook his head. His microphone was still getting camera noise.

"Then send for some more blankets, and some quilts. We'll try it again."

With blankets and quilts wrapped around it, the camera was beginning to look like a hippopotamus with the mumps; but this time the sound man smiled. It was silent.

Standing and watching near the edge of the set, having heard of the commotion, was Douglas Shearer, the head of M-G-M's sound department, one of the young men whose vision and persistence had done much to bring sound to films.

He said to me, "I see what you want, Mr. deMille. If you give me two or three days, I can bring you a camera that will make no noise and can be moved anywhere."

He came back in the allotted time with a huge and sturdy black box. In it was the camera, with its lens peeking out; and the box was thickly lined with bed blankets. It was promptly nicknamed the "blimp." Since then, camera blimps are built of more scientifically refined materials than blankets snatched from the property department. They are essential equipment in the making of every sound picture. But that was the first one, as far as I know.

I add the proviso "as far as I know," because every director in Hollywood claims to have invented every improvement in film making. They probably all did. I am exaggerating a little, but not being facetious.

For example, I think that I also invented, while I was at M-G-M, the "boom," that long and marvelously steady steel arm, at the end of which the camera, the director, and the cameramen can soar into the air, dip to the ground, swing to right or left, move forward on a scene or draw away from it, photographing all the time and getting all the broad scope, all the detail, and all the nuances of effect that the scene requires, without breaking the shot. When I invented the boom, I worked it on the principle of a see-saw, so that the camera could climb a wall and look in an upstairs window. When Woody Van Dyke invented it, he was in the jungles of Africa, making *Trader Horn* and, as I have heard the story, fastened his camera to a strong bent branch of a tree and slowly let the branch's resilience raise it to the desired height. When Lionel Barrymore invented the boom, in this case to hold a microphone above the actors' heads, out of camera range, legend has it that he used a fishpole. When Eddie Mannix invented the boom, according to Bosley Crowther, the historian of M-G-M, he rigged it "on the order of an old-fashioned well sweep." No doubt a half-dozen other claimants could rush forward to tell how they invented the boom; and they might all be telling the strictest truth. There should be nothing surprising in that. Creative minds often get the same idea independently of one another, and it is no discredit to anyone's originality if he happens to get his idea a few weeks or months later than someone else of whom he may never have heard.

Dynamite was a good picture, and a successful one. It seemed that 1929 was a good year. I had formed at Metro-Goldwyn-Mayer a promising association, and had certainly been received there royally. The studio was headed by two men as different as any two men could be, but in their respective ways unequaled in the industry—Louis B. Mayer and Irving Thalberg. Pleasant honors were coming my way. I was busy on the Community Chest. The National Museums of France were deciding to present me with the first authorized replica of Houdon's bust of Voltaire; and if that was a somewhat curious gift to make to the producer of *The Ten Commandments* (1923) and *The King of Kings*, I none the less

294

valued the honor it did me, coming from official representatives of that country where art is perhaps most highly cultivated and honored. I was serving my second term as President of the Association of Motion Picture Producers of California, the West Coast organization loosely affiliated with the Will Hays Office in New York. The sale of our Pathé stock had netted some $700,000, which wisely invested should help DeMille Productions reach its goal of independently financed pictures.

Then one day in the early autumn Julia Faye had lunch with William Randolph Hearst, Marion Davies, and Arthur Brisbane. Julia had hardly put down her napkin and pushed back her chair when she dashed to a telephone to call me. Arthur Brisbane, who next to W. R. Hearst himself was the editorial brains of the Hearst papers, had remarked at lunch that, despite glowing appearances, there was going to be a stock market crash to the like of which none of the remembered Wall Street panics was to be compared.

I immediately instructed Gladys Rosson to sell every share of stock we held; and I went back to my work.

The crash of October, 1929, came, with sickening suddenness, with no hoped-for rally, with only the steady descent into the Great Depression.

I asked Gladys for a report. She had dutifully called the brokers as soon as she received my instructions. She gave them the order which we always gave when we were selling, to offer the stocks at a half-point above the market. But the desperately tumbling market had never climbed that half-point. There were no takers at our price. Gladys's fidelity to our customary rule had cost me approximately $1,000,000.

I could not say a word of rebuke to her. She offered no alibis. Gladys never did. Nothing I could have said, not if I had burned her at the stake or flayed her alive, could have tortured her more than the self-reproach I knew she was feeling. I took the blame for not having told her more specifically that, when I said "sell" *that* time, I meant sell that minute at any price.

She was, after all, the same Gladys who, one evening when she was dining with me and I fell asleep exhausted at the dinner table, calmly sat all night with her hand under my chin, so that I might sleep undisturbed by a ducking in the soup plate. She was the same Gladys who, another night when I promised and then forgot to pick her up at a corner near her home on my way to my ranch, was still standing there when I remembered and went back a good hour or more later; and all she said was, "I saw you go by, but I knew you'd be back."

I would have given another million dollars to save her life from cancer in 1953. There is no helplessness quite like having wealth and finding it completely useless to save a precious life. All I could give Gladys Rosson, the last time I saw her, was the first 14 verses of the Gospel according to St. John; Gladys was one who knew their meaning and their worth.

13

SHANTYTOWNS OF OLD TIN and discarded packing-boxes housing human beings on the outskirts of great cities . . . the suicides of men whose pathetic inner poverty was revealed when they could not live without their money . . . in the White House, one of the most honest and able men who ever bore the lonely burden of the Presidency, but helpless to stem the black tide of economic disaster . . . apple sellers on street corners . . . breadlines . . . is it possible to convey to a generation that was in its cradle in the 1930's what the depression years were like?

It is possible if we think of "depression" as the psychologists use that term. It was more than a matter of work and bread, serious though their lack was. It was a national mood—gray, discouraged, sometimes sullen. Another people might have broken out against it in violent revolt. The American people weathered it. They even made jokes about it. But they were—there is no other word for it—depressed: and it is against that background, ever to be borne in mind, that our lives were lived in the first years of the fourth decade of the twentieth century.

People who are psychologically depressed may sometimes be helped by going to the movies; but people who are economically depressed cannot afford to buy tickets. That was one aspect of the depression that hit closest to the motion picture industry.

There was the usual economizing; but there was also another and rather curious by-product. Some producers began to inject into their pictures more and more elements which caused the menace of censorship to rumble again. Perhaps they thought that was the cheapest way to hold a dwindling audience. It was cheap, in every meaning of the word. Since the formation of the Hays Office, the producers had been guided, more or less, by an advisory list of "Don'ts" and "Be Carefuls," indicating material, words, scenes, and situations which either should not be treated in pictures for general audiences or should be treated with delicacy and good taste. But there was a growing tendency to take lightly the Hays Office's gentle admonitions, a tendency almost to retitle the list of cautions to "Do!" and "Be Careless."

I am not prudish in matters of either life or art. You cannot have drama without conflict, and the age-old conflict of good and evil demands that the evil be shown clearly for what it is. Nor do I believe that strong characters are formed by wrapping them in cotton wool, insulating them from all contact with a world in which evil is an all too prominent and potent force. In matters of language on the stage or screen, a Bowery tough simply does not speak like a kindergarten teacher. In matters of costume, you cannot swathe a Babylonian slave in the hoops and crinolines of Queen Victoria's day. If the dramatic construction of a story or its authenticity requires the portrayal of persons or scenes or situations which we might not relish having in our living rooms, they should be portrayed, as realistically as need be; and a writer or director worth his salt can portray them without offending either good morals or good taste. But what was wrong with some of the pictures of the period to which we have now come was that they were bad art as well as bad morals and bad taste. Supposedly spicy scenes were dragged in that had no relation to the plot; sometimes, in fact, the plot had to wait until Tottie Swivens had lingeringly removed her garter, before the audience could get on with the story.

When, therefore, Will Hays and Martin Quigley, the publisher of some influential motion picture trade journals, put their heads together on a plan to strengthen the industry's self-regulation, I welcomed the move. Moreover, they brought into their program at an early stage the fine, well-balanced mind of my friend, Father

Daniel Lord, to draft a "code" for the guidance of producers in their handling of the delicate problem of morals in relation to art.

These three men, all of them idealistic and practical at once, made a first-rate team. Will Hays ably represented the producing companies centered in New York, and he had an expert politician's feeling for public relations. Through his magazines, Martin Quigley was close to the exhibitors and thus to the public who passed through, or stayed away from, the doors of the theaters. Father Lord, professionally trained in ethics and theology, also had a rare appreciation of dramatic necessities and values. And all three men had a deep and personal concern for the true, the good, and the beautiful.

When their preliminary work was done, they brought to Hollywood the proposed "Code to Govern the Making of Talking, Synchronized, and Silent Motion Pictures." It was my responsibility, and honor, as president of the West Coast Producers' Association, to present their work officially to the industry. I appointed a committee, headed by Irving Thalberg, to study the Code with its framers, iron out any difficulties or differences of opinion, and bring it as near to perfection as possible. The Code was adopted by our association in February, 1930, and by Will Hays' New York group the following month.

There has been a certain amount of stupid talk about excessive Roman Catholic influence on the formation of the Production Code because Father Lord was a Jesuit priest and Martin Quigley a prominent Catholic layman, knighted by the Pope. There was no such excessive influence. Will Hays was a Presbyterian elder. I am an Episcopalian. Irving Thalberg and a majority of his committee were Jewish. No sectarian bias could have survived the scrutiny and sifting the Code had before its adoption. What all those who worked on it and adopted it had in common, and shared with the overwhelming majority of the American people, was a belief in the natural moral law and in the Ten Commandments as an expression of that law. That is the basis of the Production Code.

To my mind, quite apart from the Code's specific value to the motion picture industry, it stands as an example of the effective unity which can be achieved by men of very different beliefs, but of common fundamental principles and shared good will. There is

299

a lesson in that for the whole of the free world, at a time when its fundamental principles are under unremitting attack.

The Code and its applications have been criticized by some as too rigid and by others as too loose. I have tangled a few times, about minor points in some of my pictures, with the Code office, which now reads all scripts and reviews all finished films before they receive the seal of approval of the Motion Picture Association. The Code, after all, is a human document, and nothing human is perfect. Moreover, men of equal intelligence and integrity can differ on specific applications of the fundamental principles they hold in common. There is room, I think, for modification of the Code from time to time, in those sections of it which deal with specifics. But its basic principles have been valid since they were revealed on Mount Sinai; and

> *In vain we call old notions fudge,*
> *And bend our conscience to our dealing:*
> *The Ten Commandments will not budge—*
> *And stealing will continue stealing.*

From Mount Sinai to *Madam Satan* may seem a long leap; but, in a way, the second picture I directed for Metro-Goldwyn-Mayer illustrates some of the points I have been making. The Seventh Commandment (Sixth, if you are Catholic or Lutheran) is quite a clear, concise statement of one of the fundamental laws of marriage. But, in the human situations in which the Commandments are to be applied, it is necessary sometimes to do more than just promulgate the law. We may have to help each other keep it. *Madam Satan* is the story of a wife who goes to a masked ball to flirt with her husband because, as he puts it later, he has been wandering "far from my own fireside in search of—fire!"

Kay Johnson demonstrated to Reginald Denny that she could be an alluring siren as well as an almost oppressively respectable wife. Roland Young played the other principal male part with that wonderful touch he had for light comedy. His girl friend was a young actress whose later real life was touched by tragedy, but who has recently shared with the world the brave philosophy of her motto, "I'll Cry Tomorrow"—Lillian Roth.

Madam Satan marked the screen debut of my daughter Katherine. Katherine deMille's screen career owes little to me, and cer-

300

tainly nothing to the decorative but nonspeaking role I gave her in this film while she was still a schoolgirl. She has played larger roles in two of my later pictures, but she won them by merit, not by nepotism, for I have always believed that a son or daughter should make his or her way on the strength of his or her own abilities. Katherine deMille has a good list of credits in motion pictures: she can look back at every one of them as due to her own achievement, not to the fact that she is my daughter. One might almost say that I bent backward when I gave her her role in *Madam Satan:* at the masquerade party in the picture, I cast her as one of the wives of King Henry VIII, surely a horrid fate for anyone's daughter.

The screen had not yet got over its first infatuation with the sound of its own voice when I made *Madam Satan.* Nothing would do but that it should be a musical, my first and last venture into that form of entertainment. The characters burst into song at frequent intervals. None of their bursts need have perturbed the dreams of the young Messrs. Gershwin, Hammerstein, Hart, Rodgers, or any of the others who have delighted so many, including me, with *good* musicals.

I wonder if a sense of quiet desperation had anything to do with my decision to make *The Squaw Man* for a third time, as the final picture under my contract with Metro-Goldwyn-Mayer. In January, 1931, a month before we started on its shooting, I was writing to Father Lord: "I cannot find any inspiration at all in the type of pictures the producers want me to make. They are in a state of panic and chaos and . . . they rush for the bedspring and the lingerie the moment the phantom of empty seats rises to clutch them. . . . I cannot find a producer who is willing to do anything but follow the mad rush for destruction; so, being at a loss to know what else to do, I am putting together an organization of the six or eight directors who seem to me to be the real creative minds in the business and will endeavor to find some capital with vision enough to finance us. . . . Failing in this direction, or failing to find a producer who has confidence in the kind of pictures I want to make, I shall probably raise even the topsails of the *Seaward* and see how far I can sail without stopping."

2

We called the organization which I tried to put together the

Directors' Guild.* Frank Borzage, Lewis Milestone, and King Vidor met with me at my Laughlin Park office on February 8, 1931, when the four of us signed an agreement which was also in the nature of a manifesto, since it declared that "the conditions under which motion pictures are now generally produced are not conducive to the best creative work, and must, if long continued, result in a deadly uniformity of ideas and methods, thus seriously retarding the highest commercial and artistic development of the craft."

Among them, my three associates had directed such outstanding and still remembered films as *All Quiet on the Western Front, Front Page, The Big Parade, Three Wise Fools, Hallelujah, Seventh Heaven, Liliom,* and many others of high caliber. I could not have had abler or more enthusiastic associates than those three directors, to launch our Directors' Guild, founded on the thesis that better, more original, more varied, and more successful pictures would result if production were controlled by the creative minds in the industry rather than by financiers or bookkeepers.

Should we have been surprised that the financiers and bookkeepers did not share our enthusiasm? The producing companies preferred to keep their directors in short and tightly-held leading strings. In May of 1931, I had to write to my three associates that progress in obtaining financing and distribution for our Directors' Guild had been "difficult and slow," which was an understatement, because "the heads of the large producing and distributing organizations fear that . . . the revolutionary idea of the director selecting and making his own productions . . . might lead to a general revision of the present system" and that "the chaotic condition in which all industry is at the present time . . . has resulted in a state of panic in the mind of the producer which tends to make him fear any departure from the beaten path."

In other words, perish creativeness but don't touch the system. The financier and the bookkeeper seldom dare to think that a time of depression is the time to depart from the beaten path. It is an old story ever new in the motion picture industry. Its most recent chapter was written only yesterday, when a young revolutionary

* Not to be confused with the presently existing Screen Directors' Guild of America, which is the collective bargaining organization of motion picture directors. (*Ed.*)

302

named Michael Todd and an old one named deMille insisted upon pouring millions of dollars into their pictures at a time when nearly everyone else was quaking before the growing monster television: but *Around the World in Eighty Days* and *The Ten Commandments* (1956) brought joy to the bookkeeping departments as well as to their audiences.

But in 1931 the bravely begun Directors' Guild petered out in a desert of indifference. So I finished *The Squaw Man* to complete my contract with Metro-Goldwyn-Mayer. With Warner Baxter, Eleanor Boardman, Paul Cavanaugh, Roland Young, Julia Faye, Charles Bickford, Raymond Hatton, and with a fiery little lady named Lupe Velez as the Indian girl, it was a good picture. But in the economic condition of the times it was a predestined failure. Just before we started production, Nicholas Schenk, president of Loew's, Incorporated, which is M-G-M's parent company, came and asked me if we could stop it, since the box office had fallen off so badly that there was no hope of getting back its cost. I told him it would cost as much to stop as it would to go on, since we were bound to pay salaries and other contracted expenses; and he said to go ahead, although the picture might lose nearly $150,000, which it did. That was a state of affairs not conducive to buoyant enthusiasm.

I do not enjoy failure. Almost the only time I feel physically weary and without energy, if my health is otherwise good, is when I am doing something which is not succeeding. If I am doing something that holds any promise of achievement, I can keep at it until I drop. I may fall asleep at the dinner table; but after three or four hours' rest I am ready to do my deep breathing and push-ups the next morning, and start another day. After *The Squaw Man*, though, I do not know whether M-G-M or I was more relieved that my contract had come to an end. There was a nice dramatic irony in the fact that my farewell conversation, terminating the contract, was with the brilliant young man I had wanted to hire when we were in the old barn on Vine Street—Irving Thalberg.

The one best human asset I acquired at M-G-M came to me by accident. Her name on the payroll and the census list and the other places in this world where names are kept is Florence Cole; but on the recording angel's more accurate list of these matters, I am sure her name is "Loyalty." She was working in the M-G-M secretarial pool, and was sent to my office one day to fill in when one of our regular secretaries was absent for the day. That was more than ten thousand days ago, and Florence Cole is still with me.

Her desk now is just outside the door of my office at Paramount Studio. She is there when I come in in the morning. She is there when I leave at night, no matter if it is 8 or 9 o'clock; and she usually puts in an hour or two or three after I leave, catching up on things I have kept her too busy to do during the day. Only the oldest inhabitants of the studio can remember when she last took a vacation. If I want to consult a scrap of paper I scribbled some notes on five years ago, Florence will produce it. If I want to know when I met some visiting dignitary from Indonesia shortly after World War II, Florence will give me not only the date, but the place and the time and the names of the dignitary's wife, secretary, and all 14 members of his official party. She has the keys and the combination to all my most confidential business, and the lock on her lips is stronger than the locks of my desk or safe. If you come to see me at the studio, or if you telephone to me, you will first have to pass muster with Miss Cole unless she knows that I already know you well; and if her guardianship ever gives me a slight feeling of claustrophobia, it also enables me to get my work done. Being older than Florence, I shall probably arrive at the pearly gates before she does; but it will not surprise me at all if I find her waiting there, to hand me a small, neatly-typed card, containing all the pertinent data on St. Peter, the nine choirs of angels, and just where to go for the best selection of harps and halos.

My three years at M-G-M were not particularly happy ones, except for the persistent loyalty of those who went there with me or who joined me there and were ready to go with me wherever the next move might lead; and among those, Florence Cole's name is entitled to high place.

3

There is a saying in Hollywood that you are just as good as your last picture; and by good in this connection Hollywood means box office good. Between 1913 and 1931, my pictures had, in round numbers, cost $12,000,000 and grossed $28,000,000. But that record meant nothing. *The Godless Girl* had failed to return its cost because of the coming of sound. *The Squaw Man* was failing because of the depression. When my stay at Metro-Goldwyn-Mayer ended, I could not get a job in Hollywood.

I did not, however, as I had predicted to Father Lord, set sail on the *Seaward* for shores unknown. Mrs. deMille and I took the *Ile de France* instead.

We had never been to Europe together. When the Hollywood executives manifested their profound lack of interest in the obviously washed-up deMille, when ideas of possibly producing a play on the New York stage came to nothing, when a persuasive gentleman found it easier to persuade me to let him try to raise a million dollars to finance a picture than it was to persuade any of his wealthy acquaintances in the East to part with the million, Mrs. deMille and I decided to combine a vacation with an exploratory look at the situation of motion pictures and the theater in Europe. Mrs. deMille was vice-president of Cecil B. DeMille Productions in much more than name. She had excellent dramatic judgment and taste, and she took an active part in all the business affairs of the company.

For the first time in years I was free enough to have time for pleasant personal things. We stopped at Chester, Pennsylvania, where my old school, Pennsylvania Military College, gave me my first honorary degree of Doctor of Letters, and at Pompton Lakes, New Jersey, where a heartwarming number of old friends and schoolmates gathered for a dinner in my honor. Throughout the country, though, the gloom of the depression was everywhere evident. As our train passed through town after town, there was so little activity in the streets that every day looked like Sunday; and there was bitter hopelessness in the faces of the unemployed men on the park benches of New York.

I was unemployed myself, but I began at once, while we were still in New York, to put new irons in the fire. I knew what I wanted most to do: to make a picture from a play I had seen years before, Wilson Barrett's *The Sign of the Cross*. *The Ten Commandments* (1923) had been the story of the Giving of the Law. *The King of Kings* was the story of the Interpretation of the Law. *The Sign of the Cross*, if I could make it, would tell

305

of the Preservation of the Law. Adolph Zukor had made a silent film of *The Sign of the Cross* in 1914, but now, I found, the motion picture rights to it belong to Mary Pickford, with some subsidiary rights still belonging to the author's family. I asked John Flinn to start negotiating for the play while I was abroad, so that, whatever happened to my hopes of possibly directing some pictures in Europe, I would in any event have the play I wanted to complete the trilogy of religious dramas.

When we reached London, it was agreeable to find that Hollywood's opinion of me was evidently not shared by the British financial and film interests. I was approached by a group anxious to lift British films out of their doldrums and enter into aggressive competition for the American market. The august and potent name of Rothschild was mentioned, among others, as evidence of their financial seriousness and stability; and I was given to understand that the British government itself was friendly to the idea of my making a picture there. Moreover, the people who dealt with me liked *The Sign of the Cross*. I wrote to Gladys Rosson from London, "Their business methods are very different and certainly a great relief after the last ten years in Hollywood."

For two weeks, we spent nearly 12 hours a day in conferences and inspection of the well-equipped Wembley Studio just outside London, which was available for lease with an option to buy. But the rock upon which these negotiations foundered was the insistence of one of the British group that there must be a guarantee from the American distributor of whatever films I made in England. In vain I argued that demanding a guarantee in advance would arouse suspicion in the minds of the American companies, which had been distributing my pictures for years without any such guarantee and with such success, in general, that they would wonder why, in this case, the producer was asking for a guarantee. I have always been sorry that the British negotiations did not succeed. I have never gone to England without feeling very much at home; and I should have liked to work there for a time.

In spite of the heavy schedule of business conferences in London, I did not entirely forget that I was also on vacation. A six-page business letter to Gladys Rosson contains this "funny story on myself. I was flirting most outrageously last night at a little cafe (while talking business with the group) with a most fascinating French lady. We carried on really quite a disgraceful flirtation, and at the end of the dinner she came over and spoke to me and laughingly explained that she was Irene Bordoni!" I have often suffered embarrassment from my poor memory for names, but Irene Bordoni only enjoyed thoroughly my failure to recognize the "fascinating French lady" as the famous and beautiful actress and singer whom I had certainly seen on the stage or in pictures.

Even in midsummer, the visitor to London can find good theater every evening of his stay; and Mrs. deMille and I took advantage of it with delight. In that summer of 1931, youngsters like John Gielgud, Jack Hawkins, and Jessica Tandy were showing in relatively small parts the talents which have so beautifully matured since then. In my program of Jack Buchanan's production of *Stand Up and Sing*, I put a heavy mark in the margin so that I would remember the name as well as the delicate loveliness of Anna Neagle; but unfortunately I have never had the opportunity to work with that fine actress. When I saw *Payment Deferred* at the St. James' Theatre, however, I knew that I had found the only man to play Nero if I ever achieved my dream of making *The Sign of the Cross*. He was a fat man with a heavy mustache, dressed in drab business suits for his role as a Dulwich householder, as far removed as might be imagined from the decadent splendors of Imperial Rome; but he was inevitably Nero to my eye, for I saw in Charles Laughton the incredibly wide range of talent which makes every role he plays seem as if it had been tailored just for him.

4

We had planned to visit Russia, to see for ourselves the revolutionary social and economic experiment taking place there and possibly to find in it some picture material; but when we reached Paris, an invitation came which made a visit to the Soviet Union more interesting still. An official of the Soviet Embassy came to ask if I might be interested in staying in Russia long enough to produce a picture there.

I resolved to go into Russia with an open mind, but also with open eyes and ears. I arranged for Theodore Kosloff to meet us in Berlin and come to Russia with us, so that I would have my own trustworthy interpreter and not be dependent upon the official and, I was sure, very clever guides who would make certain that I saw and heard only what the Soviet government wanted me to see and hear. Mrs. deMille and I took a leisurely trip through prosperous Belgium and the smiling Netherlands, stopping in Haarlem to visit the church where Anthony deMil was married in 1653, then went up the Rhine and through the Black Forest to Baden-Baden, from where I wrote gratefully to Gladys Rosson, "There have been no reporters and few people knew me." I told Gladys I was going on to Russia and added: "Tell the family to be careful of wisecracks in their letters, as mail will probably be read before it reaches us. . . . Theodore was afraid to go in alone, but he feels that with us he will be safe. I hope he has not over-estimated my influence with the Soviet."

Theodore got in and out of Russia safely, to the surprise of some of his friends, but not without some harrowing moments: there was little we could do to help his sister, whom he met on the street in Moscow, selling cigarettes.

An official guide, Mme. Levina, was assigned to us. She was the soul of courtesy and efficiency and friendliness; but I adopted the practice of letting her accompany Mrs. deMille to the museums and other sights, while Theodore and I wandered about, talking to people in the streets and parks, dropping in on any surviving old friends of Theodore's that we could find and engaging them in as much conversation as they would vouchsafe. My freedom of move-ment was never interfered with. On the contrary, when I was caught in a crush in the crowd while I watched a thrilling muster of nearly half a million Russian youth pouring from three great avenues into the Red Square in Moscow to be reviewed by Stalin, a courteous Red Army officer was suddenly there to extricate me. Another time, on a train, a Russian passenger complained that Mrs. deMille and I had a room to ourselves while he had none: quickly two Red Army officers appeared, one on either side of the man, and as quickly his complaints subsided. I got the distinct impression that I was free, though constantly guarded and watched, but that the Russian people certainly were not free.

They would talk freely only in the open air. The Hotel Met-ropole in Moscow lived up to its advertisement of "Good meals and excellent wines served in restaurant. Music every evening," but Mrs. deMille, Theodore, and I were often the only guests

308

enjoying the orchestra and the attention of the entire corps of waiters in the huge dining room. No one would sit with us or talk with us there, except Valentine Kataev, the playwright, from whom I bought the motion picture rights to his then popular play, *Squaring the Circle*.

In almost every conversation we did have with Russians, their misconceptions about America were appalling. "Why do you hate us?" they would ask again and again. I would try to explain that the American people did not hate the Russian people, but that both peoples were suffering from lack of knowledge of each other. I felt then and still do that motion pictures could be a strong bridge of understanding between peoples. This is why I was interested in the Soviet film proposal in 1931 and why I have approved the recent arrangement made by Eric Johnston of the Motion Picture Association and Turner Shelton of the United States Information Agency for an exchange of selected American and Russian films, provided the Russians live up to their agreement and do not doctor our pictures for their own purposes, as they did with *The Godless Girl*.

Weird notions about American life and history were not confined to the people we met on streets and in parks. A Moscow University professor told me that Abraham Lincoln was a capitalist and that his only reason for freeing the Negro slaves was to serve capital. The professor had no reply when I asked him if in that case he thought the Negroes should be returned to slavery.

It was easy to see where these ideas of the outside world came from, when we observed in a schoolyard large cut-out figures of a bloated capitalist, a sinister-looking churchman, and a doddering czar, set up as targets for the children's stones and mudballs.

Yet there was no denying that one felt a certain exhilaration in the Russian air. The people were not free. They were terribly poor. It was a land of bewildering contrasts, from the bright and airy prisons shown to foreign visitors, in which the prisoners were apparently well cared for and cheerful, to the hotels so primitive and filthy that at least once Mrs. deMille slept fully dressed on a sofa rather than brave the uninviting bed. The Red Army was very much in evidence and the presence of the secret police, if less evident, was everywhere felt; yet I have no doubt that the average Russian was as thrilled as I was to watch the soldiers marching by, swinging their arms and singing their stirring songs. However much it was due to false propaganda, there was a sense of dedication, typified by the small boy who acted as our guide through a deserted monastery. I tried to get him to sell me one of the sacred ikons thrown carelessly around the floor. It would never have been missed; but, he said, it belonged to the Soviet, and he was true to his trust.

I believe that most Americans in Russia at that time shared what I have called my own guarded optimism about the still young Soviet experiment. Shortly after my return to this country, I read a speech delivered in New York by Colonel Hugh L. Cooper, American consulting engineer on the Dnieper River hydroelectric station, in which he spoke of what he termed "the fallacious theory that Russia is or may become a menace to our economic and political institutions." There is at the present time no better informed or more intelligent anti-Communist writer in the United States than Eugene Lyons. He was United Press correspondent in Moscow in 1931 and during my stay there he often entertained me at his quarters in an old palace, bringing such other writers as Walter Duranty, Maurice Hindus, and Louis Fischer to meet me and give me their impressions. I think Gene Lyons would agree with me that we have all learned a great deal more about the true face of Communism than we knew in 1931, though even then Louis Fischer told me that I was a "hopeless bourgeois."

When it came to discussing making a film in Russia, I admit that I was struck by the contrast between all the doors closed to me in Hollywood—which I had reason to believe was the spearhead of a concerted effort on the part of the producing companies to depress the position, influence, and pay of all motion picture directors—and the recognition given to directors in Russia. In any list of Russian films, the director was given the same kind of credit an author is given in a list of books: *Potemkin* by S. Eisenstein, *Storm Over Asia* by V. Pudovkin, and so on.

However, in my discussions with the officials of Mejrabpom-Film, I learned that a film director in the Soviet Union did not have the individual freedom we had in the United States, even with all our harassment by the financiers. Not for nothing were the studios in Russia called "film factories." The Soviet principle was applied to their operation: in my conference at the Mejrabpom

310

Studio, not only the officials, but representatives of all the classifications of studio workers took part; and decisions, I gathered, were all made collectively by this large group. I am always ready, as I have said, to take good suggestions from anyone; but I did not feel that I could make a good picture under those conditions of Soviet control. Proposals and counterproposals were exchanged; but I was neither surprised nor too sorry when it became evident that I was not cut out to be a Soviet director!

All was friendliness, though, when we finally left Moscow for Nizhni Novgorod and down the Volga by boat to Stalingrad, where we took a train for Vladikavkas, stopping at Rostov for two hours and the first bath in eight days, without soap, of course, and using the bedsheet for a towel. It had to be a quick bath too, to leave time for the first regular meal since we had been on the train, eating tomatoes, watermelon, and bread bought from the people crowded around every station. Our car on the train was lighted by one candle. The car porter, an old lady, had another in a lantern to help her eyesight when she peered out from beneath her shawl to examine our tickets. At night the moon illumined the car, and Mrs. deMille, Theodore, and the pretty young girl who, finding no other place to sit, appropriated our luggage for that purpose, looked like a tableau of ghosts, as we passed over the steppes and in sight of the snow-capped peaks of the Great Caucasus Range.

The most fascinating part of the whole journey through Russia was over the Georgian Military Highway from Vladikavkas through the mountains to Tiflis. We had a private open bus, built to carry 14 or 16 people. Our luggage filled the back seats. At least we thought it was private. First the driver asked if he could take two friends part of the way. That was all right. Then, when it came time for one of the friends to drop off at his destination, his mother was waiting to take his place in the bus. Then the hospitable driver picked up two more friends. Surprisingly, though, he objected strenuously when a Red Army officer and a civilian began to board our bus after a stop for lunch. A hot argument ensued, which of course I could not understand, but the officer and his companion withdrew in defeat. Then it was explained to me that the civilian was a prisoner being taken to trial or prison, and our Russian guardians were afraid that he would try to escape and

311

there might be some shooting. When the officer was asked what crime his prisoner had committed, he replied, "We never say what the crime is."

Driving through the mountains of Georgia was like entering a new world. In contrast to the beaten look of many of the peasants in northern Russia, the men we saw here, in their big white sheepskin hats and with long knives at their belts, had the air and the good humor and the independent swing of mountaineers. Every ox-cart carried a gun. Almost every house had a high stone watchtower, where, at the first sign of any trouble, provisions and water were hauled up, and the men and their strong, good-looking women went up to barricade themselves and fight off any invader. Farther back in the mountains, we were told, in the Valley of Svanetia, accessible over rugged roads open only two months out of every year, lived a tribe descended from a band of lost Crusaders, still using armor and weapons bearing inscriptions in Latin, speaking a language understood by no one else in the whole area, and following a religion composed of scraps of paganism, Christianity, and Mohammedanism. In travel, as in life, there is always some fascinating place, just off the highroad, where one never has time to go.

In Tiflis, the officers of the Kino film factory proudly showed us their studio, still making silent films since there were not yet theaters wired for sound in Georgia; and in the evening they gave us an open-air Georgian banquet. Each guest, except me, was toasted with a charming speech and a glass of Georgian wine. No one's glass was ever permitted to be empty. Then the toastmaster explained that when Georgians received a distinguished guest, the toast to him was drunk from horns of wine. Two horns appeared, each holding about a quart of wine. The toastmaster made an eloquent speech to me. I made what I hope was an appropriate response. Then we each drained our horn of wine at one draught. Mrs. deMille expected me to topple over at any point in the evening from then on, but the wine was so good and the shashlik and roast chicken so plentiful that I kept both my head and my feet. However, I did beat time vigorously, as everyone else did, to accompany the lively Georgian dancing which entertained us; and when we left the banquet at a late hour, it was amid cheers.

Another train journey brought us to Batum and to still another

312

world, a semi-tropical world where the 150 days of annual rainfall brought out lush foliage and necessitated the building of houses on stilts. The women veiled their faces at our approach, but, on a drive to visit a 12,000-acre tea farm, one of the frequent tire punctures enabled us to stop and strike up acquaintance with a Georgian who had been a prince, a very pleasant man in a white blouse and the inevitable fur cap. He let Theodore Kosloff and me try his horse and admire its interesting saddle. Then Theodore made the mistake of offering him a tip. We would have been slain with princely anger if the guide had not explained that, being foreigners, we did not know any better. The prince remounted and rode away without a word.

5

All the way from Berlin we had been safeguarding our tickets for reservations on a ship from Batum to Istanbul. Now we learned that it would be another ship, on another day, and that that ship was delayed by storms in the Black Sea. For five days we were told, "It will probably be here tomorrow." On the fifth day, when an Englishman whom Mrs. deMille happened to meet at lunch told her that he had come in on a French boat which was sailing out again that day, and when we found that the French boat had a cabin open, *with bath,* there was a wild scramble to pack and get to the dock. But at the dock there was Russian officialdom. I had in my luggage a couple of scenarios, some letters of introduction, and financial statements of DeMille Productions and the Bank of America. The latter, which was the kind of statement American banks publish in the newspapers every few months, seemed to the customs official particularly incriminating. He impounded the bag containing these mysterious documents, and I had to board the ship without them; but Mme. Levina, as her last friendly service to us, rounded up a higher official who had the bag delivered to me shortly before we sailed. Mrs. deMille asked Mme. Levina if we could send her some gifts from America. She said, "Yes, but be sure that they are very plain, cotton stockings, not silk, and things like that. It wouldn't do for me to be receiving any fancy or luxurious things from outside the Soviet Union."

Only someone who has spent time in Russia can fully understand what a beautiful sight the French steward in his clean white collar was, when we went in to dinner and he showed us to a table with a clean cloth and napkins; we sat down and breathed the air of freedom.

A young American aboard ship told me that I had seen more of the inside of Russia than the American engineers who had spent years there. In Istanbul, the American Ambassador, Joseph C. Grew, and counselor of the embassy, G. Howland Shaw, who later became Assistant Secretary of State, kept me talking about Russia for an hour without stopping. The ambassador invited me back for luncheon the next day and for dinner the evening after that, saying that he had not had as clear a picture of Russia from any other source. That was the beginning of my friendship with Joseph Grew, one of the ablest and wisest men in the American diplomatic service. When in the 1940's he was excluded from the high councils of our government by men who, for whatever reason, did not see the menace of communism as accurately as he measured it, I was privileged to join him and others, at his invitation, in sponsoring Radio Free Europe and the Crusade for Freedom as a contribution of private citizens to freedom's warfare for the minds of men.

There is no need to pause long over the continuation of our journey to Greece, Egypt, and the Holy Land, all described innumerable times by better pens than mine. A three-day expedition by camel caravan into the Libyan Desert, riding by day through the eternal silent combat of blazing sun and cold desert wind, camping by night in the crisp silver moonlight, with our tents so tiny in the vast expanse of desert sand, taught me how true and wise is the instinct that for so many centuries has led men who have sought to come close to God into desert solitudes.

In Egypt, I formed another lifelong association when Dr. Charles R. Watson, president of the American University at Cairo, made himself, as he put it, our dragoman for a tour of the Cairo antiquities such as only so learned and sympathetic a guide could give us. When we visited the 1,000-year-old Moslem university of Al Azhar, we had a taste of that exquisite Arab courtesy which is one of the most attractive characteristics of that great people. An aged Moslem professor was discoursing to his pupils on a point of doctrine from the Koran; but with a smilingly tolerant bow to Dr.

314

Watson, he added, "There are, of course, some who think differ-
ently about this subject. Allah knows which is right."

Dr. Watson invited me to serve on the committee of Sponsors
of the American University at Cairo, which I have gladly done
ever since, as a very small contribution to the very great work of
a university which is a model of what American cultural centers
in foreign countries can and should be. We have kept a print of
The King of Kings at the American University in Cairo for frequent screening through the years and through all the troubled
changes in Egypt's history in the past quarter-century. When the
first print wore out, Ambassador Stanton Griffis urgently asked us
to provide new ones, which Jeremiah Milbank and I did, because
of the value which the ambassador and the university attached to
the film as a healing influence upon religious tensions. That was
brought out in a story told me, I believe, by Dr. Watson. One day
when the students of the American University were watching *The
King of Kings*, the muezzin's call to prayer was heard from a
near-by mosque. The screening was stopped. The Moslem students knelt, facing toward Mecca. The Christian students waited
respectfully until their classmates had finished their prayer, then
all together resumed following the story of Him whom Moslems
honor as the Prophet Jesus and Christians call the Saviour of mankind.

Tensions later to break into fierce open war were noticeable
when we visited Jerusalem. At the Wailing Wall we saw and heard
devout Jews mourning their still lost land of Israel. Near-by were
Arabs watching the Jews with utter and unconcealed dislike. Between the two groups marched, back and forth, a single British
Tommy, armed, impartial, impassive, sole but sufficient symbol
of the power that kept an uneasy peace in the homeland of the
Prince of Peace.

No religious or national tensions, not even the encrustation of
centuries of unhappy bickering among Christians themselves,
could overlay the moving experience of walking where Jesus of
Nazareth walked, worked, suffered, died, and rose again. Even
when I watched one Christian priest or monk playfully singeing
the beard of another with a lighted candle, as they went in pious
procession near the Holy Sepulchre, I was amused, not shocked. It
is not unnatural to be playful when one feels at home.

315

All throughout my long absence overseas, I was of course in constant touch with affairs at home, through Neil McCarthy and Gladys Rosson. American business was sliding deeper and deeper into depression. The motion picture industry was sliding with it. Pictures were not even returning their negative cost. Although DeMille Productions was, perhaps fortunately, not making pictures, it had found other ways of losing money just as quickly. A construction company and a brokerage house in which we were interested were in bad shape. We had to borrow on my life insurance policies, as well as from banks, and eventually to mortgage our Laughlin Park properties, including my home, to meet our obligations. And then the Bureau of Internal Revenue informed us that DeMille Productions, Mrs. deMille, and I were delinquent in our income taxes, over a period of years, to the grand total of $1,676,563.85.

The government's claim rested principally upon a charge that DeMille Productions had been incorporated for tax avoidance purposes and that the corporation had hoarded its income, instead of distributing it to the shareholders, so that Mrs. deMille and I could avoid paying tax on it as personal income. If the government made good its claim, we were ruined financially. We could not possibly pay the amount claimed. It would mean bankruptcy, personal as well as corporate. Mrs. deMille and I, now both past fifty, would be financially where we had been in 1913 when I took the train to Flagstaff. We might even be worse off: this time we might have to sell the family silver instead of putting it in the pawn shop.

We resolved to appeal the claim, of course; but for the next six years it was to hang over us like one of those avalanches poised over an Alpine village, ready to fall at the slightest jar.

That was the situation we faced at the end of 1931, when we came home to our children and to the staff, reduced in numbers but not in loyalty, who had stayed in the service of their unemployed employer.

The early months of 1932 did, however, bring to completion one of the most satisfying projects I have ever undertaken. As long before as October, 1929—a fateful month and year for starting any financial enterprise!—I had received from a gentleman I did not know, Thomas S. Evans by name, a letter that began, "Out in

Westwood Hills there is building a new university—the University of California at Los Angeles." It was evidently a form letter. The gist of it was that, although the Constitution of California forbade the teaching of religion *by* a state university, the official representatives of the Protestant, Catholic, and Jewish faiths in Los Angeles had joined "for the first time . . . without any compromise of their own positions," to make religion a vital influence *at* the new U.C.L.A.; wherefore Mr. Evans requested "a substantial contribution" to the University Religious Conference, of which the letterhead identified him as executive secretary. I was entirely in sympathy with Mr. Evans' statement that "religion is essential in education"; but I receive many letters asking for contributions, usually "substantial." I had Gladys Rosson write one of the politely noncommittal letters at which she was so expert, asking for more information and sending Mr. Evans my "kindest regards."

As a result, I came to know Tom Evans and, later, the remarkable man who had stimulated this daring and improbable venture of bringing Protestants, Catholics, and Jews together in a common religious cause, Dr. O. D. Foster of the North American Conference on Religion and Higher Education. I found that the Roman Catholic and Anglican bishops of Los Angeles, the rabbi of the largest Jewish congregation in the city, and the ministers of the principal Protestant churches were not merely co-operating. They were almost vying with each other, not for denominational advantage, but to do their utmost to make this equally shared venture a success. The upshot was that I became a member of the board of trustees, chairman of the business and building committee, and eventually treasurer of the University Religious Conference.

It is the worthiest of causes that suffer most during a depression. Mr. and Mrs. Edward L. Doheny made an initial gift of $30,000 to purchase land near the Westwood campus; but from then on it was a grueling struggle even to keep the Conference alive, not to mention putting up a building. There were months when Tom Evans and his assistant, Adaline Guenther, went without salary. There was one point when the Conference's bank balance amounted to $1.96. But the University Religious Conference's building was dedicated on the last day of March, 1932; and it stands today a busy center for student activities of all the religious groups represented in the Conference—a monument to the Prot-

317

estant, Catholic, and Jewish ministers, laymen, and laywomen whose efforts made it possible, and an example, which America and the free world badly need, of interfaith co-operation without compromise.

I have not been active in the affairs of the University Religious Conference for many years; but I had a touching echo from its early days when I learned in 1956 that Dr. O. D. Foster, the father of the Conference, then nearly 80 and living in retirement, was rapidly losing his sight and had expressed a wish that he might see *The Ten Commandments* (1956) before his eyes were veiled by total blindness. I had only an unfinished rough cut of the picture at the time. This I never show to anyone but people connected with film production and hence able to make the necessary allowances for occasional missing scenes, faulty sound, incomplete editing, and other work which still needs to be done on the film; in this case it would take several months. But we brought Dr. Foster to the studio for a special screening; and the last film he saw was the story of the giving of the Law, the fountainhead of all the religions he had spent an unselfish lifetime in bringing closer together.

Edward L. Doheny's connection with the University Religious Conference brings to mind another contact I had with him, on a very different matter. It was a few years after the so-called "oil scandals" of the Harding Administration, but while they were still fresh in the public memory, that Edward L. Doheny invited me to lunch one day. He wanted, he said, to discuss a possible subject for a motion picture. I knew him slightly, as one of the wealthiest men in the West. The whole country knew him as the man who had been acquitted of bribing President Harding's Secretary of the Interior, Albert B. Fall, with $100,000 which Fall had been convicted and sent to prison for accepting! But the size of the alleged bribe was small in the public mind compared to what Edward Doheny was supposed to have received in return: a lease on the fabulous Elk Hill naval oil reserves. What Edward Doheny wanted to tell me was his side of the story; and it would have made one of the most talked of motion pictures of the decade.

As he told it to me, the U.S. Navy, with a prudent eye on future defense needs, wanted to build and stock facilities for 1,500,000

318

barrels of fuel oil at a place where it would be handy to the fleet in a possible future theatre of war. But talk of disarmament was filling the air in the first years of the Harding Administration. For the Navy to put in its budget the necessary appropriation for such an immense installation and the oil to fill it might have disturbed the efforts of the President and Secretary of State Hughes to secure international agreements for a world reduction in naval strength; and it would certainly have given notice to a potential enemy that we were anticipating trouble from his direction. The problem was discussed at high levels in Washington, and the Secretary of the Interior remembered his old and intimate friend from their youthful days together on the western frontier, who had now made an immense fortune in oil, Edward L. Doheny. An appeal was made to Doheny, and he agreed to build the storage facilities and stock them with fuel oil, in exchange for crude oil from the Navy's reserves. It was, in Doheny's mind, a patriotic service to his country, for which he had had to stand trial and for which his friend Fall had been crucified.

The $100,000 delivered to Fall in a little black bag Doheny regarded as a personal loan between old friends, of what was to him a relatively small sum of money, not at all related to the oil leasing arrangement.°

The public did not see it that way, however; nor did the court that convicted Albert Fall. But one of the high names in Washington which was never smeared with oil was that of the Assistant Secretary of the Navy, Theodore Roosevelt, Jr.; and he said that the building of the storage facilities for fuel oil for the Navy was "an essential part of the Navy's plan of defense." The majority of Americans never heard of the place where that fuel oil was to be stored for ready use, until several years later. It was a place in the Pacific Ocean, called Pearl Harbor.

The Doheny story would have made a good movie. But the New York executives thought that it was too political and controversial; so it joined the list of pictures that were never made.

That would be a long list, if I named all the pictures I have wanted to make and those I still want to make. However, I shall

° It is interesting to note that David Hodges Stratton came to very much the same conclusion regarding this loan, after doing his research for *Albert B. Fall and the Teapot Dome Affair,* an unpublished Ph.D. dissertation, University of Colorado, 1955. (*Ed.*)

319

not repeat the error I made once when an interviewer asked me what pictures I would like to produce. I told; and the day after the interview was published, every one of the subjects was registered with the Hays Office by some other producer, thus disbarring me from making any of them. The heights to which human stupidity can soar are unbelievable—or would be, if I hadn't reached them on occasion.

7

In the years since I had left Famous Players-Lasky, that company had changed both its Hollywood habitation and its name. From 1927 to 1930, it was called Paramount-Famous-Lasky. Then it became Paramount-Publix, recognizing the importance of the Publix theaters which it had acquired. In 1932 it was to become Paramount Productions, Inc. I may as well bring the list of changes up to date: in 1936 it became Paramount Pictures Inc., and in 1950 returned to the name it began with in 1914, Paramount Pictures Corporation. Joining in the reader's sigh of relief, I can call it simply Paramount from now on.

It had also moved from the old Lasky lot at Vine and Selma, where we had first found the barn, to a new site on Melrose Avenue, where a studio had been in existence for some time and had passed through several hands before coming into Paramount's. Then the Melrose Avenue frontage was sold and Marathon Street cut through behind it, and Paramount settled into its present location, one of the few Hollywood studios which is still actually in Hollywood.

There was new blood in the company, too. Adolph Zukor and Jesse Lasky were still at the top, but under them the studio was headed by a capable and understanding executive, Ben P. Schulberg. His days there were numbered, but no one knew that, except those who were numbering them, when early in 1932 he and Neil McCarthy negotiated the contract for me to return to Paramount and make one picture, *The Sign of the Cross*.

While Waldemar Young and Sidney Buchman were working on the script, before we were ready to begin production in July, 1932, B. P. Schulberg was succeeded as head of the studio by Emanuel Cohen, known to everyone as Manny Cohen, tiny in stature, but a giant in importance.

His greeting to me, when I went to discuss *The Sign of the Cross* with the new studio head, was: "Remember, Cecil, you are on trial with this picture."

Manny was my greatest trial. Of my old staff, I was allowed to bring back to Paramount with me only Mitch Leisen and Roy Burns. I was assigned a secretary, a conscientious girl, scrupulous in the performance of her duties, particularly the duty of watching the clock. One evening I returned to my office a few minutes after 6 P.M. The office was locked, and the conscientious keeper of the key had gone her way. She did not return. The next day Florence Cole rejoined my studio staff. I was also assigned a film cutter. The head of the cutting department did not like me very well. The cutter he assigned did not know me very well. Soon Anne Bauchens rejoined my studio staff. Perhaps Manny Cohen found me something of a trial too.

But I had a picture to make; and I wanted it right.

Jesse Lasky agreed with me that Charles Laughton would be the ideal Nero; but when he informed the new executives, who had brought new money into the company, that he had signed Laughton for the part, they told him that he had made a frightful mistake, that Charles Laughton would be the worst possible selection to play Nero. I feel sure that the new executives had nothing against Charles Laughton. It was just that the ax was out for Jesse. He has told in his own memoirs how, in the spring of 1932, John Hertz, the new chairman of Paramount's finance committee, suggested to Jesse that he take a leave of absence, that he needed a rest and change. Twenty-five years passed before that "leave of absence" ended and Jesse returned to Paramount, to offices in the same building with me, to start work on *The Big Brass Band*, the picture he wanted most to make, and lived only long enough to begin.

Mr. Zukor still sat in the president's chair; but he must have begun to feel it shake a little.

In signing Charles Laughton, however, Jesse had done an immense last service to *The Sign of the Cross*, to me, to the career of Charles Laughton, and to the public whose appreciation of his performance as Nero made him a star.

Fredric March was cast as Marcus, a Roman officer charged with the extermination of Christians, and Elissa Landi played

321

Mercia, the Christian girl whose steadfast faith and pure love lead Marcus to embrace Christianity and a martyr's death. For the part of Poppaea, Nero's wife, I thought of a young actress, born in Paris but experienced on the American stage and screen, whom Paramount had been using in a succession of fluffy, light-headed roles which, I felt, did not give scope enough to the talent she had. I stopped her one day on the Paramount lot and without any warning or explanation asked her, "Claudette, how would you like to play the wickedest woman in the world?"

Claudette Colbert's beautiful big eyes opened wider. She said, "I'd love it!"

Still, the part of Poppaea would be such a change for her that I thought she had better be tested in it before being definitely cast. I gave her a page of the script containing a scene between Marcus and Poppaea, asked her to prepare it, and scheduled a screen test in costume. When Claudette appeared in the costume of a Roman empress, there was no doubt that she fitted the part visually. But how would she handle the acting and the lines? I asked the empress and the upstanding, noble Roman soldier to run through the lines once before we turned the camera for Claudette's test. It was the shortest dialogue test on record. Between them they spoke only five words of the script before I called a halt. It ran like this:

March: "You harlot!"

Colbert: "I love you!"

DeMille: "That's enough. There's no need for a test. You have the part, Claudette."

Would that all casting, testing, and directing were as easy. We did not think to test the elephants we hired from a circus for one of the scenes of Roman triumph. All they had to do was march past the camera in their lumbering, dignified way. But they too, they decided, were actors. When they entered the scene and heard the clapping and cheering of the Roman multitude, they remembered their circus training and promptly responded to the applause by standing on their heads. One of them at least redeemed that *faux pas* later when, alarmed by something or other, the whole herd of elephants stampeded. One of our players, Bob Miles, was caught in the very middle of the stampede. But the female elephant carrying him in her trunk put Bob on the ground and stood over his body and stayed there immovable, shielding Bob with her sturdy bulk and her four great legs like trees, until the other crazed pachyderms were corralled and quieted. If that one elephant had not had presence of mind or protective instinct or whatever it was that made her a nonconformist among the herd, nothing could have saved Bob Miles from being trampled to death. I kissed the elephant. She was a grand lady.

We had lions in *The Sign of the Cross*, too. The problem with them was not to keep them from stampeding, but to make them move. For one scene I wanted them to go up a flight of stairs into the bright sunlight of the arena, into which the Christians about to be martyred were being driven from another dungeon. The lions' reluctance made it clear that they preferred their cool underground waiting room; and our expert lion-wrangler told me flatly, "Mr. deMille, these cats don't climb stairs." I have little patience with temperament in any of my actors. I took a chair in one hand and an ax-handle in the other and started after the lions. They looked all around, puzzled, as if to say, "Where's the trainer? Why doesn't he protect us from this wild man?", but then they saw the stairway as their only route of escape, and up they went.

There is one scene which caused considerable comment, public and private, and which sheds no little light on the question of censorship. In his effort to seduce Mercia away from her Christian faith and its moral dictates, Marcus brings her to his home and makes her sit through an orgy typical of the pagan Rome of Nero's reign. She is proof against all the enticement of it. Then, as a last resort, a dance is performed before her by one of Marcus' wanton guests. It is an alluring dance. Dramatically, it had to be, to bring out by contrast the greater strength and purity of Mercia's faith. But some thought it too alluring.

As some Jews had opposed *The King of Kings*, the life story of the greatest Jew who ever lived, so some Catholics were most prominent in opposition to *The Sign of the Cross*, a story of the magnificent faith and heroism of the infant Christian community of Rome.

I love the spirituality of the Catholic Church; and this is not a new love either with me or with my family. Staunch Episcopalian as my father was, his diary records his attending Catholic services in Holy Week. Whenever I am in New York, I like to walk down

Fifth Avenue from my hotel, and there are two stops I never fail to make: at the Catholic Cathedral of St. Patrick and at St. Thomas' Church of my own faith. I can meditate equally well in both. When I visited the great church of St. Gudule in Brussels in 1931, I noted in my travel diary, "The Catholic churches seem to have the atmosphere of greater spirituality than the Protestant." But spirituality is one thing and pressure tactics are another. When opposition to *The Sign of the Cross* began to swell, based, as I believed, on an unwarrantable misunderstanding of the dramatic necessity of the dance in question, I determined to resist it.

Will Hays called me on the telephone. As always, he went straight to the point.

"I am with Martin Quigley," he said. "What are you going to do about that dance?"

"Will," I said, "listen carefully to my words because you may want to quote them. Not a damn thing."

"Not a damn thing?"

"Not a damn thing."

The dance stayed in the picture. It was severely criticized, by my good friend Father Daniel Lord among others. That was their right. I have never questioned the right of any individual or group to criticize, even to boycott, a picture. I will always resist, as far as I am able, the claim of any individual or group to the right of censorship.

After première openings in New York and Los Angeles, *The Sign of the Cross* went into general release on February 10, 1933. What American who was adult or adolescent then can fail to remember that month? The pall of depression was at its darkest. Banks were failing, wiping out the meager savings of men and women who had already lost their jobs or were too old to work. Thousands were homeless and hungry. Government seemed paralyzed, caught as it was at the changeover between the Hoover and Roosevelt administrations.* Then came the general "Bank Holiday," as it was called, when every bank in the country was closed in order to prevent a catastrophic collapse of the entire banking system.

* Prior to 1937 the incoming President was inaugurated on the 4th of March following his election, not in January as at present. (*Ed.*)

Without cash, people offered and theater managers accepted unsecured I.O.U.'s, scribbled on little pieces of paper, as admission to see *The Sign of the Cross*. Nearly every one of them was redeemed when cash began to flow again.

The gods of materialism had failed. The foreword to *The Sign of the Cross* bade people "glance back through human history to men and women who held their ideals dearer than their lives.

"Through untold suffering they struggled to keep lighted for us the torch of faith and hope.

"The sacrifice of those martyrs who gave their lives on blood-red sands of Roman arenas preserves for us an eternal Truth.

"The faith born then is still available."

14

I VOTED FOR FRANKLIN D. ROOSEVELT in 1932 for one reason: prohibition. I am a Republican, and I supported my fellow-Californian, Herbert Hoover, in 1928 with the largest contribution I have ever made to a political campaign. Of the five Presidents whom I have met, Herbert Hoover still holds the highest place in my esteem for his sheer brain power and his dogged, uncompromising, selfless honesty. But I felt so strongly that prohibition, however noble in motive, had brought so many evils into American life that in 1932 I turned to the candidate who held out the promise of ending the cause of those evils. No one foresaw then how handily many of the racketeers, deprived of their bootlegging profits, would move into the more respectable and still more lucrative field of labor unions. That too, in my opinion, has been an indirect result of prohibition, which gave the racketeer his first big chance to entrench his parasitic, lawless power.

It was to call attention to the evil of racketeering, and to point to the uncontaminated idealism of American youth, that I made my next picture, *This Day and Age*, in the spring of 1933. The scenario was written by Bartlett Cormack from Sam Mintz's story, "Boys in Office." Charles Bickford played the racketeer boss, Garrett, as convincingly as he had played the noble-hearted miner in *Dynamite:* but most of the principal players were youngsters, portraying the group of high school students who bring Garrett to justice after he slips through a murder charge by legal technicalities and the connivance of cynical public officials. The ever-appealing Richard Cromwell played the student leader, with Judith Allen as his sweetheart. Ben Alexander appeared as one of the students; and there was another youth, who still responds when I call him "Gus," his name in *This Day and Age*, though the present-day television audience knows him better by his real name of Oscar Rudolph, director of the Ann Sothern show and other well-liked television programs.

Some critics thought that *This Day and Age* was Fascist because the youngsters did kidnap Charles Bickford and lower him slowly into a pit full of very businesslike rats, in order to extract from him the confession which they then turned over to the lawful authorities. This, again, like the dance in *The Sign of the Cross*, was a case of painting in heightened colors for dramatic effect. It was not the intention, nor did it so result, that high school students all over America should tackle their local racketeers in the same way, letting rats nibble their toes. And the same critics, as is their wont, made no mention of the very sympathetic presentation of members of minority groups, Jews and Negroes, which was explicitly inserted into the story of *This Day and Age*.

An interesting sidelight was thrown on the unconscious plagiarism of which any writer can be innocently guilty, when I screened the film for my staff in 1953. One of the lines in the picture is: "I like my olives green but I don't pick 'em myself." After that screening, Jack Gariss, one of the writers working with me at the time, told me that he had used that line many times, completely forgetting that he had first heard it twenty years before in *This Day and Age*.

We finished shooting the film on June 21, 1933, at 9:27 A.M. At 9:35 A.M., I began tests for *Four Frightened People*. The lost eight minutes, I suppose, were my vacation that summer.

One of the reviewers of *Four Frightened People* wrote that "Mr. DeMille . . . must have been thinking all the time of his silent version of Barrie's *The Admirable Crichton* which he called *Male and Female*." There was a basic similarity of situation, although *Four Frightened People* was based on a story by E. Arnot Robertson and written for the screen by Bartlett Cormack and Lenore

Coffee. The four people, Claudette Colbert, Herbert Marshall, William Gargan, and Mary Boland, were frightened because, fleeing from cholera and the bubonic plague while on a cruise, they found themselves stranded in the jungles of Malaya.

One would hardly recognize Nero's wicked wife in the prim, demure schoolteacher, with her hair severely parted in the middle and combed straight to frame a face devoid of make-up and wearing large horn-rimmed spectacles; but Claudette Colbert could never be really unattractive. Claudette, however, does not enjoy the creeping and crawling creatures of the jungle, and I had to assure her solemnly that she would not meet any such unpleasant companions in the parts of Hawaii where we were to shoot the film. Almost the first thing she did when she arrived at the location was to sit on an eight-inch centipede.

Having described Claudette's appearance in character at the beginning of the picture, I must hasten to say that the rigors of jungle life brought out all the little schoolteacher's strength and womanly charm, so much that her two male companions were fighting over her before they finally reached the safety of a British outpost.

Some of the scenes of *Four Frightened People* are played at the base of an enormous stone idol, left in ruins in the thick of the jungle. Constructing it was not an easy matter, especially in view of the provision that we had to leave the Hawaiian forest as we found it, after we finished shooting; but Roland Anderson, our art director, built a magnificent idol and shrine, some 60 feet tall, and I found a spot on a jungle trail which would be a perfect location for it. I was told that we could put the idol there, since the trail was used very little, except occasionally by the patients or staff of a near-by mental hospital when they were out for walks.

Two of the patients, presumably soon due for discharge as cured, happened along while we were still working there. When they returned to the hospital, one of the doctors asked them about their walk, if they had enjoyed it, if they had seen anything unusual. The patients did not want to risk being confined again, by telling any unlikely stories about suddenly coming upon an ancient idol blocking the familiar path. They said, "No, nothing unusual."

"Come, come," the doctor said, "you must be honest with me. I

328

know there is a motion picture company working down there and they've built a great head of Buddha or something. We'll go down together tomorrow and I'll explain it all to you."

But late that afternoon Roy Burns came to me and explained that the only way we could catch the boat on which the company had reservations to go home would be to move the idol to our next scheduled location and finish the scenes there. I pointed out the huge cost of dismantling and moving the 60-foot idol; but Roy, with his usual efficiency, had the figures to prove that it would be much more costly if we missed the boat, and he added that he had a crew ready to work all night taking down the idol and packing it for transport. Roy is like that. When Roy says, "We can't do it, Boss" or "We can," he is one expert whom I am inclined to believe.

Came the next morning, as the subtitle of a silent picture would put it, and the conscientious doctor shepherded his two patients to the spot where, they said, they had seen nothing unusual. The forest and the trail looked exactly as they had looked before any movie company had come near them. The doctor said, "Well . . ." The patients said, "You were going to show us . . . ?" And all three returned to the hospital in, I am sure, a thoughtful silence.

2

While we were editing *Four Frightened People,* back in Hollywood, Mrs. deMille and I were summoned to Washington to testify before the Board of Tax Appeals in the government's $1,-600,000 suit against us. A rough cut of the picture had been put together, but I had to leave the vitally important final decisions on editing to the none too tender mercies of the same cutting department which had so resented my insisting that Anne Bauchens be brought back and her name written into my contract. I should not like to say that anyone in that department seized the chance to cut my throat as well as my picture; but the degree of intelligence applied to the editing may perhaps be manifested by one example. At one point in the picture, William Gargan, wanting Claudette Colbert to stand up and start moving through the jungle, says to her, "Come on, Little Miss Muffett." I was informed from Hollywood that that line was being cut out, because Claudette's name in the picture was Jones, not Muffett, and it would confuse the audience!

329

Four Frightened People was one of my few spectacular failures at the box office. It fell about $500 short of returning its cost. It comforts me to think that this was due to the final editing; but perhaps it should also confirm me in sticking to my own last and leaving whimsical stories to directors like Preston Sturges or Leo McCarey or Billy Wilder who are so good at that type of picture.

Mrs. deMille and I were more successful before the Board of Tax Appeals, however. Supported by the evidence of Neil Mc-Carthy and John Fisher, and by the minutes of Cecil B. DeMille Productions for the years in question, Mrs. deMille and I testified that the corporation had been formed with the sole intent of being ready to go into independent picture-making and that it had retained its earnings instead of distributing them to the shareholders, not to avoid taxes, but to build up, if possible, a reserve large enough to let us finance our own pictures without needing the help or suffering the interference of outside capital.

I did not see how any court could interpret the facts in the record other than as Mrs. deMille and I understood and testified about them. But everyone who goes into court thinks he is right; and government agencies, including courts, are unpredictable. I have seldom felt so relieved of anxiety as when the majority opinion of the Board, delivered by Judge Edgar J. Goodrich, declared, referring to our testimony and the minutes of DeMille Productions:

> We are not ready to disregard this testimony or to say that the recorded thoughts of the company's guiding heads, the writing of which was begun more than a decade ago, was artfully drawn for self-service against a future day of trial. Those denials of wrongful intent, those declarations of a purpose other than the avoidance of taxes in the building of a surplus, we believe. . . . It is apparent that the company, when producing under contracts for others, was beset with controversies and difficulties and frequently, if not constantly, endangered by the possibility of cancellation of its contracts. The desire and determination of the stockholders to advance the activities of their company from those of a producer under contract to others, to those of an independent producer, financed sufficiently to insure the making and marketing of its own pictures, seem not unreasonable . . . and . . . we cannot say that the surplus accumulated by this corporate petitioner was beyond

330

that necessary to its ends. . . . Consequently, for these reasons, we have made our finding, and hold that respondent erred in imposing upon petitioner the taxes provided by these sections of the statutes.

Behind Judge Goodrich's majestic legal phrasing lay all the years since *The Ten Commandments* (1923), years of struggle and frustration, of pictures I often did not particularly want to make but still made to the best of my ability, years in which I was reaching a stage of life when time grew ever shorter to make the pictures I wanted to make, and finally the year in which every door in Hollywood was closed against me until Ben Schulberg reopened that at Paramount to me to make *The Sign of the Cross*. If the government had won its case, they would have been lost years. I would have been so mortgaged to the government, to pay off that crushing tax load, that I would have lost, probably, any chance of ever being independent. I would have had to take whatever contract terms and whatever picture subjects any producing company would give me, probably for years to come.

I did not know Judge Goodrich, except for having seen him on the bench at our hearing, but he has held one of the warmest spots in my heart ever since. His judicial decision not only saved me *from* losing a very large sum of money and some of the best years of my life, it saved me *for* the possibility of making some of the kind of pictures I wanted to make. I have come to know Edgar Goodrich since, as one of the most genial and erudite gentlemen I am privileged to number among my friends; and he wears his erudition with a grace and lightness which remind me of the men of the Renaissance, who could tune a viol as readily as they could turn a couplet or discourse on the philosophy of Plato. In Judge Goodrich's case, the viol is a guitar; and the verses are touching, profound or comic, as suits his fancy; and Plato would enjoy knowing him.

The pleasantest social afternoon I have ever spent, I think, was one Saturday, nearly 20 years after our hearing before the Board of Tax Appeals, when Judge Goodrich took me to a little old brick building, whose address in Washington I would not reveal even if I remembered it, where he and a dozen friends used to foregather —I hope they still do—on any random Saturday whenever enough of them could spare the time from their busy official lives, for a manly luncheon and an afternoon of talk and song. Neither will I reveal the name of their informal club, nor the names of those who were present on the afternoon when I was allowed to be with them. Outside that little brick building, they were generals, judges, men high in government, the professions, and the world of business. But on those Saturday afternoons, the stars, the robes, the cares and worries of their high responsibilities were shed for a few hours. Around the plain long table where I sat with them, they were just themselves, Ed, Jimmy, or whatever; and the talk was both light and brilliant, and the songs, many of their own composition, delightfully hilarious. In fact, the only people who may not have enjoyed that afternoon were the efficient and courteous waiter who attended us, because he had to make so many trips to the telephone for calls to me, all of which I resolutely refused to answer, and the officials of the morgue, not far away, who complained that our singing disturbed the inhabitants of that institution.

The good companions of that afternoon may not remember it as well as I do: but I remember it because they made this stranger among them feel at home.

And when in 1956 Judge Goodrich was kind enough to tell me that he liked *The Ten Commandments,* released that year, my mind went back to our case before the Board of Tax Appeals, and I said to him: "You made *The Ten Commandments* possible."

No tax collector will ever be deterred by an initial reverse, of course. The government carried our case to the Circuit Court of Appeals and eventually to the Supreme Court of the United States. But Judge Goodrich's decision in our favor was upheld all the way.

It is a sobering thought that this book may perhaps be read in some countries where the puzzled reader may ask himself, "An individual private citizen, winning a case against the government, in the government's own courts?" That is liberty under law, next to religion the most precious possession of the free world.

Others were not faring so well in the courts at the time, however. Paramount was heading into bankruptcy. Like my own tax case, Paramount's corporate troubles dragged on for several years. In both cases, I have to do here what it is necessary to do in a

332

motion picture sometimes: telescope history a little, to show the connections of events perhaps widely separated in time.

A cruelly pathetic image of Adolph Zukor was drawn by *The Hollywood Reporter* of October 28, 1933, when it chronicled: "The Paramount 'inside' came out in the open today and from it emerged a picture of a weary old man who had built a great institution—and then reached a point where everybody else was running it but him."

Old? Adolph Zukor was 61. Weary? If he was weary, he had reason enough to be. Again, I must leave the full story of Paramount in those troubled years to be told by some general historian of motion pictures when all the archives are opened and all the participants in that drama have had their final say. But I believe that no one, no Cecil Rhodes, no Croesus, no Napoleon, could have kept Paramount afloat on the bitter waters of The Great Depression. I believe that Adolph Zukor did all he could. If not all his decisions were wise, whose are? His reward was a demand by the trustees in bankruptcy that his contract be canceled.

The trustees and creditors did not stop there. At one point some of the bankers were insisting that no one connected with motion pictures should be on the reorganized board of directors of this motion picture company! Mr. Zukor was forced out of the presidency. But fortunately the stockholders had power enough at least to keep him on the board, and he was left in general charge of production.

I went to see Mr. Zukor on some business during this time. He was showing the strain, in ways that saddened me. Adolph Zukor and I had fought in 1924; but while I am a pretty good fighter, I am a very poor hater. Being Dutch, I talked to this man, nine years my senior, like a Dutch uncle. I told him what he had meant to the motion picture industry, how much it owed to him and how it still needed him, that if he accepted defeat, not only he but Paramount and the whole industry would be irreparably the losers. Perhaps my words helped a little. But Adolph Zukor has always been a good general; and one of the marks of a good general is an ability to throw his attackers off balance.

Daringly, he called his opponents' bluff. He invited the new managers to run the company without him. Soon the bankers themselves were ready to plead with him to stay.

There would be little point in listing the names of those who came and went, like ships that pass in the night, sometimes barely speaking to each other in passing, in and out of high executive positions in Paramount, until the present administration, with Barney Balaban as president and Adolph Zukor as chairman of the board, took hold in 1936. The permanence of the Balaban regime for more than 20 years is testimony to the stability and strength it brought to a tottering structure.

If DeMille Productions or I had had money enough, we could have entered into control of Paramount at a time when its stock was selling for $2 a share; but our whole surplus was $600,000 short of what was needed to go into the deal John Hertz offered us in 1934. As it was, we had to sacrifice monies still due us from *The Ten Commandments* (1923) in order to effect a compromise with the trustees and obtain our entitled share of the earnings of *The Sign of the Cross.*

Among the comings and goings of executives, there was one change which touched me amusingly. When Manny Cohen took his departure, he was succeeded for a time as studio head of production by Ernst Lubitsch. Like myself, Lubitsch was a director, not an executive type. As directors, we had a high and healthy respect for each other. Our pictures were very different indeed, but I recognized Lubitsch as the top director in his field, and he apparently thought that I did well in mine. Whenever I went to him for decisions which only the production head can make, he invariably got flustered and red in the face with embarrassment at having to give me instructions and permissions. Fortunately for the millions who enjoyed his uniquely delightful films, the great talent that was Lubitsch's was not long wasted behind an executive's desk; he resigned to give his full time to his own pictures.

It is time for me to get back to mine.

3

With the exception of *The Greatest Show on Earth,* produced in 1952, all my motion pictures since *Four Frightened People* have been on historical themes. (Perhaps even *The Greatest Show on Earth* must be considered an historical picture now, since "circus day" in the small cities and towns of America has become, alas, a thing of the past.) Whether Paramount was frightened by *Four Frightened People*, or simply came to the conclusion that a man does best what he enjoys doing, or was influenced by the fact that in the past 20 years or so I have been able partially to finance my own productions, I have had greater freedom in the selection and treatment of subject matter during these years with Paramount than I had ever had before. Not that I have always had perfectly clear sailing or a total absence of difference of opinion with the Paramount executives, even in these happy years. Hollywood would not be Hollywood, nor would New York be New York, if suddenly the twain should meet in perfect harmony. But all in all they have been happy years. How much that has been due to one man I shall try to express when it comes time to tell what I feel about Frank Freeman.

Looking back over the series of historical pictures that began with *Cleopatra* in 1934, I see each one as a step closer to a goal that I have yet to reach. In my last two pictures, *The Greatest Show on Earth* and *The Ten Commandments* (1956), I believe that I have come closer than ever before to getting on the screen the conception that was in my mind. If the Lord gives me time, I hope to come closer still; for I still have some ideas, not yet realized.

People sometimes ask me which of my pictures is my favorite. That is like asking a mother which of her children she likes best. There are parts of nearly every one of my pictures that I do not think I have equaled in any other; and there are places in every one of them that make me want to shrink down inside my coat and hide whenever I see them on the screen. I exempt from all these comparisons only one picture: *The King of Kings*, because of its subject. As Will Rogers said to me after seeing it, "You will never make a greater picture, because there is no greater subject."

One of my longest and closest professional and personal associations began because I was impatient about waiting my turn for the use of a projection room at the studio, while I was casting *Cleopatra*. I had already engaged Claudette Colbert for the title role, but had not yet found a satisfactory Marc Antony to play opposite her. However, I did have some film footage of horses that I wanted to see, for possible use in the picture. I took it to a

335

projection room, but found the room in use by some other producers who were looking at test films, so I carried my horse footage up to the projectionist's booth and asked him if he would run it for me as soon as the room was cleared of those other people. While waiting in the booth, I heard, coming from the sound track of the test film, a resonant, manly voice, with only a pleasant trace of an English accent. I peeked through the projectionist's little window toward the screen, and saw that the owner of the voice that had caught my ear was a young actor, with a handsome, strong, sensitive face, a finely-shaped head, and a powerfully-built frame.

"Never mind the horses," I said to the projectionist. "I want you to run that test again for me."

I watched the second running of the test critically, but I was as much impressed by it as I had been by the first. I asked who the young actor was.

"Oh," I was told, "he's a young Englishman that Paramount signed from the London stage. Name of Harry Wilcoxon, but the executives don't think 'Harry' is dignified enough, so we're changing his name to Henry Wilcoxon."

"Harry or Henry," I said, "he is Marc Antony."

That was my first glimpse of my present closest associate in production. Henry Wilcoxon, I found, is a man of many talents in addition to the acting ability which had impressed me in his test. His office is decorated with his own paintings, and they are good. He is a good swordsman and rider. In story conferences with our screenwriters, he is an active shaper of ideas and craftsman of dramatic construction. He has a capacity for detail which is most important in the work of production. As an actor, he has played with distinction the leads or important supporting roles in six of the twelve pictures I have made since 1934, as well as in many other pictures. His appearance as a clergyman in *Mrs. Miniver* gave the screen one of its most memorable moments, when he summed up the whole meaning of that moving story of English bravery and hope in a short sermon he gave in a bombed-out church. That sermon, widely reprinted in many languages during World War II, brought its message of courage and faith to many who never knew that it was written overnight by Henry Wilcoxon and William Wyler and filmed the next morning. Its message was

336

needed in the picture because the war had come to America just a few days before, and the haste of its writing and filming was necessary because Henry Wilcoxon was already on active duty with the United States Navy. His five years in the service inter-rupted our professional relationship, but nothing has interrupted our friendship since I cast him as Marc Antony in *Cleopatra;* he has been my associate producer since 1948.

For the part of Julius Caesar I chose Warren William. Perhaps he was overshadowed in the public mind by the other talent in the picture or by the fact that, true to history, Caesar was killed halfway through the story; but I have always felt that neither the critics nor the public did justice to Warren William's per-formance. I have seen other fine actors playing Julius Caesar; I have never seen any that surpassed Warren William.

Joseph Schildkraut played Herod; he was surprised when I told him only a year or so ago that "that small part," as he called it, was in my opinion one of the best performances he has ever given. Another of my favorite players, Ian Keith, was Octavian; and the part of Marc Antony's friend, Enobarbus, was played by C. Aubrey Smith, not yet knighted as Sir Aubrey, but showing to the full those qualities as an actor which made him a delight to work with, and those qualities as a man which brought him honors from his sovereign and the respect and affection of everyone in Hollywood. His scene with Henry Wilcoxon, when Enobarbus bids farewell to Marc Antony, stripping himself, one by one, of the badges and chains that commemorate events in their long comradeship in arms, is one of the most moving scenes in any picture I have made.

Remembering Claudette Colbert's squeamishness about centi-pedes when we were making *Four Frightened People* in Hawaii, I thought it well to have a serious private talk with her before finally signing her for the role of Cleopatra.

"You remember," I said, "how Cleopatra died. She committed suicide by putting an asp, which is a venomous snake, to her bare breast and letting it kill her."

I seemed to have an uncanny faculty for saying things that made Claudette's beautiful big eyes grow bigger, but not always with pleasure.

"Oh, Mr. deMille," she said, "I couldn't do that! A snake? I couldn't possibly——"

"Wait, Claudette," I interrupted. "Don't say positively that you can't, or I cannot give you the part. You want to play it, don't you?

"Yes, but——"

"No, now wait, please. I want you to play it. I don't want anyone but you for Cleopatra. Will we just not say any more about the snake until we come to it, and will you trust me if I tell you that you can play the scene?"

With the greatest lack of enthusiasm I have ever seen in an actress being offered a desirable role, Claudette reluctantly agreed.

In all her scenes with Warren William, Henry Wilcoxon, and the rest, she was perfect. She was the imperious Queen. She was the vivacious, alluring woman. She was Egypt. Then came the final big scene. Caesar and Antony were dead. The armies of Rome were massed before the very gates of her palace. Cleopatra was alone, helpless, with both love and power gone; but she was still the Queen. She would not be dragged behind a conqueror's chariot to make a Roman holiday. She would die first. In regal robes, she mounted for the last time the splendid throne of Egypt. Claudette and I had not mentioned snakes for quite some time.

I had been thinking about them, though. I had borrowed from the zoo the largest snake the zoo would lend me. I coiled it around my body and came on the set with one hand behind my back, in the pose that always betokens arrogance, and in my other hand the head of the huge serpent pointed straight at Claudette on her throne.

As soon as she saw me coming, she cried, "Oh, Mr. deMille, don't come near me with that!"

Steadily I advanced until I was at the foot of the throne, into which the Majesty of Egypt was shrinking like a very frightened girl.

She pleaded, "I *cannot* touch it, Mr. deMille!"

"Well," I said, "how about this?" And I brought from behind my back my other hand and in it a tiny, harmless snake, the proper size of an Egyptian asp.

"Oh," Claudette said with relief, "that little thing! Give it to me!"

I uncoiled the large borrowed reptile from my body, with gratitude for his temporary services; and Claudette played her death scene with the proper little snake, and played it very well.

I was less successful, in one of the big crowd scenes in *Cleopatra*, in getting quite the performance I wanted from a few of the extra players. They were not acting. They were just there. After working most of the morning and still not getting the general crowd performance that I wanted, I made a little speech, with some forcefulness pointing out that even a few indifferent, careless extra players could spoil a whole scene just as one rotten apple can spoil a whole barrel. I suppose that everyone's nerves were a little raw after the frustrating morning, but my phrase about the apple must have been the last straw to one of the extras, an old man, who stepped out of the crowd, came over to me, and, shaking his fist under my nose, told me loudly, among several other uncomplimentary things, that I was a sour old crabapple. That seemed to me an appropriate time to call lunch. The set had hardly broken for lunch when the old man came to me again and apologized. He said he did not know what had got into him, that he should never have said such a thing; he was profusely sorry.

"Well," I said, "maybe it's true."

"No, it's not true."

"Well, it could be. I suppose I am sour sometimes."

Now he became vehement. "No, you're not! It's not true at all."

The old man and I spent the lunch hour sitting together on some steps, arguing about my vices as a director, I maintaining that I had plenty of them and he stoutly defending me.

4

Among the cartoons which I keep on the wall of my office at the studio is one entitled, "One of Cecil B. DeMille's Yes-Men Says 'No.'" The cartoonist has drawn me, or a reasonable facsimile of me, standing on a high platform directing a cast of, undoubtedly, thousands in a scene which appears as if it might be the storming of a medieval castle. At the foot of the platform is a man, in a posture of brave defiance, uttering the horrendous, the unheard-of, word, "No." The battlements of the castle are shaking like leaves of the aspen. Stalwart men are fainting or frozen with shock. The very earth seems to shudder. All in all, it is a clever, amusing vignette of a peculiarly persistent lie.

I have no use for yes-men. I have never understood why anyone should be paid a salary for giving back to me my own thoughts. I have a number of mirrors in my house and a tape recorder in my office which could serve that purpose, if I were interested in it, much more economically. What I want, what I need, from the people who work with me is not that they be echoes, but experts. I want their ideas, not mine repeated. If we differ, I want them to defend their ideas against mine. With any member of my staff, I will sometimes argue against an idea of his which I know is good, in order to get him to make it still better. If he really believes in his idea, he will fight for it; and out of that creative contest is likely to be born a better idea than either he or I might have produced alone. Yes-men contribute nothing. They simply waste my time.

I cannot think of any more disgusting, and indeed insulting, form of sycophancy than for anyone to agree with me only because he thinks that is the smart thing for him to do. I have had a very few like that around me at times, in whose mealy mouths butter would not melt when they were talking to me, but gall would seem sweet compared to what they said about me elsewhere. Sometimes I saw through them early. Sometimes it took me a little longer. Sometimes I kept them on because of some other value they had, while I suppose they were congratulating themselves on pulling the wool over the old egomaniac's eyes.

Yet I can see how the deMille yes-man legend may have grown up. I have not much use for no-men either; by which I mean people who cannot admit that they are ever wrong, who always adopt and never budge from a negative attitude toward anyone's ideas but their own. Then, too, there are the people to whom a cynical attitude toward everything and everyone else seems a necessary cover for their own pettiness of mind and heart. Twisted themselves, they must always be looking for the "angles." They can never see anything as it is: they see only what can feed their sense of their own smartness. They are the people who can never afford to say a whole-souled "yes" to anything. I have known some like that too; and I am afraid I have not always remembered that perhaps they deserve more pity than contempt. But to such poor souls I suppose anyone who ever says yes is a yes-man.

It must have been around 1934—I do not want to be too exact—

that I first made the acquaintance of a persistent gentleman whom I shall call Mr. Whitman, since I do not remember ever having known anyone whose real name was Whitman. Mr. Whitman wanted me to produce a picture on a certain Biblical subject. He also had aspirations as a songwriter, I believe. Since there is dramatic material on almost every page of the Bible, it would take more than a lifetime to bring it all to the screen; and Mr. Whitman was courteously informed by my office, as many others have been, that my production schedule did not permit me to consider his suggestion. Mr. Whitman did not give up easily, however. He sent me gifts. I sent them back. He sent me letters in which a strict lawyer might have scented hints at extortion; but I declined to press charges on these.

When he appeared somewhat vociferously outside my dining room window while a dinner party was in progress, however, and particularly when he began to direct his rather threatening attention toward my daughter Katherine, I felt that something should be done. Mr. Whitman was arrested, given a psychiatric examination, and committed to a state mental institution. Mr. Whitman did not feel at all kindly about my part in these proceedings.

For years afterward, life was made interesting by telegrams from the mental hospital, advising me in effect, "Whitman escaped. Look out for yourself." My family and staff would see to it that I was surrounded by adequate protection until another message came, informing me that I could relax, Whitman was back in custody. Finally, he was discharged as cured. Occasionally he would be seen in the neighborhood of the studio, whereupon my secretary would invariably summon the studio police to action stations: my family and staff did not view his discharge with the scientific detachment of the state psychiatrists. Sometimes he would write to me. Once he wrote from Europe, asking me for a letter of recommendation for a job there. It took me nearly a week to write the letter in terms that would in all fairness put the prospective employer reasonably on his guard without spoiling Mr. Whitman's chances of possibly making a fresh start in life.

Then, many years later, I had occasion to go to Europe myself with certain members of my family and staff. I have already remarked, I believe, on my unreliable memory for names. The first day aboard ship, at dinnertime, I called the attention of those with me to a man on the other side of the large dining room and said, "I've seen that man somewhere. There's some important connection, but I cannot, cannot place him." None of my companions knew him, and I wracked my brain in vain all through dinner. It was, of course, Mr. Whitman: he was waiting for me at the door, to reintroduce himself, when I finished dinner. The two men with me, my son-in-law and my executive assistant, quickly went around a corner to double up in unholy glee at my predicament, much to the disgust of my granddaughter who stood stanchly by me, expecting to see grandfather assassinated on the high seas.

All Mr. Whitman wanted then was to greet me effusively and ask if he could have a private chat with me. Against the advice of everyone with me, I sent him word later that I would see him alone in my cabin the following afternoon. I did not know until afterward that, during his visit with me, the male members of my party were poised behind the half-open doors of the two adjoining cabins, ready to pounce to my defense. Their stalwart services were not needed, however. Mr. Whitman chatted most amiably. But the crowning touch came when he presented me with his picture, autographed. The inscription read: "In memory of our twenty years of association."

Soon after the completion of *Cleopatra*, I began work with Harold Lamb on the script of my next picture, *The Crusades*. As the readers of his many books know, Harold Lamb has the gift of combining sound scholarship with stirring and colorful writing. It is such a pleasure to work with him that I have always welcomed picture subjects on which he could collaborate with me. To *The Crusades* especially he brought his rare and sympathetic understanding of the peoples of the Middle East, which helped achieve one of my objectives: to bring out that the Saracens were not barbarians, but a highly cultivated people, and their great leader, Saladin, as perfect and gentle a knight as any in Christendom. Another of Hollywood's best writers and my good friend, Dudley Nichols, collaborated on *The Crusades* with Harold Lamb and Waldemar Young; Jeanie Macpherson, Howard Higgin, and Charles Brackett also contributed to the writing, as indeed Jeanie did to most of my pictures from then on, whether or not she took screen credit for her work.

342

My chief cameraman at this time was the award-winning Victor Milner; and Cullen Tate was joined as assistant director by a young Scotsman named David MacDonald, who had come to me in 1933 with a letter of introduction, a long-standing ambition to be a motion picture director, and absolutely no preparation for it except the hardly useful experience of having spent several years on a rubber plantation in Malaya. But the time he came was just when we were getting ready for *Four Frightened People* and needed someone who knew the Malayan language and the ways of Malayan jungle dwellers. He was so competent on *Four Frightened People* that I kept him with me until he learned film production thoroughly and was ready to return to Great Britain and make a name for himself in the British film industry with his picture on the African campaign of World War II, *Desert Victory*.

If I tried to pay due tribute to all who contributed to what the public knows as "DeMille pictures," there would be room for little else in this book; but perhaps the public may learn from this book to be patient with and grateful for the long list of credits they see on their theater screens. In *The Crusades*, for example, audiences have marveled at the scene in which Saladin, demonstrating the fineness of his sword, lets fall on its edge a flimsy veil, which the sword at a touch cuts in two; but the audience could not know the patient skill of the technicians who made that scene possible to photograph.

Henry Wilcoxon was the obvious choice for the lion-hearted King Richard. I have often wondered, though, what a certain patient in a Los Angeles hospital thought of that choice. While we were preparing *The Crusades*, I was confined to the hospital for a time with some minor illness that did not interfere with my work or with my running pictures every night in the hospital's projection room, much to the joy of the other ambulant patients. We were at the stage of approving costume designs for *The Crusades*, and I pressed nurses into service to model the women's costumes and had men from the studio clanging in and out of my room attired as knights, monks, Saracens, and what not. One day a patient from a near-by room was just being wheeled out for an operation when he beheld, striding by, the noble figure of Henry Wilcoxon in full regalia as the King. I have wondered if that pa-

343

tient may have thought fleetingly that his operation was all over, and had not been a success.

Thanks to our treatment of the subject and the wonderfully sensitive performance of Ian Keith as Saladin, *The Crusades* has been one of my most popular pictures in the Middle East, where one might least expect that subject to be well received. Queen Berengaria, Richard's wife, was played by Loretta Young, who was just as lovely then as she is now; and my daughter Katherine had the part of Richard's rejected fiancée, the Princess Alice. A story such as *The Crusades* has many parts for good character actors, and I was glad to be working again with C. Aubrey Smith, Joseph Schildkraut, Montague Love, Pedro de Cordoba, Hobart Bosworth, and others whose talent and experience made for gemlike performances in the supporting roles. Apart from Berengaria and Alice, the best parts in a picture about warriors naturally were parts for men; but there was one young girl, briefly glimpsed in the first reel when she is sold at a slave auction, whose name, Ann Sheridan, would later head many a cast list, though it was not mentioned among the cast of *The Crusades.*

The Crusades is an example of what I have called telescoping history. In historical fact, there were several Crusades extending over two centuries. It would be impossible to tell the story of them all in 12,000 feet of film; and if one tried, the audience would leave the theater confused, bored, and anxious to tell all their friends to stay away from that breathless dash through medieval history. Audiences are not interested in dates: they are interested in events and their meaning. We chose the year 1187 as the focal point for our story, but did not hesitate to bring in elements from other Crusades before or after that exact time. For instance, the Hermit, played by C. Aubrey Smith, was meant to embody Peter the Hermit, Bernard of Clairvaux, and all the zealous preachers who stirred Europe to arise and take the Cross. The history conveyed to the audience by *The Crusades* was simply that there was a time when Christian men, kings, knights, and commoners, with motives ranging from the purest faith to the blackest treachery and greed, left their homes by the thousands and sought to wrest the Holy Land from its Moslem possessors, who were not, as the propaganda of the time would have it, infidel dogs, but highly civilized and chivalrous foemen. I submit that if

344

anyone in the audience took that conception home with him, he had a very good idea of what the Crusades were all about. The personal story of Richard and Berengaria, told against that historic background and amid such stirring scenes as the great battle of Acre, held the audiences' interest, and perhaps conveyed too the truth that the men and women of the history books were men and women of flesh and blood.

The Crusades was released in the United States in October, 1935. In England, where it might have been expected to be a great success, its release came at the time when, in Lord Dawson of Penn's unforgettable phrase, the life of King George V was moving peacefully to its close; and the stricken nation, mourning its beloved King, had no heart for going to the theater.

It is very seldom that a film which does not do well at the start of its release ever catches up later on. Perhaps that is one reason why *The Crusades*, in my opinion one of the best pictures I have ever made, was not a greater financial success in its first release. It did, however, give me the unusual experience of being flattered by a tax collector. In one of the Bureau of Internal Revenue's periodic scrutinies of my books, the Bureau's agent expressed amazement that so good a picture as *The Crusades* did not at the time show a profit; but there was nothing in it for him to tax.

Cecil B. DeMille Productions was slowly, very slowly, working its way out of its own private depression. *The Crusades* was my last picture under the then existing contract with Paramount, and as usual in those days there were the lengthy negotiations about a new contract. Sam Goldwyn invited DeMille Productions to go over as a unit to United Artists, but it would have taken a $1,400,-000 investment, which we did not have. Then Sam made one of the gestures characteristic of him: he offered to finance us for one-half of what was needed; but, with the ominous income tax case still unresolved, we could not afford even to accept that generous offer.

For a time in 1935, Mrs. deMille and I even discussed retiring from motion pictures altogether. I had directed 60 films in all. Most of them, we felt, were a credit to us. We would have left with that record, a name that for 50 years had lived in the American theater, not without distinction. But I suppose we both should have known that we were idly dreaming when we talked about retirement or concentrating on other business interests. Mrs. deMille has always been brave and loyal, but I just wonder how she would have survived my trying to be interested in nothing but real estate or oil wells, with the Champion Driver straining at the leash to storm the walls of Acre, launch Cleopatra's royal barge, or chase a pride of lions upstairs. Paramount's co-operation helped us decide what undoubtedly we would have decided anyway, somehow: the final terms of the new contract gave me the right to have my own production unit, with Paramount retaining only approval of story and budget; and we were at least in a position to finance part of the budget.

5

If we had been foolish enough to retire in 1935, I wonder if I might have missed the experience which brought me closer to the American people than anything else I have ever done. It began in 1936, when I was approached by representatives of Lever Brothers, the powerful international firm of soap makers, with an idea. Their idea was a new radio program. Lever Brothers thought, very accurately as it turned out, that the program would sell soap. I saw in it an opportunity to bring the living theater, good drama, possibly great drama, into the living rooms of American homes; and I hasten to add that I was not repelled by the salary offered me if I would take part in this enterprise—some $2,000 a week. In the 1930's, radio was almost, if not quite, as bad a word among motion picture people as television was to become later; but I thought, also accurately I believe, that the proposed radio program would help, not hurt, motion pictures, for its basis was to be the dramatization of stories that had been filmed, played by actors and actresses from motion pictures.

The first broadcast of the Lux Radio Theatre went on the air on June 1, 1936, when I first spoke the words, "Greetings from Hollywood, ladies and gentlemen." The play was *The Legionnaire and the Lady*, starring Clark Gable and Marlene Dietrich. The program originated in the old Music Box Theatre in Hollywood, where week after week we had a live audience of about 1,000 people, to give the players and the director the lift that only a living audience can provide.

But the great audience of the Lux Radio Theatre was America.

346

For nearly nine years after that June evening in 1936, I spoke "Greetings from Hollywood" on Monday nights to an ever-growing audience, in homes across the whole broad country, in hospitals, later in camps and installations of the armed forces, wherever there was a radio within range of the Columbia Broadcasting System; and every Monday night, after an hour of good entertainment, I signed the program off the air with "This is Cecil B. deMille saying good-night to you from Hollywood."

There were times when I went from a hospital on a stretcher to the broadcasting theater. There was one time when the passengers on a crack transcontinental train fretted and, I trust, believed that their delay was caused by a hotbox or some other small mechanical difficulty, while I finished saying good-night from Hollywood and raced to where the train was held for me on the outskirts of Los Angeles. Once, when I visited the White House, the President's secretary showed me a chart which Franklin D. Roosevelt kept to gauge the size of the nationwide audience of his renowned "fireside chats": the program the President used for comparison of audience appeal was the Lux Radio Theatre. On peak Mondays, there were sometimes 40,000,000 listening to the Lux hour.

I like big numbers; but what the Lux program meant to me cannot be measured by any numbers. It meant families in Maine and Kansas and Idaho finishing the dishes or the schoolwork or the evening chores in time to gather around their radios. It meant the shut-ins, the invalid, the blind, the very young, and the very old who had no other taste of the theater. It meant people, not in the mass but individuals, who did me the honor of inviting me into their homes; people to whom I was no longer a name filtered through the wordage of imaginative press agents, but a person whom they knew. And I would be less human than even my critics would allow, if I were not touched when people, recognizing me on trains or in stores or on the street, in almost any city I visited, told me that they liked those Monday evenings, and the little comments I made between the acts of the Lux plays, and my "greetings" and "good-night." It cost me very much more than $100,000 a year when a letter came to me in 1944, telling me that I could no longer conduct the Lux Radio Theatre; but it is not yet time to tell that story and all that came of it.

Not that I was allowed to increase the size of my hatband because of the popularity of the Lux program. My granddaughter Cecilia saw to that. When one of those annoying adults asked her what her grandfather did, she answered with the candid truthfulness of childhood, "He sells soap." Another time her mother came downstairs in the evening to announce rather distressfully that Cecilia had refused to say her prayers. The great director rose to the occasion. "She will say them for me," I said, and proceeded up to her room.

"Don't you want to say your prayers?"

"No"—curt, clipped, and determined.

"Well, I will say them for you then." I sat down by the bed and began, "Our Father which art in heaven . . . ," confidently expecting to hear a soft childish treble joining in. But the two small lips stayed in that tight line which means only one thing—that a woman has made up her mind. Not until I reached "the kingdom and the power and the glory" did little Cecilia's lips part; and what they firmly said was, "This is Cecil B. deMille saying *good-night* to You from Hollywood!"

I have had some unkind things to say about press agents, but the year 1936 brought me from their ranks one of the ablest assistants I have ever had, William H. Pine. He had had a long and successful career in theatrical publicity, and was head of the Paramount Studio advertising department, when he decided that he wanted to learn production and I welcomed him as my first associate producer. If I had to name the most difficult jobs in the motion picture industry, I believe that of associate producer would rank near the top of the list. He must know or, as in the case of a neophyte like Bill Pine, must quickly learn all the phases of production. Working under the producer, he is without complete official authority, yet he must have enough personal authority and knowledge to command the respect of all the specialized departments which co-operate in a production. He must be able on occasion to subordinate his way of doing things to the producer's views and ways; yet he will not make his full contribution unless he has originality and initiative. He must walk a straight line between the pitfalls of becoming a mere errand boy for the producer or stubbornly engaging the producer in a constant tug-of-war. If he succeeds as an associate, he undoubtedly has the qualities it takes

348

to be a full-fledged producer. Bill Pine was a conspicuous success. He remained with me four years, then entered partnership with William C. Thomas to make their own productions. They were known in Hollywood as the "Dollar Bills" because they wisely began with low budget pictures, which were so very successful that Pine-Thomas Productions was moving into a major position in the industry at the time of Bill Pine's unexpected death in 1955. If he had lived, he would be challenging the deMilles and Goldwyns of today; and no one could be happier than I to remember that Bill Pine learned his trade as my associate producer from 1936 to 1940.

The first picture on which Bill Pine worked with me was *The Plainsman*, the story of Wild Bill Hickok and the roaring days after the Civil War when the West was being opened to law and lawlessness, order and disorder. *The Plainsman* started out to be the story of Wild Bill Hickok and Buffalo Bill Cody, but, despite a good performance by James Ellison as Buffalo Bill, the character of Hickok took over and dominated the story, as a character can do sometimes whatever the original intention of author or director may have been. Perhaps this was not surprising in the case of *The Plainsman*, since the part of Wild Bill Hickok was played by Gary Cooper.

6

With the name of Gary Cooper, we are coming into an era of motion pictures whose stars will be more familiar to the average reader of today than is, perhaps, a Geraldine Farrar or a Thomas Meighan. I need hardly describe to anyone who ever goes to the movies that combination of assured authority and apparently effortless ease of manner which makes Gary Cooper so distinguished a performer. Gary is an embodiment of the old saying that art consists in concealing its own artfulness. After seeing him on the screen, any young man might say, "Shucks, I could do that." The young man would be wrong. Gary Cooper, off screen as well as on, is an affable, modest American gentleman; but he is also an accomplished artist in his profession. How much I have enjoyed working with him may be judged by the fact that he has played the lead in *North West Mounted Police, The Story of Dr. Wassell,* and *Unconquered,* as well as *The Plainsman.*

The part of Calamity Jane in *The Plainsman* was taken by Jean Arthur. I confess to taking some liberties with authenticity in that casting: pictures I have seen of the real Calamity Jane were far removed indeed from the piquant loveliness of Jean Arthur. But, if I may say so, it was good casting none the less; and Jean threw herself into the role with appropriate gusto. One of the most touching love scenes in any picture, at least any I have made, is the brief, laconic, almost inarticulate exchange between Wild Bill Hickok and Calamity Jane, when they are both tied and awaiting probable death as captives of the hostile Indians.

I was also touched in another way by Miss Arthur during the making of *The Plainsman*. I insist upon authenticity; and so Jean had to learn how to manipulate a 10-foot bullwhip as competently as Calamity Jane did when she was driving a stagecoach. I offered my wrist as a convenient target for the curling end of the whip during Jean's practice sessions. The wrist bore lash marks for days; but Calamity herself would have applauded the skill of her portrayer.

As I have had some unkind things to say about experts also, it is only fair to say that sometimes the experts can be right. Among the technicians working on *The Plainsman* was Farciot Edouart, who had started with me in the photographic laboratory at the old Lasky Studio and was now becoming, as he is today, one of Hollywood's best authorities in that specialized branch of motion picture photography known as "transparencies." It is the use of transparencies, that is, of projecting background scenes from behind a transparent screen, in front of which the principal players are then photographed, that enables us to play a scene on a street in Paris or at the foot of Mount Fujiyama without our actors, director, or first camera crew having to leave the studio on Marathon Street, Hollywood. For one important scene in *The Plainsman*, the second unit director, Art Rosson, had gone on location and photographed a band of Indians riding at breakneck speed into a river and then, horses and riders, falling in wounded confusion just as they neared an island in midstream. This film was brought to the studio and turned over to Farciot Edouart to be projected on his one big transparent screen while, in front of it, Gary Cooper and a few other beleaguered white men lay behind a crude barricade, supposedly on the midstream island, holding their fire until the oncoming Indians were almost on top of them, ready to be shot on cue.

Farciot rehearsed the scene carefully. The muzzles of the white men's guns had to be within three feet of the transparent screen. They were supplied with gunpowder specially treated so that the smoke would dissipate rapidly and not stain the screen. Then Farciot called me to see a rehearsal.

"Not enough smoke," I said. "It doesn't look real."

Farciot warned me that to make the shooting any more real, at that close range, would imperil Paramount's one and only 8 x 12 foot transparency screen.

What I thought was, "Experts again." What I said was, "Oh, you can get that screen stuff by the yard at the ribbon counter of Sears and Roebuck."

Farciot, without any excessive air of martyrdom, issued the regular blanks and powder that would ordinarily be used by the players. The reader will have anticipated the result. After the first volley, the precious, the unique screen hung in shreds.

Farciot slowly turned around toward me and quietly said, "Shall I go up to the ribbon counter at Sears' now?"

But Farciot Edouart is an expert not only in his own line, but in foreseeing the vagaries of directors whose zeal may not always be according to knowledge. He knew that R-K-O studio possessed an exactly similar screen. He had already made arrangements to borrow it. It was wheeled in and the shot successfully made—with Farciot's formula in the beleaguered plainsmen's guns.

There are two villains in *The Plainsman*. Charles Bickford played the unscrupulous mastermind of a ring selling high-powered arms illegally to the Indians, and Porter Hall gave one of his excellent performances as the historical character, Jack McCall, shown in the picture as a rather sniveling, cowardly underling in the conspiracy.

As every historian of the Old West knows, Jack McCall killed Wild Bill Hickok by shooting him in the back. It was worrisome enough to the Paramount executives that we were making a picture in which the hero, and Gary Cooper at that, was to be killed in the last reel instead of riding off into the sunset with Jean Arthur in the happy ending which audiences are always expected to demand. First the executives asked me not to kill Wild Bill; I

351

told them I could not remake history to that extent. "Well then," Adolph Zukor said finally, "if he has to be killed, don't let him be killed by that little rat, McCall. At least let Charles Bickford kill him!" But history was adhered to, and the audience did not object to the much more effective, as well as truer, tragedy of Hickok's being killed by a "little rat" rather than by a more manly villain.

After the picture was released, a man in the Middle West saw in it a chance, as he thought, for some easy money: he wrote to me that he was Jack McCall's son and that he was aggrieved by our presentation of his parent, but he hinted that his grief could be solaced by a suitable poultice of cold cash. I am sometimes criticized for spending as much money as I do on research for my pictures; but sometimes it pays off in unexpected ways. I was able to present my grief-stricken correspondent with evidence that Jack McCall had never married. I heard no more from him. He evidently thought better of pressing his—shall we say?—not quite legitimate claim.

The musical score of *The Plainsman* was composed by George Antheil, deftly incorporating some of America's best-loved folk music, and directed by a pleasant, stout, little man whose later life was to include more exciting drama than any of those for which he skillfully arranged and directed screen music: but in 1936 not even Boris Morros himself would have guessed that in less than 20 years he would be one of the most celebrated and courageous intelligence agents in the service of the United States.

In addition to such veterans of DeMille Productions as Victor Varconi, John Miljan, Francis McDonald, Edwin Maxwell, and others, a memorable performance of the part of Abraham Lincoln was given by Frank McGlynn, living again the role which theatrical history has always linked with his name since he portrayed it first in John Drinkwater's play. But the actor in *The Plainsman* whose association with me was to be most constant and most intimate was a young man whose part is listed in the cast only as "Northern Cheyenne Indian": his name is Anthony Quinn and, as well as being a highly talented and popular star today, he is also my son-in-law, the husband of my daughter Katherine.

While preparing to tell a chapter of America's frontier history in *The Plainsman*, I was given an opportunity to play a small part in her current political history when I was named as a delegate to the national convention of the Republican party, held in Cleveland, Ohio, in the summer of 1936. If my temporary defection to vote for Franklin D. Roosevelt in 1932 was known to my fellow Republicans, they must have forgiven it.

The quadrennial national conventions of our two major political parties are curiously each very different, yet all very much alike. I have attended three Republican conventions, as either a delegate or an observer, and I shall have something to say about those of 1944 and 1952; but in 1936 my part was too insignificant to merit more than passing mention. Our California delegation went to Cleveland united in support of our state's favorite son, the rising young District Attorney of Alameda County. He has now risen as high as any American can rise in the legal profession, and is known as the Honorable Earl Warren, Chief Justice of the United States. The 1936 convention did not accept California's offer of that promising young lawyer for either the Presidency or the Vice-Presidency, but nominated instead Alfred M. Landon of Kansas and Frank Knox of Illinois.

When I returned home after the convention, I issued to the press an optimistic statement about the Republican campaign to elect Messrs. Landon and Knox. The following November, Maine and Vermont agreed with me.

15

WHEN A MAN nears sixty the projection of his life upon the screen of time seems to move more swiftly; and as the later years go by, more swiftly still. I am not even yet accustomed to the little shock that always strikes me when I ask Florence Cole to look up for me some incident, some visitor, some letter, that my memory recalls as of perhaps six months or a year before, and Florence brings me the letter or her notes, dated six years ago.

The youngest member of my staff, bright and pretty little Mary Bennett, was not nearly old enough for kindergarten when *The Plainsman* was released in January, 1937, and I made plans for a trip to Louisiana in preparation for my next production. The years between then and now must undoubtedly seem to Mary Bennett a fairly mature lifetime. To me, why, that was only yesterday, wasn't it? If I seem at all to foreshorten those years—in many ways the most important years of my life—I am not indulging a movie-maker's license to telescope history: I am only telling the story as it is recorded on the film of memory. Is it, perhaps, a blessing of the Divine Projectionist, that the reels nearest "The End" should move more swiftly? Is He gently reminding us that the work we have left to do must be our best work, for there is not time for anything less than our best?

Important years, and good years, these past twenty, not without strife, but not without great satisfactions too. I had achieved, if

354

not complete financial independence in matters of production, at least the great boon of being freed from pressure to make pictures with nothing but commercial values. I could make the kind of pictures I had so long wanted to make; and the pleasant irony of it is that—so far—they have all been much greater successes commercially than any of the pictures I have made under commercial pressure.

Following *The Plainsman,* I decided to make the story of another kind of pioneer, the man to whom in some measure America owed all its vast West: for if Jean Lafitte, the pirate with a price on his head, had accepted the British offer of gold and a commission in the Royal Navy, instead of bringing to General Andrew Jackson the fighting power of his pirate band and the flints desperately needed for American muskets at the Battle of New Orleans, the War of 1812 might have ended with a foreign flag at the mouth of the Mississippi. The picture that told this story, produced in 1937, was *The Buccaneer.**

In preparation for it, I went to New Orleans early in 1937, accompanied by Bill Pine, Gladys Rosson, and others, to look over the actual scenes of the Battle of New Orleans and Lafitte's pirate lair and to initiate research in the archives of the New Orleans Cabildo, which were generously opened to us by their curator, James J. A. Fortier. Among my party was Frank E. Calvin, who had begun work with me as my "chair-boy" and been graduated to the post of research consultant. At the time, he and my daughter Cecilia were awaiting their final decree of divorce; but, even if I was losing a son-in-law, there was no reason to lose a good research consultant. Frank remained with me for several more pictures.

Mention of Frank Calvin's humble start in motion picture work calls perhaps for some comment on a subject which has added to Hollywood's merriment for many years: the DeMille chair-boy. When a director is working on a motion picture set from morning till night, day after day, his work demands every ounce of his energy and constant attention. If he has a chance to sit down for a few moments, he should take it; and he should not have to search

---

* Not to be confused with the picture of the same name, produced in 1958 by Henry Wilcoxon and directed by Anthony Quinn, with some supervision by Mr. deMille, who made his final appearance on the screen in a filmed foreword to the Wilcoxon-Quinn production. References to *The Buccaneer* in Mr. deMille's text are all to his own 1937 production (*Ed.*)

around for his chair or walk all over the set trying to find where he left it the last time he had a minute to rest. I have solved that by appointing one young man on each production whose job it is to see that my chair is where I am whenever I need it. In that way, I lose no time, and my mind need never be distracted from its concentration on the work in hand.

Frank Calvin was one of several "DeMille chair-boys" who have realized that that particular job is an unequaled opportunity to learn the business of production and direction; that is why Frank took the job. The chair-boy is always right behind or beside the director; he sees the whole complex activity of production from the director's own unique vantage point; he hears everything the director says; he sees why the director makes this or that decision, this or that change; and, if he is apt, he can learn also from the mistakes he sees, including the director's. Far from being a flunky, he has a front row seat in a most practical school of film-making. I have made it a practice, on several of my pictures, to invite one or two young students of the cinema from foreign countries to go through a production with me, coming on the set every day, observing, picking up whatever points of information or technique they might find useful in their future work in their own countries. My chair-boys have the same advantage, in addition to being paid for carrying a light piece of furniture from place to place on the set.

I could wax lyrical about New Orleans' charm and hospitality, which I have experienced many times. So have many other visitors; but not all have had New Orleans' arms and heart opened to them under the guidance of so genial a host as E. V. Richards, Jr. Until his semi-retirement, E. V. Richards headed a powerful chain of motion picture theaters in the South. He is a very strong-willed businessman. I doubt that any exhibitor in the country is more skilled at getting favorable terms from the distributors, which decreases my profits when it is a DeMille picture that he is bargaining for!—but, like some few of the other really great businessmen I have known, Rich is more than a businessman. He is a good citizen, a keen student of Louisiana history, and one of the most stalwart moving forces in the Navy League. A municipal art gallery is one of his major interests. And he is an embodiment of all the South's finest traditions of gracious living. For any producer to say such things of any exhibitor is a measure of my affection for E. V. Richards.

In fact, it was E. V. Richards who directed my attention to Lafitte as a subject for a motion picture. For years, I had been interested in the buccaneers, perhaps as a throwback to one of my ancestors who accepted the surrender of the notorious Blackbeard. But it was not until I went on a tarpon fishing trip with E. V. Richards, which took us past Lafitte's stronghold of Barataria and in and out of the moss-hung, mysterious bayous of lower Louisiana, that I found *the* buccaneer, a man who deserved America's gratitude, yet also merited Byron's description of the corsair who left a

> . . . *name for other times,*
> *Linked with one virtue and a thousand crimes.*

Fredric March made a dashing and completely believable Lafitte, a man of curiously mingled ruthlessness and honor, a vagabond of the high seas who wanted desperately to be rooted somewhere. The English actress, Margot Grahame, played the high-born New Orleans girl he loved, and Franciska Gaal the little Dutch "powder monkey" who loved him. One of the screen's most finished and endearing performances was given by Akim Tamiroff as Dominique You, the boastful, soft-hearted "cannoneer of Napoleon" and Lafitte's first lieutenant. I was hard put to find an Andrew Jackson until one evening Mrs. deMille came home from attending a play produced by the Works Progress Administration's theater project and told me that I must go to see it, for, she said, I would find my Jackson in a former stockbroker who had turned to the theater when the 1929 crash wiped out his business—Hugh Sothern. Oddly enough, Hugh Sothern turned out to be not only a good actor, but a distant kinsman of the Andrew Jackson whom he portrayed. In the small part of Dolly Madison, Spring Byington gave the picture one of its most memorable scenes when, fleeing from Washington moments before the British entered the city to burn the capitol, she stopped her carriage and dashed back into the deserted White House to rescue an old piece of rolled-up parchment; and when her impatient escort asked what it was she had gone back to save, when every minute's delay meant the risk of capture, she replied calmly, "The Declaration of Independence."

There is always one serious problem in making a picture about the American Revolution or the War of 1812: our enemies then, the British, are our best friends now. Foreign nationals are always sensitive about being made villains in American films. I once proposed that the motion picture industry buy outright the island of Cedros, off the west coast of Mexico, and handsomely subsidize its inhabitants, for the right to make all movie villains "Cedrans," thus sparing the feelings of other countries and sparing the industry the effects of protests and boycotts by nations which imagined that we were casting them in a bad light. My suggestion came to nothing; probably a Cedran Protective Association would have sprung up anyway, with vociferous accusations that Hollywood was engaging in anti-Cedran activities.

The British have better sense and more tolerance, by and large, than some other groups; but even the British do not enjoy seeing Britannia beaten by a parcel of Yankee sharpshooters. In *The Buccaneer,* we took pains to show British gallantry on the field of battle; the most ardent Yankee could not fail to be moved by the scene of the British troops advancing across Chalmette, and the British flag being passed from hand to hand as the color-bearers were shot down by Jackson's backwoodsmen and Lafitte's buccaneers from behind their ramparts made of cotton bales. The British at the Battle of New Orleans were commanded by Major General Sir Edward Pakenham who was killed in the battle. Many years later, his descendant, Lord Pakenham, presented me, with a glowing and deeply moving introduction, to a distinguished gathering at a luncheon in London; and on my return to America I had the pleasure of sending Lord Pakenham a contemporary print of his ancestor's heroic death for King and country in far-off Louisiana. I had found the print in New Orleans in 1937 and kept it for twenty years as a memento of the brave general; but I am glad that it is now in the keeping of his family.

While we were writing *The Buccaneer,* a new bond was forged with a dear and familiar name when Jesse Lasky, Jr., a youngster of 26, came to me and said that he would like to have a job of writing. I gave him the script of *The Buccaneer* and asked for his suggestions. He wrote a number of new lines which I liked and wanted to incorporate in the script, but the other writers at work on it did not welcome the addition of another name to share their credit, so I had to ask young Jesse if he would let me use his lines in return for a promise that he would work on my next picture, whatever that might be. I also sent him a present, a case of champagne, the most appropriate symbol for the bubbling good nature he has inherited from his father. Jesse, Jr. has worked on all but two of my pictures since 1938. He was away for a time fighting the Japanese—who, he said, held no terrors for him, after working with me!

We opened *The Buccaneer* first in E. V. Richards' Saenger Theatre in New Orleans, then went on to Atlanta for a performance which was to be in a special way a tribute to a lovely young Georgia girl who is one of the stars I can truly claim to have discovered, Evelyn Keyes. She had a small part in *The Buccaneer*, but her beauty and talent made her one of the very few players to whom I have ever given a personal contract with DeMille Productions in the past 30 years or so. But Evelyn did not attend the Atlanta opening. She came to Atlanta, warmly received by her adoring family and loyal fellow-townsmen. It was an exciting homecoming for a young girl, and Evelyn reacted to it all by having to be put to bed with a pretty red rash, which I ungallantly told the press was just plain measles; but of course Bill Pine and Bill Hebert, my publicity representatives, saw to it that I was corrected and a more appropriately impressive diagnosis duly released.

Southern chivalry was in full flower when Margot Grahame accompanied me to a joint session of the Georgia legislature, which postponed its adjournment in order to have a glimpse of Margot and incidentally listen to me speak. I began my speech by referring to the tremendous historical importance of the occasion: it was probably the first time, I said, that a Republican had ever addressed the legislature of Georgia. Instantly Atlanta's Representative William G. Hastings was on his feet to assure me of my safety: Republicans, he announced, were fully protected by Georgia's fish and game laws. As we were leaving the stately chamber, a venerable white-haired senator named Flynt left his aisle seat and, embracing Margot Grahame, gave her a resounding kiss. The newspaper, of course, could not resist headlining, "Movie Beauty Melts Heart of Flynt."

It was on this occasion too that I had my first meeting with Atlanta's perennial Mayor W. B. Hartsfield, whom his fellow-citizens have had the great good judgment to keep re-electing for term after term ever since. Six years later, Mayor Hartsfield would be one of the very first and very few public officials with courage and stamina enough to support my stand for political freedom and the right to work.

In Boston, on the same tour, I met another mayor, the newly-elected Maurice J. Tobin, who was so strikingly handsome that I boldly offered him a contract if he would come to Hollywood. His Honor said he preferred to remain in Boston. I said the people of Boston might not let him stay where he was; I paused only long enough to let the shock register, before adding that the people of Boston might decide to send him to a city farther south, namely, Washington. My prophecy was fulfilled, not by election indeed but by appointment from the highest source, when President Harry S. Truman named him Secretary of Labor.

At several stops on the tour I had been asked by reporters about my own political ambitions, if any. As early as November, 1937, Leo E. Anderson, the Los Angeles County Chairman of the Republican party, had come to me, with an impressive group of other party leaders, to ask if I would permit my name to be proposed as a candidate for the United States Senate, to run against William Gibbs McAdoo, President Wilson's son-in-law and the Democratic Senator from California, whose term was about to expire. No man could be unmoved by that honor; no American with a sense of history could fail to be inspired and awed by the possibility of sitting as a member of that body in which so much history has been made. It was a literally tremendous challenge and opportunity; but it would mean abandoning one career which was at last becoming established firmly, for another in which I would be, I fully realized, an untried novice. I might have remembered what my father once wrote to Henry George, "I never do anything by halves, and am *half* hearted in *no* cause that I embrace." All I could tell Leo Anderson and his group was that I would think it over very seriously and take advice on it from minds whose political experience and judgment were greater than my own.

Then, in Boston, a reporter brought me word that the California

360

State Republican Committee had met and endorsed me for the senatorial nomination, with only three dissenting votes.

But by then I had already made up my mind; and the tour itself had helped me decide. I had seen in every city the increasing power of motion pictures, the trade I knew: a power for good, for bringing not only entertainment but the influence of religion and patriotism to a constituency not of one state, but of the world. On my weekly radio program, I was speaking not to 95 fellow senators, but to 9,000,000 American families. The decision facing me was not unlike that which my father had faced, between the pulpit and the stage; and the decision I made was the same as his. With gratitude to the leaders of my party in California, deeper than I could adequately express, I declined the nomination.*

My critics may think that my decision was more of a calamity to Hollywood than to the nation; but I think my father would have approved. He would have been pleased, too, that while on that same tour I was invited to speak at Harvard, and in New York the Division of Film Study of his own university, Columbia, gave me a luncheon at which President Nicholas Murray Butler made the principal address.

The reader will probably not need to be reminded of how indulgent Mrs. deMille and my children have had to be to the demands that my work makes upon my time. It has often bothered my conscience: like every father, I suppose, I have asked myself if I have let work take me too much away from my family. The extent of those demands, and my family's patience with them, could hardly be better shown than by the fact that my daughter Cecilia's second marriage had to be fitted into the schedule of my tour with *The Buccaneer!*

After her divorce from Frank Calvin, Cecilia became engaged to Joseph W. Harper, a young Los Angeles businessman who had been a friend of our family for many years. Naturally, she wanted both her parents at her wedding; and she and Joe were planning a honeymoon in Europe, to begin early in February, 1938. The

* On November 26, 1958, Mr. Edward S. Shattuck, Republican National Committeeman for California, wrote to the editor: "I was among those who called on Mr. deMille to urge him to run for the United States Senate. . . . We were very enthusiastic to have him run and I am still sure that if we had been successful, we would have had one of the greatest senators that this country ever knew." (*Ed.*)

only way all the dates could coincide was for Mrs. deMille, Cecilia, and Joe to meet me in Kansas City and have the wedding there the same night as the opening of *The Buccaneer*. With only fifteen guests present in the penthouse of the Muehlebach Hotel, I gave the bride away and stood beside Mrs. deMille as our daughter was married by the Rev. G. Charles Gray to the young man who in the years since then has been as close to us as if he were our own son.

The wedding took place near midnight of January 21, 1938. It was perhaps truthful, if not altogether flattering, of the Kansas City *Star* to say that at that late hour "the bride had become a bit weary and even Mr. DeMille's smile had lost some of its luster." I do not know about Mr. deMille's smile; but I remember, with squirms of mental pain, what the lateness of the hour, the excitement of the première that same evening, and the emotion of a father at his daughter's wedding did to Mr. deMille's memory, poor enough at best. I presented Joe Harper to the press as "my son-in-law, Mr. Calvin."

Joe Harper is the gentlest, most sweet-tempered, most charitable of men; but he also has a quick and penetrating sense of humor. Both qualities shone in his response to that introduction. Smiling sweetly, he bowed and said to me, "Thank you, Mr. Goldwyn."

3

The subject of my next picture was suggested to me by Martin Quigley, I am grateful to record. We had begun work on a story of Hudson's Bay, with Jesse Lasky, Jr., doing the preliminary research and writing, but abandoned it when we learned that 20th Century-Fox had a similar subject almost ready for production. Martin Quigley's suggestion struck fire in my mind at once: to tell the story of the spanning of America by steel, the first transcontinental railroad. A President of the United States had thought that episode in our history so important that, when he signed the bill authorizing government co-operation with the building of the Union Pacific Railroad, he wrote out his name in full, Abraham Lincoln, instead of his more usual signature, A. Lincoln.

Union Pacific was the picture's obvious title; and it brought me the sturdy friendship of the great American who was then president of the Union Pacific, William M. Jeffers. Strength of character and conviction are qualities that I admire in any man; and no man had more of them than that Nebraskan of Irish immigrant descent, who went to work on the Union Pacific Railroad at 14, rose to be president of the road, and served his country and her allies as Rubber Administrator during World War II, when only the intelligence and drive of a Jeffers could keep the armies of freedom moving forward after the supplies of natural rubber from Southeast Asia had been cut off. He was a devoted member of his church, highly honored by its Supreme Pontiff; but he leaped to my side in a controversy with a bishop of that church, because he thought that right was on my side. He could be hard-fisted and he was always outspoken; but he held the respect and often the affection of men who differed violently with him politically and otherwise. His big, heavy frame, topped by a face that matched it, with his cigar clenched in his strong teeth, made him a striking, perhaps to some a formidable, figure; but no face has ever worn a broader, warmer smile, and no frame has ever held a stouter or more loyal heart.

From the start of work on *Union Pacific*, Bill Jeffers put all the resources of the railroad at our disposal. He assigned two railroad superintendents and a roadmaster to us as advisers. He opened the company's archives to Frank Calvin's research, and they proved a mine of information for the authenticity we were seeking, even if we could not use all the intriguing material in them, such as the letters from proprietresses of certain establishments who complained to the railroad that some of its workmen had taken their pleasures without paying the tariff customary in those ladies' line of work.

For the scenes showing the frantic race between the Irish builders of the Union Pacific and the Chinese workers on the Central Pacific, Bill Jeffers lent us his railroad's fastest track-laying crew, whose speed and precision were such that footage from our picture, showing them at work, was used in government training films during World War II.

For the leading roles in *Union Pacific*, I cast Joel McCrea and Barbara Stanwyck. I am sometimes asked who is my favorite actress, among those I have directed. I always dodge the question by explaining that I have to continue living in Hollywood. But if the tortures of the Inquisition were applied and an answer extracted from me, I would have to say that I have never worked with an actress who was more co-operative, less temperamental, and a better workman, to use my term of highest compliment, than Barbara Stanwyck. I have directed, and enjoyed working with, many fine actresses, some of whom are also good workmen; but when I count over those of whom my memories are unmarred by any unpleasant recollection of friction on the set or unwillingness to do whatever the role required or squalls of temperament or temper, Barbara's name is the first that comes to mind, as one on whom a director can always count to do her work with all her heart.

The dramatic situation in *Union Pacific* is provided by the conflict between Joel McCrea, pushing the railroad west, and the forces represented by Brian Donlevy, who for their own venal reasons wanted to stop the westward march of steel. Caught between these forces, and Joel McCrea's rival for Barbara Stanwyck's affections, is a young man, more weak than wicked, played by a young actor to whom I gave the part as his first big role in a big picture. He was discovered by Sidney Justin, of Paramount Studio's legal department, at the Pasadena Playhouse, whose program listed him as Preston Meservey; but since Meservey is not a name too easy to pronounce, it was as Robert Preston that he made his first big hit in *Union Pacific*. It was in this film, too, that I first teamed those two superb scene-stealing character actors, Lynne Overman and Akim Tamiroff, who were to enact again in *North West Mounted Police* the high comedy and the pathos of their rivalry.

A visitor to the set of *Union Pacific*, at one stage of its production, might have seen me enacting the role of the man on the flying stretcher. Needing some major surgery but not having time for it, I kept working until one day I collapsed at the studio and had to be brought home in an ambulance. I also had a radio broadcast to make for Jesse Lasky, which I made from my bed at home; fortunately television had not yet come into prominence. Then I recalled the ambulance and had myself brought back to the studio. Since the director must see the picture he is making from the camera's eye, I had my stretcher fixed to the camera boom and for ten days swung with it up in the air and down again, for whatever camera angles were required.

Continuing the production on schedule was not my only motive for that adventure, upon which I fear that my good doctor did not look with complete favor. My other and perhaps deeper motive was my horror of ever letting myself be made a coddled invalid. I believe that invalidism can become an addiction, if one lets it, as insidious as an addiction to drugs, alcohol, or any other delusive comfort of the flesh. You begin by obeying your doctor, which is quite right, within reason; but then you begin to enjoy it. You can always command a sympathetic audience, sympathetic to your face anyway, by telling, with increasing gravity and wealth of detail, how careful the doctor says you must be. If anything is proposed which calls for some exertion, you smile, a little sadly, and say that that is not for you. You forget that sloth is one of the seven deadly sins. You need a jolt. *Union Pacific* was mine.

Having been called on occasion a master of spectacle myself, I had the awed pleasure of meeting a real one, in the person of Bill Jeffers, when we made plans to open *Union Pacific* in Omaha in April, 1939. With the ardent co-operation of the Paramount publicity department, headed then by Robert Gillham, Mr. Jeffers determined to make this a première to dwarf all premières; and when Mr. Jeffers determined upon anything, that was usually the way it turned out. The opening was scheduled for Omaha on April 28, but it began in Los Angeles five days before that.

4

With Mayor Fletcher Bowron at the station to see us off, with a dozen stars and featured players in the party, and with Bill Jeffers sporting a very tall silk hat, we left Los Angeles on a special Union Pacific train, drawn by not one engine, but two. The engine that did the work was the Union Pacific's latest and most powerful steam-electric turbine, but in front of it puffed the wood-burning "Old 58" of the railroad's pioneer days. We had used Old 58 in the picture, and it was in perfect working order, though it had to stop every 50 miles to take on water; and to find someone capable of running it, we had had to call out of retirement a veteran engineer past 80 years of age. The train stopped at every major station, and several minor ones, along the route from Los

Angeles to Omaha; and at every station, if there were not open carriages or cars for a parade through the town, there was at least a decorated platform right beside the train, for speeches to what seemed like the assembled population of all the surrounding counties, with many of the people dressed in pioneer costume, the men with beards grown for the event and hats that rivaled Mr. Jeffers' own.

Omaha itself was transformed. One whole street had been made over, with its business buildings given false fronts to make it a replica of a street in the roaring West of the 1860's. Indians camped on the courthouse lawn. The crowds of bewhiskered, beaver-hatted men and bonneted women could make one believe the press reports that the city's population had doubled for the celebration of "Golden Spike Days," so called to commemorate the spike of gold used to fasten the last rail to the last tie when the Union Pacific was completed in 1869.

The first big event was a dinner in the Ak-Sar-Ben coliseum, another triumph of the Jeffers drive and generalship: 3,000 people were served in 18 minutes! As always when Americans gather together to consume food, there were speeches, of course. Civic officials spoke. Officers of the railroad spoke. Unlike the railroad, some banquet orators have extremely inadequate terminal facilities. When one gentlemen, representing some quite important shipping interests, pursued his dogged way through a lengthy discourse on the deplorable state of the beet sugar industry under current government policies, the audience was dying; and particularly since the gentleman had not mentioned our picture, so was I. Then the chairman of the board of the Union Pacific, W. Averill Harriman, arose. He was bright and brief. He said, "I hear there's a great show in town. Let's see it." New Deal Democrat that he is, I have loved Averill Harriman ever since.

Another Democrat, but of the unreconstructed rebel variety, came into one of the most honored and cherished places anyone has ever held in my life when Y. Frank Freeman came to Hollywood. Proudly hailing from Greenville, Georgia, Frank Freeman came up in the motion picture industry through the exhibition side, of which his knowledge is unsurpassed. A vice-president of Paramount since 1935, he came to Hollywood as head of the studio when Mr. Zukor retired from that post in 1938. For 20

366

years, he has been closer to me, professionally and as a friend, than anyone else in the industry. There is no one in the industry more universally and sincerely respected than Frank Freeman. If my relations with Paramount in the last 20 years have been happy, as in the main they have, if I have been enabled to put anything worthwhile on the screens of the world in that time, it is largely because Frank Freeman is a man with whom I have perfect understanding and in whom I have perfect confidence. There is some mystery about the initial letter of his name, the "Y" in "Y. Frank." Personally, I think it is a typographical error. Perhaps the registrar of births in Greenville, Georgia, in 1890 couldn't spell very well. It should be "I"—for Integrity.

In February, 1939, I joined the American Federation of Radio Artists. While I have never believed in the closed shop, I do believe in the necessity of unions. I remember well the low wages, long hours, and atrocious working conditions which were all too prevalent in American industry when I was a boy and young man. When Mrs. deMille and I were touring in plays, we sometimes saw from the window of our train little children, carrying their lunch pails, going to work at dawn. When AFRA was formed, the men and women working in radio undoubtedly needed organization to put them in a more equitable bargaining position with management. I joined the union willingly. I saw, then, no more likelihood of conflict with it than many Americans saw, at the same time, any likelihood or need of conflict with Adolf Hitler.

America, in fact, was celebrating prosperity and peace in 1939 with a World's Fair in New York and the Golden Gate Exposition in San Francisco. As the motion picture industry's contribution to these events, I was asked to supervise the making of a film, in which all the producing companies would collaborate, to show the highlights and the meaning of America's history. With a narration written by Jeanie Macpherson and Jesse Lasky, Jr., the scholarly technical assistance of Professor James T. Shotwell of Columbia University, and the herculean labors of Francis S. Harmon, Arthur H. DeBra, Herbert L. Moulton, and Bill Pine, *Land of Liberty* was a compilation of scenes clipped from 124 different motion pictures and hundreds of newsreels, woven together in what Howard Barnes of the New York *Herald-Tribune* called an "undeniably impressive . . . effective educational screen project."

367

There was a rather amusing difference of opinion between Professor Shotwell and me on how *Land of Liberty* should conclude. Professor Shotwell, more New-Dealish in tendency than I, wanted to end with a speech by Franklin D. Roosevelt. I wanted one by Chief Justice Charles Evans Hughes. We used both.

Shown first at the New York and San Francisco fairs, *Land of Liberty* was released, in a shortened form, to theaters in January, 1941. The exhibitors did not welcome it with any cheers. Exhibitors never welcome anything that will lengthen their shows and thus possibly reduce the number of audiences they can turn in and out in one day; which is a not unnatural point of view for an exhibitor, when it does not run away with him to the extent of slicing great swathes out of a picture in the projection booth, to shorten its running time. But 1941 was a good year for *Land of Liberty* to be seen: perhaps some of those who saw it had a better idea of what they were called on to defend, when bombs fell on American soil on December 7, 1941.[*]

5

The only war which concerned me closely in 1939, however, was the Riel Rebellion in Canada, which was the subject of my next picture, *North West Mounted Police*, my first film to be shot entirely in Technicolor. With marvelously cordial co-operation from the Royal Canadian Mounted Police, as that handsome and intrepid corps of redcoats is now called, Frank Calvin spent a month in Canada in research on the history and traditions of the Mounted Police and their part in crushing Louis Riel's last abortive attempt to raise the Indians in revolt against Queen Victoria's rule. The historical facts gave us all the color we needed for the broad canvas of the background; and we had a good story, by Alan LeMay, Jesse Lasky, Jr., and C. Gardner Sullivan, to tell within the framework of the facts.

Our biggest problem was casting. Movie fans, after seeing a picture may complain, "Why didn't they cast So-and-so in that part? He would have been much better." It is not as easy as all that. The player a producer wants may have other commitments

---

[*] *Land of Liberty* is still widely used in schools. At the time of his death, Mr. deMille was engaged in bringing it up to date by the addition of new material, which work has been completed by Henry S. Noerdlinger. (*Ed.*)

at the time; or he may decline a role the producer offers him, as Cornel Wilde declined the role of Joshua in *The Ten Commandments* (1956), thus giving John Derek his opportunity for a noteworthy performance; or even after he is cast, he may strongly wish to take another part in another picture, if he can get the producer's consent, as Joel McCrea did when I agreed to his leaving *North West Mounted Police*. I replaced him with Gary Cooper, who fitted perfectly into the part of Dusty Rivers, a Texas Ranger whose search for an outlaw led him into Canada and into adventures both hair-raising and romantic.

There was no question about the suitability of beautiful Madeleine Carroll for one of the feminine leads, or of Preston Foster, Robert Preston, and Francis McDonald for other important roles. Walter Hampden, wearing contact lenses to change the color of his blue eyes, made a wonderfully dignified and impressive Chief Big Bear. But the part that stumped us was that of Louvette, the fiery, seductive half-breed girl.

We considered a half-dozen or so, without finding the one actress who would be exactly right, until one day Florence Cole came into my private office and said, "Louvette is here to see you." Florence is not given to making practical jokes, and she is extremely careful not to let anyone waste my time. With no idea of what was in the wind, I told her to usher Louvette in.

Florence stepped back from the door, and a dark girl, with eyes that could smolder or melt, came in, made up as a half-breed and costumed as such a girl would dress on the wild Canadian frontier in the 1880's.

She gave me one insolent look and said, "You teenk you wan beeg director, hah? Me, Louvette, show you!"

That was enough; Paulette Goddard had the part.

North West Mounted Police had its world première in Regina, Saskatchewan, on October 21, 1940. Three days before the stars of the picture left Hollywood for the première, Madeleine Carroll's sister was killed in one of Hitler's bombing raids on England; but she made the tour, was beautiful and glamorous everywhere, charmed everyone, and showed in her own way as much pluck as was being shown by her stricken parents, who refused to leave England, and by the whole English populace, whom Hitler was so foolish as to think he could cow. In addition to her other activities on behalf of the war effort, including the support of orphans lodged in her house in France, Madeleine kept her fingers constantly occupied in knitting for the troops and refugees. Some of the press commented that this was, of course, a publicity stunt. A worm's-eye view, I suppose, is all that one can ever expect from a worm.

I have always been glad that *North West Mounted Police* appeared just when it did, to give American audiences a warm and true conception of the valor of the British Commonwealth and its peoples. I never had any doubt, from the outbreak of World War II, where America must and eventually would take her stand. In domestic policies, I felt that the New Deal had done a certain amount of good and a great amount of harm; but in foreign policy, when Franklin D. Roosevelet looked at Hitler and Mussolini, he saw straight and true, from the start. When, like other reserve officers, I was placed on one-minute call by the War Department as early as December, 1939, I realized of course that my age was too advanced and this new kind of war too grim a business for any exploits by the Champion Driver; but I felt that, in preparing early for what must come, Roosevelt was right.*

The summer of 1940, however, brought me a peaceful and nostalgic interlude, when I went yachting with E. V. Richards off the Carolina coast, and made my last visit to my family's old home in Washington, North Carolina. Since then, I never saw again the house where my father and brother were born; as I have mentioned earlier, it is now torn down. Its last use, I believe, was as a tourist home, not an unfitting end for a house that was always hospitable. The Washington *Daily News* announced that the entire town was planning to turn out to welcome me. It did, heartwarmingly; and I daresay that most of those who turned out were cousins of mine in the Carolinian sense, for the blood of Blounts, Bragaws, deMilles, Hardings, Hoyts, and many others is all intermingled in that sturdy stock. But it remained for the enthusiastic local theater manager to cap the occasion. It so happened that my visit coincided with the first run of a picture dealing with the notorious outlaw, Frank James, and his return to plague the marshals, sheriffs, and peaceable folk of the Old West. The theater

* Mr. deMille held a reserve commission as a major in the Signal Corps. (*Ed.*)

marquee of little Washington heralded my visit with these welcoming words: THE RETURN OF FRANK JAMES AND CECIL B. DEMILLE. But if I smile at that reminiscently, the smile lingers for another reason: the warmth with which little Washington embraced a faraway, but not forgetful, son.

The year 1940 saw another one of my briefer ventures into the world of business, when I took part in organizing a firm to manufacture and distribute something called a "movie slot machine." This was a device which, by the deposit of a coin in the appointed slot, would project for the eye of the depositor a three-minute short subject film. Our device won first prize at the Western States Coin Machine Convention, winning out, to my satisfaction, over one in which James Roosevelt had an interest; but the public did not award the prize of its favor to any of these hopeful products. For the sake of the English language, that may have been just as well: for the machines would almost certainly have come to be called "slotties."

6

Now I must record an experience which, fortunately, comparatively few men have: the death of a grandchild. In March, 1941, little Christopher Quinn, not yet three, with a big and wonderful world to explore, somehow escaped our watchfulness for a few minutes, trudged across the street from our home, was drawn by the magic shimmer of a pond on the property of my neighbor, W. C. Fields, slipped or in his eagerness leaned over it too far, and was drowned. His father and I had to stand by, helpless, while a rescue squad worked in vain to revive him. Katherine and Tony were too grief-stricken to go to the cemetery. I went, and watched the little coffin laid to rest. He would be in college now, perhaps beginning to think of a life work, perhaps of marriage. But he left us when the world was still big and wonderful and unexplored; when his world was untouched by anything but innocence and love; and of such is the kingdom of heaven.

7

Having told in *Union Pacific* what railroads had meant to a growing America, I turned next, after *North West Mounted Police,* back to the year 1840, when America's lifeline was the sea, when the great sailing ships linked the Eastern seaboard with the rich valley of the Mississippi. *Reap the Wild Wind* was based on a magazine story by Thelma Strabel; and our screenplay, by Alan LeMay, Charles Bennett, and Jesse Lasky, Jr., told of the salvage masters of Key West who reaped the wind's harvest, fighting the hurricanes to save lives and cargo from vessels wrecked on the Florida reefs.

On *Reap the Wild Wind,* as later on *The Story of Dr. Wassell* and *Unconquered,* we had the advice of Fred F. Ellis, a retired captain of the British Merchant Marine, whose knowledge of sailing vessels and of all the usages, language, and lore of the sea kept us technically correct and gave us so thorough a course that we might all have qualified as old salts after working on one picture with him. Captain Ellis was always punctiliously correct, yet always reasonable, which some technical advisers are not. If any viewer of *Reap the Wild Wind* was shocked to see that the peak and throat halyards were tied close together on the fife rail starboard side, I could show him a note of Captain Ellis' in my working script of the picture, conceding that "Mr. DeMille wishes to take the dramatic liberty of tying" them that way, so that Paulette Goddard could cut both ropes with one stroke of an axe.

Two fine actors new to working with me, Ray Milland and John Wayne, joined Paulette Goddard to head the cast. Raymond Massey was a snarling but strong villain; and again Walter Hampden, Robert Preston, Lynne Overman, and Charles Bickford brought their talents to help tell our story, while Martha O'Driscoll, Louise Beavers, and Elizabeth Risdon played the principal feminine supporting roles. In *The Buccaneer,* Evelyn Keyes had gone down in a scuttled ship early in the picture. In *Reap the Wild Wind,* that same fate was the portion of another young actress whose talent would raise her also to stardom, Susan Hayward. In one sequence, a party at a fashionable home in Charleston, the audience could note with delight that one of the most prominent guests was none other than Hedda Hopper.

The musical score by Victor Young continued a collaboration begun on *North West Mounted Police* with that composer whose round and rumpled appearance and well-chomped cigar belied the airy magic and vibrant might that he could draw from wood-

372

winds, brass, and strings. He composed the scores of all my later pictures until his early death in 1956.

Another good workman, whose career was also cut off too soon, Edward Salven, came with me as first assistant director on *Reap the Wild Wind,* having previously worked on *Union Pacific* and *North West Mounted Police.* I have said that an associate producer has one of the most difficult jobs in the motion picture industry. A first assistant director has the same, less steadily but in more concentrated form, perhaps especially if he is working with me. In addition to being responsible for the extra players, for rehearsals, and for the full direction of some scenes, it is his job to police the whole set, to see that everything the director wants done is done by everyone including the director. He must be forceful and resilient by turns, and intelligent and diplomatic all the time.

To all these gifts Eddie Salven added a puckish sense of humor that saved many a tense situation. Nerves sometimes get badly frayed on the set. There have been times, I am sure, when players have looked upon me as an incurably mad ogre; there have certainly been times when I have looked upon certain players as unmitigated dolts. Those were the times when one of Eddie Salven's quips could change glares or sulks to grins; and the play, which is always the important thing, could go on. I hope that he knew, and that Chico Day, Mickey Moore, Danny McCauley, and all my other assistants know, how much I know about how much they do for me.

Among the most valuable members of my staff is the one we call field secretary. It is her job to be with me at almost every minute when I am working away from my office. She is my memory; and the reader knows by now how much I need one. She must be intelligent, attentive, and alert. On the set, I may give an order for something to be done tomorrow, which I will forget unless it is noted down; in the studio restaurant, I may meet an exhibitor from the Philippines or a missionary from the Sudan or a congressman concerned with legislation affecting some cause in which I am interested, whose words I may need to refer to a year from now; I may be trudging over the Sinai desert and suddenly see something or think of some incident from years ago that I want to put in this book. The field secretary is there to see and hear

373

everything and to use her own good judgment, in many instances, of what is important to record and what is not.

In the midst of shooting *Reap the Wild Wind,* we were in urgent need of a new field secretary, and Bill Pine prevailed upon a young girl who had worked temporarily on some of my earlier pictures to come and help us out for the seven weeks remaining of the production schedule. The seven weeks have lengthened to more than twice as many years, and Berenice Mosk is still my field secretary. Her endurance is no less remarkable than her efficiency. In her spare time, that is, when I am in my office and Florence Cole and Doris Turner are bearing with me, Berenice works with our writers; and they would acknowledge, I think, that she not only keeps track of their most soaring flights of fancy, but helps to keep them in orbit and quietly contributes not a few of the ideas and lines which find their way into the finished scripts and onto the screen.

My sixtieth birthday came while we were shooting *Reap the Wild Wind.* I could not have summed up better my feeling about Paramount, and especially about Frank Freeman, than by what I said at the luncheon the studio gave me that day: I enjoyed my work then more than at any other time, I said, "because now for the first time I am being helped to make a picture instead of being dared to make one." I also achieved a symbol of Hollywood immortality in an unusual way on that birthday: I was too busy on the set to go up to Hollywood Boulevard, so Sid Grauman brought a block of wet cement to the studio to receive the prints of my hands and feet, which tourists will inspect in the forecourt of the Chinese Theatre for generations to come, and ask each other, "Cecil B. de Mille? Who was he?"

The climactic scenes in *Reap the Wild Wind* were in a sunken ship, photographed under water by Dewey Wrigley, with the special effects done by the consummate skill of Gordon Jennings. Much as I have berated some of my actors and actresses, on occasion, for their inability to take direction, I must admit that no human player has presented me with the problems encountered in directing fish. Rehearsal did not do them much good. Most of them would not stay within camera range, but there was one who had the hardest time of all in learning the first rule of film acting: he would swim straight to the camera and, until he

374

Our Golden Wedding Anniversary,
August 16, 1952.

Grandchildren are, from left, back row: Constance Harper, Kathleen Quinn, Christina Quinn, Peter Calvin, John Harper, Alan deMille, and Cecilia Calvin. Middle row: Joseph W. Harper, Jr., Johnny deMille and Duncan Quinn. Billy deMille stands with his grandfather and Diane deMille with her grandmother.

Our sons John and Richard and daughters Katherine and Cecilia help celebrate fifty years of marriage.

Cinematographer Peverell Marley and Anne Bauchens. My association with these co-workers extends back over several decades. "Annie B." has edited every one of my pictures since 1918.

Elmer Bernstein and Anne Bauchens; the newest and oldest of my co-workers, at my 76th birthday party at the studio.

Dwarfed by Gary Cooper and Charlton Heston.

My studio office on my 76th birthday.

Stellar help in celebrating my 77th birthday. My son-in-law, Anthony Quinn, Henry Wilcoxon, Mary Pickford and Bob Hope.

Jerry Lewis with the older Paramount generation: Frank Freeman and Adolph Zukor.

My pictures are made at my desk: my studio office when *The Ten Commandments* (1956) was in the sketching stage.

Ascending Mt. Sinai on location for *The Ten Commandments*.

Charlton Heston's towering performance of Moses in *The Ten Commandments* evolves.

One of many conferences at the Red Sea camp, Abu Rudeis, Egypt. Henry Wilcoxon at left, Edward Salven and Kenneth DeLand.

The end of the day's shooting at Abu Rawash, Egypt, October, 1954. Beyond the airplanes provided by the Egyptian government as wind machines is our tent city.

Egyptian villagers as extras at the Beni Youssef location.

Seeking a telling effect.

Yul Brynner as Rameses, Anne Baxter as Nefretiri.

Anne Baxter in costume on the set of *The Ten Commandments* (1956) visited by Julia Faye, who portrayed in the 1923 production the role played by Anne Baxter in 1956.

Marjory Collins caught some of the physical strain that came in the making of *The Ten Commandments* at Mount Sinai, October, 1954.

Julia Faye, John Carradi and Charlton Heston wi Nina Foch, Olive Deeri and John Derek in the Pa over scene from *The T Commandments*.

A fine study reveals aspects of great character in Frank Freeman and the Rev. Billy Graham.

The Screen Producers Guild dinner in 1956 renewed for an evening the association of Jesse Lasky, Sam Goldwyn and myself going back over forty years.

With the President of the Church of Jesus Christ of Latter-Day Saints, at Brigham Young University, May, 1957: "David McKay, almost thou persuadest me to be a Mormon!"

Queen Elizabeth II is truly Her Most Gracious Majesty. Sir Henry and Lady French at left; Lord Rank at right.

ith Pope Pius XII at Castelgan-
lfo, October, 1957.

ELICI,   FOTOGRAFIA   PONTIFICA,
MA)

e Cross of the Legion of Honor presented by M. Arthur Conte,
nch Minister of Industry and Trade, in Paris, October, 1957.

Homecoming from Europe, November, 1957; Cecilia was there to meet Grandfather.

Leaving the studio on my 76th birthday, with the two Cecilias, granddaughter and daughter.

With Mrs. deMille at home.

was frantically scared away, give the audience a real idea of what it is like to be stared at with a fishy eye.

The audience's eyes, however, were on the giant squid. Nature has produced few terrors of the deep as fearsome as that creation of the Paramount prop shop. It was truly a marvelous piece of work, with its heavy red tentacles 14 feet long weaving realistically and menacingly through the water to grip and crush John Wayne, until Ray Milland drove a cargo hook between the monster's malevolent eyes.

The creators of the giant squid, and even I, were very proud of it. That opinion was not shared by one member of my staff, though. After the preview, my publicity representative, Theodore Bonnet, came to me in the lobby of the theater with consternation in face and voice.

"You're going to cut the squid scene out, aren't you?" he said. "Why?" I asked.

"Why, all the women around me in the audience hid their heads when they saw it!"

I have never had a more graceful writer, nor many more pleasant persons in any capacity, on my staff than Ted Bonnet; but he had not yet learned the paradox of the show business—that audiences will come in droves to see something that will make them hide their eyes when they do see it.

Some of the Paramount executives may have had their doubts about *Reap the Wild Wind*, too. One of them screened it for an internationally famous expert in public opinion research. That learned man pronounced that the picture could not be a success, and gave the reasons why. *Reap the Wild Wind* broke Paramount's record for grosses at the box office, previously held by *The Ten Commandments* (1923), and held the new record until it was surpassed by Leo McCarey's *Going My Way*. I did not have to wait until the Presidential election of 1948 to have my faith in public opinion polls somewhat shaken.

After *Reap the Wild Wind*, I planned to produce and direct *For Whom the Bell Tolls*. Jeanie Macpherson worked on a screenplay for it for six and a half months; but then came an official request from John Hay Whitney, Co-ordinator of Commercial and Cultural Relations between the American Republics, asking that I make a picture on a Latin-American theme. This struck a responsive chord, for I had been working ever since 1939, with no less than six different writers, on a Mexican story with its historical background laid in the early part of this century. I revived that project, relinquishing to Paramount my plans for *For Whom the Bell Tolls,* and transferred Jeanie to working with Theodore St. John on the Mexican story.

It was never produced, however. I had the most cordial negotiations about it with General Maximino Ávila Camacho, brother of the President of Mexico, and with Miguel Alemán Valdés, who later became President; but I could never quite overcome my misgiving that, as I wrote to Frank Freeman, no matter how good and true a story we had, "some political schemer" opposed to the Mexican Government might use "the sensitive Mexican people to bring ridicule on the picture for the purpose of discrediting the present political leaders of Mexico" and estranging "the Mexican people from the people of the United States." Rather than risk that, I shelved the subject; and DeMille Productions absorbed its share of the preparatory costs.

In any event, a faint droning sound heard over Hawaii one Sunday in December, 1941, was to grow into a thunder that would shake the whole world, the seas and the dry land, and change the plans and dreams and lives of everyone. Again America was at war.

There was no quaintness about World War II. All but my very youngest readers will remember it, its grimness and its hard-bought glory. For me to chronicle any personal contribution of mine to the war effort would be intolerable foolishness. I did for it what all Americans did, and infinitely less than many.

But one contribution of mine to international good will must not go unrecorded. Although the Academy of Motion Picture Arts and Sciences has never deemed me qualified to receive its award for direction, it did ask me to make the presentation of its 1941 award for best achievement in directing; and I was glad thus to join in honoring John Ford for his direction of the beautiful and touching *How Green Was My Valley.* At the Academy dinner held in February, 1942, I should have qualified without dispute if there had been an award for how red is my face. Among the distinguished guests at the dinner was the Ambassador of China, that country for which all our hearts bled as it suffered, at that stage of the war, its fearful, ruthless conquest by Japan. When I introduced the Ambassador, I spoke feelingly of how honored we were by the presence of "His Excellency, the Japanese Ambassador"! In the stunned and frozen silence which followed that gargantuan blunder, I fear that my immediate correction of it did not help matters much; and my own confusion and chagrin at such stupidity may explain the same evening's later diversion when I presented the "Oscar" to John Ford, who was a commander in the Navy, and addressed him warmly as "Major Ford." Driving home after the dinner, Mrs. deMille remarked to me thoughtfully, "Well, Cecil, at last you have done something that Hollywood will remember."

8

One evening late in April, 1942, Florence Cole, Berenice Mosk, and I stayed at the studio to hear, on the radio in my office, one of those wartime broadcasts by President Roosevelt which did so much to inspire and unify the American people in their war effort. In the course of his speech, the President told the story of the heroism of a Navy doctor named Corydon M. Wassell, who at great risk had saved some wounded American sailors by single-handedly getting them out of Java just ahead of the triumphant onrush of the Japanese invaders. We had no sooner clicked off the radio at the end of the President's speech when my telephone rang. It was Ted Bonnet. Had I heard the President? Yes. Did I hear him tell the story about that Navy doctor? Yes. Did I see what a great picture could be made of that story? I did!

But what neither Ted nor I knew was the real drama of the story—that Dr. Wassell had been ordered to leave the men behind because they were too badly wounded to be moved, and had taken it upon himself to countermand the order of his superior officer.

Frank Freeman had gone home to dinner, but I telephoned him at once, and he was back at the studio within minutes, putting in a call to Washington to the President's secretary, Stephen Early. The word came back that Mr. Early had retired and left orders not to be disturbed. There was nothing we could do until morning, except one all-important thing: inform the Motion Picture Producers' Association of our intentions ahead of any other producer who might well have the same idea, as in fact some did.

Late that evening, Florence Cole despatched a telegram to the Association, registering the title of my next picture: *The Story of Dr. Wassell.*

The following morning I telephoned the Secretary of the Navy, Frank Knox, whom I knew. Having no idea why I was calling, he pleasantly asked what he might do for me.

I said, "I want Dr. Wassell and the United States Navy."

"You can have Dr. Wassell," the Secretary replied, "but as for the Navy, they're rather busy right now. There is a war on, you know."

At that moment Dr. Wassell was in Australia. He had reported to Admiral William A. Glassford there with quaking knees: the Navy does not look kindly upon disobeying or changing orders, even if the result is saving men from capture by the enemy. He had been relieved to learn that, instead of being court-martialed on the spot, he had been cited to receive the Navy Cross. But now arrived a signal from the Navy Department in Washington, ordering him to report immediately to San Francisco, where he would receive further orders. Meanwhile he was not to talk with the press or anyone about his adventures or his sudden recall to the United States. None of the American naval officers in Australia could give the puzzled doctor any information on this sudden and surprising order, but one captain, who was a close friend of his, said, "I guess you're going to get hell, so you might as well go."

Nor was any further light vouchsafed when another officer met Dr. Wassell in San Francisco and whisked him not to Washington, but to Los Angeles. It was a thoroughly baffled doctor who soon found himself facing not a naval disciplinary board, but me.

The hero facing me, I found, was in appearance, speech, and manner a typical American country doctor, from Arkansas. I learned later, in many hours of conversation with him, that while serving as a medical missionary in China, he had discovered the cause of the dread disease, schistosomiasis Japonica, only to find that it had been discovered one day earlier by another doctor 800' miles away. In his broadcast, President Roosevelt had spoken of Dr. Wassell as "almost like a Christ-like shepherd, devoted to his flock." He was, I found, a convinced, devout Episcopalian, but all the sailors I interviewed later confirmed that there was no sanctimonious preachiness about him: he was the kind of Christian whose faith was shown by his works. How true that was came out after the war when, as a retired rear admiral in his middle sixties, Corydon Wassell went out again as a medical missionary, to a leper colony in Hawaii.

His modesty, in fact, made the idea of filming his story almost more of an ordeal to him than facing the Japanese or a court-martial would have been. I was able to persuade him to agree to it only when I told him that we had already promised to give 10 per cent of the picture's gross receipts to the Navy Relief Fund. For that cause, he would do anything.

With the Navy's co-operation, we rounded up the survivors of Dr. Wassell's rescue operation and spent many hours with Berenice Mosk taking down their individual verbatim accounts of it, to add to Dr. Wassell's own account. One of the survivors, Melvin Francis, appeared in the motion picture as himself. After we filmed the bombing scene in our picture, he remarked, "Take me back to Java!"

There was one of the wounded men, however, whom we could not interview. Benjamin Hopkins, seaman first class, had not got out of Java. He was badly wounded internally, and had to be left in the care of a British officer who promised to get him out if he could; but the Japanese came on too fast. It was assumed that "Hoppy" had died; and our picture showed him making a last hopeless stand against a Japanese ambush. Not until our picture was finished did we learn that he was a prisoner-of-war. Then I did something I have never done before or since, something against all the rules of motion picture construction: I tacked onto the film, after the last fade-out and end title, a piece of sound track, with no picture, but only my voice coming from the blank screen to tell the audience that Hoppy's mother had received word that he was still alive. And many months after the war ended, Hoppy came to Paramount Studio for a special screening of *The Story of Dr. Wassell,* just for him and his new bride.

The credits on the title of *The Story of Dr. Wassell* state accurately that the screenplay, by Alan LeMay and Charles Bennett, is "based upon the story of Commander Corydon M. Wassell, U.S.N. (M.C.), as related by him and fifteen of the wounded sailors involved . . . and also upon the story of James Hilton." We commissioned James Hilton, the author of *Goodbye, Mr. Chips*

379

and many other novels, to write the Wassell story in book form—
and gave him nine weeks to do it, from start of research to
finished manuscript. Incredibly, he accomplished it in eleven
weeks and three days. I did not know as much about writing
books then as I do now, or James Hilton's feat would have seemed
even more marvelous than it did. The actual writing of this
autobiography has been going on since 1953; but I have been
rather busy living since then, too.

If, from my description of Dr. Wassell, the reader has not
already thought of the one actor ideally qualified to play him,
then the reader deserves a low mark as a casting director. Important though speed of production was to us, it was well worth
waiting until *For Whom the Bell Tolls* was finished so that we
could obtain Gary Cooper. Laraine Day played Madeline, who in
actuality is Mrs. Wassell; but for story purposes we took the liberty
of postponing the marriage of Dr. and Mrs. Wassell for some
years. That is an instance of the perfectly legitimate dramatic
license which sometimes helps a story without doing any damage
to essential historical truth. The date on Dr. and Mrs. Wassell's
marriage certificate is important to them, but it is their relationship as two human beings which is important to an audience.

Dennis O'Keefe played Hoppy, and his moving performance
added to the audience's joy at the news that the real Hoppy was
still alive. Signe Hasso's refreshing loveliness, amid the pain and
noise of battle, increased the charm of her portrayal of Bettina,
a Dutch nurse; and Carol Thurston lent an appealing warmth
to the part of Tremartini, who incidentally was a real character,
whose fate after the Japanese invasion we were never able to
learn.

The critics received *The Story of Dr. Wassell* with almost unprecedented unanimity. They lambasted it particularly for departing from the facts, though of course to the critics that was
only one of its vices. But Dr. Wassell himself said, in a radio
broadcast from Little Rock before the opening of the picture
there in his home town, that it was 98 per cent true. Such statements, of course, do not affect critics. What, indeed, can ever
affect the affectation of omniscience?

One of Gary Cooper's lines in *The Story of Dr. Wassell* was,
"There'll be a special place in heaven for the Dutch," because it

was a small Dutch ship that brought Dr. Wassell and his men from Java to Australia. Perhaps it was our portrayal of Dutch heroism, which was surely no more than was due to the Dutch military and naval personnel and the Dutch civilians in Java, that moved Queen Wilhelmina of the Netherlands to decorate me with the Order of Orange-Nassau. But I also had a personal reason, in addition to my own Dutch ancestry, for cherishing that decoration: when I was about eight years old, the picture of Queen Wilhelmina, then aged about ten, appeared in a New York newspaper, and I fell madly in love with her. Her Majesty certainly never knew that; but I was able to tell the story to her daughter, Queen Juliana, when the latter visited Hollywood many years later.

9

We also had an American President of Dutch descent when *The Story of Dr. Wassell* was made; and Franklin D. Roosevelt was gracious enough to intimate that he would receive me at the White House, together with Dr. and Mrs. Wassell, when we went to Washington for the special opening of the picture in Constitution Hall. In wartime—need I remind older readers?—transportation was not easy to secure; but an invitation to the White House is a command, and I managed to get reservations on a small southern airline for Gladys Rosson and myself.

That was the only time, I believe, that Mrs. deMille ever voiced any hint of an objection to the company I kept.

She asked me rather ominously, "Are you and Gladys going to Washington?"

"Yes."

"Traveling together in the same small plane?"

"Yes."

Mrs. deMille's face assumed a still more worried look. "My," she said, "it would be terrible if anything happened to Gladys!"

The plane skirted some tree-tops along the way; but it landed safely, and Mrs. deMille could set at rest her worries about the secretary upon whom we both depended so much. The President was ill when we reached Washington, but he received us in his study. As we were waiting to go in, Mrs. Wassell said to me, "Are you nervous, Mr. deMille?" She was not, at all.

I might have been nervous, however, if I had listened to the advice of my staff. Appreciating President Roosevelt's co-operation and interest in *The Story of Dr. Wassell,* I had decided to bring him some gifts—a print of the picture, some Dutch stamps which he did not have in his collection, and one of the so-called "DeMille half-dollars," a special issue commemorating the first English settlement in Virginia, of which I had bought about half the entire issue, to use as awards for fellow-workers who make some extraordinarily original or hazardous contribution to my productions. My staff thought that that was just fine. But, I added, I also intended to present the President with a small clay tablet from my collection of antiquities. It was a tax receipt, and hence, I said, a clear proof that the Democratic party was 4,000 years old. The suggestion of telling that to President Roosevelt horrified my staff; but I counted on his sense of humor, and I was not wrong. He threw his head back in that characteristic laugh, and hugely enjoyed my gentle dig at his party's policy of "tax and tax, spend and spend."

He could afford to enjoy it. That same year, 1944, the American people were to elect him President again for an unprecedented fourth term. In the American way, I did my best to help defeat him. I attended the Republican National Convention in the summer of 1944; and, remembering that much of President Roosevelt's political strength came from labor unions, I was shocked to find that the Republican Convention program included no national labor leader among its speakers. The national president of the carpenters' union, William L. Hutcheson, was a Republican. I found out that he would be willing to speak from the convention platform if asked. Then I cornered the man who was a great power in the Republican party in Pennsylvania, Joseph Newton Pew, Jr., and said to him, "We've had people from every race, every religion, every part of the country, every segment of humanity, speaking up there—except a leader of organized labor. The unions have been slighted. Bill Hutcheson will speak. Can you get him on?"

Mr. Pew shook his head. The convention was rolling so fast toward the nomination by that time, he said, that it could not be stopped to hear another speech. If there is any man in the United States who knows politics, it is Joe Pew. All I could do was shrug resignedly. That was the inauspicious and unlikely beginning of one of the strongest and warmest friendships of my life, my friendship with Joe Pew.

J. N. Pew, Jr., if known to the public at all, is known as a very wealthy man, chairman of the Sun Oil Company, and a pillar of the conservative wing of the Republican party. If that is all the public knows of him, it knows very little indeed. I will not offend him by telling all I know about those facets of his character which would greatly surprise any of the public who have perhaps fixed upon him the unreal image of the typical tycoon. But I wonder how many men would pay for the printing of a political tract, diametrically and violently opposed to their own views, simply because they thought the opposing viewpoint deserved a hearing, which the author of the tract could not afford to pay for. I wonder how many men, no matter how wealthy, when presented with plans for an invention which promised to advance the science of medicine by a tremendous leap, would instantly say, "Yes, we ought to form a company for this, so as to fix it that no one will make any money out of it." Joe Pew's name will occur again in these pages, not as often as it should if I were not respectful of his modesty, but at least twice, for he has given me two demonstrations of friendship unequaled in my lifetime.

He has been a tower of strength to me in an activity into which I was unwillingly launched in 1944, which has taken much of my time and energy since then, and which I will not drop until I die.

So, in another way, was the man who came with me as associate producer while we were making *The Story of Dr. Wassell*. Sidney Biddell, a New Englander by birth, with a fine education and a background in publishing and writing for the stage and screen, was my associate producer for approximately three years, at the end of which he became a full-fledged producer of his own films. Those three years coincided with the finishing of *The Story of Dr. Wassell* and the making of *Unconquered*, in connection with both of which Sidney functioned with all the skill and tact which his difficult job required, and with that special grace of manner he has, which can only be described by the old-fashioned word, gentlemanly, which makes him so pleasant a person to work with and to know.

10

But those three years also coincided with the bursting and first reverberations of a bombshell, which gave me another reason to be grateful that Sidney Biddell was at my side. I have never made agreement with me, on politics or any other such subject, a condition of membership on my staff. When the present members of my studio staff are in a baiting mood, they like to remind me that three of the four men among them are Democrats; they particularly like to manifest this with satisfied smiles at luncheon the day after an election when the Democrats win, though I must say that they bear manfully with my smug smile when the Republicans win. I have never asked any member of my staff to do anything counter to his own personal convictions; but naturally I have been glad when their convictions enabled them to join wholeheartedly with mine. I should have been handicapped indeed if Sidney Biddell, being closest to me, had not conscientiously and thoroughly agreed with me about a certain letter which reached me on August 16, 1944. But he did agree; and his support of the stand I took in response to that letter has never wavered.

The letter was from one of the two unions to which I belong, the American Federation of Radio Artists.* It informed me that the board of directors of the Los Angeles local of AFRA had voted to assess each member of the local the sum of one dollar, for a fund to be used in opposing a proposition scheduled to appear on the California ballot in the coming general election in November.** The proposition in question, known as Proposition 12, would have abolished the closed shop in California and given to every Californian the right to get and hold a job whether or not he belonged to a union. The $1 assessment to fight this proposition, my union informed me, was due and payable by September 1, under pain of suspension from membership in the union. Since AFRA had a form of closed shop contract with the radio industry,

* The other union to which Mr. deMille belonged until his death, and on whose board of directors he served, was the Screen Directors' Guild of America. (Ed.)

** In California, amendments to the state constitution and certain other legislative measures are submitted to the direct vote of the people: such measures appear, as numbered "propositions," on the same ballot with the names of candidates for public office. (Ed.)

suspension of an AFRA member meant that he could no longer work in radio.

When I received the letter, I knew very little about Proposition 12. But I knew, or thought I knew, something about an American citizen's right to political freedom. When I studied Proposition 12, I decided to vote for it. And here my union was demanding that I pay $1 into a political campaign fund to persuade other citizens to vote against Proposition 12: was demanding, in a word, that I cancel my vote with my dollar. Even if I were opposed to Proposition 12, I asked myself, did my union, did any organization, have the right to impose a compulsory political assessment upon any citizen, under pain of the loss of his right to work?

To me, the issue was clear from the first time I read the letter. What was at stake, as far as I personally was concerned? My job with the Lux Radio Theatre, which paid me approximately $100,000 a year and which, because of its contact with the American people, meant much more to me than could be measured in money. On the other side of the scale was $1—with my political freedom pinned to it. There are very few men who lightly toss away $100,000 a year; I am not one. I took advice. Most of it was the advice of appeasement. "Pay the dollar. Don't give up the Lux show. Fight the thing some other way if you want to—but pay the dollar."

I saw, moreover, that if I did not pay the dollar, my refusal would become a national issue. That was no exaggerated self-esteem: if a voice that had been listened to by 20- to 30,000,000 people every Monday evening for nine years was suddenly banned from the air, some of those people would undoubtedly ask why. I was certain that the answer to that question would hurt the union in the public mind; and I had no wish to hurt my union. I therefore invited some of its officers to a conference with Neil McCarthy and me, told them I thought they had made a great mistake in imposing this compulsory political assessment, and offered to contribute to the union, as a voluntary gift, a number of dollars equal to the number of members in the Los Angeles local, if they would rescind the assessment and return their dollars to the members who had paid them under compulsion. The union refused. I saw then that the fundamental issue was not Proposition 12. It was an issue of union power: the power to control the individual member's political freedom through control of his right to work.

It was not until several years later, when Louis F. Budenz visited me shortly after his defection from the Communist party, that I learned how the high councils of that party had marked two men on the American radio for silencing: Fulton Lewis, Jr., and Cecil B. deMille. As Louis Budenz put it to me, "We never could get Fulton Lewis; but we got you." I do not maintain that the officers of AFRA were Communists. The Communists always score their best victories when non-Communists do their work for them.

When the issue was finally drawn, when the deadline and the extended deadline for paying the assessment passed and the union remained adamant, I sat down for one last discussion of it with Mrs. deMille. Not since 1913 had we had so serious a decision to make together. I told her again what refusal to pay the assessment would mean to us: the loss of the $100,000 a year, the loss of my radio program, the likelihood that I would be pilloried as anti-labor and drawn into a controversy that might last for years, with what effect upon our work and our lives no one could say; and on the other side, the simple solution of paying $1 to a cause in which I did not believe.

"Which," I asked her, "should I choose?"

Generations of Adamses, reaching back to the Revolution, spoke in her answer:

"You have no choice."

I conducted the Lux Radio Theatre of the Air for the last time on January 22, 1945. AFRA has since become AFTRA, the American Federation of Television and Radio Artists. Its ban still holds. Television, as a medium of general entertainment, was almost unknown in 1945; but I am banned as completely from television as from radio.

Since the passage of the Taft-Hartley Act in 1947, no one can be denied the right to work for refusal to pay a political assessment. Not being retroactive, that law is of no benefit to me; but Senator Taft told me that that law would not have been enacted if my refusal to pay the dollar had not drawn public attention to the abuse of union power.

For sounding the first tocsin of what was to become for him and for many thousands a crusade, the credit must go to William M. Jeffers, my old friend of *Union Pacific* days. Supporting my stand, he invited me to come to Omaha again, on a day dear to his good Irish-American heart, March 17, 1945, and over a nationwide broadcast, which he would arrange, put before the American people the case of political freedom and the right to work. I had lost the right to work in radio; but I still had the right of free speech. I accepted Bill Jeffer's invitation.

The response was overwhelming. No motion picture, with the exception of *The King of Kings* and *The Ten Commandments* (1956), has brought me so many letters. They came from every part of the country and from every fighting front where Americans were still at war. They were from Democrats and Republicans, rich and poor, men, women, and even children in all walks of life. Many of the most touching of them came from union members or their wives. The gist of them all was much the same: "Do something to keep what has happened to you from happening to the rest of us."

That it was happening to others, as well as to a rich producer who could afford to lose $100,000 a year and not starve, was brought home to us in Hollywood when six members of the Screen Office Employees Guild, clerical workers at Metro-Goldwyn-Mayer, were dropped from their union and lost their jobs because they opposed political assessments; and what was happening in Hollywood was happening throughout the nation.

The letters I received, in their numbers and their warmth of sympathy and approbation, went far to make up for the excoriation and abuse in which union publications and the then flourishing Communist press joined in a strange and alarming chorus. But the letters also created a problem. Many of them had money in them. To those who sent dollar bills, asking me to pay the assessment with them and return to the air, I returned their money, explaining that if I could not in good conscience pay the dollar myself, I could not let anyone pay it for me. But others sent money—$1, $5, $10, in some instances as little as a dime, all they could afford—for me to use to fight the power that could cut off a man's livelihood if he refused to obey its dictates. This money was a sacred trust. I opened a special account in the little branch of the Bank of America a block from the studio; and, as it grew to hundreds of dollars, wondered how I could discharge that trust.

Again Bill Jeffers helped me decide. "You must form an organization," he said, "a foundation for political freedom; and you must put your name on it, because your name is associated with this incident that gave birth to the movement and is a guarantee of the foundation's purpose."

The result was the DeMille Foundation for Political Freedom, organized first as a trusteeship with Neil McCarthy, Sidney Biddell, and me as trustees, and incorporated in September, 1945, with William M. Jeffers as chairman of its board until ill health caused him to resign, when he was succeeded by Y. Frank Freeman.

The history of the DeMille Foundation would be a book in itself. In this book I can only touch upon some of its highlights, some which most affected me personally and some which have never been told before. Yet in another sense its history can be told in two sentences. In 1945 there were two states which had on their statute books laws giving men and women the right to work regardless of their membership or non-membership in a union. Now there are 18; and the DeMille Foundation has been active in every one of them.*

* Now there are 19, Kansas having joined the list in November, 1958. The DeMille Foundation for Political Freedom was dissolved by vote of its board of directors in February, 1959. Its valedictory *Bulletin* to its members throughout the United States said in part: "This was a hard decision to make, because of what the Foundation has meant to us all and especially to Mr. DeMille; but the large majority of the Directors felt it wiser and better to close the Foundation than to carry on without the active presence of him who was its inspiration and main driving force. No one can take Mr. DeMille's place. No one else should use his name. . . . The cause of the Right to Work lives on." (*Ed.*)

16

ANTI-SEMITISM WAS THE FIRST major problem the DeMille Foundation had to face, oddly enough. For some reason which it will take a better psychologist than I to fathom, any movement which is considered as being generally "conservative" seems to attract peculiar brands of crackpots. Perhaps the "left wing" has its own lunatic fringe; I am not so closely acquainted with that. At all events, very soon after my Omaha speech, I received a lengthy telegram offering $25,000 to the cause if I would make an address under the auspices of an organization with a high-sounding religious and patriotic name. This sum—$25,000—was very much more than we had in the little account in the little branch bank; but the telegram was signed by a name which we recognized as that of an anti-Semitic agitator better known in another section of the country than he was in California. His offer was turned down.

That may seem obvious and unimportant; but it set a policy from which the Foundation has never deviated, though on another occasion it cost us four times $25,000. Our purpose was to work for political freedom and the right to work. A number of people, some interested in very good causes as well as some in very bad ones, have shaken their heads sadly when we have declined to depart from our one goal. But strength lies in integrity;

389

and certainly no racial or religious "ism" has any part in a movement to secure for all Americans their God-given freedom and rights.

One of the most sickening experiences I have ever had was when I was asked to speak about the DeMille Foundation at a private dinner in an exclusive New York club. One of the moving spirits behind the dinner was a retired army officer, very proud of his association with scores of patriotic societies, whom I shall promote in rank and call by the fictitious name of Colonel Jones. The business affiliations of the men on the guest list included some of the richest and most powerful corporations in America. I was allowed to bring a few guests of my own. Among them I invited Adolph Zukor. When he walked into the room, where most of the guests had gathered and were chatting affably, you could feel the temperature drop to below freezing. Mr. Zukor, you see, is a Jew.

We had dinner. I spoke on the DeMille Foundation's principles. Two members of the Foundation staff spoke on its detailed plans. Then a number of the guests spoke, all endorsing the principles, all explaining why they and their companies, just then, could not give any support to the plans, though they certainly wanted us to know that they were 100 per cent with us in spirit. Then J. N. Pew, who had come up that afternoon from Philadelphia, spoke. Drawing on his marvelously detailed knowledge of conditions in every part of the United States, he told where the DeMille Foundation had been active and what, from his own investigation, he knew it had accomplished, and how much it merited the support he pledged it. Quietly, without half trying, he made the other men around the table look like the pygmies which, with a few exceptions, they were. And riding back to my hotel with me after the dinner, Joe Pew said to me, "The reason I came up for this was that I knew they'd break your heart."

I can remember only one time in my life when I have ever cut a man dead. That was the following day, at a luncheon, when the man whom I have called Colonel Jones came up to greet me effusively. He finished his greeting, if he finished it at all, to my back.

I think of that dinner and some other occasions like it when I

390

read in some propaganda sheet that the DeMille Foundation is a rich men's instrument for crushing labor. There was the time when a prominent lawyer, much too bright to have done it accidentally, took an hour and a half to introduce me, so that the audience was completely exhausted before I began to speak. There was the time when a trade association was so fond or fearful of its cozy deals with certain union bosses that it withdrew its invitation to me when it learned that I was going to speak for the freedom and rights of the rank-and-file union members, caught between their bosses in the union and their bosses on the job. There are a few wealthy men, like Mr. Pew, with vision and heart, who support the DeMille Foundation; but when I think of its members throughout the country and look for a typical one, I am much more likely to think of Nettie Bailey.

Mrs. Nettie B. Bailey was an old lady in her eighties. She lived in a small town on Maryland's Eastern Shore. I forget, if I ever knew, how she learned of the DeMille Foundation, but, a good Marylander, she remembered "Carroll's sacred trust" of freedom and, every month until the month she died, she never failed to send to the Foundation office her few dollars and a letter that was passed from hand to hand and lifted all our hearts. It is not the Colonel Joneses, with all their patriotic publicity, but the Nettie Baileys, whether they are 18 or 80, who are the real America.

2

It should not be surprising that, for my next picture after *The Story of Dr. Wassell*, my thoughts turned to the birth of freedom, and the beginning of the death of slavery, in Colonial America. Ideas for motion pictures can come from anywhere, as I have said many times. The germ of *Unconquered* was born one Sunday afternoon when I was reading a work on colonial history and learned that in the eighteenth century, on American soil, white men and women were bought and sold as slaves. I was familiar with the indentured servants, of course; but these were slaves, convicts from England, shipped to the American colonies to be sold by private transaction or at public auction, in conditions often as degrading as those which aroused the nation's conscience against Negro slavery a century later.

At the time I began thinking out a story to convey the theme of freedom against the background suggested by that idea, I was losing my good research consultant, Marion Crist; and the correspondence, invitations to speak, and all the other details concerning the DeMille Foundation were piling up to a degree that bade fair to swamp us. I needed help, with the research for the new picture and with the whole new world of activity that was opening up as the result of my refusal to pay the $1 political assessment. Whenever Sidney Biddell comes to see me now, characteristically omitting to mention his own labors for both *Unconquered* and the increasing civic activity of 1945, he always reminds me of two claims he has to my gratitude: that he brought me the help I needed, in the persons of Henry Noerdlinger and Donald Hayne.

No man who has ever worked with me has come closer to the deepest places of my mind than Donald Hayne. It is typical of him that at our first meeting in March, 1945, he said that he admired my courage in refusing to pay the dollar, but he did not say that he agreed with me. He had voted against Proposition 12, but still he did not believe that anyone should be taxed for a political campaign. It was not until he was convinced by his own study of the issues, undertaken in his own deliberate manner, that he was willing to go almost all the way with me in my opposition to the closed shop. His work soon expanded beyond the letter writing and organization work which he originally came in to do. Since his first few months with me, there is almost no activity of mine in which he does not have a part, except matters of business, for which he has little taste or skill.

When I ask him a question, he will always give me a scrupulously weighed and honest answer, whether I like it or not; and that is what I want. I do not always agree with him either, but whatever the subject, from showmanship to theology, each of us always understands the other's meaning, with a mental sympathy and communication that are altogether rare. Once I spent a long evening alone with Joe Pew, discussing the most abstruse yet most important question that can engage the human mind—the nature of God. As the night wore on, Mr. Pew smiled and asked me, "How many people do you know who would know or care what we've been talking about?" "I know one," I said. "His name is Donald Hayne."

Henry S. Noerdlinger joined my staff as research consultant in August, 1945. A Swiss by birth, from the canton of Saint Gallen, he has a European's command of languages, an American's sense of the practical, and the judicial temperament, the industry, and the exactness of a born scholar. I had Henry in mind when I wrote this paragraph for the introduction to his book, *Moses and Egypt:*

> The research consultant on a producer's staff must become familiar with all the principal sources of information on the historical characters and the historical period of the picture; he must assemble an adequate working library for constant use as well as a voluminous collection of reference notes, photographs, photostats, excerpts, and other data from the great libraries and museums of the world; and he must approach his task with the steady objectivity of the scholar—even if this means that he must sometimes be, quite firmly, a "no-man" to the producer, the writers, the art department, and the others engaged in actual production!

From *Unconquered*, through such varied subjects as *Samson and Delilah*, *The Greatest Show on Earth*, and *The Ten Commandments* (1956), Henry Noerdlinger has been the most thorough and accurate research consultant I have ever had, making himself as much at home among the pyramids of the Pharaohs as in the tinsel and spun-candy world of the circus. He is beginning to read for me now on the subjects of what, at my age, will probably be my last pictures. When we are ready to shoot the next one, *On My Honor*, there is nothing worth knowing that Henry will not know about the Boy Scouts and their founder, Lord Baden-Powell.* I shall not say anything here about the other subject which I call "Project X"; but if the scientists of the world have agreed as between the cosmic theories of Lemaître and Hoyle by that time, Henry Noerdlinger will know all about that too.

Research was particularly important on *Unconquered* because the story is laid in the year 1763. Many Americans seem to be

* A screenplay of *On My Honor* is now being prepared by Henry Wilcoxon and Jesse L. Lasky, Jr. (*Ed.*)

393

under the impression that American history began in 1776. There are seldom sharp breaks in history: what we know as the American way of life, with its growing passion for freedom and its two poles of settled stability in the East and pioneering in the West, was already being born when Americans were still British colonials. But the westward expansion of America might have been halted, and people in Ohio today might be speaking French if the Indian uprising under Pontiac had succeeded in destroying the English outposts on the frontier, chief of which was a small fortified settlement, later called Pittsburgh, in the western part of Virginia. This is the historical background of *Unconquered.*

That Pittsburgh was in Virginia, until two English astronomers named Charles Mason and Jeremiah Dixon surveyed a line to settle a boundary dispute, is one of the little surprises which, I confess, I enjoy putting in a picture, especially for the benefit of critics who will say "What nonsense!" until they go and look it up.

There are other little surprises, however, which I do not enjoy finding in a picture after it is made. One of the lines in *Unconquered* is "These men is possum hunters," spoken by a sergeant bragging of what deadly sharpshooters his militiamen are. I could only bow in merited shame before the letters which came in after the film was released, pointing out that opossum are trapped, not shot. I could not blame Henry Noerdlinger, as I do not believe that the American opossum is very common in the canton of Saint Gallen; and I could not blame the writers, Charles Bennett, Fredric M. Frank, and Jesse Lasky, Jr., since neither English schools, Dartmouth, nor the University of Dijon normally include many courses in possum-hunting in their curricula. I could, however, blame the Champion Driver, with his peerless knowledge of hunting game both big and small, for not catching that error in the script.

With all due respect for the performances of Gary Cooper, Paulette Goddard, Howard da Silva, Boris Karloff, Cecil Kellaway, and Ward Bond, my two heroes in *Unconquered* were Sir C. Aubrey Smith and Robert Baughman. Sir Aubrey, well past 80 years of age, would come on the set each morning with his lines letter perfect, giving the director a joy which much younger players, alas, sometimes deny him. You will not find the name of

394

Robert Baughman in the cast of *Unconquered*, not even among the "small parts and bits"; but I made it a point to find out the name of the young drummer boy who, during our filming of the siege of Fort Pitt, had a fireball accidentally fall on his drum, but kept on drumming right through the scene, though his hand was badly burned. That was Bob Baughman; and that is what makes the difference between an actor and someone who comes to the studio to collect a certain number of dollars for standing in front of a camera a certain length of time.

3

Paramount was very patient with me when I had to interrupt my work on *Unconquered*, a story of freedom in 1763, to accept invitations to speak in various parts of the country on the subject of freedom in 1945. If there is anything less interesting than talking about one's surgical operations, it is reciting one's old speeches. But there were two I made that year which were not without their exciting overtones.

When I spoke in Wichita, Kansas, one of the events planned for me in that hospitable city was a tour of the Boeing aircraft plant. We visited the plant in the evening, but it was humming with full activity to meet the nation's need for more and more war planes. We saw every part of it, climbed in and out of fuselages in various stages of construction, and the ex-president of the Mercury Aviation Company felt very much an amateur amid the complexities of modern aircraft. At the end of the tour, the head of the plant, who had guided us, made a mysterious remark. "I wish I could tell you what you have seen," he said, "but you will hear of it in a few weeks, and it will be the most terrible thing you have ever heard in your lifetime." We did hear, in August. Without knowing it, we had seen, and perhaps been in, the plane whose destination was Hiroshima.

That was destruction. But I also saw in the same city what amounted almost to creation, when I watched the infinite patience of skilled men and women teaching children with cerebral palsy to talk and walk and pick things up from a table and put them down, at the Institute of Logopedics, on whose national advisory board I have gladly and humbly served ever since.

In September, 1945, I was invited by a post of the American

Legion to speak from one of the most historic platforms in America, the steps of the old Sub-Treasury Building in New York. Wichita may have escaped the attention of the unions. New York did not. My hosts were flooded with telegrams protesting the appearance of this notorious labor-hater. Pressure was brought sufficient to cause some of the bands to walk off the musical program planned for the day. My hosts were not daunted; but the air was electric with the possibility of a rowdy and hostile demonstration, when I walked out of the historic building to take my place at the front of the platform. I noticed then that a man had quietly slipped out of the place where he had been waiting unnoticed, and was standing beside me. It was Barney Balaban, the president of Paramount. I do not know what Barney Balaban's politics are, or whether or not he agrees with me on the subject of the right to work. But I know that America has no finer citizen, and the Bill of Rights no firmer supporter, than Barney Balaban; and I have never forgotten that quiet demonstration of his friendship, when he came to stand beside me on a day when friends were few.

We had a share of excitement at the studio itself in 1946, when the motion picture industry was rocked by a jurisdictional strike. It was a dispute between two unions, not involving management in the essential issue; but the strike leaders were determined to close the studios and halt production, if need be, in order to beat the rival union. Early one morning, the word spread somehow that a mass picket line would be thrown around Paramount that day. Donald Hayne telephoned me at my home to ask if I was going to the studio. When I said yes, certainly, he said, "Then I'll meet you at your home and go down with you." When we reached the studio, the pickets were massed outside both gates on Marathon Street. Their aspect was not friendly. Donald and I went to the front door of the DeMille Building, a couple of hundred feet from the nearest gate, and I proceeded to unlock it.

A couple of pickets detached themselves from the mass and came down to us. One of them said to me politely, "Would you mind going in through the gate?" What he had in mind I do not know, since the approach to the gate was jammed with rather angry humanity, but his manners were perfect.

As politely, I replied, "I always use this door, so I am going through it today."

I had often heard about the effect of a soft answer upon wrath, but I never saw it so clearly demonstrated. The polite picket looked nonplused. He withdrew, and we went in. Others were less gently received. One man announced to the pickets, "I am an American citizen and I want to go to work." For answer, he was thrown over a hedge.

Most of the studio workers simply stayed home. I went around the studio to visit the few who had braved the picket line. On one of the sound stages I found a very famous male star, literally shaking with terror because his car had been rocked as he drove it through the densely packed crowd at the gate. The studio was an empty, deserted place; but when I reached the research building I found the head of that department, all alone, sitting behind her desk doing her work, with not a one of her neat gray hairs out of place, as calmly as if it were any ordinary day. I had known her since she started work as Bessie McGaffey's assistant in 1923, but her unruffled courage that day, in contrast to most of the males who stayed home, added a new dimension to my admiration for Miss Helen Gladys Percey. I give her Hollywood's high accolade of "Miss": for she earned star billing in my esteem that day.

For some weeks during the strike, my staff and I lived in the studio, sleeping on cots in our offices, so as not to risk being shut out if we happened to meet less polite pickets another day. Eventually the strike petered out, with no tangible result for the workers except a great loss of wages; but the losing union kept one token picket at our gate for a year or two afterward. He was a very amiable old gentleman. He and I became such friends that a stop to chat with him was a fixed event in my daily routine. I am sure he did not regard me as an evil labor-hater, any more than I regarded him as a dangerous subversive. But how bored he must have been.

When *Unconquered* was released in the autumn of 1947, I had long since ceased to be surprised by critical reviews; but I had reason to be shocked when Bosley Crowther hinted that I had borrowed our scene of the relief of Fort Pitt from *Beau Geste*. The film critic of *The New York Times* really should know his theatrical history better than that; but then, Bosley Crowther may be too young to remember the old play about the Sepoy Rebellion, called, I think it was, *Jessie Brown*, which my father read to me when I was a little boy at Echo Lake. That is where the scene came from. I do not remember how many times I have used it. The next time I use it, I trust that no one will hint that I am plagiarizing *Unconquered*.

4

For more than a decade, I had been thinking on and off about one of the greatest love stories in history or literature, which is also a poignant drama of faith, the story of Samson and Delilah. Again and again I had gone back to the Book of Judges to read it; but every time I was stopped by the fact that I could not find the one thread that would tie together the separate incidents in Samson's life as it is recorded in the Bible. Then I came upon a little-known novel, *Judge and Fool*, by Vladimir Jabotinsky; and the problem was solved. The Bible tells of Samson's rage when his Philistine bride was given to another man by her father, and of his contemptuous rejection of the father's offer of the bride's younger sister. The Bible does not name the younger sister, Jabotinsky did. He named her Delilah. By that simple, plausible, and entirely legitimate device, the story came together as a drama rather than a narrative. Narrative answers the question, "What?" Drama answers the question, "Why?" If the younger sister, so humiliatingly rebuffed by Samson, were named Delilah, she had a motive to destroy him, more powerful, more burning, than the merely mercenary one of the bribe offered her by the Philistines.

I had not made a Biblical film since *The King of Kings*, nor any with a religious theme since *The Sign of the Cross* and *The Crusades*. A new generation of executives had grown up since *The King of Kings*; and most of them greeted my suggestion of *Samson and Delilah* with the expected executive misgivings. A Biblical story, for the post-World War II generation? Put millions of dollars into a Sunday school tale? Anticipating this familiar chorus, before the meeting held in my office to decide on my next production, I asked Dan Groesbeck to draw a simple sketch of two people—a big, brawny athlete and, looking at him with an at once seductive and coolly measuring eye, a slim and ravishingly attractive young girl.

When the executives trooped in, ready to save me and Paramount from the ruinous folly they were sure I had in mind, I greeted them, saw them to their seats, and brought out the Groesbeck sketch.

"How is that," I asked them, "for the subject of a picture?"

They were enthusiastic. That was movies. That was boy-meets-girl—and what a boy, and girl!

"That, gentlemen," I said, "is *Samson and Delilah.*"

"Oh, well, if *that's* what you mean. . . . You see, we thought . . . But that's different. . . . That's okay."

I am sometimes accused of gingering up the Bible with large and lavish infusions of sex and violence. I can only wonder if my accusers have ever read certain parts of the Bible. If they have, they must have read them through that stained-glass telescope which centuries of tradition and form have put between us and the men and women of flesh and blood who lived and wrote the Bible. Clothing them in what we think is reverence, we have too often stripped the men and women of the Bible of their humanity; and I believe that that same process strips them of much of their religious value, too. If we are forced to remember that Samson was swept by a surge of sexual passion but redeemed the breaking of his vows when, being blinded, at last he saw, or that Moses had a murderously violent temper but mastered it and turned its force to weld and lead a people into freedom, or that Jesus Himself sweat blood from fear but rose and faced His captors in the calm strength of the will of God, it becomes less easy to excuse our own lusts and hates and faithless cowardices.

My friends in the front office are always right when they say that people will not come to see a picture in which Biblical characters walk around looking and acting like Biblical characters. But, when they walked the earth, they did not know they were Biblical characters. They were men and women. And that is how I portray them.

It is not easy. Our eyes are all too accustomed to that stained-glass telescope. Sometimes, as in showing the executive group what I meant by *Samson and Delilah*, I have to use some device of surprise like the sketch by Dan Groesbeck. Sometimes, in trying to convey the concept to writers or actors, I have to translate the Bible's glorious and hallowed English into the crudest vernacular. It shocks, but it makes real.

For the roles of Samson and Delilah, I selected two players quite deliberately because they embody in a large part of the public mind the essence of maleness and attractive femininity, Victor Mature and Hedy Lamarr. That casting was risky. If it turned out that my two leads had nothing to give to the story but the appearance of male strength and female beauty, however superlatively they shone in those qualities, the real point of the story would be lost. But when I saw the rushes of the scene in the grist mill, of Samson mocked in his agony and Delilah discovering that the man she has loved and betrayed is now blind, I knew, if I had not known before, that the talents of Victor Mature and Hedy Lamarr are more than skin-deep. George Sanders gave the finished performance one always expects of him as the Saran of Gaza; and Henry Wilcoxon made a stalwart Ahtur, Samson's rival for Delilah's older sister, played by Angela Lansbury. There were parts, as there will always be in my pictures, for veterans who had worked with me, such as Victor Varconi and Pedro de Cordoba; and among the several featured players who gave excellent performances was one whose talent and dedication to her art should carry her very far in the theater, whether on screen or stage, Olive Deering, who played Miriam, the Danite girl who loved Samson to the end of his life and beyond.

There is, of course, a spectacle in *Samson and Delilah,* when blind Samson, having prayed for the return of the strength he had lost through his folly, crashes the Philistine temple down in ruins upon the enemies of his people and their God. If the scene is spectacular, credit is due to the Book of Judges, not to me. It did, however, give us an interesting architectural problem: to construct a temple which would come down in total ruin by the dislodging of only two columns. The Bible does not give blueprints; but we found a description of just such a building, and just such a spectacular collapse, in the writings of Pliny, the Roman historian of the first century A.D., and we constructed our temple set accordingly, with only such modifications and safeguards as the needs of our story required and modern engineering made possible.

400

When I screened *Samson and Delilah* for Harold Lamb, who had worked on my first treatment of it in 1935, he said, "This is a great picture, and the critics will slaughter you for it." "Preposterous" and "essentially worthless," *The New Yorker* called it; but, surprisingly enough, many of the critics found good things to say about it, even if it is sometimes difficult to understand what is being said when the sayer's tongue is in his cheek.

The reader may think that I have a constitutional allergy to critics. That would be a false impression. I respect intelligent criticism. What I deplore in many critics is not that they criticize, but that they do not see. I may illustrate that, once and for all, by referring to what was perhaps the most intelligent review of *Samson and Delilah*, written by George Barbarow in the Winter, 1950, number of *The Hudson Review*.

As a critic should be, Mr. Barbarow was unsparing in pointing out what he considered flaws in the picture. "Coarse, raw, garish, oversimple" were some of his adjectives; he chided us for omitting some of Samson's feats of strength from the construction of our story; and he chastised us for presenting too much of the motivation of characters "by the lazy means of speech" instead of showing it visually. But Mr. Barbarow saw the whole picture, and knew what he was looking at. He knew the Bible, he knew drama, and he knew cinema. Thus he was able to see that "the constant use of drastic visual contrast throughout the picture is thoroughly appropriate to the representation of conflicts that are in themselves merciless and barbaric" and that "what is significant about this eye-blasting contrast is its harmony with the spirit of the Old Testament, pregnant with *wrath* and saturated with *blood*." No other critic, even the most favorable, seemed to see, for example, *why* and *how* Samson is suddenly vested with "terrifying pathos" when, blind and stumbling, "enmeshed in a ridiculous, gracelessly draped red net," he is baited "by a swarm of dwarfs" to make sport for the crowd in the Philistine temple: Mr. Barbarow knew enough about film direction and editing to know that such effects are "no accident," that it was "by the visual arrangement of this sequence" that Samson, "who has previously been a mixture of rustic comedian and arrogant fool . . . becomes the object of immeasurable sympathy . . . invoked at the right moment, which is shortly before the hero performs his final, most devastating feat."*

It is stimulating to read criticism, even adverse, when it is based on knowledge and understanding, when it is written by critics who have eyes to see all that the screenwriters, director, actors, technicians, and film editor have put into a picture. But I think one may be forgiven an ever so slight allergic reaction when all that effort and skill on a picture like *Samson and Delilah* are airily summed up, even by a friendly critic, as "the most expensive haircut in history."

People see in any motion picture only what they have eyes to see. The young Presbyterian minister in East Grand Forks, Minnesota, who wrote to me, "I trust my ministry will be more according to God's will for having seen *Samson and Delilah*," told me as much about himself in those words as he did about the picture. So did *The New Yorker.*

One whose critical views are more pronounced on matters of music than motion pictures also had kind words for *Samson and Delilah*. It was not the best of nights. James F. Byrnes, the former Secretary of State and a powerful Democratic leader in the South, had just announced his break with the Truman policies, and it was an unsmiling, grim-looking President who came to see our picture of a strong man fighting off enemies. But he was very affable to me, and I was impressed by his extensive knowledge of the Bible. I could hardly be farther apart from anyone politically than I am from President Truman, but he has one quality that I admire in any man: his great courage.

I met President Truman's successor around the same time, but in much less formal circumstances. I was in Washington to attend the Gridiron dinner with Roy A. Roberts, the publisher of the Kansas City *Star*. After arraying myself in white tie and tails, I repaired to Roy Roberts' hotel room, where I found him and some other gentlemen wrestling with the intricate problem of

* No one interested in film technique or film history should neglect reading Mr. Barbarow's review of *Samson and Delilah* in full, as a model of acute and informed criticism. Cf. also Joseph and Harry Feldman, "Cecil B. DeMille's Virtues," *Films in Review*, December, 1950, for a brief but also well-informed and objective analysis of Mr. deMille's technique and a wholesome antidote to what the Messrs. Feldman decry as the "accepted critical practice to condemn his works without examination, which is the very essence of prejudice." (*Ed.*)

402

getting his necktie fixed in a suitable and proper bow. Never one to shirk a call for first aid, I took the problem in both hands and succeeded in tying the bow, with the help of General Dwight D. Eisenhower as technical adviser. Tying a bow tie is an operation which always calls for a bold attack, confidence, ability to maneuver, knowledge of when to lengthen or shorten the lines, when to infiltrate the center, when to throw all your reserve strength into the final assault on both flanks: I could not have had a better coach than the commanding general of the greatest military operation in history.

5

Sometimes, as my staff could feelingly relate, it takes me a long time to reach decisions. Sometimes, however, I hear and heed opportunity's first knock. One such time was a day early in 1949 when I saw an inconspicuous item in *The Hollywood Reporter*. It said that Ringling Bros. and Barnum & Bailey were interested in the possibility that a motion picture might be made about their circus. Within five minutes I was closeted with Henry Ginsberg, then head of production at Paramount, closing the deal for my next picture: *The Greatest Show on Earth*.

There had been several good, and some not so good, pictures with a circus background, but there had never been what I would call a circus picture: one in which the circus itself was the star. There is no other institution on earth like the American circus. It is an army. It is a family. It is a city, always on the move. It is an agile giant. It is sweat and fatigue and danger endured to send a rippling wave of thrills and laughter across a continent. All the nations of the world are represented in it, but those who are "with it" form a tight clan set apart from everyone else in the world. Yet those men and women, who walk casually into cages filled with snarling lions, who seem to fly through the air as if it were their native element, who drive the stakes and haul the ropes and reef the canvas that turn some vacant lot into a magic wonderland, are men and women very much like those who, from town to town, sit on the hard benches under the big top and for a few hours taste the wonder of childhood again, on circus day. That—all of that—is what I wanted to put on the screen.

But first I had to learn it from the inside. I literally joined the

403

circus: in the summer of 1949, I traveled and lived "with it" on its trek through heat and rain across several states of the Middle West. Gladys Rosson was with me and trouped as wholeheartedly as if she had been to the sawdust born. Her notebook of 135 pages is crammed with incidents comic and terrifying, anecdotes and bits of business for possible use in the picture, circus slang carefully noted, vignettes of life in the "backyard" when the make-up is off and there are washing and mending to be done and babies to be bathed and gossip exchanged, as in any other small-town neighborhood; and if Gladys' notes run only from A for Accident to W for Wire Walker, you may be sure that we saw nothing starting with X, Y, or Z, or it would be there.

The most thrilling moment in the circus, I found, is one that there is no way to photograph. It is at night, when the big top is empty except for one man: the man whose job it is, in the darkness, to release the last rope, the "main fall," and let the great tent drop to the ground. I insisted on going in with him one night, over the murmurs of some who not unreasonably felt that a headline in the next day's paper, "Movie Producer Killed In Circus Tent Fall," might not be the best kind of circus publicity. When the last pin of the main fall rope is pulled, the 60-foot high canvas roof of the big tent drops instantaneously 30 feet. Then the air catches it, and it settles slowly down the rest of the way as air is pushed out at the open sides. But in that first instant you run. No nightmare holds terror any greater than the thought of being smothered under hundreds of square yards of heavy canvas. To the man who pulled the main fall, however, it was all in a day's, or night's, work. He took time to remark to me casually, "My aunt was your first leading lady": he was a nephew of Redwing, the Indian girl I had cast in *The Squaw Man* in 1913.

Various claims have been made through the years about which director has used the greatest number of extras in any one picture. The zero key must be the most worn part of every press agent's typewriter: it is so easy to multiply by thousands with one finger. I shall, however, make my modest entry in this mathematical derby: there must have been more than 50,000 people on the streets of Sarasota, Florida, the circus's winter home, when we let it be known that we were going to film the circus parade there and, of course, photograph the crowd. After

404

a month's work of shooting at the winter quarters in Sarasota, we returned to Hollywood for two months of studio production, then rejoined the circus in Washington and went on with it to Philadelphia, photographing actual performances under the big top in both cities, with our stars playing their roles on the trapezes, astride the elephants, and rollicking with the clowns, before the actual circus audiences.

Lighting and photographing under those conditions, so different from the sound stages in the studio, was a triumph of the cinematographers, George Barnes, Pev Marley, and Wallace Kelley. Only a trained eye can tell which audience shots were made under the big top and which in the studio—except, of course, for such close-ups as the delightful bit in which Bing Crosby and Bob Hope consented to appear with no listing of their names in the cast or any other warning before our audience in the theater suddenly sees them, side by side, solemnly swinging their heads left and right as their eyes follow the swinging of a trapeze.

I shall not recount the plot of *The Greatest Show on Earth:* I am hoping that Paramount will re-release it soon! I never realized that I was so popular until it became known in Hollywood that the leading feminine roles in this film were parts for which any actress would give her eye teeth. I was not offered any eye teeth, but my office was adorned with floral tributes from aspiring young ladies until it looked like an exotic garden or a funeral parlor. Those leading roles, however, were assigned not on the basis of flower arrangement, but to three good actresses who are also good troupers. When the audience sees Betty Hutton on a trapeze and Dorothy Lamour hanging by her teeth in the "iron jaw" act and Gloria Grahame letting an enormous elephant graze her pretty nose with its hoof, it is actually Betty and Dorothy and Gloria that they see.

When Cornel Wilde was studying art in Budapest in his not distant early youth, he may not have imagined that attuning his ear to European speech would ever stand him in good stead; but the accent he used in *The Greatest Show on Earth* added to the debonair charm of his performance. Charlton Heston's talent had not matured as much as it has now, but he was an effective, hard-driving boss of the circus. Jimmy Stewart, as Buttons, a clown, gave

405

one of those performances that look so easy, and for that reason show such artistry.

But one of the best performances in the picture was given by a little lady who must now be all of ten years old. I do not know her name. She was in the circus audience, in Philadelphia I think it was. At the end of the show, she was a tired little girl. Our camera was set up to make a shot of the audience leaving the tent. Just as she was passing by, carried in her father's arms, her little head dropped and she fell asleep on his shoulder. It was the perfect visual summation of the whole scene: a child, filled with the happiness of the circus, slipping gently from that wonderful dream world into the wonderful world of dreams. Thank you, little lady, for giving us that lovely moment.

One might hope that a picture about the circus, of all subjects, would not be subject to any group's disapproval; but *The Greatest Show on Earth* was condemned, for different reasons, by some Catholics and some Freemasons. Father Thomas F. Little, representing the Legion of Decency, disapproved, and tried unsuccessfully to get me to change, our photography of certain costumes worn at every performance of the circus, and our sympathetic treatment of Buttons, the clown, who had committed, but who also atoned for, a crime. The barrage from the Masonic side came in the form of an article in *The New Age*, organ of the Southern Jurisdiction of the Scottish Rite, whose author saw "the sinister hand of Rome" in the fact that we had shown the pastor of the Catholic church in Sarasota, Father Charles L. Elslander, blessing the circus train as he does every year when it sets out from winter quarters. As I have already made some observations on censorship, it would be tiresome to repeat here the replies I made to Father Little and to my brother Mason who chose to sign his articles with the initials "E.R."

The only refreshing aspect of those two episodes is the evidence they brought that neither Catholics nor Masons are as totally regimented as is sometimes believed by non-Catholics and non-Masons. Among the letters I received from Catholics who saw and enjoyed *The Greatest Show on Earth*, I cherish particularly one from a convent of nuns who screened the picture for the young girls and children in their charge; and a number of

Freemasons agreed with my published reply to our brother of the Southern Jurisdiction, Scottish Rite.

It is pleasant to record that both Monsignor Little and the Masonic Grand Lodge of New York, to which I belong, warmly commended *The Ten Commandments* (1956).

6

In 1951, I began to receive intimations that I ought to make a trip to Paris. The strongest of them came from Harold Talbott, who was prominent among those who felt that the commander of the North Atlantic Treaty Organization forces would make a winning candidate and a good President of the United States. I admired General Eisenhower. I had no doubt of his ability or of his appeal to the American people. But I did not go to Paris to join those who were urging him to run for President. If I had gone, it would have been to tell him what I believe I told his chief aide and my old friend, Major General Wilton B. Persons, that I could not understand why a man whose place in history was secure, as a liberator of Europe from the Nazi yoke, should want to step out of that historic niche and put himself into the hazards and headaches of domestic politics, even for the sake of being President. Besides, the man I thought best qualified for the presidency was Senator Robert A. Taft.

In my opinion, Robert Taft was one of the most misunderstood men of American history. I met him first in 1947, when he invited me to testify before the Senate Labor Committee at the hearings out of which grew the Labor-Management Relations Act of 1947, better known as the Taft-Hartley Act. An hour or so after I appeared before the Senate Committee, Representative Francis Case, now Senator from South Dakota, asked me to remain in Washington long enough to give the same testimony before the Committee on Education and Labor of the House of Representatives. One member of the latter Committee was kind enough to say that my analysis of the evils of closed shops was the best he had ever heard; but the only partly original contribution I can claim to have made to the resultant legislation was in calling attention of the Congress to the so-called "Rand Formula," a plan devised by Mr. Justice I. C. Rand of the Supreme Court of Canada, whereby a worker who does not wish to join a union is not compelled to do so, but may be required to pay the union a reasonable and proper fee for representing him in collective bargaining. Some months later, in the Senate debate on the Taft-Hartley Bill, Senator Taft stated on the Senate floor that it was the intent of the authors of that bill to provide for the application of the Canadian formula to labor relations in the United States.

Senator Taft's cousin, Hulbert Taft, the Cincinnati publisher, and his great friend, Ben E. Tate, had long been supporters of the DeMille Foundation. Through them, and after my appearance before the Senator's committee at his invitation, I came to know Robert Taft fairly well. No one could question his monumental intelligence and integrity; but hostile propaganda, within and without his own party, painted him as a cold, austere, arrogant, unappealing man, a tory of the tories, too far removed from any common human sympathies to be a successful candidate. In whatever personal dealings I had with him, in the Senate Office Building or in his cousin's home or wherever we met, I found him always sharply incisive mentally, but warm, gracious, self-confident but humble, and gifted with a shy, almost elfin sense of humor. I could see why men like Ben Tate not only admired but loved him.

To give what little help I could to his candidacy for the Republican presidential nomination of 1952, I went to the National Convention in Chicago, not as a delegate but as a visitor, and indeed not particularly welcomed by some of the California delegation, which was pledged to Governor Earl Warren. Among the incidents of that convention, so packed with drama and emotion, one small one stands out in my memory. One morning I was asked by the Taft headquarters to have breakfast with two delegates from Arizona who were thought to be wavering and might perhaps be won over to vote for Taft. I failed to win them; and the reason why I failed was instructive. Taft, one of them said, was too liberal; look at his stand in favor of public housing. Those two smart young politicians knew the real Taft better than that portion of the public which accepted his enemies' caricature of him.

But in spite of the dogged, do-or-die enthusiasm of the Taft supporters, in spite of all the oratory and tense parliamentary maneuvers on the floor and all the backstage conferences lasting well into the night while bands marched bravely up and down

408

Michigan Boulevard keeping spirits high with the Taft campaign song, the convention nominated General Eisenhower. The party closed ranks behind him. No one gave him more generous support than Bob Taft; and the American people have endorsed the choice by overwhelmingly electing President Eisenhower to two terms.

After Senator Taft's courageous death from a cancer which he refused to let interfere with his leadership on behalf of the Eisenhower policies in the Senate until his illness totally incapacitated him, I was privileged to join with Ben Tate and others in sponsoring the Taft Memorial on the grounds of the Capitol in Washington. I am convinced that history will recognize his stature, just as I am convinced that the American people will come to see the soundness of his principles, especially his championship of the rights of the individual rank-and-file worker, including his right to work.

7

It may be apparent that, whatever other trials they have to bear, my staff cannot complain of lack of variety in their work. As both the work and the variety seem to increase as time goes by, I have been fortunate in finding new helpers as I have needed them. Donald MacLean joined my staff in 1949. With a background of wide experience in advertising, radio, and film production, and a fine taste in literature and the arts reflecting his education at Cambridge, he brought also that rare and welcome gift, a huge appetite for hard work. If tomorrow's mail brings a request from a university professor for information on the right-to-work laws of 18 states, and a reminder that the American Cancer Society needs a new film for its annual campaign, and a batch of letters from young people seeking advice on how to break into the movies, I will write "D. MacL." on the corner of each one; and they will all be done.

On other letters and memoranda I will write other initials, depending on their subject matter. My staff does not decrease my work. They enable me to do much more and better work; and they are, as Barney Balaban once said in public tribute to them, "a team of co-workers whose loyalty is unmatched in the film world" —or, I would add, anywhere else.

Among them is one who came to me as an unexpected by-product of my small part in the Taft campaign of 1952. One of the friends I made at that time was the leader of the Taft forces in Wisconsin, Thomas P. Coleman. Not long afterward, when Tom Coleman's secretary was moving to California, he gave her an introduction to me. By one of those happy chances that are more than chance, there was just at that time a vacancy on my immediate secretarial staff at the studio; and so Doris Turner became the latest of those secretaries whose ability, patience, cheerfulness, and above all loyalty have been of such help to me through the years. When I say that Doris Turner reminds me in many ways of Gladys Rosson, I cannot pay her a truer or higher compliment.

My studio "family" was becoming rounded out to its present complement, and grandchildren and great-grandchildren were bringing Mrs. deMille and me the happiness of new, ongoing life; but the years bring too the realization that life has other rooms than this, and that doors must close, for a time, on lives that we have loved. My brother Bill died at his home in Playa del Rey, California, on March 5, 1955. After his career as dramatist and director, he had become Professor of Drama at the University of Southern California. His scholarship, his long experience in the theater and motion pictures, his brilliance, and his wit, all flowered there; and generations of students keep him in that special place of memory reserved for great teachers. A few days before he died, I was visiting him in the late afternoon, as the sun was lowering in golden glory over the Pacific Ocean visible from his house. He was very weak, and I was prepared to go when his wife, Clara, remarked that he seemed to be getting tired. Bill called her over to his bed. "Let him stay," he said, "till the sun sets." He loved beauty. In our more than seventy years we had watched together many times the infinitely varied splendor of the setting sun; and one day, together, we shall see it rise again.

17

You won't call it *The Ten Commandments,* of course."

That was the climax of one of the executive sessions with which the reader is by now familiar. It was at the studio, with Barney Balaban, Mr. Zukor, and all the other top policy makers of Paramount in attendance, to reach a final decision on what my next picture should be, following *The Greatest Show on Earth.*

It was a rather long session, for I had a rather long story to tell. For more than twenty years, and increasingly in the years since World War II, people had been writing to me from all over the world, urging that I make *The Ten Commandments* again. The world needs a reminder, they said, of the Law of God; and it was evident in at least some of the letters that the world's awful experience of totalitarianism, fascist and communist, had made many thoughtful people realize anew that the Law of God is the essential bedrock of human freedom.

That, I felt, was worth telling. But how? I had discussed it with my staff, first along the lines of the 1923 production of *The Ten Commandments*—a modern story with, possibly, a Biblical prologue. Someone suggested that we might tell the story of a public official in an American city, an honest politician, and the forces aligned against him, and through that story show, as we had done in the 1923 production, the effect of keeping the Commandments

411

or of breaking them and being broken by them. My own mind kept going back to the Biblical part of the 1923 film. That was still not dated. It was timeless. Then it was proposed that we tell the story of the Exodus of the Children of Israel, under Moses' leadership, but illustrate each of the Ten Commandments through the inter-weaving personal stories of individuals in that Exodus. But the final decision, and I think the soundest, was simply to put the Bible story on the screen and let it speak for itself.

The Bible story was timeless. It was also timely. It is a story of slavery and liberation, two words that the world's experience since 1923 had saturated with more vivid meaning, with more real fear and more anxious hope. When Moses stood before Pharaoh, voicing the divine demand, "Let my people go!", the same two forces faced that confront one another today in a world divided between tyranny and freedom. When Moses led his people to Mount Sinai, they learned, as the world today must learn, that true freedom is freedom under God.

The deeper we went into research on the story of Moses, the more it loomed as a dramatic human story as well. The Bible told us that he had been reared in Pharaoh's court as the adopted son of Pharaoh's daughter, in other words, as a Prince of Egypt; but the Bible is silent about the years from his early childhood to his young manhood, when he killed the Egyptian overseer. How did he learn that he was Hebrew? What moved him to turn his back on the splendors and power of the court to take up the burdens of his own enslaved people? What happened to Moses during those missing years?

Research gave some exciting hints. Good authorities placed the time of the Exodus during the reign of Rameses II, 1301-1234 B.C. If this was so, then the Pharaoh in whose court Moses was reared as a prince was Sethi I. On a temple wall at Karnak there is a carved image of Sethi I with Rameses II as his crown prince. But the figure of Rameses has been carved over another figure which has been obliterated. Who was this crown prince whom Rameses supplanted? What had he done to merit sending the stonecarvers to blot out his figure and his name? Had he perhaps rebelled against the Pharaoh and stirred up the Pharaoh's slaves to long for freedom under an unknown God? Was he, perhaps, Prince Moses?

412

We learned too that succession to the Egyptian throne was nominally through the female line: a man could become Pharaoh by marrying the heiress to the throne. The wife of Rameses II was Queen Nefretiri. If Moses was crown prince before Rameses, would not Nefretiri have had to be his destined bride?

All that the modern scholars told us about the Egypt of the thirteenth century B.C. fitted in with the legends handed down in the Hebrew *Midrashim* and the writings of such ancient authors as Philo, Josephus, and Eusebius, who told of Moses as a prince indeed and the victim of a court intrigue fomented by jealous rivals.

The plot of our picture took shape out of the very pages of the Bible, the venerable legends of the Jewish people, the still standing monuments of ancient Egypt, and the conclusions of some of the best modern authorities on the Bible and Egyptian history.*

But as always the idea had to be "sold" to the Paramount executives. It had a strong champion in Hollywood, Frank Freeman, and one in New York, Adolph Zukor. Some others, to put it mildly, were less enthusiastic about another Biblical picture.

Finally the idea was accepted, at the Hollywood meeting referred to at the beginning of this chapter. But at least one of those whose job it would be to sell and distribute the picture was still none too happy. One could see the wheels turning in his head: if only the picture had a good snappy title, well, it might squeak through to a modest box office success. "You won't call it *The Ten Commandments,* of course," said he.

Mr. Zukor had been sitting quietly through the meeting, his small form almost lost in his great chair. But when he heard that remark, he leaped with all the flashing vigor he had ever shown in the boxing ring sixty years before. Not call it *The Ten Commandments?* Mr. Zukor, in his eighties, may not gird for battle as often as he did in years gone by; but when he does, much younger men may well find it prudent to retreat. We called it *The Ten Commandments.*

Once the decision was made, I could not have asked for finer co-operation than Paramount gave me. The contract was settled the way Frank Freeman and I always make contracts: a few

* For complete documentation of the research for *The Ten Commandments,* the reader may be referred again to Henry S. Noerdlinger, *Moses and Egypt,* University of Southern California Press, 1956. (*Ed.*)

penciled notes on a small piece of paper, and a handshake. When Frank looked over the figures I had jotted down, he said to me, "You know, C. B., these figures won't give your company, Motion Picture Associates, as big a percentage of return as you got from *The Greatest Show on Earth* or *Samson and Delilah.*"

"I know it," I said, "and the reason I wrote it that way is because I am asking Paramount to take a bigger risk. I can't tell you what *The Ten Commandments* will cost, except that it will be over $8,000,000. I don't know how much over."

The final production cost was $13,282,712.35*

Not once was any question raised about budget. For the first time in my life I had a completely free hand. For that I have to thank Frank Freeman and Adolph Zukor, and especially Barney Balaban, the president of Paramount. They had faith in me, at last. They also had faith in faith: in the subject of *The Ten Commandments.*

2

Everything I have written about the preparation for a motion picture could be written about *The Ten Commandments*, only it would have to be magnified about ten times. I have sometimes compared a producer to a commanding general, who must see that all the units of his armies, with all their distinct functions in the coming battle, are ready to strike simultaneously on the target date. Jesse Lasky, Jr., and Fredric M. Frank began work on the script, joined by two writers new to working with me, Æneas MacKenzie, with his Scottish burr, his piercing insight into dramatic values, and his fine sense of story construction, and Jack Gariss, deeply thoughtful and sensitively attuned to the spiritual no less than the dramatic values of our theme, both of them men of strong and independent mind, able to hold their own in the long, hard process of forging a story into a finished screenplay. In

* This figure is inserted in Mr. deMille's text from the latest statement of Paramount Pictures Corporation to Motion Picture Associates, Inc., dated April 4, 1959. As of August 12, 1959 (which would have been Mr. deMille's 78th birthday), *The Ten Commandments* had grossed, in round numbers, $83,600,000 and had been seen by approximately 98,500,000 people. These latter figures were kindly supplied by Mr. Y. Frank Freeman, who is also authority for the estimate that the total audience for all Mr. deMille's pictures, from 1913 to 1959, is not less than 4,000,000,000 people, about one and a half times the present population of the world. (*Ed.*)

414

our story conferences, producer and writers may alternate in the roles of hammer and anvil. If sparks fly sometimes, it is good when they glow with the intelligence and wit of writers like the four who worked with me on this film.

The script was three years in the writing. Meanwhile, Edith Head and her staff were designing costumes, John Fulton was calmly preparing to part the Red Sea again, LeRoy Prinz was studying Egyptian wall-paintings four thousand years old for his authentic choreography, Elmer Bernstein, that unusually gifted young composer whose mind meshed so well with mine, was working on the musical score—if I named all those whom I would like to name, the list would be longer than the credit titles at the beginning of the picture. When the reader sees *The Ten Commandments*—as of course he will, I hope!—let him read each of those names as a grateful bow from me to a goodly company of fellow-workers, whose picture it is as much as it is mine.

I was never in any doubt about who should play the part of Moses, and my choice was strikingly confirmed when I had a sketch made of Charlton Heston in a white beard and happened to set it beside a photograph of Michelangelo's famous statue of Moses. The resemblance was amazing; and it was not merely an external likeness. Charlton Heston brought to the role a rapidly maturing skill as an actor and an earnest understanding of the human and the spiritual quality of Moses. He set himself to study the character and the period with a diligence worthy of a student for an advanced degree. On the sands of the Egyptian desert or on the rocky slopes of Sinai, before each of his big scenes he would go off by himself for a half-hour, in costume, and walk up and down, in solitary thought. I never asked him what he was thinking at those times, but when he came back to the set and walked through the crowd of Arab extra players, their eyes followed him and they murmured reverently, "Moussa! Moussa!": to them, Moslems almost all, he was the Prophet Moses. Charlton Heston's fitness for his role, and what he thought and felt about it, shine in what is to me one of the most moving scenes in the film: that in which Moses, after his divine encounter at the Burning Bush, walks barefoot down the mountainside, his face lifted and filled with the glory and the rapt awe of a man who has seen God.

The casting of the Pharaoh Rameses, a part equal in dramatic strength to that of Moses, was done very quickly. I happened to be in New York with my granddaughter Cecilia, Gladys Rosson, and Donald Hayne, and one evening Gladys insisted that, instead of having a quiet, leisurely, peaceful dinner in my hotel, I take my three companions to see *The King and I*, then still in its long Broadway run. As often happens when someone makes me go out of an evening against my will, I enjoyed it thoroughly, especially the King. At the end of the second act, I went backstage and found the dressing room of Yul Brynner, whom I had never met. I told him my name and that I was planning to make a picture called *The Ten Commandments*. There are not many minutes between the acts of a Broadway musical, but in that space of time I told Yul Brynner the story of *The Ten Commandments* from the viewpoint of the Pharaoh, I offered him the part, he accepted, we shook hands, I went back to my seat in the theater, Yul became King of Siam once more; and I did not see him again until we were ready for him to become King of Egypt.

Some critics, I believe, have said that Yul Brynner in any role is still playing the King of Siam. I advise them to look again. Let them see *The King and I* and *The Ten Commandments* in quick succession, and they will see the subtle differences in characterization between the barbaric, puzzled, arrogantly defensive King of Siam and the no less arrogant but sophisticated, self-assured Pharaoh of *The Ten Commandments*. There are similarities in the two performances, for Yul Brynner, after all, is only one man; but it is the subtle differences which show his great artistic competence.

I cast Yvonne De Carlo as Sephora, the wife of Moses, after our casting director, Bert McKay called my attention to one scene she played in *Sombrero*, which was a picture far removed in theme from *The Ten Commandments*, I sensed in her a depth, an emotional power, a womanly strength which the part of Sephora needed, and which she gave it. The critics were less than kind to my selection for the other feminine lead, Anne Baxter as Nefretiri. I think the critics went farther wrong there even than they usually do; I think Anne Baxter's performance was very good. Perhaps the critics were too busy thinking what clever things they could write about our misspelling of Nefretiri's name. Why, every critic knows that it should be Nefretiti. What every critic does not know is that Queen Nefretiti and Queen Nefretiri were distinct royal personages, living about 150 years apart, and to confuse them, as some critics did, is like confusing President Washington with President Coolidge or mistaking Queen Elizabeth II for Queen Anne.

I could say something good, something specific and distinct, about every one of the principal players in *The Ten Commandments;* but I remember my promise, many chapters back, not to become one of those who sit you down and make you listen to every detail of the movie they saw last night. Nor could I stop with the principal players if I once began to talk about the actors in this picture. I will tell only one incident, about one of the extra players, a girl whose name I do not know. It happened while we were shooting a part of the Exodus at the studio. It was a warm day. Again and again the crowd of extras trudged before the camera, packed together, laden down with their babies and their household goods, jostled not only by each other but by water buffalo, wagons, and the whole surge of a nation on the move. There were clergymen among the visitors on the set practically every day, and this day one of them happened to be the Prior Provincial of the Dominican Order in the western United States, Father Joseph Fulton. Standing at the very edge of the set as the Exodus swept just out of camera range, Father Fulton remarked to one young girl, an extra, as the crowd eddied around him, "You must be tired."

"No," she said. "On a picture like this you don't get tired." That extra girl never imagined that I would ever hear about her answer to an unidentified clergyman's kindly remark. She could have made that answer for only one reason: she meant it. For her, and for most of those who worked in and on *The Ten Commandments,* it was more than a movie. Their names run into thousands. The reader can see them, and can sense what they felt, when he sees the film. He will see what he has eyes to see.

What he will not see, however, is all the drama that took place behind the camera.

Some of it was on a world stage. There was a revolution in Egypt shortly after we decided to go there on location, to film the scenes of the Exodus and the giving of the Law. King Farouk was exiled. General Mohammed Naguib became President of the new

417

Republic of Egypt. Since the co-operation of the Egyptian government was essential, I immediately communicated with President Naguib, cabling him the very day the Republic was proclaimed and continuing a correspondence which was so cordial that we felt safe and justified in sending a company of technicians, headed by the production manager Donald Robb, to Egypt in mid-1954 to contract for the construction of the huge set of the gates of the city of Per-Ramses, the manufacture of the thousands of properties needed, the housing and feeding of the rest of us when we arrived, and the engagement of whole villages of Egyptians—men, women, and children, with their flocks of cattle and camels and domestic fowls—to take part in the Exodus. It was a gigantic task that Don Robb, Kenny DeLand, Walter Tyler, Ray Moyer, Jerry Cook, Bob Goodstein, and their helpers accomplished. The reader can see that in the picture too, and can appreciate it if he has ever had any experience of building, equipping, and peopling a city in a foreign country.

3

My announcement that I was going to Egypt was taken by some, I believe, as a publicity stunt. DeMille might go over for two or three days, get his picture in the papers, then come back to Hollywood and leave the location work to others. I trust that no one conveyed that impression to Anis Serag El Dine before that splendid Egyptian gentleman offered me and my immediate party the use of his own family's penthouse, of two stories with a lovely roof garden and swimming-pool, atop his apartment building in Giza, a half-block from the Nile. We stayed nearly two months, but until the last one of us left nothing could persuade the Serag El Dines to return to their home and let any of us go to an hotel. Hospitality can hardly go further than when a man and his wife and children move out of their home and leave it for two months, fully staffed with the most perfect Sudanese domestic help, to foreign guests whom they had never met and with whom they had had only indirect business dealings.

But before we left Hollywood, there were certain arrangements I felt it wise to make. A motion picture can be made with all the skill and all the devotion in the world, all the technical acumen of a John Fulton or a Farciot Edouart, all the confidence of a Barney

418

Balaban or a Frank Freeman, all the dedication of our players from Charlton Heston to the girl who said she was not tired after hours of working in the dusty, sweaty Exodus; and that picture can be ruined by bad publicity. I had had experience of that on some previous pictures. I did not propose to let it happen to *The Ten Commandments.*

With some blessed exceptions, press agents tend to develop a strangely simple sense of values: merit is measured solely by the column inch. It does not seem to matter what you get in print as long as you get in print. Truth? Understanding? Common decency? Good taste? Who but an incurable old fogy would weigh those corny considerations against the triumph of getting a snappy squib in somebody's column? A press agent who was sent out to Egypt with us furnishes an instructive example. I have said that in my opinion one of the most moving scenes, emotionally and spiritually, in *The Ten Commandments* is the scene of Moses coming down the mountain after meeting God in the Burning Bush. We shot that at Sinai. Charlton Heston was barefoot, since the Bible says that God commanded Moses to take off his sandals because he was standing upon holy ground. The stones over which Charlton Heston had to walk were uncomfortably warm from the blazing desert sun. And all that the clever press agent saw in that tremendous scene was what he was inspired to write in the despatch he sent back to the studio, which ran something like this: "DeMille gave Moses the hotfoot today." I do not remember the exact wording, because that summation of one of the highest spiritual moments in the picture never reached the press. I had seen to that when, passing over some eager applicants for the job of my public relations representative at the studio, I managed to secure one whom I had to persuade to take the job, but who took it because he knew what *The Ten Commandments* was about and had the good sense, good taste, and downright doggedness to see that it was presented to the public with a dignity worthy of its theme.

That man was Art Arthur. He was surprised and may have felt overburdened when I circulated what amounted to an edict that not one word of publicity was to go out without first passing over his desk and getting his approval; but I could go to Egypt with confidence, knowing that Art Arthur was sitting and working until

419

midnight, night after night, at that desk. In addition, upstairs in the DeMille Building his assistant, Ann del Valle, was handling the public relations in religious, educational, and other special areas with the combination of keen news sense, taste, and tact which made her the obvious and unanimous choice to succeed Art Arthur as my present public relations representative, when Art returned to his own professional work as a producer. No motion picture has ever had a more intelligent and successful publicity campaign than that planned and executed for *The Ten Commandments* by Art Arthur and Ann del Valle. The best technique of public relations, after all, is to tell the truth. Rare beings in a world where truth is often a neglected waif, Art and Ann saw that and acted on it. Hence their success.

October, 1954, came; and we were in Egypt. I sailed with Cecilia and Joe Harper, their children Cecilia and Jody, Donald Hayne, Berenice Mosk, my secretary Joan Catterlin, and untiring Joseph Mullin, who relieves me of all the worry and work involved in traveling, never complains of long hours or changed plans, and keeps me looking presentable whether I am in the Ritz in Paris or in a tent on the Sinai Peninsula. The magnanimous Serag El Dines' apartment was ready to receive us all into its comfort, after a voyage on a small boat from Naples to Alexandria, on which we were all sick, except my daughter, who simply cannot be bothered being ill. She always has too much else to do.

This, I think, is the place to tell Cecilia what I would never dream of saying to her face. She is so much like me that she can read my mind at times, which can be most annoying. But she is not only my daughter. She is also her mother's, with all her mother's balance and patience and grace and keenness of mind and consummate skill in human relations—qualities for which her father has not always been conspicuous. When Cecilia and Joe travel with me, they are not on a pleasure cruise. They work, hard. When the nerves of anyone in the company are rubbed raw, as they well may be on a grueling location, Joe Harper is the best doctor in the world for them. On that small boat from Naples to Alexandria, Donald Hayne, sick in his cabin, asked the Italian stewardess to take a message to Signor Harper. She did not know Signor Harper, so Donald described him for her: "a little large, and always smiling." From that, she knew him instantly.

420

Cecilia is not always smiling, especially when she is differing from me with a stubbornness whose origin I would never acknowledge, of course, anywhere but in the unanswerable privacy of this printed page, but she is always there, for me to depend upon for all the things that she can do and I cannot. And they are many. On the Egyptian location, Cecilia was out at the set every day, no matter how late the night before she had been representing me at social functions which I thought up all manner of excuses to escape; and on the set I watched how, more and more, if I was occupied and then later whether I was occupied or not, members of the company would come to Cecilia for decisions and would get them, quick and right. I do not often use the word "proud," but this is one place where it belongs: for is there any word that any father would rather be able to use, to tell his daughter what he thinks of her?

Before we could start work, there were the Egyptian press to meet and the official calls to make. At the press conference, the Egyptian journalists were uniformly intelligent and courteous. Their only misgiving seemed to be a wonder about what strictly orthodox Moslems would say about portraying a character as saintly and revered as the Prophet Moses on the screen. I could answer that one of the strongest voices urging me to make *The Ten Commandments* had been that of the distinguished Moslem Prime Minister of Pakistan, Mohammed Ali, who saw in the story of Moses, the prophet honored equally by Moslems, Jews, and Christians, a means of welding together adherents of all three faiths against the common enemy of all faiths, atheistic communism. But seated in the midst of the courteous Egyptian journalists was an American gentleman who is something of a phenomenon in that he is almost a professionally pro-Arab Jew. He tried to embarrass me. In his view of things, it seemed, *The Ten Commandments* was going to be a piece of pro-Israeli, anti-Arab propaganda; and it would have been a large, if dubious, feather in his cap if he could make me admit that publicly, my first week in Cairo. He asked me, so innocently, who those people were that my hero Moses led out of Egyptian bondage? What were they called? I suggested that he look up the answer in the Koran, which was one of the primary sources for our production of *The Ten Commandments*. The Egyptians in the audience seemed to enjoy my answer. Most people prefer fair play.

From the time we stepped off the ship at Alexandria, the Egyptian government had surrounded us with every courtesy. I thought, naturally, that my first official call should be on President Naguib. Then I had my first lesson in Middle East diplomacy. My first call, I was told, should be on the rising strong man of the revolution, Colonel Gamal Abdel Nasser, who was then Prime Minister. After that, I might go to the President's palace and sign the visitors' book if I wished. President Naguib was being edged out as coolly as if he had been a Paramount executive in the whirling 1930's. A few weeks later, while we were still in Egypt, he was finally deposed and placed under what was practically house arrest. I was not allowed to meet him.

I had two meetings with Colonel Nasser and his Minister of War, General Abdel Hakim Amer, now Field Marshal of the armies of the United Arab Republic. I was impressed. Some of Colonel Nasser's actions since then have raised serious questions in my mind, but in those still early days of the Egyptian revolution I received a strong impression of its leaders as young men perhaps inexperienced in government, but sincerely dedicated to the welfare of their people, facing manfully the enormous task of raising living standards, sensitive about their new-found independence, but by no means unfriendly to America, then at least.

On the lighter side, both Colonel Nasser and General Amer admitted to being confirmed fans of American movies from their childhood; and General Amer revealed a secret out of the past of his chief. The young Gamal Abdel Nasser's fellow-officers had nicknamed him "Henry Wilcoxon"!

The most interesting man I met in Cairo was our Ambassador to Egypt, Jefferson Caffery. The only trouble with the American diplomatic service throughout the world is that there are not enough Jefferson Cafferys, and that he and those like him in the service are not able to postpone indefinitely their arrival at retirement age. What other foreign diplomat in a country torn by revolution has equaled Jefferson Caffery's feat of saving King Farouk's life by walking with him to the very deck of the yacht which took the King into exile, then returning to Cairo to enjoy the complete confidence of the very revolutionists who had ousted the King and formed the new Republic? Ambassador Caffery is retired now. I met him last in Rome in 1957. I do not know whether he was there on business or pleasure or pilgrimage. I did not ask: for wherever Jefferson Caffery is, officially or unofficially, there America is being represented perfectly.

I made time for several visits to our embassy in Cairo, not only to call on the Ambassador and Mrs. Caffery, but also to inspect the facilities of the United States Information Agency, of which I am chief consultant on motion pictures. There was a touching eloquence in the tin cans of film, battered and dented from their many trips to and from Egyptian towns and villages with their message of what America means. The evening I dropped in unannounced at the U.S.I.A. library, I found the large, well-lighted, well-stocked reading room literally jammed with young Egyptians eagerly reading American books. I think of those experiences when I read criticism of this agency. I daresay there is waste in it, just as I am sure there is waste and perhaps even some graft occasionally in the making of one of my pictures or any enterprise involving a large number of fallible human beings. But in a struggle for the minds of men, the only bullets we can shoot, thank God, are the bullets of ideas; and it seems to me both sad and senseless to scrimp the sinews of the one agency of our government designed and equipped to wage that all-important struggle.

4

There is a book entitled *Once to Sinai*. Anyone who has ever been there, seeing that title, must wistfully ask himself, "Only once?" There is a compelling attraction about Mount Sinai which draws me, at least, to want to go back there, not with a motion picture company of sixty people and a big production on my mind, but with nothing more urgent to do than sit on the roof of the Monastery of St. Catherine at night and watch the moon rise over the sheer granite face of that mountain which was mysterious, holy ground as far back as the memory of man can reach and beyond.

But, apart from the austere beauty of the mountain itself, the attractions of Sinai are certainly not physical. The journey can be made from Cairo by motor car in one long, hard day. Our caravan of Plymouths took two, pausing to inspect possible location sites and stopping overnight in a tent camp at Abu Rudeis on the Sinai Peninsula. I speak of our caravan: I would not like to make that journey with only one automobile. If it broke down, it might stand for a day or two or longer under the broiling sun in the most desolate country I have ever seen, before another car happened along. A few miles east of Suez, beyond the oasis still called the Well of Moses, the road fades out into a track hardly distinguishable from the sand all around; for more than half the journey down the peninsula, we could tell our way only by the whitewash marks our advance party had left on rocks every few hundred yards. We reached the Monastery of St. Catherine at sundown of the second day.

St. Catherine's, one of the three or four oldest monasteries in Christendom, has had a motley assortment of visitors in its long history: pious pilgrims from the earliest centuries of Christianity, great churchmen in the days a thousand years ago when the nearby oasis of Wadi Feiran was a thriving metropolis, scholars come to delve in its fabulous archives where Tischendorf found (and, according to the monks, stole) the *Codex Sinaiticus,* one of the oldest manuscripts of the Bible, soldiers from the Crusaders to Napoleon's army and British troops in World War II. But I feel sure that somewhere in the monastic annals there is a note that the oddest visitors of all arrived in October, 1954, when we sixty Americans descended on the peaceful scene, with a fleet of Plymouths, cameras, light reflectors, tents, furniture, costumes, foodstuffs, and all the other baggage necessary for the filming we planned to do high up on the holy mountain.

But monastic hospitality was ready to cope even with us. There are now only about a dozen monks in the once flourishing and wealthy community. Only one of them spoke English. I think of him as old Father Gerassimos, though he is eight or ten years younger than I, and his long white beard was belied by his merry eyes and ready smile and the briskness with which he bustled around in his blue denim work gown and the brimless stovepipe hat of the Greek Orthodox clergy, taking care of all our needs. He met me at the gate, escorted me through courtyards and corridors and up wide staircases, pointing out the narrow slits in the massive walls through which archers could shoot their arrows if the monastery were attacked, and installed me in the

424

suite of rooms of the Archbishop of Sinai, His Grace Porphyrios III.

The Archbishop resides for most of the year in Cairo, where the monks of Sinai have a large school for boys, but his rooms in the monastery are kept in readiness for his visitations and for such guests as he chooses to admit to them. In those rooms I stepped back into an era older even than my own childhood. In the bedroom a tall, fat wood-burning stove shared space with the high and downy bed. On the Archbishop's desk there was no blotting-paper: a small silver canister of black sand was there for that purpose. In the bathroom, however, was a gleaming white modern tub. Could the influence of DeMille pictures, I thought, have reached even unto Sinai?

The morning after our arrival I was up early and ready to go out scouting locations when a deputation of monks, black-bearded and black-robed, appeared at my door, bearing a vessel of holy water. They had come to invoke the blessing of God upon me and the work I was about to begin. The prayers recited and the symbolically purifying water sprinkled, I set out to tramp over the countryside around the monastery. Climbing one hill ahead of the group with me, I suddenly came upon a veiled Bedouin woman and a child, gathering sparse fodder for their camel. The woman drew herself up to full height and spoke to me in rapid, forceful Arabic. As the others with me came up the hill, I turned to the interpreter assigned to me by the Egyptian government, Captain Salah, and asked him to translate. I was expecting him to tell me that the woman was ordering us off her land, fast. But what she said was: "Sirs, you are welcome. We are too poor to offer you any gifts, but we offer you our welcome."

The devoted thoughtfulness of the Christian monks, the majestic dignity of the Moslem Bedouins, are among my most vivid memories of Sinai. When I returned to Cairo, I asked Colonel Nasser if I might subsidize a physician to spend all his time on the Sinai Peninsula, going from one Bedouin settlement to another, teaching hygiene and taking care of the people's ills, especially the eye infections which made so many of the children pitiful to see. The Prime Minister said regretfully that he did not think he could find one city-bred young doctor who would be willing to bear the rigors of living on Sinai.

In spite of the hospitality of the monks and the marvelous provision made by an Egyptian catering company for our cleanly cooked food and pure water, we tasted some of those rigors, especially in the days and nights we lived in tents on a plateau high above the monastery, near the very top of the holy mountain. The only way to get there was by a two-hour camel ride or a still more arduous trek on foot. We had to dismantle the cameras and other equipment, load the parts on camels, and reassemble them at the tent camp. The days were hot and the nights cold. We were all stricken, on and off, once or more often or steadily, with the illness that so often affects travelers from more northerly and more hygienic climes. We all lost weight, almost visibly from day to day.

But every day we shipped back to Cairo the precious film, packed in ice to keep the desert heat from damaging it, and from Cairo it was flown daily to Hollywood to be developed and then flown back to Cairo for us to project. When we saw it on the screen at the Misr Studio, it made the rigors seem well worth while. We were bringing to the screens of the world for the first time, in all their awesome grandeur, the very places where Moses talked with God and received the Law by which mankind must learn to live, or perish. Of those, Christian, Jew, or Moslem, who revere Moses as the man who came closer, perhaps, than any other mere man to the Divine Mind, very few can make a pilgrimage to Sinai. We were bringing Sinai to them.

At last our work there was done. It was time to return to Cairo for the big scenes of the Exodus. The monks rang all their church bells in farewell, an honor reserved usually for the visits of the Archbishop. Just outside the great wall of the monastery, the Bedouins who had worked with us gathered to bid us good-by and to stage for us what must be one of the oldest plays in the world, *The Wolf and the Sheep.* Its plot was simple, but essential drama: some of the players browsed around the improvised stage as sheep, a bad and horrifying wolf leaped among them to spread havoc and to kill, then good dogs and men with sticks came to the rescue, barking and beating the wolf off the stage. No one knows for how many centuries the Sinai Bedouins have enacted this unwritten drama or dance, woven out of their own nomadic shepherd life. It has never occurred to me before now—but Moses himself might have seen the same play performed on the same spot.

426

The return trip to Cairo was broken for a day or two to photograph the Red Sea, which incidentally is one of the bluest seas in the world. If any viewer of *The Ten Commandments* has an ear quick enough to catch a tiny break in the sound track, during one of the scenes when the Children of Israel are gathering at the shore of the Red Sea, the reason for it is that, after the sound track was made and matched to the visual part of the film, we decided that we must snip the word "Red" out of the dialogue referring to "the Red Sea," because there in the background was the expanse of water so beautifully and deeply blue that the audience might have laughed at hearing it called red!

Out on the desert at Beni Youssef, a few miles southwest of Cairo, all was in readiness for the start of the Exodus. From the great set of the city gates of Per-Ramses, 107 feet high and nearly a quarter of a mile long, stretched the avenue of sphinxes between which Moses would lead his people forth to freedom and, soon after, the Pharaoh's chariots would thunder in pursuit. Some journalists had fun with the notion that DeMille, not satisfied with the real and ancient pyramids, built some of his own. We did, and for the very simple reason that the actual pyramids of ancient Egypt have changed in appearance in the past 3,000 years. The pyramids we built on the horizon, visible from the city gates, were white and unweathered, as the real pyramids were in Moses' time.

Behind our set of the gates there was a city, but it was not Per-Ramses. It was Paramount: offices, huge storage sheds for properties and costumes, a medical and first-aid station, facilities for feeding the thousands of Egyptian extras and watering their cattle, tents for the Egyptian cavalry lent us by the government to act as Pharaoh's army, corrals for the horses which had to be trained for months to draw chariots without shafts since Pharaoh's chariots had none, and parking space for the fleet of cars which shuttled constantly between Beni Youssef, the Misr Studio, and the Mena House where most of our company was quartered.

Directing scenes in which as many as 8,000 people take part at one time is never easy. It becomes somewhat more difficult when the people speak only Arabic and the director only English. The Bible solved that problem for us. Moses had appointed "rulers . . . of hundreds, of fifties, and of tens." We engaged twenty

427

assistant directors who spoke both Arabic and English, briefed them each day on the next day's work, and sent them, in costume, into the midst of the Exodus, each one responsible for directing a certain segment of the great moving mass of people, animals, and wagons. An interpreter was at my side all the time to translate my directions into the microphone; and Henry Wilcoxon, in addition to sharing with me the burden of the whole production, usually donned a costume and was ready to dart unobtrusively in and out of the scene to handle any emergency that might arise within camera range.

All moved toward the big day: when, to the age-old, thrilling cry, "The Lord our God, the Lord is One!", Moses led his people forth. The cinematographers, Loyal Griggs, Jack Warren, and Wallace Kelley, had studied every angle of shots that had to be right the first time. Yul Brynner flew over from New York to be ready for his scenes, accompanied by his old friend and mine, Dr. Max Jacobson, who planned to stay in Egypt for a few days and then go on to Europe.

Meanwhile, at Abu Rawash, another few miles farther out of Cairo, with all the same gigantic preparation, another tent city was going up, this one with airplanes added to serve as wind machines, for some of the later shots of the Exodus on its way to the Red Sea.

5

One November afternoon, while we were shooting at Beni Youssef, I ran up the steep 107-foot ladder to join John Fulton, who was making a special effects shot from the top of the Per-Ramses gates. When I reached the narrow platform at the top, my chest filled with pain. I am afraid John Fulton's explanation of his shot may not have received my full attention. I was thinking that if I wanted to reach the ground under my own power, I had better go down the ladder again quite soon. I did.

My daughter Cecilia and Berenice Mosk were waiting for me at the bottom. Walking with them to the front of the set, I remarked that I had never had quite that sensation in my chest before. They badgered me to sit down and rest. Just then Dr. Jacobson and his wife, Nina, turned up on the set. They had been out sight-seeing; but the doctor had felt some sort of impulse to

428

come to Beni Youssef. He took one look at me and sent Nina dashing into Cairo for medications. Then I learned that I had had a heart attack.

My room in the Serag El Dines' apartment was a busy place for the next twenty-four hours. It happened that Mme. Serag El Dine's brother, Dr. Hussein Ibrahim, was one of the best heart specialists in Egypt. With four other good Egyptian doctors and Dr. Jacobson, he held a consultation and announced the findings of himself and his colleagues: I must stay on my back, in bed, motionless, under an oxygen tent, for two weeks, and then have further rest in bed for an indefinite number of weeks after that. I reminded the doctors that I was in the middle of a big production. Paramount had sunk millions of dollars in it, without question, because Barney Balaban, Adolph Zukor, and Frank Freeman had faith in me. Hundreds of people were involved, dependent upon the completion of *The Ten Commandments* for their employment. I did not tell the doctors what I was also thinking, that if my motives in making the film were what I thought they were, I would be given the strength to finish it. I was 73 years old. That was a lifetime long enough for a man to have learned something about the ways and power of God; and long enough to make it not so very important if one's greatest effort turned out to be his last. But what I told the doctors was that I proposed to be on the set a little after nine o'clock the next morning and to go on with my work.

Then Dr. Jacobson came into my room alone. He is a blunt speaker. He is also a man of understanding. He told me, with no polite varnish on his words, the risk I would be taking; but he showed too that he realized why I felt that I must take it. "It is a calculated risk," he said, "but with medication, and if you will agree not to walk upstairs in this apartment more than once a day and to ride in a car or jeep instead of walking on the set, in my judgment you can get up tomorrow."

If I had followed the advice to stay flat in bed, medically sound and prudent as it was, I would have died of frustration. I do not recommend anyone else to follow my example, for not everyone else has a Max Jacobson at his side. He had come over to Egypt for a few days on a social visit. He stayed for a month. We finished

429

our work there on December 3, and flew home to take it up again in Hollywood.

The biggest technical problems in *The Ten Commandments* were more than technical. How do you photograph the direct and mighty action of the hand of God? How, if you dare attempt it, do you reproduce His very voice? In a way, the scenes of the opening and closing of the Red Sea, though they took 18 months, cost $1,000,000, and were made by a blending of shots taken at the Red Sea itself, at Abu Rawash, and in the studio, were easier than some of the scenes of divine manifestation which may look much simpler.

How to illustrate the angel of death passing over Egypt, striking the first-born of the Egyptians, sparing the Hebrew families whose doorposts were marked with the blood of the lamb? Looking out her window over the San Fernando Valley one night, Lynn Hayne saw an oddly shaped cloud stretched across a patch of sky, with long streamers or fingers of cloud reaching down from it toward the earth. She drew a sketch of it and sent it to me the next day. In *The Ten Commandments* that is how the effect of the angel's passing is shown, as a breath of pestilence coming down from a greenish cloud and creeping over the earth, to kill and to spare.

Doris Turner brought me the idea which unlocked the problem of how to show the Burning Bush as the Bible describes it, burning but not consumed. Doris happened to see in a shop window a clock, shaped like a fireplace, with wavy light from a hidden source playing over small artificial logs. That does not sound like the sort of clock a good interior decorator would let one have around the house, but I keep and cherish it because, as soon as I showed it to John Fulton, he immediately caught the effect I wanted and produced it on the screen.

Those two instances, out of many, may show why I value so highly the members of my staff who live and breathe a picture, who become as wrapped up in it as I do, to whom their work is not a nine to six o'clock job, but an absorbing vocation. I do not think they work that way for me. We all work for goals bigger than any one of us. That, I think, is why some of my staff stay with me for ten, twenty, forty years; and that, or rather the failure to see that, may be why some do not stay so long.

430

The greatest single problem in *The Ten Commandments* was the Voice of God. To reproduce the Divine Voice is of course an obvious and literal impossibility. Yet somehow Moses heard Him speak; and somehow we had to bring the audience to share with Moses in that tremendous experience. But what human actor could essay that role? Marvelous as the techniques of sound engineering are, what mechanical device could be equal to that impossible assignment? We tried everything suggested by anyone. Individual actors with fine voices recorded the lines. It seemed most fitting to try a chorus of individuals of all races and creeds, speaking in perfect unison. Was there some way to use a musical instrument, a great organ, and through the magic of the sound department shape its majestic tones into words? We recorded voices under water. We amplified them in deep canyons and from one mountain peak to another and re-recorded their reverberations. We tried everything; and everything was wrong.

An ancient Jewish legend solved half our problem. The *Midrash Rabbah* says that from the Burning Bush God spoke to Moses in the voice of Moses' father, Amram, so as not to frighten him. That lovely courtesy of God suggested that our audience too might accept a not unfamiliar voice, a little slowed and deepened: and so the Voice of God at the Burning Bush is Charlton Heston's voice, which is fitting also because, in our script, when Moses returns to tell Sephora and Joshua of his experience at the Burning Bush, he says to them, "He revealed His Word to my mind."

There remained the Voice of God at the giving of the Commandments. Here we could not use Charlton Heston's voice. Here God is the Transcendent Lawgiver, the *mysterium tremendum* as the theologians call Him. This must be a Voice unique, powerful, fatherly indeed but not without a touch of austerity and even anger: for at the foot of Sinai His chosen people are worshiping the Golden Calf. It was impossible to find that voice, until one day Henry Wilcoxon asked me to come to the projection room and listen to some readings of the Commandments by different voices. One was right.

Henry asked me if I recognized the voice. I did not. He told me then whose it was: a man I had known for many years, not a professional actor, whom Henry had persuaded to come to the dubbing-room and record the lines spoken by the Voice of God at

431

the giving of the Commandments, without telling me that it was being done. It was agreed among us that, out of reverence for the part of the Voice of God, the name of the man who played it should not be revealed. I will not reveal it here.

Our solution of that whole problem was imperfect, of course. Any solution of it would be. But I liked the comment of Mary-vonne Butcher in her review of *The Ten Commandments* in the English magazine, *Blackfriars,* on our treatment of the manifesta-tion and voice of God, that if you were going to attempt the im-possible, that was a very good way to do it.

The studio filming of *The Ten Commandments* was finished on August 13, 1955, the day after my 74th birthday. The doctors were still making me give them electrocardiograms every month or so. They were perfect. The Lord had been very good to me.

6

Then began the months of work of which the public knows little, but which is so important, the editing, the musical scoring, the dubbing, and that marvelous weaving together of a half-dozen or more different sound tracks, done in that room in the studio which many studio workers themselves hardly know, where the expert sound technicians sit at a keyboard like a multi-manual organ and, as the picture is projected silently on a screen before them, play into it, with perfectly precise timing, all the sounds that have been recorded separately.

While all this work was going forward, I received a somewhat cryptic message from Joseph Pew. Could I meet him in San Francisco on a certain date? For the past year or two, I had been closer to the politics of Pharaoh's court in the thirteenth century B.C. than to some of the civic interests I share with Joe Pew: I could not guess why he wanted to see me, but Donald Hayne and I flew up to San Francisco on the appointed day, because Joe Pew is the kind of friend that one always trusts to have a reason for whatever he asks. I did not know how great a friend, however, until we were alone with him in his hotel room. He had heard a rumor, he said, that I was in financial trouble with *The Ten Commandments.* If it were true, he just wanted me to know that he was there to relieve me of that trouble. I was able to assure him that the rumor was false, that Paramount was supporting the production magnificently. But in my 74 years I had never had a demonstration of friendship like that, offered as simply and readily as I might offer to lend someone $10. I had had no friends like that in 1925 or 1931. But then, there is no one else quite like Joe Pew.

We previewed *The Ten Commandments* in Salt Lake City. I always preview my pictures away from Hollywood, because it is almost impossible to get a typical audience reaction so close to the center of the motion picture industry: Hollywood people react as professionals or would-be professionals rather than just as people, and I make my pictures for people. The Paramount publicity department and most of my staff warned me that I would not get a typical reaction in Salt Lake City either: it would be too heavily weighted in favor of a religious theme because of the preponderant number of Mormons in any Salt Lake City audience. But all along I had in mind reaching, in addition to the regular motion picture audience throughout the world, the audience that motion pictures had lost or never won. If the deeply religious, serious-minded Latter-day Saints of Salt Lake City approved of *The Ten Commandments*, so would millions of others, of other faiths, throughout the world. They did approve it, enthusiastically.

And I may have had a personal, almost a selfish, reason for wanting to preview in Salt Lake City: it gave me another chance to spend some time with that great-hearted, lovable man who is literally a latter-day saint, the President of the Mormon Church, David O. McKay. There are men whose very presence warms the heart. President McKay is one of them. I spoke from the heart when, in the middle of a commencement address I was giving at Brigham Young University, I turned to him on the platform and said, "David McKay, almost thou persuadest me to be a Mormon!"

I am not a regular church-goer. I do not boast of that: I state it as a fact. I might be a better man if I were. To me, prayer is contact of the human mind with the Divine Mind, and that is possible anywhere, perhaps more possible in solitude than in a crowd. As I conceive of God, He is that Mind behind the universe we see, of which our minds are like small reflecting sparks struck off; and that Mind is always there, ready for us to touch and draw upon and reflect in our own minds more and more. Whenever I read the first chapter of the Gospel according to St. John, I sub-

433

stitute "Mind" for "Word." I do not know Greek, but I think it is closer to what the Gospel writer meant by *logos* to read the text, "In the beginning was Mind, and Mind was with God, and Mind was God. . . . In Him was life; and the life was the light of men. . . . And Mind was made flesh, and dwelt among us."*

I may have had some unflattering things to say about some churchmen who seemed to me more concerned about power and prestige than prayer; but I have known men of every church through whom the Divine Mind shines crystal clear. Some I have known for years, like President McKay or that dynamic Pres-byterian, Dr. Louis H. Evans, who always gives me the impression that his mind is busy with God's business. Others I met for the first time on my tour before the opening of *The Ten Command-ments:* men like Rabbi Abraham Shusterman of Baltimore, whose prayer at a luncheon made the Divine Presence almost tangible in the room, and the manly, self-sacrificing Catholic Archbishop of Boston, Richard J. Cushing, with whom one meeting was enough to show me that here was a man whose friendship I want to keep as long as I live, and after. I have known others like them, min-isters, priests, rabbis, in personal meetings and in the letters they write to me. Others like me might be more regular church-goers if there were more McKays, Evanses, Shustermans, and Cushings in the church: but I am grateful for those there are.

Another friendship I made through *The Ten Commandments* was with that grand American who is by no means ready to be called a grand old American, Bernard M. Baruch. We invited him to a special screening in New York. The word came back that Mr. Baruch accepted with pleasure; but it was hoped that we would understand if he found it taxing to sit through a picture nearly four hours long and consequently had to see part of it one evening and part the next. He sat through it all without moving, and at the end he said to me, "This could be a turning-point." He saw, with his sharp clarity of mind, exactly what I hoped for *The Ten Commandments:* that it might be a turning-point in the thoughts and lives of at least some of the millions who would see

* We are indebted to Mr. Gilbert Highet for the interesting information that one as competent in Greek and sensitive to English as Robert Bridges also trans-lated *logos*, in the context of the Fourth Gospel, as "mind." Mr. deMille could not have been aware of this when he hit upon the same rendering: he was not familiar with Robert Bridges' work. (*Ed.*)

434

it, and through them perhaps be in some measure an influence upon a world hungry for freedom under God.

My hopes began to be realized soon after the picture opened in New York on November 9, 1956. Letters began to come to me, in increasing numbers, as the picture opened in other cities across the whole United States and Canada. I cannot quote any of them because, as I leaf through them again in their still growing thousands, I cannot make a selection of a few without slighting so many more that are equally moving. But there is one thought that runs through them like a refrain: "This picture has made God real to me."

I cannot read that without thinking of Henry and Beatrice deMille, my father and mother, and the evenings at Pompton, the red-bearded minister, the years of my youth, my teachers Belasco and Sothern, the years of my marriage, the more than half a century of my wife's loyalty and love, the years of struggle and often failure, the years of conflict, of fighting to make the kind of pictures I wanted to make, of friendships strained to breaking, the years of standing alone. "This picture has made God real to me." One letter like that is recompense enough, for all the years.

7

Before the opening of *The Ten Commandments* in Europe in the autumn of 1957, Paramount asked me to go over there; and Europe was most kind to me. In Italy, I was received in audience by Pope Pius XII and President Giovanni Gronchi, blessed by the Pope and decorated by the Republic. In Germany, President Theodor Heuss received me and I had long talks with Chancellor Konrad Adenauer and the heroic mayor of brave Berlin, Willy Brandt, both men who understood *The Ten Commandments* because they know what it means to stand like Moses facing a world in which freedom and God are outlawed. France gave me, with her welcome, the Legion of Honor; the city of Paris engraved my name upon a medal and the name of Paris in my heart. All this was very wonderful. But most wonderful was the response of the people. They seemed to like my pictures. They even seemed to like me.

For Beatrice deMille's son, of course, going to England is always like coming home. The most amusing and the most moving events of my tour took place there: that is the way it is in a family. The

London Critics' Circle gave me a luncheon and a breathtaking experience: if I live another 76 years, I shall never be paid a higher compliment than to have critics ask for my autograph!

The film critics were kind, but one art critic was out for some gentle fun when he heard that I owned a Van Dyck painting of Moses in the bulrushes. That cannot be, he wrote, because that painting is owned by the Duke of Devonshire and is safely hanging at the Duke's place in Ireland. The Duke's painting was in Ireland, but he was in London; and when he read the little piece in the paper, he came to call on me and compare notes on Van Dycks, true or false. I confess that I was expecting the Duke to be a rather formidable person: except in the adventures of the Champion Driver, dukes have been outside my normal orbit. When, instead, a friendly, charming, incredibly young man walked into my sitting-room in the Dorchester Hotel, I could not refrain from asking him, "What should I call you, 'Your Grace' or 'Andrew'?" Delightedly, he chose "Andrew." We talked about Van Dycks. I showed him a photograph of mine and its authentication by an expert whose authority he recognized immediately and with respect. On the strength of that, the Duke conceded that my Van Dyck was probably the authentic one; but I think we both admitted that Van Dyck and his pupils might not be altogether above the suspicion of turning out two identical paintings, one for an earlier Duke of Devonshire and another for quick transport to the Continent, from where mine had come. The art critic had no more to say on the subject. The Duke and I had all the fun.

When I travel, I have to take a suite of rooms at each hotel, for press interviews and the like; and my sitting-room tends to become a sort of grand central station for those who are traveling with me. One morning in London, I walked out of my bedroom draped in nothing but a towel, to find Dr. Max Jacobson in the sitting-room, in conference with the eminent English physician, Lord Moran. Introductions were made, and I said, "Gentlemen, I just came in to do my exercises. Go ahead with your talk and, if you will excuse me, I'll do my push-ups." I got down on the floor and began my daily stint.

Lord Moran watched me with one eye, then finally said, "How old are you, Mr. deMille?"

"Seventy-six," I said without breaking the rhythm of the push-ups.

436

Lord Moran turned back to Dr. Jacobson with evidently renewed interest in Max's theories and powers.

If I had been asked the one person in England, or in the world, whom I would most like to meet, it would have been the great man who invited me to call on him at his house in Hyde Park Gate early one evening. Sensible man that he is, Sir Winston Churchill was in bed, but not without either his huge cigar or his complete and keen alertness. I do not think it right to quote directly a conversation with the greatest man of the twentieth century; but we talked for a good half-hour, and Sir Winston was as gracious as he is great. I have never climbed Mount Everest, nor been elected President, nor discovered a new galaxy in the heavens. But I have met Churchill.

And at the Royal Film Performance, I was presented to the radiant young Queen. Elizabeth II is Her Most Gracious Majesty indeed. If only the Champion Driver had had a cloak to lay before her feet!

From the Queen to the youngsters who greeted me in the street, there was a warmth in England that touched me deeply. I shall always be grateful to the British Broadcasting Corporation and Derek Bond for giving me, on my last evening in England, the opportunity to meet the British people in their homes, by television. My English mother would have liked the letters her people wrote me after that appearance.

And then I flew to Denmark, Iceland, skirted the North Pole, to Canada, and home, November 8, 1957.

Mrs. deMille was a little more frail, but her hand held mine as firmly as it did when we sat on the steps of No. 9 Beacon Street, Boston, and saw the twentieth century begin. The house, the garden, the offices looked the same: well cared for by the people who have served us so faithfully for so long.

The deer at Paradise were glad to see me. Deer are good and patient friends. They do not reproach you when you go away. They welcome you whenever you come back. They are not inquisitive. But if they did ask me the same question that was asked me at every stop in Europe and America—"What are your future plans, Mr. deMille?"—I could give them only the same answer I gave at every stop and must give you, patient reader:

"Another picture, or another world."

Epilogue

by the Editor

THE EDITING of this book was completed at 2010 DeMille Drive, in an upstairs study which Mr. deMille sometimes used, from whose windows I look out on the lawn and rose garden kept green and trim and lovely by Joseph Dizman, the gardener who still speaks to me of Mr. deMille not as employer but as friend. At the end of the garden, I can see the house where Mr. deMille lived for more than half his lifetime. Sometimes I see playing on the lawn his three-year-old great-grandson, Hussein Peter El Boughdadly, and I call out the window to him, "Hi, Bo!", for the sake of his solemnly cheery answer, "Hi, Hayne."

Downstairs, Russel Treacy, Florence Cole, and Carol Bogden are busy at their desks. Nothing is changed, except that Mr. deMille's awards and decorations are arranged around the walls of his office; and that he is not here. And that, still, sometimes seems unreal.

❋　　❋　　❋

On June 16, 1958, Mr. deMille testified before a sub-committee of the United States House of Representatives in Washington, on behalf of the right to work. On June 18, back at his home, he suffered another heart attack, much more serious than the one in Egypt; but he made a partial recovery, came in to the studio

438

nearly every day, spoke at a studio luncheon honoring his 77th birthday on August 12, and took an active, though limited, part in the campaign for the right-to-work amendment on the November ballot.

In December, against the advice of his family and staff, he insisted upon keeping his promise to attend the New Orleans and New York openings of Henry Wilcoxon's production of *The Buccaneer:* his last public appearance was on December 22, at the Capitol Theatre, New York.

He made his last visit to his Paramount Studio office on January 9, 1959. As he was leaving the studio, he said, "We have a lot to do in the next three years." Persuaded then to stay at home and husband his strength, he continued to work on the two pictures he was planning, as well as on this book, his correspondence, and his business affairs. The last member of his staff to work with him was Doris Turner, who spent each day and many evenings at his bedside, trying to give him just enough work to satisfy his demand for it and still keep him from overexertion.

He died at five o'clock in the morning of January 21. Cecilia and Joseph Harper were at his bedside, together with his physician, Dr. Hans Schiff, and his nurse, Mrs. May Carter. Mrs. deMille, in a nearby room, was too ill to be told. The funeral was held at St. Stephen's Episcopal Church, Hollywood, on January 23, followed by burial in the simple family tomb in Hollywood Cemetery.

The night before Mr. deMille's funeral, I was asked to write something about him. What I wrote ended with these words:

> He was human. He had faults, irritating smallnesses, blind spots, vanities—and a prince's grandeur, and astonishing humilities. Famous in every corner of the world, he was unknown to most, misunderstood by many, cordially disliked by some, beloved by those who knew him best. . . . He was a man of unquenchable faith and hope and a courageous heart. . . . He was a man of vision. Now he sees.

*　　*　　*

The last words of this book must be his. Among the papers in her father's room, Cecilia Harper found these notes, penciled in his handwriting:

"The Lord giveth and the Lord taketh away. Blessed be the the name of the Lord. It can only be a short time . . . until those

439

words, the first in the Episcopal funeral service, are spoken over me. . . . After those words are spoken, what am I? . . . I am only what I have accomplished. How much good have I spread? How much evil have I spread? For whatever I am a moment after death—a spirit, a soul, a bodiless mind—I shall have to look back and forward, for I have to take with me both."

THE END

Appendix

Motion Pictures Directed by Cecil B. DeMille

This chronological list of Cecil B. deMille's 70 feature pictures was compiled by Florence Cole and Jane Mounts from Mr. deMille's original working scripts of the films listed or other contemporary sources in his files. Pictures supervised but not personally directed by Mr. deMille are not included. Following the practice of film historians, the dates are those of the years in which the respective pictures were released, with the exception of the first version of *The Squaw Man*, for which it was thought proper to retain the traditionally accepted date, 1913, to denote the beginning of Mr. deMille's activity in film production in that year. Any discrepancy between dates in this list and dates given in the text of Mr. deMille's autobiography is explained by the fact that in writing or speaking of his films, Mr. deMille usually assigned to a picture the date of the year in which its production was completed, which in some instances was prior to the year of its release. Re-releases are not listed; but it may be noted that when *The Sign of the Cross* was re-released in 1944, a new prologue, directed by Mr. deMille, was added. Names listed after each title are those of the principal players in the film. (*Ed.*)

1913: *The Squaw Man.* (Co-directed with Oscar Apfel) Dustin Farnum, Winifred Kingston, Redwing, Dick La Strange, Foster Knox, Monroe Salisbury, Joe E. Singleton, Billy Elmer, Fred Montague, Baby de Rue, Dick La Reno.

441

1914: *The Virginian.* Dustin Farnum, Winifred Kingston, Billy Elmer, Monroe Salisbury, Anita King, Tex Driscoll, Jack Johnstone.

1914: *The Call of the North.* Robert Edeson, Theodore Roberts, Winifred Kingston.

1914: *What's His Name.* Max Figman, Lolita Robertson, Sydney Deane, Fred Montague.

1914: *The Man from Home.* Charles Richman, Theodore Roberts, Mabel Van Buren, Anita King, Fred Montague, Monroe Salisbury.

1914: *Rose of the Rancho.* Bessie Barriscale, Jane Darwell, Monroe Salisbury, Dick La Reno, J. W. Johnstone, Jeanie Macpherson.

1915: *The Girl of the Golden West.* Mabel Van Buren, Theodore Roberts, House Peters, Anita King, Sydney Deane, Billy Elmer, Jeanie Macpherson, Raymond Hatton, Dick La Strange.

1915: *The Warrens of Virginia.* James Neill, Mabel Van Buren, Blanche Sweet, Page Peters, House Peters, Marjorie Daw, Gerald Ward, Dick LaReno, Raymond Hatton.

1915: *The Unafraid.* Rita Jolivet, House Peters, Page Peters, Billy Elmer, Larry Peyton, Theodore Roberts, Marjorie Daw.

1915: *The Captive.* Blanche Sweet, House Peters, Page Peters, Jeanie Macpherson, Theodore Roberts, Billy Elmer.

1915: *Wild Goose Chase.* Ina Claire, Tom Forman, Lucien Littlefield, Helen Marlborough, Raymond Hatton, Theodore Roberts.

1915: *The Arab.* Edgar Selwyn, H. B. Carpenter, Milton Brown, Billy Elmer, Gertrude Robinson, Sydney Deane, Theodore Roberts, Raymond Hatton.

1915: *Chimmie Fadden.* Victor Moore, Raymond Hatton, Mrs. Lewis McCord, Ernest Joy, Anita King, Camille Astor, Tom Forman.

1915: *Kindling.* Charlotte Walker, Thomas Meighan, Raymond Hatton.

1915: *Maria Rosa.* Geraldine Farrar, Wallace Reid, Pedro deCordoba, Ernest Joy, Anita King, H. B. Carpenter, James Neill.

1915: *Carmen.* Geraldine Farrar, Wallace Reid, Pedro deCordoba, Billy Elmer, H. B. Carpenter, Jeanie Macpherson, Anita King.

1915: *Temptation.* Geraldine Farrar, Pedro deCordoba, Theodore Roberts, Elsie Jane Wilson, Raymond Hatton.

1915: *Chimmie Fadden out West.* Victor Moore, Camille Astor, Ernest Joy, Mrs. Lewis McCord, Raymond Hatton, Tom Forman, Florence Dagmar.

1915: *The Cheat.* Fannie Ward, Sessue Hayakawa, Jack Dean, James Neill.

1916: *The Golden Chance.* Cleo Ridgley, Wallace Reid, H. B. Carpenter, Ernest Joy, Edith Chapman.

442

1916: *The Trail of the Lonesome Pine.* Theodore Roberts, Charlotte Walker, Earle Fox, Thomas Meighan.

1916: *The Heart of Nora Flynn.* Marie Doro, Elliott Dexter, Ernest Joy, Lola May, Billy Jacobs, Margaret deMille, Charles West.

1916: *The Dream Girl.* Mae Murray, Theodore Roberts, James Neill, Earle Fox, Charles West, Mary Mersch, Mrs. Lewis McCord.

1917: *Joan the Woman.* Geraldine Farrar, Wallace Reid, Theodore Roberts, Charles Clary, Hobart Bosworth, Raymond Hatton.

1917: *A Romance of the Redwoods.* Mary Pickford, Elliott Dexter, Charles Ogle, Tully Marshall, Ray Hatton, Walter Long, Winter Hall.

1917: *The Little American.* Mary Pickford, James Neill, Ben Alexander, Guy Oliver, Edith Chapman, Jack Holt, Ray Hatton, Hobart Bosworth, Lillian Leighton.

1917: *The Woman God Forgot.* Geraldine Farrar, Raymond Hatton, Hobart Bosworth, Wallace Reid, Theodore Kosloff, Walter Long, Charles B. Rogers, Olga Grey.

1917: *The Devil Stone.* Geraldine Farrar, Wallace Reid, Tully Marshall, Hobart Bosworth, Lillian Leighton, Horace B. Carpenter.

1918: *The Whispering Chorus.* Raymond Hatton, Kathlyn Williams, Edythe Chapman, Elliott Dexter, Noah Beery, Guy Oliver.

1918: *Old Wives for New.* Elliott Dexter, Sylvia Ashton, Wanda Hawley, Florence Vidor, Theodore Roberts, Helen Jerome Eddy, Marcia Manon, Julia Faye, Parke Jones, Edna Mae Cooper, Gustav Seyffertitz, Tully Marshall, Lillian Leighton, Maym Kelso.

1918: *We Can't Have Everything.* Kathlyn Williams, Thurston Hall, Elliott Dexter, Sylvia Breamer, Wanda Hawley, Sylvia Ashton, Charles Ogle, Tully Marshall, Theodore Roberts, Ernest Joy, Billy Elmer, James Neill.

1918: *Till I Come Back to You.* Bryant Washburn, Florence Vidor, Gustav Seyffertitz, Winter Hall, Clarence Geldert, George Stone, Julia Faye, Lillian Leighton.

1918: *The Squaw Man.* Elliott Dexter, Thurston Hall, Katherine McDonald, Helen Dunbar, Winter Hall, Ernest Joy, Herbert Standing, Julia Faye, Theodore Roberts, Noah Berry, Ann Little, Ray Hatton, Jack Holt, Monte Blue.

1919: *Don't Change Your Husband.* Elliott Dexter, Gloria Swanson, Lew Cody, Sylvia Ashton, Theodore Roberts, Julia Faye, James Neill.

1919: *For Better For Worse.* Gloria Swanson, Sylvia Ashton, James Neill, Elliott Dexter, Tom Forman, Wanda Hawley, Theodore Roberts.

443

1919: *Male and Female.* Lila Lee, Theodore Roberts, Ray Hatton, Mildred Reardon, Gloria Swanson, Thomas Meighan.

1920: *Why Change Your Wife.* Thomas Meighan, Gloria Swanson, Bebe Daniels, Theodore Kosloff, Sylvia Ashton.

1920: *Something to Think About.* Elliott Dexter, Claire McDowell, Theodore Roberts, Gloria Swanson, Monte Blue, Theodore Kosloff, Julia Faye.

1921: *Forbidden Fruit.* Clarence Burton, Agnes Ayres, Kathlyn Williams, Theodore Roberts, Winter Hall, Theodore Kosloff, Forrest Stanley.

1921: *The Affairs of Anatol.* Wallace Reid, Elliott Dexter, Gloria Swanson, Wanda Hawley, Theodore Roberts, Theodore Kosloff, Ray Hatton, Agnes Ayres, Monte Blue, Bebe Daniels.

1922: *Fool's Paradise.* Theodore Kosloff, Mildred Harris, Dorothy Dalton, Conrad Nagel, Clarence Burton, Jacquelin Logan, Kamuela Searle.

1922: *Saturday Night.* Edith Roberts, Sylvia Ashton, Jack Mower, Leatrice Joy, Conrad Nagel, Edith Chapman, Julia Faye.

1922: *Manslaughter.* Leatrice Joy, Thomas Meighan, Jack Mower, Julia Faye, Jack Miltern, Dorothy Cummings, Edythe Chapman, Lois Wilson.

1923: *Adam's Rib.* Anna Q. Nilsson, Milton Sills, Pauline Garon, Theodore Kosloff, Elliott Dexter.

1923: *The Ten Commandments.* *Cast of the Prologue:* Theodore Roberts, Charles DeRoche, Estelle Taylor, Julia Faye, Gino Corrado, James Neill, Lawson Butt, Clarence Burton. *Cast of the Story:* Edythe Chapman, Richard Dix, Rod La Rocque, Leatrice Joy, Nita Naldi, Robert Edeson, Charles Ogle, Agnes Ayres.

1924: *Triumph.* Leatrice Joy, Rod La Rocque, Victor Varconi, Theodore Kosloff, Charles Ogle, Robert Edeson, George Fawcett, Julia Faye, Spottiswood Aiken, ZaSu Pitts, Raymond Hatton, Alma Bennett, Jimmie Adams.

1924: *Feet of Clay.* Vera Reynolds, Rod La Rocque, Julia Faye, Ricardo Cortez, Robert Edeson, Theodore Kosloff, Victor Varconi.

1925: *The Golden Bed.* Lillian Rich, Henry Walthall, Vera Reynolds, Theodore Kosloff, Robert Cain, Rod La Rocque, Warner Baxter, Robert Edeson, Julia Faye.

1925: *The Road to Yesterday.* Joseph Schildkraut, Jetta Goudal, William Boyd, Vera Reynolds, Trixie Friganza, Casson Ferguson, Julia Faye, Clarence Burton, Charles West, Charles Clary.

1926: *The Volga Boatman.* William Boyd, Elinor Fair, Victor Varconi, Theodore Kosloff, Julia Faye.

444

1927: *The King of Kings*. H. B. Warner, Dorothy Cumming, Joseph Schildkraut, Rudolph Schildkraut, Ernest Torrance, Jacqueline Logan, Julia Faye.

1928: *The Godless Girl*. Lina Basquette, George Duryea, Marie Prevost, Noah Beery, Mary Jane Irving, Gertrude Quality, Kate Price, Hedwig Reicher, Julia Faye, Emily Barrye, Jacqueline Dyrese.

1929: *Dynamite*. Kay Johnson, Charles Bickford, Conrad Nagel, Julia Faye, Muriel McCormick.

1930: *Madam Satan*. Kay Johnson, Reginald Denny, Roland Young, Elsa Peterson, Lillian Roth.

1931: *The Squaw Man*. Warner Baxter, Eleanor Boardman, Paul Cavanaugh, Roland Young, Julia Faye, Lawrence Grant, Eva Dennison, Desmond Roberts, Lillian Bond, Harry Northrup, Lucille McIntosh, Lupe Velez, Mitchell Lewis, Charles Bickford, J. Farrell McDonald, Dickie Moore, DeWitt Jennings, Raymond Hatton.

1932: *The Sign of the Cross*. Fredric March, Elissa Landi, Charles Laughton, Claudette Colbert, Ian Keith.

1933: *This Day and Age*. Charles Bickford, Judith Allen, Richard Cromwell, Harry Green, Eddie Nugent, Oscar Rudolph, Billy Gilbert.

1934: *Four Frightened People*. Claudette Colbert, Herbert Marshall, William Gargan, Mary Boland, Leo Carrillo.

1934: *Cleopatra*. Claudette Colbert, Warren William, Henry Wilcoxon, Gertrude Michael, Joseph Schildkraut, Ian Keith, C. Aubrey Smith.

1935: *The Crusades*. Loretta Young, Henry Wilcoxon, Ian Keith, C. Aubrey Smith, Katherine DeMille, Joseph Schildkraut, Alan Hale, C. Henry Gordon, George Barbier, Montagu Love, Lumsden Hare, William Farnum, Hobart Bosworth, Pedro de Cordoba, Mischa Auer, Jason Robards, J. Carrol Naish, Oscar Rudolph.

1937: *The Plainsman*. Gary Cooper, Jean Arthur, James Ellison, Charles Bickford, Helen Burgess.

1938: *The Buccaneer*. Fredric March, Franciska Gaal, Akim Tamiroff, Margot Grahame, Walter Brennan, Ian Keith.

1939: *Union Pacific*. Barbara Stanwyck, Joel McCrea, Robert Preston, Lynne Overman, Akim Tamiroff, Brian Donlevy.

1940: *North West Mounted Police*. Gary Cooper, Madeleine Carroll, Paulette Goddard, Preston Foster, Robert Preston.

1942: *Reap the Wild Wind*. Ray Milland, John Wayne, Paulette Goddard, Raymond Massey, Robert Preston.

1944: *The Story of Dr. Wassell*. Gary Cooper, Laraine Day, Signe Hasso, Dennis O'Keefe, Carol Thurston.

1947: *Unconquered.* Gary Cooper, Paulette Goddard, Howard da Silva, Boris Karloff, Cecil Kellaway, Ward Bond, Henry Wilcoxon, Sir C. Aubrey Smith.

1949: *Samson and Delilah.* Hedy Lamarr, Victor Mature, George Sanders, Angela Lansbury, Henry Wilcoxon.

1952: *The Greatest Show on Earth.* Betty Hutton, Cornel Wilde, James Stewart, Charlton Heston, Dorothy Lamour, Gloria Grahame, Lyle Bettger, Henry Wilcoxon.

1956: *The Ten Commandments.* Charlton Heston, Yul Brynner, Anne Baxter, Edward G. Robinson, Yvonne De Carlo, Debra Paget, John Derek, Sir Cedric Hardwicke, Nina Foch, Martha Scott, Judith Anderson, Vincent Price, John Carradine, Olive Deering, Douglass Dumbrille, Frank DeKova, Henry Wilcoxon, Eduard Franz, Donald Curtis, Lawrence Dobkin, H. B. Warner, Julia Faye.

Index

447

448

451

452

453

454

455

Hotel Metropole (Moscow), 308-309
House of Commons, 99
Howard, Bronson, 24
Howard, Clifford, 278
How Green Was My Valley, 376
Hoyle, Fred, 393
Hudson Review, The, 401-402
Hughes, Charles Evans, 319, 368
Hughes, Rupert, 216
Hugo, Victor, 31
Hungary, 124
Hutcheson, William L., 382
Hutton, Betty, 405
Hyatt, Charles E., 37, 42, 43, 44, 45, 73
Hyatt, Theo, 2

Ibrahim, Dr. Hussein, 429
Ibsen, Henrik, 16
If I Were King, 51, 53, 56
Ile de France, 305
Illustrated London News, The, 123
"Impact of the Paramount Decision on Motion Picture Distribution and Price Making," 154
Imperial School of Ballet, 188
Ince Studio, 264, 266, 267
Ince, Thomas H., 264
Ince, Mrs. Thomas H., 264, 267
Indiana, 273
"Inserts," 83
Institute of Logopedics, 395
Internal Revenue Bureau, 316
Inter-Ocean, The, (quoted), 29
In the Barracks, 66
Intolerance, 125-26
Iribe, Paul, 231, 232, 233
Irving, Sir Henry, 125, 219, 228
Istanbul, 313, 314

Jabotinsky, Vladimir, 398
Jackson, Andrew, 355, 357
Jacobson, Dr. Max, 428-29, 436-37
Jacobson, Nina, 428, 429
James, Frank, 370-71
James, Smith, and McCarthy, 117
James, William, 61
Japan, 377, 379
Java, 379, 381
Jazz Singer, The, 288
Jeffers, William M., 363, 365, 366, 387, 388
Jefferson, Joseph, 32, 48
Jeffries, Jim, 200
Jehlinger, Charles, 46
Jennings, Gordon, 116, 272, 374
"Jenny," 197

Jensen, John, 204, 205
Jerusalem, 315
Jesse L. Lasky Feature Play Company, 70, 76, 79, 87, 89, 91, 96
finances, 88
first location, 77-80
Jessie Brown, 398
Jester, Ralph, 204
Jesus of Nazareth, 267, 315
Jewel, Edward, 278
Joan of Arc, 169, 171, 173, 174, 176, 179
Joan the Woman, 169-72, 175, 179, 180, 187
John Delmer's Daughters, 16, 17
Johnson, Kay, 291, 292, 300
Johnson, Noble, 251
Johnston, Alva, 101
Johnston, Eric, 241, 309
Jolivet, Rita, 127
Jolson, Al, 288
Jones, Grover, 215
Joy, Leatrice, 247, 248, 251, 262
Judge and Fool, 398
Judith of Bethulia, 76
Juliana, Queen, 381
Julian Petroleum Corporation, 285
Jungmeyer, Jack, 278
Justin, Sidney, 364

Kansas City Star, 362, 402
Karloff, Boris, 394
Kataev, Valentine, 309
Kaufman, Al, 117
Keenan, Frank, 58
Keith-Albee-Orpheum Company, 289, 290
Keith, B. F., Corporation, 273
Keith, Ian, 337, 344
Kellaway, Cecil, 394
Kelley, Wallace, 405, 428
Kennedy, Joseph P., 289, 290
Kent, Sidney R., 250, 259, 264, 270
Kenyon, William S., 197
Keyes, Evelyn, 359, 372
Key West, 372
Kiesling, Barrett, 249, 260
Kindling, 138
Kinetoscope, 74
King and I, The, 416
King of Kings, The, 11, 31, 165, 267, 274-85, 295, 305, 335, 387, 398
Jewish opposition to, 323
Kingsley, Charles, 13, 25, 28, 31, 32
Kingston, Winifred, 85, 89, 97, 102
Kino Film factory, 310
Klaw, Marc, 48

456

Lyon, Ben, 223
Lyons, Rabbi Alexander, 282
Lyons, Eugene, 309

McAdoo, William Gibbs, 360
McCarey, Leo, 330, 375
McCarthy, Justin Huntly, 51
McCarthy, Neil, 117-18, 120, 164-65, 194, 242, 257-58, 261, 316, 320, 330, 385, 388
McCauley, Danny, 373
MacCormac, Muriel, 277
McCrea, Joel, 292, 363, 364, 369
McCutcheon, George Barr, 106
MacDonald, David, 343
McDonald, Francis, 352, 369
McDowell, Claire, 230
McGaffey, Bessie, 115, 116, 278, 397
McGlynn, Frank, 352
McKay, David O., 433, 434
MacKaye, Steel, 15, 18, 19, 24, 26
McKee, Singer Jim, 220
McKeighan, William W., 198
MacKenzie, Aeneas, 414
McKinley, William, 45
MacLean, Donald, 409
MacLean, Grace, 162
Macpherson, Jeanie, 113, 120, 145-46, 149, 171, 190, 192, 220, 223, 225, 230, 231, 247-48, 264, 278, 342, 367, 375, 376
Madam Satan, 300, 301
Madison Square Theatre, 15, 16, 17, 18, 20
Maine, 45
Maine, 66
Main Line, The, 19, 29
Make-up, 47
Male and Female, 222, 223, 224, 327
Mallory, Rev. Dr. George S., 15, 17, 28
Mallory, Marshall H., 15
Man From Home, The, 107, 108
Manhattan, 13
Mannix, Eddie, 294
Mansfield, Richard, 48
Manslaughter, 247, 248
Mantz, Paul, 203
Mao Tse-tung, 192
March, Fredric, 321, 357
Maria Rosa, 141, 142, 147
Marion, Frances, 181, 182
Mark, Mitchell, 185
Marley, Peverell (Pev), 252, 264, 405
Marsden, Fred, 17
Marshall, Herbert, 328
Marshall, Tully, 172, 215-16
Marsh, Mae, 171

Martel, Charles, 179
Martha, 57, 146
Martin's brigade, 8
Mason Opera House, 56, 115
Massey, Raymond, 372
Matthew, Father Francis J., 188-89
Mature, Victor, 400
Maugham, Somerset, 231
Maxim's, 233
Maxwell, Edwin, 352
Mayer, Louis B., 100, 186, 285, 294
Meighan, Thomas, 138, 224, 225, 226, 247, 349
Mejrabpom Studio, 310, 311
Melford, George, 135, 138, 173
Méliès, Georges, 73, 116, 117
Men and Women, 26, 27
Mena House, 427
Mennonites, 4-5
Mercury Aviation Company, 197-203, 205, 242
Mercury Export Corporation, 201
Mérimée, Prosper, 145
Metro-Goldwyn-Mayer, 186, 273, 290, 291, 293, 294, 299, 300, 301, 303, 304, 387
Metropolitan Opera Company, 57
Mexico, 67, 68, 82, 201, 238, 284, 376
Mexico City, 201
M-G-M (see Metro-Goldwyn-Mayer)
Mikado, The, 57
Milan, 95, 146
Milbank, Jeremiah, 266, 267, 274-75, 289, 315
Miles, Bob, 322-23
Miles, Harold, 278
Milestone, Lewis, 302
Miljan, John, 352
Milland, Ray, 372, 375
Miller, Alice Duer, 247
Million Dollar Theatre, 199
Milner, Victor, 342-43
Minnesota, 95
Minter, Mary Miles, 229, 237
Mintz, Sam, 326
Misr Studio, 426, 427
Mitchell, Billy, 234-35
Mizner, Wilson, 63
Mohammed, 263
Mohammed Ali, 421
Mohammedanism, 312
Monastery of St. Catherine, 423, 424-25
Montana, 194
Montezuma, 188
Montreal, 54
Mood music, 134, 143, 255
Moon, Lorna, 231

458

461

463

465